Elements of
FREIGHT TRAFFIC

PUBLICATIONS OF THE

REGULAR COMMON CARRIER CONFERENCE

Elements of
FREIGHT TRAFFIC

by

William Way, Jr.

Professor of Transportation and Chairman,
Transportation & Public Utilities Department
College of Business Administration
The University of Tennessee

1956

REGULAR COMMON CARRIER CONFERENCE, ATA
WASHINGTON, D. C.

COPYRIGHT, 1956, BY REGULAR COMMON CARRIER CONFERENCE, ATA
1424 SIXTEENTH STREET, N.W.
WASHINGTON 6, D. C.

First Printing, May, 1956
Second Printing, December, 1956

PRINTED IN THE UNITED STATES OF AMERICA

FOREWORD

To provide suitable text material for Lesson No. 4 (Introduction to Traffic) of the Motor Transportation In-Service Training Program, sponsored by the Regular Common Carrier Conference, and conducted by The University of Tennessee, and to provide a much needed writing on a subject which is of major importance to the transportation industry, the Conference commissioned Professor William Way, Jr. to undertake the compilation of this book.

It was agreed with the author that he would be accorded complete freedom in his presentation, and he accepts complete responsibility for the views expressed and the conclusions reached in this book.

This study has been made with the hope that it will contribute to a clearer understanding of the complex subject of Motor Carrier Traffic.

REGULAR COMMON CARRIER CONFERENCE

Washington, D. C.

v

PREFACE

This volume was prepared under the auspices of the Regular Common Carrier Conference, American Trucking Associations, Inc., for use in the Conference's Motor Carrier In-Service Training Program. It is designed to assist motor carrier employees in understanding certain phases of traffic and, possibly, as a specialized reference for use by educational institutions in traffic instruction. This publication should not be considered as an all-encompassing text on traffic similar to those which have been adopted by numerous institutions of higher learning. It covers shipping documents, freight classification, and an introduction to tariff publishing rules and tariff interpretation. Included is a detailed explanation of all the shipping rules contained in the published classifications.

Originally, there was a separate Education Committee of the Conference whose first chairman was R. A. Goodling, President of Dixie Highway Express, Inc., Meridian, Mississippi, and later Chairman of the Conference. In the opinion of the writer, it was largely due to Mr. Goodling's intense and active interest in education for the motor carrier industry that the many educational pursuits of the Conference have received national recognition both within and outside the motor carrier industry. Mr. Goodling was succeeded by A. E. Greene, Jr., when he was Vice President—Traffic, Mason & Dixon Lines, Inc., Kingsport, Tennessee, and who is now Vice President & General Manager of Great Southern Trucking Company, Jacksonville, Florida. It was Mr. Greene, in a conversation with the writer in November, 1954, who first suggested the feasibility and development of a Motor Carrier In-Service Training Program by means of correspondence courses.

Subsequently, educational matters were included with fiscal affairs in what is now known as the Education and Fiscal Committee with J. F. Smalley, President of Central Truck Lines, Inc., Tampa, Florida, as chairman. Mr. Smalley continued the interest in education of his predecessors. With adoption of the Motor Carrier In-Service Training Program by the Conference's Board of Governors, Mr. Smalley appointed a sub-committee to determine details of the program, as follows:

A. J. Novick, Sub-Committee Chairman
President, Novick Transfer Co., Inc.
Winchester, Virginia

F. G. Freund, Director
Traffic Department
American Trucking Associations, Inc.
Washington, D. C.

T. R. Glick, Traffic Manager
Cooper-Jarrett, Inc.
Philadelphia, Pa.

E. Ward King, President
Mason & Dixon Lines, Inc.
Kingsport, Tennessee

A. E. Greene, Jr., V.P. & G.M.
Great Southern Trucking Company
Jacksonville, Florida

E. L. Murphy, Jr., President
Murphy Motor Freight Lines, Inc.
St. Paul, Minnesota

M. B. Rose, Vice President—Traffic
Central Truck Lines, Inc.
Tampa, Florida

John M. Miller, Chief
National Freight Claims Council
American Trucking Associations, Inc.
Washington, D. C.

H. M. Sell, General Traffic Manager
General Expressways, Inc.
Chicago, Illinois

J. R. Wyatt, Vice President—Traffic
Mundy Motor Lines
Roanoke, Virginia

William Way, Jr.
Professor of Transportation
The University of Tennessee
Knoxville, Tennessee

Kenneth R. Hauck, Secretary
Education and Fiscal Committee
Regular Common Carrier Conference
American Trucking Associations, Inc.
Washington, D. C.

Mr. Smalley was succeeded as chairman of the Education and
Fiscal Committee by

H. N. Beiter, President
The Beiter Line, Inc.
Elyria, Ohio

Many persons have assisted in the preparation of this book. My colleagues in the Transportation Department of The University of Tennessee, Professors J. W. Bennett, Jr., and J. L. Frye, have read and criticized the entire manuscript. Likewise, the manuscript has been read and valuable suggestions have been made by Mr. F. G. Freund, Director of the Traffic Department, American Trucking Associations, Inc., Washington; and by Mr. W. M. Miller, Executive Vice President, Mr. C. J. Ackerman, Chief Rate Analyst, and Mr. E. C. Moss, Chief of the Tariff Bureau, Southern Motor Carriers Rate Conference, Atlanta, Georgia. To the above named gentlemen, grateful acknowledgment is made both for their criticisms and especially for the unquestioned valuable time consumed. Finally, I wish to express my profound gratitude to Mr. Kenneth R. Hauck, a member of the staff of the Regular Common Carrier Conference and Secretary of its Education and Fiscal Committee, for his continued interest, cooperation, and energy since inception of the Motor Carrier In-Service Training Program.

WILLIAM WAY, JR.

College of Business Administration
The University of Tennessee
Knoxville, Tennessee
February 14, 1956

Shortly after the Author's manuscript was placed in the hands of the printer, Professor Way passed away, March 18, 1956. It was necessary for his colleagues and associates to complete certain minor details in reference to the manuscript.

Samuel W. Earnshaw prepared the Index, and the reading of the printer's proofs was accomplished by the Staff of the Regular Common Carrier Conference, ATA. Dr. Clarence E. Kuhlman of the staff of The Department of Transportation and Public Utilities, The College of Business Administration, The University of Tennessee, also proofread the printer's proof.

It is hoped that this work has been accomplished in the manner in which Professor Way would have completed it.

JAMES W. BENNETT, JR.

Professor of Transportation
The College of Business Administration
The University of Tennessee

TABLE OF CONTENTS

Chapter 1

INTRODUCTION

This volume, as its title implies, is an introduction to traffic. Its purpose is to provide some information for those persons whose daily work does not bring them in close association with traffic matters. Its reading may serve as a "refresher" for traffic personnel. An effort has been made to present the subject in as simple language as possible so that it may be understood by an individual who has absolutely no knowledge of the subject. Possibly, the simple method of presentation will seem boring to the traffic expert; but it should be remembered that it is not the expert, but the novice for whom this study has been prepared.

It is not unusual for people to shy away from both study of traffic and employment in the traffic department of a firm. To a large extent, this attitude is caused by a lack of understanding. Yet, traffic is a most important phase of business activity both for carriers, and for shippers and receivers of freight. The annual expenditure for transportation services in the United States is about 55 billions of dollars,[1] which amounts to between 10 and 20 percent of total costs of production.[2] Sometimes, "without apparent justification," shipping costs exceed all other costs of producing an article.[3]

The transportation companies contribute about 10 percent of the national income;[4] and the transportation industry consumes 48 percent of all petroleum products produced in the United States, 62 percent of all rubber, 28 percent of all steel, 17 percent of the alumi-

[1] An address by the late D. D. Conn, Executive Vice President, Transportation Association of America, as reported in *The Chicago Shipper*, Curtis C. Stewart & Associates, Chicago, July, 1953, p. 30.
[2] Landon, C. E.: *Transportation*, William Sloane Associates, Inc., New York, 1951, p. 7.
[3] Butterbaugh, W. E.: *Industrial Traffic Management, A Survey of Its Relation to Business*, United States Department of Commerce, Bureau of Foreign & Domestic Commerce, Government Printing Office, Washington, 1930, p. 2.
[4] Locklin, D. P.: *Economics of Transportation*, 4th Edition, Richard D. Irwin, Inc., Chicago, 1954, p. 14.

num, and 14 percent of the copper. The industry paid $11.7 billions in federal taxes alone, or a contribution of $32 millions per day in support of the federal government. The federal government also collected over $3 billions in 1953 in excise taxes on transport equipment and services, another $3.5 billions in corporate income taxes, and over $5 billions in individual income taxes from employees of the carriers.[5] Motor carrier transportation alone provides a livelihood for one out of every ten persons gainfully employed in the United States.[6]

At the outset, two points must be kept in mind. First, many matters are involved in a study of traffic. A logical sequence of presentation of those matters is difficult to determine, particularly since one phase overlaps another. Frequently, to explain one point necessitates reference to something which has not been mentioned, with the result that the reader may imagine he is going around in a circle. Eventually, the subject will take definite form and the fundamentals will assume a positive pattern whereby they can be applied. The beginner can console himself with the realization that no one person knows all the answers to everything pertaining to traffic.

The second point is most important for a comprehensive understanding of the subject. So frequently, a person directs all his attention to a single part of the mode of transportation in which he is primarily interested. Unquestionably, such an attitude has its merits, and the loyalty of an individual, first to his immediate carrier-employer and secondly to his general mode of transportation, cannot be questioned. But an intelligent approach to a study of traffic cannot be restricted to the affairs of a single carrier nor even to a single mode of transportation. The development of most traffic matters stems from the experiences of railroads. To ignore railroad history is impossible in a comprehensive study of the subject. Further, a knowledge of railroad rules and practices is helpful not only to broaden one's background, but more particularly to enable a motor carrier employee to better understand his competition. Although primary emphasis will be devoted to motor carriers, consideration of comparable railroad matters is deemed advisable as well as necessary.

What Is Traffic? There are several meanings of the word "traffic." One is that it is to barter, to buy and sell, as, to carry on traffic with the Indians, or the illicit traffic in narcotics. Also, it is trade between communities or countries. Common uses of the term refer to ship-

---

[5] "Transportation in America," Chamber of Commerce of the United States, Washington, 1954.
[6] "Motor Truck Facts," Automobile Manufacturers Association, Detroit, 1954 Edition, p. 26.

ments of goods and the travel of people. The "perishable traffic" of the carriers refers to the quantity of perishables transported. "Export traffic" is the amount of property shipped out of the country in foreign trade. The "traffic" of a manufacturing company constitutes all the different commodities that are brought into the plant, such as raw materials and fuel, and the products which are shipped out. Traffic is trade: trade in particular commodities or trade in general.

Another definition is that traffic is the business of transporting passengers and property.[7] The control, or the supervision of trade in the technical sense is traffic management. Traffic is the business, not the means, of moving persons and property from one place to another, the business of shipping and receiving freight, the business of transportation. The physical movement of persons and property is performed by the transportation industry.

Traffic & Transportation. There is a definite and close relationship between "traffic" and "transportation"; but there is a positive difference in the meaning of the terms. As was mentioned above, transportation is the physical movement of persons and property from one place to another. Transportation is a service. Frequently, one hears the phrase, "the service of transportation." The history of the United States portrays its indispensability; and its unprecedented technical developments in recent years causes one to think of distance in terms of time rather than miles.

The several modes of transportation (air, motor, rail, and water carriers) move fruits, steel, textiles, and thousands of other commodities to places where they are needed and consumed by individuals and by industries. The value of all these thousands of articles are increased by the service of transportation. For example, what value does iron ore possess while it is still unmined in the Mesabi Range? What is the value of steel in a steel mill at Pittsburgh or Birmingham without transportation facilities to move it to places where it will be used? Of course, there could be no steel if raw materials, including fuel, could not be transported to the steel mills. What is the value of an orange on a tree in Florida or California before it is picked, packed, and made ready for shipment to a consuming market? The answers are obvious. Without adequate and efficient transportation facilities, articles would have very little or no value at the localities where they are produced by nature or by man.

Traffic is a highly specialized, technical science. In recent years it

[7] Neilson, W. A., Editor in Chief: *Webster's New International Dictionary,* 2nd Edition, G. & C. Merriam Company, Springfield, Mass., 1948, p. 2685.

has become increasingly complex, but its complexity adds to its fascination. "Something different every day" is what makes traffic work so appealing to the many men and women who are engaged in it. Changes in methods of production and distribution, as well as in transportation services themselves, have accelerated the pace for new opportunities in the ever-growing field of traffic.

Terminology. Traffic has its own technical language, its terminology frequently differing from that of other forms of business enterprise. For example, the word "tariff" to the uninitiated implies some special tax or fee assessed by government on imports, or something relating to customs duties. To the traffic man, a tariff is something entirely different; it is a duly authorized publication setting forth the charges and/or rules of transportation companies—that is, a price list for the service of transportation. A tariff will state in terms of dollars and cents how much it will cost to ship a certain article from one place to another, and the rules applicable to such a shipment.

Brief definitions of some of the terms commonly used are listed below.

RATE—The price for shipping freight—that is, the price for the service of transporting property.

FARE—The price for transporting persons.

CHARGE—The price of a carrier for performing any service other than actual transportation, such as, the amount for storing goods.

TARIFF—A publication setting forth the rates, fares, and charges of a carrier, and the rules applicable to such transactions.

CLASSIFICATION—The grouping of articles into a limited number of classes for the application of rates.

CARRIER—Any individual, partnership, company, or corporation engaged in the business of transportation.

BILL OF LADING (abbreviation, B/L)—A document required when shipping goods by a common carrier which serves as a receipt from the carrier to the shipper for the goods which have been entrusted into the carrier's possession, a contract of carriage, and evidence of title of ownership of the goods covered by it.

SHIPMENT—Property which is transported on one bill of lading, from one shipper, from one point of origin, on the same day, to one receiver, at one destination.

ROUTE—The manner in which a shipment moves—that is, the carrier, or carriers, which transport the shipment from origin to destination.

4

CLAIM—The demand on a carrier by the owner of a shipment for reimbursement to cover pecuniary loss for which the carrier is responsible.

INTERLINE TRAFFIC—Traffic that is handled by more than one carrier between origin and destination.

CONSIGNOR—The shipper of goods.

CONSIGNEE—The receiver of a shipment.

TRUCKLOAD (TL)—A shipment which weighs at least the minimum amount required for application of a truckload rate. In motor carrier traffic terminology, the word "volume" is frequently used interchangeably with "truckload." A shipping rule to be discussed later uses the term "volume or truckload," but there is no definition of "volume," and "truckload" is not fully explained.[8] For instructional purposes, it is believed "truckload" is a bit more realistic to the beginner than "volume." Although, to be technically correct, both words should be used together as they appear in the rule mentioned above; but, in the interest of simplicity "truckload" will be used in this volume rather than "volume or truckload."

LESS-THAN-TRUCKLOAD (LTL)—A shipment weighing less than the minimum amount required for application of a truckload rate.

ANY QUANTITY (AQ)—A shipment which is accorded a rate regardless of its weight.

INTRASTATE COMMERCE—The movement of persons or property wholly within the borders of one state. The points of origin and destination, as well as the entire route over which the shipment moves, must be within the same state.

INTERSTATE COMMERCE—The movement of persons or property across the boundary of any state or the District of Columbia.

FOREIGN COMMERCE—The movement of persons or property between the United States and a foreign country.

Scope. This presentation has been compiled to serve a particular purpose in the motor freight industry, and it is designed primarily for the common carrier of general commodities. No attempt has been made to cover all the numerous ramifications of traffic; instead, the content of this volume is restricted to certain topics which were found advisable by a special subcommittee of Education and Fiscal Committee of the Regular Common Carrier Conference, American Trucking Associations, Inc. For convenience, the contents may be divided into four general headings, as follows: (1) shipping docu-

[8] *National Motor Freight Classification No. A-2*, American Trucking Associations, Inc., Washington, effective July 7, 1954, Rule 13, pp. 163-A, 164-A.

ments, (2) freight classification, (3) an analysis of the rules of the published motor and rail Classifications, and (4) a preliminary explanation of rates and tariffs. Considerable detail has been devoted to each of the four general subjects which not only should serve to explain them but also indicates the vast amount of technical knowledge required to master these segments of traffic.

Chapter 2

SHIPPING DOCUMENTS—
Part I

THE BILL OF LADING

Many an individual engaged in business keeps his records in his head and his finances in his pocket. Particularly was this true in the early days of the motor freight industry. Granted, such simplicity is admirable; and faith in one's fellow man *always* to live in accordance with the Golden Rule is commendable, although, unfortunately, idealistic. If there were literal compliance by everyone with, "Do unto others as you would have them do unto you," there would be no reason for laws, other than the Law of God, to regulate human behavior and business activities. In so far as the business of shipping is concerned, there would be no need for court actions, no need for an Interstate Commerce Commission to regulate carriers, no need for shipping rules which shippers and carriers are required to observe. Likewise, the several papers used in shipping transactions would be unnecessary, other than strictly for informative purposes. The shipping documents which are described in this and subsequent chapters came into being because of necessity. Long ago, government recognized that an innocent shipper should be protected against the actions of an unscrupulous carrier and, likewise, that a diligent and upright carrier was entitled to protection from a dishonest or scheming shipper.

Every business organization has various papers or forms of one kind or another which are used in the conduct of its affairs. The transportation industry is no exception. However, unlike most non-public utility industries, many of the papers used in shipping are required by law; therefore, they have a legal aspect and they must conform with provisions of the applicable laws. There are numerous forms, of course, adopted by carriers and shippers for their own convenience which have no legal significance.

Just as in all business and professional enterprises, contracts must be made and records must be kept by an efficient traffic organization. Maintenance of accurate records is of particular importance, both to substantiate legal actions which may arise at some future date, and to show transportation costs. These various papers set forth, in part, the legal rights and obligations of the shipper, the responsibilities of carriers, and shipping costs for each item of carrier service.

It is conceivable that the respective businesses of managing the shipment and receipt of freight (industrial traffic management), and the transport of goods with its positive obligations to shippers and receivers (carrier traffic management), are second only to the government in the extent of required papers. It is a common opinion among laymen, whether or not justified, that with anything pertaining to a government operation, completion of the numerous ramifications of paper work, and the "shuffling of papers," is more important than the job to be accomplished. Many a GI who may read this section, accidentally or otherwise, will agree! Notwithstanding that the American system of regulation of transportation unquestionably necessitates compliance with various documents which have been prescribed legally for use of both carrier and shipper, the fact remains that the carriers and industrial traffic managers are overburdened with "formal formalities" in protecting their respective interests. To use a trite expression, the paper work associated with traffic management is "colossal." Whether the necessity for so many documents actually is real is another matter. The extension of regulation to include the many shipping documents, to say nothing of the numerous statistical reports carriers are required to compile, increases the operating costs of both carriers and shippers; and it should be understood, any increase in carrier costs inevitably are reflected in increased freight rates which shippers as a whole must pay. Be that as it may, the fact remains that certain documents are required by law for the protection of both shippers and carriers; and the legality of those various documents, and the purposes they serve, must be accepted by shipper and carrier.

Considerable effort on the part of personnel in a traffic department is devoted to the extensive and exacting responsibility of dealing with papers pertaining to the shipment of goods. For those individuals who enjoy that kind of work, it soon becomes fascinating. It provides an excellent opportunity for a person possessed with a curious mind to discover errors and to track down responsibility.

Shipping documents which are of greatest importance to the traffic manager are: (1) the bill of lading, (2) the shipping order, (3) the arrival notice, (4) the freight bill, and (5) the delivery

8

receipt. Usually, the first two are prepared by the shipper. Accuracy in their preparation, execution, and recording constitute a grave responsibility of the shipper; and failure in any feature thereof is likely to result in an unnecessary increase in shipping costs. The last three documents always are prepared by the carrier; but, as a receiver of freight, the industrial traffic manager has a vital interest in them.

Of tremendous importance to the carrier for operating purposes is another document known as the "waybill." A waybill is to a shipment of freight as a ticket is to a passenger; the waybill accompanies a shipment to destination just as a ticket goes with a passenger. There are other papers which are used in connection with different phases of shipping, but they will be mentioned later at the appropriate time when discussing those shipping practices and procedures.

Shipping Order. A document signed by the shipper known as the "shipping order" must be submitted to the carrier's agent at the time a shipment is tendered to a carrier to be transported. It is an official document required by law which directs the carrier to provide the transportation service. Upon the consignor rests the responsibility of having it in the hands of the carrier's representative; otherwise, the carrier has the legal right to refuse acceptance of the shipment, and properly so. In practice, however, there are exceptions to a strictly literal compliance with the preceding statement. Where the veracity of the shipper cannot be questioned, or where there is a close personal relationship or understanding between the shipper and the carrier's representative, loaded truck trailers are pulled from the shipper's loading dock before the shipping order is in the hands of the carrier's agent. It is common practice for a reputable firm which ships many truckloads of freight daily, for the loaded carrier equipment to be removed from the shipper's premises at varying intervals throughout the day, and the shipping orders covering all shipments to be delivered to the carrier's agent in the late afternoon.

In practice, the shipping order is not a separately prepared document. Instead, it is a carbon copy of the bill of lading, which is discussed in the next section. Hence, the shipping order contains exactly the same information as the bill of lading. This procedure eliminates extra clerical work and possibility of error in preparing the two documents individually.

The shipping order must be signed by the shipper and, as a general rule, it is prepared by him. In effect, it serves as formal confirmation of a previous request on a carrier to provide the desired equipment for loading a carload or truckload shipment, because, usually, the shipping order is not received by the carrier's agent until the shipment is ready to move. It is a directive to the carrier to transport and deliver the shipment as described by the bill of lading.

Bill of Lading. The most fundamental of all shipping documents is the bill of lading. Its common form of abbreviation is: "B/L." It has been said that the bill of lading "is one of the most extensively used documents in our commercial life"; but also, it "is the least read document in our commercial life." [1] Every student of traffic should possess a thorough knowledge of the bill of lading, for it is the basic and by far the most important document in shipping. It is of vital concern to both shippers and carriers.

Bill of Lading Functions. The bill of lading used in domestic commerce serves a number of positive uses which are combined into the one document. Frequently, the functions of the bill of lading are said to be that it is a receipt, a contract, and documentary evidence of title. However, there are additional purposes, the more important of which are summarized below.

1. RECEIPT. The bill of lading is a receipt or acknowledgment by the carrier to the shipper that the carrier has received into its custody from the shipper, and has accepted for transport, certain described property of a specified quantity and weight. It is a receipt for a shipment consisting of goods in the amount and kind as stated in the bill of lading. In the words of the Interstate Commerce Commission, "As a receipt for the goods, it recites the place and date of shipment; describes the goods, their quantity, weight, dimensions, identification marks, condition, etc., and sometimes their quality and value." [2]

The receipt portion of the bill of lading in common use by railroads and motor carriers reads, as follows: [3]

> RECEIVED, subject to the classifications and tariffs in effect on the date of the issue of this bill of lading,
> From...................... Date.............. 19....,
> At.............. Street,.............. City,............
> County,................ State,................
> the property described below in apparent good order, except as noted (contents and condition of contents of packages unknown) marked, consigned, and destined as shown below.....

---

[1] Braden, C. W.: "The Story of the Bill of Lading," National Distillers Products Corporation, New York, undated, p. 3.
[2] *In the Matter of Bills of Lading,* 52 I.C.C. 671 (681), 1919.
[3] *National Motor Freight Classification No. A-2,* American Trucking Associations, Inc., Washington, effective July 7, 1954, p. 170-A.

Although classifications and tariffs have not been explained up to this point, both are legal publications, and the rates and charges contained in the latter are the official legal prices for transportation services; also, among other things, each published classification and tariff must show the effective date.

If a shipment, when tendered to a carrier, does not appear to be in good order—such as, a broken container or package—the carrier's agent should make an appropriate notation thereof on the face of the bill of lading in order to protect the carrier from possible liability by the consignee claiming the damage was done while the goods were in the custody of the carrier. Also, since the shipper packs his shipment at his place of business in packages, crates, or whatnot, and since it would be utterly impractical for the carrier to open and inspect the contents of each container, the carrier relieves itself of any actual knowledge of the contents of packages.

2. CONTRACT. The bill of lading is a contract between the carrier and the shipper in which the carrier agrees to transport the shipment at the legal applicable freight rate from point of origin to point of destination and there deliver it to the specified consignee, and in which the shipper agrees to pay the legal charges. Like any legal contract, the bill of lading shows the conditions under which it is binding to both parties. The terms of the contract include not only the conditions which are printed on the back of the bill of lading, which will be discussed later, but also they are in part implied by both the common law and statutory law. These provisions are most important from a liability standpoint.

Further similarity to other contracts is that the bill of lading should be signed by both parties, or their duly appointed agents, in order to be legally binding. However, with the bill of lading there is a notable difference because if either party through error or oversight fails to sign the bill, it remains valid and it is not voided. In 1919, the Interstate Commerce Commission held; "It is sufficient if the shipper accepts the carrier's bill of lading without himself signing it. It becomes binding upon him by his acceptance, he being presumed to know and accept the conditions of the written bill of lading." [4] In confirming the finding of the Commission, the Supreme Court of the United States stated: [5]

The respondent (shipper), by receiving and acting upon the receipt (B/L), although signed only by the petitioner (carrier), assented to its terms and the same thereby became the written agreement of the parties . . . In the absence of a statutory requirement, signing by the re-

[4] *In the Matter of Bills of Lading, op. cit.*
[5] *American Railway Express Co. v. Lindenburg*, 260 U. S. 584 (591), 1923.

11

spondent was not essential . . . His signature, to be sure, would have brought into existence additional evidence of the agreement, but it was not necessary to give it effect.

In further clarification, Dean W. J. Knorst, of the College of Advanced Traffic in Chicago, states: "Were the carrier's agent to neglect to sign the Bill of Lading, the same reasoning would hold true. The carrier, by executing the Bill of Lading, would be presumed to have accepted the terms thereof." [6]

The statement in the first paragraph of this section that the shipper agrees to pay the legal charges does not mean the shipper must pay the freight rate in advance of shipment, for it is well known that many shipments move "collect" and the consignee pays the charges. It means the shipper is liable to the carrier for all lawful charges, except when the "Non-Recourse" clause of the bill of lading, which will be explained later, is signed by the shipper wherein the carrier is directed not to deliver the shipment until the consignee has paid the charges. For the present, exceptions and certain conditions will be ignored, and suffice it to say that the consignor is liable to the carrier for the lawful charges when the consignee refuses to pay.

Another point needing clarification is when there are two or more carriers involved in the transaction. The contract is executed between the shipper and a single carrier who will initiate movement of the shipment at point of origin. Only the representative of the originating carrier signs the contract, *not* representatives of each of the carriers participating in the through movement. Hence, it might be assumed the contract is binding upon the originating carrier only, since it is the sole carrier actually signing the document; but such is not the case. Assume a rate is published from point X to point Y, X is located on the line of railroad A, Y is on the line of railroad C, and railroad B is intermediate between A and C. Such a rate is known as a "joint" rate, and the through route from X to Y would be a "joint" route. The contract specifying such a route is binding, not only upon originating railroad A, but also on the other two railroads. At the time the contract was signed and the shipment was turned over to carrier A at point X, it is probable neither carrier B nor C knew anything about the transaction; but when A accepted the shipment and signed the contract, B and C automatically became parties to the transaction. In effect, therefore, B and C serve

---

[6] Knorst, W. J.: *Transportation and Traffic Management,* Vol. 1, Fourth Edition, College of Advanced Traffic, Chicago, 1952, p. 313.

as agents for A in performing the through transportation service from X to Y.

The contractual provision of commonly used bills of lading, which immediately follows the receipt portion, reads as follows: [7]

It is mutually agreed, as to each carrier of all or any of said property over all or any portion of said route to destination, and as to each party at any time interested in all or any of said property, that every service to be performed hereunder shall be subject to all the conditions not prohibited by law, whether printed or written, herein contained, including the conditions on back hereof, which are hereby agreed to by the shipper and accepted for himself and his assigns.

3. TITLE. The bill of lading serves as documentary evidence of title to ownership of the goods described therein. Although there has been no explanation of the different kinds of bills of lading, for the present let it be assumed that there are two classes, namely: (1) a "straight" bill wherein a shipment is consigned directly to a particular consignee, and (2) an "order" bill which is negotiable and wherein a shipment is consigned "to the order of" someone. Should a dispute or litigation arise concerning a shipment, the bill of lading will be accepted by the courts as *prima facie* evidence of ownership. *Prima facie* evidence, of course, is rebuttable, which means the burden of proof is on the contesting person to show that the facts so stated are false. Questions pertaining to the passing of title to goods from consignor to consignee can become most complex and can involve many complications, which is well demonstrated by Thomas G. Bugan devoting almost 500 pages to the matter in his excellent book entitled, *When Does Title Pass.*[8]

Legal questions regarding the passing of title are governed by laws of the several states other than the Interstate Commerce Act. In general, a law known as the "Uniform Sales Act" covers matters pertaining to title to goods, including those goods which are in the custody of a carrier. The law has been adopted by 34 states, Alaska, Hawaii, and the District of Columbia.[9] In those states where the Act does not apply, local laws and the principles of the common law prevail; but, generally, they differ little from the Uniform Sales

---

[7] *National Motor Freight Classification No. A-2, op. cit.,* p. 170-A.
[8] Published by William C. Brown Company, Dubuque, Iowa, 1951.
[9] The Uniform Sales Act has been adopted as follows:

Alabama, 1931	Delaware, 1933	Kentucky, 1928
Alaska, 1914	District of Columbia, 1937	Maine, 1923
Arizona, 1907	Hawaii, 1929	Maryland, 1910
Arkansas, 1941	Idaho, 1920	Massachusetts, 1909
California, 1931	Illinois, 1915	Michigan, 1913
Colorado, 1942	Indiana, 1929	Minnesota, 1917
Connecticut, 1907	Iowa, 1919	Nebraska, 1921

13

Act.[10] Unlike so many phases of traffic management, it should be understood the Interstate Commerce Commission possesses no jurisdiction whatsoever in determining questions concerning the ownership of goods in transit, which person had title to a shipment at a particular time, or responsibility for loss or damage to such goods. Legal actions involving these matters usually are brought in state courts of competent jurisdiction.[11]

In the relationships between buyer and seller, in practically all instances the buyer is the consignee and the seller is the consignor. In cases where a shipper consigns a shipment to himself, he becomes both consignor and consignee. The sales contract between buyer and seller may specify the conditions under which ownership of the goods being shipped passes from the seller to the buyer. As the eminent authority John M. Miller has stated: "As between buyer and seller of merchandise shipped, the question of determining when title passes from one to the other usually depends upon the intentions of the parties. In the absence of an agreement to the contrary, ordinarily a delivery by the consignor to the carrier conveys title to the merchandise to the consignee." [12] The specified "intentions of the parties" in a sales contract are most important.

Likewise, delivery of a shipment to the carrier is important. It is not the purpose here to explain exactly what constitutes delivery. Let it be assumed for the present that delivery is accomplished when the bill of lading has been issued and the shipment is placed in the hands of the carrier or the carrier's agent. Pick-up and delivery services usually are performed by most carriers for small shipments not falling within the category of carload or volume freight; hence, delivery can be made either to the carrier's terminal or to the driver of a pick-up truck. It is an inherent characteristic of both motor carriers and the Railway Express Agency to provide this service with their own employees and motor vehicles; but frequently, the railroads contract the service to a local motor operator. Under the latter situation, one might assume delivery is not com-

Nevada, 1915	Oregon, 1919	Utah, 1917
New Hampshire, 1923	Pennsylvania, 1916	Vermont, 1921
New Jersey, 1907	Rhode Island, 1908	Washington, 1926
New York, 1911	South Dakota, 1921	Wisconsin, 1912
North Dakota, 1917	Tennessee, 1919	Wyoming, 1917
Ohio, 1909		

Bugan, T. G.: *When Does Title Pass*, William C. Brown Company, Dubuque, 1951, p. 429.

[10] *Ibid.*, pp. 1–2.

[11] *Ibid.*, p. 7.

[12] Miller, J. M.: *Law of Freight Loss and Damage Claims*, William C. Brown Company, Dubuque, 1953, pp. 259–261.

pleted until the local cartage operator actually delivers the shipment to the railroad's depot, but that is not the case because the local operator is the agent of the carrier, *not* the agent of the shipper.[13]

The function of a bill of lading as a document representing title to the shipment it covers involves the common commercial expression "f.o.b.," the abbreviation for "free on board"—i.e., that the consignor has delivered the shipment to the carrier "free" of charges for the consignee. However, there are a number of f.o.b. bases which govern the applicability of the term in contracts of sales, such as: "f.o.b., point of origin," which means the consignee pays the freight charges from shipping point to destination; "f.o.b., destination," wherein the shipper pays the charges; "f.o.b., freight charges deducted by consignee"; and others. Unless a contrary intent is expressed in the sales contract, the phrase "f.o.b." determines both the place of delivery and the passage of title of a shipment to the consignee by the consignor; and both parties to the sales contract by agreement may "specifically provide for the time, the place, and the circumstances under which title and risk will pass."[14] The f.o.b. specification determines the responsibility for the payment of freight charges and indicates the conditions under which or the time at which title to the shipment passes from the consignor to the consignee, thus:[15]

(1) *"F.o.b., point of origin."* The consignor (seller) delivers the shipment "free on board" to the carrier at point of origin at which time title to the goods passes to the consignee (buyer) in the absence of an agreement, expressed or implied, to the contrary, and the consignee is responsible for the payment of freight charges. In other words, ownership of the shipment passes from the consignor to the consignee at the time the shipment is delivered to the carrier

---

[13] Tedrow, J. H.: *Regulation of Transportation,* William C. Brown Company, Dubuque, 1951, p. 15.

[14] Bugan, *op. cit.,* p. 119.

[15] A different view is expressed by Professor Van Metre, as follows: "Not a few writers state that the expression 'F.O.B.' (free on board) has to do with the time of the passage of title to goods turned over to a carrier for transportation under a straight bill of lading, saying that if the goods are shipped 'F.O.B. point of origin' the title passes to the consignee at that point, but if they are shipped 'F.O.B. point of destination' the shipper retains title until the goods reach the point to which they are consigned. There is no legal justification for such a belief. The term F.O.B. has to do only with responsibility for freight charges and has no bearing upon the time of the passing of title. If a shipper wishes to retain title in goods entrusted to a carrier, he should consign them to himself under a straight bill of lading or ship them under an order bill of lading." Van Metre, T. W.: *Industrial Traffic Management,* McGraw-Hill Book Company, New York, 1953, p. 192.

at point of origin by the consignor, and the consignee henceforth bears the risk of any loss or damage to the shipment.[16] "It is a familiar general rule that delivery to a carrier is delivery to the buyer on an F.O.B. origin shipment."[17] In quoting from the case of Standard Casing Co. v. California Casing Co., in Bugan's book, the court held: "The general rule is that, upon a sale 'f.o.b. the point of shipment,' title passes from the seller at the moment of delivery to the carrier, and the subject of the sale is thereafter at the buyer's risk . . . The operation of the rule is, of course, subordinate to intention."[18] The terms of f.o.b. origin may be more specific, such as: f.o.b. cars, f.o.b. factory, f.o.b. mines, etc. Under such circumstances, title passes to the consignee only after the shipment actually has been loaded in or on the cars, or other type of carrier equipment as may be specified, and the cars have been delivered to the carrier. On f.o.b. origin shipments, in the absence of contrary intent as may be specified in the sales contract, it can be concluded that title passes to the consignee upon delivery of the shipment to the carrier at point of origin by the consignor.[19]

(2) "F.o.b., point of origin, freight charges to be deducted by consignee." Under this provision of a sales contract, the consignor pays the freight charges—that is, the freight charges are deducted from the invoice value of the shipment. Since the shipper pays the freight charges, it might be assumed title remains with the shipper until delivery of the goods to the consignee at destination; but that is not the case. The word "origin" in the contract shows an agreed intention on the parts of both buyer and seller regarding payment of freight charges and passing of title. Therefore, title itself passes to the consignee in exactly the same manner as with a plain "f.o.b. origin" shipment, the difference here being that the consignor rather than the consignee pays the freight rate. Payment of freight charges, even if added to the seller's invoice and subsequently paid by the buyer, does not change the effect of the "f.o.b. origin" provision.[20]

(3) "F.o.b., point of origin, C.O.D." The C.O.D. provision added to a "f.o.b. origin" shipment does not change the situation regarding title. Here, the purpose is to withhold possession of the shipment by the consignee until he pays the C.O.D. amount to the delivering carrier. Title, however, passes to the buyer upon delivery of the shipment to the carrier at point of origin in exactly the same

---

[16] Matters pertaining to risk, carrier liability, loss and damage, etc., are discussed in Lesson No. 6, *op. cit.*
[17] Bugan, *op. cit.*, p. 8.
[18] *Ibid.*, p. 9.
[19] *Ibid.*, Chapter 2.
[20] *Ibid.*, Chapters 3 and 4.

manner as with a simple "f.o.b. origin" shipment. The same is true for a shipment moving on an "order" bill of lading wherein the goods are deliverable to the order of the consignor if he is retaining control of the goods solely to secure payment of the purchase price.[21]

(4) *"F.o.b., destination."* Under a "f.o.b. destination" sales contract, the shipper is required to pay the freight charges to the destination specified in the bill of lading. The title to the shipment remains with the shipper until delivery of the goods to the consignee at destination, in the absence of an agreement to the contrary. "Even in the absence of the term 'F.O.B.,' if the shipper is *required* to pay the freight, then the title does not pass until delivery at destination, unless there be circumstances surrounding the agreement which indicate a contrary intent. It is, therefore, entirely proper to infer, that if the shipper is required to pay the transportation costs, then the agreement, in effect, constitutes an F.O.B. destination shipment."[22] Continuing, Bugan states, "that under an F.O.B. destination agreement, the carrier is the agent of the seller for purposes of transportation."[23] Arrival of such a shipment at destination city does not necessarily constitute delivery, because if the sales contract stipulates delivery at a particular warehouse, factory, residence, etc., title does not pass to the consignee until actual delivery at the specified place.[24]

The above brief explanation of f.o.b. bases should indicate their great importance to the shipper and carrier. Not only do the various conditions of f.o.b. determine who pays the freight charges, but also they are important in deciding issues involving ownership of the goods. Usually, the f.o.b. base that is specified will establish conclusively the ownership of the shipment.

It has been stated previously that, in accordance with the contractual provisions of the bill of lading, the carrier is bound to deliver a shipment to the consignee so specified in the bill of lading or to comply with subsequent instructions of the owner of the shipment. If, however, the shipper learns that the consignee has become insolvent after the goods are in the hands of the carrier, the consignor may repossess the shipment through what is known as "stoppage in transitu." In such instances, the shipper extends due notice to the carrier directing that the goods be held in the carrier's possession subject to further instructions from the shipper. Insolvency of the consignee is essential to a "stoppage in transitu" action and,

---

[21] *Ibid.*, Chapter 5.
[22] *Ibid.*, p. 90.
[23] *Ibid.*, p. 92.
[24] *Ibid.*, Chapter 7.

usually, it will be exercised only when a shipment is moving on a "straight" bill of lading; but if the shipment is covered by an "order" bill of lading, which is described later, "stoppage in transitu" can be accomplished only by surrender of the original copy of the bill to the carrier.[25] This right has been accorded to a shipper in order "to prevent the property of one person being applied to the debts of another. When the shipper exercises this right, the carrier is excused from making delivery." [26]

In instances where a shipper consigns a shipment to himself or to his order, title remains with the consignor until he disposes of the shipment by negotiating the bill of lading to someone else.[27]

4. BASIS FOR CLAIMS. Up to this point, there has been no mention of the word "claim," other than the definition in Chapter I. Generally speaking, a claim is a demand for reimbursement from a carrier to cover actual loss in terms of dollars and cents—that is, for failure of the carrier to deliver the goods in the same condition as when tendered to the carrier by the shipper.

The provisions and conditions of the bill of lading determine to a large degree the extent of carrier liability for loss and damage to shipments. The bill of lading is proof of the contract between shipper and carrier. Therefore, to substantiate the existence of a contract of carriage, the original bill of lading must accompany a claim. It is sound practice for shipper to keep bills on file so that they may be available if and when it should become necessary to make a claim at some future date, because it is the simplest way of proving there was a contract of carriage with a given carrier. Such tangible evidence is required in the settlement of a claim. If, however, the original bill of lading has been lost, destroyed, stolen, or for any reason cannot be produced, the carrier paying the claim will require suitable indemnity against payment of a duplicate claim to some other party who may have acquired the original bill.[28]

5. NEGOTIABILITY. It will be explained later that there are two forms of bills of lading called the "straight" and the "order" bill of lading. When a bill of lading is drawn to the shipper's order and is properly endorsed, it is a negotiable document which is acceptable for credit,[29] and it may be negotiated by any person who has pos-

---

[25] *The Freight Traffic Red Book,* Traffic Publishing Company, New York, 1950 Edition, pp. 371, 381.
[26] Miller, *op. cit.,* pp. 303–304.
[27] See, p. 51, below.
[28] Miller, *op. cit.,* p. 558.
[29] Prof. Van Metre takes exception, as follows: "Some writers call the order bill of lading a negotiable instrument, but such a statement is incorrect, because a negotiable instrument is an order or promise for the payment of a stipulated

session of the bill, "however such possession may have been acquired."[30] The legitimacy of the negotiability of an order bill of lading is well established in the Pomerene Bills of Lading Act, adopted by Congress in 1916, Section 3 of which reads, as follows:

A bill in which it is stated that the goods are consigned or destined to the order of any person named in such bill is an order bill. Any provision in such a bill or in any notice, contract, rule, regulation, or tariff that it is nonnegotiable shall be null and void and shall not affect its negotiability within the meaning of this Act unless upon its face and in writing agreed to by the shipper.

A "straight" bill of lading is not negotiable.

6. DESCRIPTION OF SHIPMENT. The bill of lading, when prepared in a proper manner, describes the shipment in technical traffic language, together with the number of packages, marks on the packages, and the weight. Those detailed and accurate data are essential in determining the price of the shipping transaction, because two of the determining bases of a freight rate are the articles being shipped and the weight thereof.

7. FREIGHT CHARGES. The freight rate, and any other charges which may be applicable, appear on the bill of lading. Hence, it shows the amount paid, or if moving "collect," the amount to be paid in compliance with the contract of carriage. On the face of the bill of lading is a space in which to indicate if the freight charges have been prepaid, viz:[31]

If charges are to be prepaid, write or stamp here. "To be Prepaid."
....

Received $..........
to apply in prepayment of the charges on the property described hereon.
....
Agent or Cashier
Per ....
(The signature here acknowledges only the amount prepaid.)

sum of money, such as a check, note, or draft, and the bill of lading is not such an order or promise. It is nevertheless negotiable."—Van Metre, *op. cit.*, p. 191.
[30] Bills of Lading Act, Sec. 30.
[31] *National Motor Freight Classification No. A-2, op. cit.*, p. 170-A.

8. ROUTE. Under Section 15, Paragraph 8, of Part I of the Interstate Commerce Act, a shipper by rail has the positive right to decide the route over which his shipment is to move, and he so specifies it in the bill of lading by naming the carrier or carriers which are to participate in the movement. The railroad, if it is a local movement, or the railroads, if a joint route is involved, so named are bound to comply with the shipper's routing. However, there is no similar provision in Part II of the Act pertaining to motor carriers. In an outstanding case involving a joint motor route, the Interstate Commerce Commission ruled in 1942, "There is no provision in Part II of the Act which gives the shipper the right to specify the route of movement . . . , and defendants (the motor carriers) herein were under no compulsion to follow the instructions given them by complainant (the shipper)." [32] Therefore, it should be understood that the Act does not contain the same requirements for motor common carriers of general commodities as it does for railroads in complying with routing instructions.

9. IDENTIFICATION OF CONSIGNEE. Under the contract of carriage, the carrier is required to deliver the shipment to the proper person who is entitled to receive it by law. "From the earliest times, shippers have enjoyed the choice of naming a consignee to whom the goods were to be delivered." [33] A consignee must be named in every bill of lading, and the carrier is required to deliver the shipment to that named consignee in accordance with the bill of lading contract. It is well established that if a carrier delivers a shipment to someone not lawfully entitled to receive it, the carrier is liable to the owner of the goods.[34] Hence, the bill identifies the lawful receiver of the shipment. If the consignee is unknown to the delivering carrier, the easiest means of identification is by the consignee merely presenting the bill of lading which, usually, he will have received from the consignor.

The most commonly used bill of lading provides space for the name and address of the consignee immediately following the contractual provisions quoted in section No. 2 above, on page 21.

10. SPECIAL INSTRUCTIONS. Should the shipper desire something to be done to a shipment in addition to transporting it from origin to destination, instructions to cover such a request must appear on the face of the bill of lading; otherwise, the carrier will have no way of

---

[32] *Hausman Steel Company v. Seaboard Freight Lines, Inc., et al.*, 32 M.C.C. 31 (34), 1942.
[33] Miller, *op. cit.*, p. 34.
[34] Bills of Lading Act, Sec. 10.

(Mail or street address of consignee—for purposes
of notification only.)

Consigned to...
Destination................. Street................ City
.... County.................... State
Routing ....
                        Vehicle or
Delivering Carrier........ Car Initial........ No.........

knowing what is desired. If the carrier holds itself out to perform
such special services, as covered in duly published tariffs which
state the conditions under which the service or services will be performed and the charges therefor, it is required to comply with those
instructions. Note, there must be specific provisions in the carrier's
tariff! Such special instructions, for example, may include orders to
re-ice a carload of perishable commodities, to stop a carload or
truckload shipment at some intermediate point for partial unloading, and others.

Background of the Bill of Lading. Use of the bill of lading began
in the overseas trade many centuries ago. Its origin is somewhat ob-
scure, for history has left no record of the early document. Prior to
the thirteenth century, the "Law Merchant of Europe" consisted of
various customs and practices which were understood by all merchants and which were applied throughout the continent with more
or less uniformity. It was unwritten law, efficiently enforced by
local courts. Quite often, those local courts were composed solely of
merchants and, hence, there existed a thorough understanding of
the problem or case to be heard. Gradually, the large trading cities
codified their "Law Merchant."

With the passing of feudalism and the reign of sovereign cities,
the local codes, or, as they were known, "Customs of the Sea," were
revamped and cast into national statutes by the various rising mon-
archies. The early local tribunals were replaced by national courts
of admiralty.

Excerpts from local codes seem to show that, previous to the tenth
century, it was customary for shippers to forward goods on vessels
without any further evidence than a verbal acknowledgment of
their receipt by the master of the vessel, and a mutual unwritten understanding as to the shipper's and shipowner's rights and liabilities.
Gradually, written evidence of the receipt of goods was substituted.
When cargo was delivered to the vessel, an entry was made in the
"Ship's Book." This book was a written record, retained on board
the vessel, in which was recorded all transactions of the vessel in

21

regard to its receipts, expenses, and cargo. It appears that the cargo entries also contained the conditions under which the goods were transported. By the fifteenth century, there was universal use of the "Ship's Book."

International trade increased in volume and permanency during the sixteenth century. Shippers began to make definite trade connections in foreign lands and to ship their goods by impersonal methods. The long-established custom of the owner, or his representative, accompanying his shipment began to wane. As a result of this gradual evolution, the slow but positive development of the bill of lading was inaugurated.

Until the beginning of the nineteenth century, the bill of lading used for ocean shipments was very brief. It was a document of not more than 200 words, which simply acknowledged receipt of the goods in apparent good order and agreed to deliver them in the same condition. No long list of exemptions from liability were included, as is common today with ocean carriers, although there was always a clause which excepted the perils of the sea. Sometime around the middle of the nineteenth century, ocean carriers began to append one exemption after another to their liability under the contract of carriage. At first, it was done through the device of granting lower rates to those shippers who would sign bills of lading relieving the carrier from liability under certain circumstances not usually contained in the contract. These early rate reductions were *bona fide* and such contracts were upheld by the courts. Finally, however, the practice became ubiquitous, and the reductions became mere fiction.

Prior to federal legislation, the Supreme Court of the United States repeatedly had held that in the absence of a special contract, there was an absolute warranty upon the part of a shipowner to provide a seaworthy vessel for the particular purpose for which it was engaged.[35] Many shipowners took advantage of these rulings by inserting so many clauses which exempted the carriers from liability for cargo loss and damage that a number of commercial associations began to insist upon amendments to the then existing maritime law. The objections to the prevailing liability conditions in the bills of lading were based upon unreasonable provisions which protected the shipowners from practically all losses. Many of

---

[35] *The Southwark,* 191 U. S. 1, 1903.
  The Edwin L. Morrison, 153 U. S. 199, 1894.
  The Caledonia, 157 U. S. 124, 1895.
  The Irawaddy, 171 U. S. 187, 1898.

the bills of lading contained clauses which exempted the carrier from loss or damage occasioned by its own employees, by the unseaworthiness of the vessel, and others. The carrier's common law responsibility virtually was nullified. Bills of lading contracts became so long, complex, and involved that shippers were unable to check the all too numerous conditions in a manner to protect their own interests. A most peculiar clause that appeared in some bills gave the shipowner the right to sell a shipper's goods, not only if freight charges were due on the shipment itself, but also to satisfy former debts to the carrier either by the shipper or the consignee, even though those debts might have arisen on bills which had no connection with the shipment involved.[36]

Development of Uniformity. It should not be difficult to understand from the above brief description that carriers had used various kinds of documents in shipping transactions long before there were any statutory laws governing bills of lading. The primary purpose of the carriers was to restrict their liability.

An early American bill of lading on record is one dated at Rogersville, Tennessee, July 12, 1815, in which the carrier, presumably a wagoner, promised to deliver a shipment of saltpeter at Baltimore in 35 days at a rate of $3.00 per 100 pounds.[37] What a contrast to the modern service of approximately 30 hours by certificated motor carrier at rates of $1.04 per 100 pounds on a truckload basis and $1.69 for less-than-truckload! [38]

Bills of lading of the pioneer American railroads were modeled after those of their predecessor ocean, wagon, and canal companies, and, usually, they were restricted to purely "local" shipments. "They were completely deficient in uniformity regarding form, rules, and conditions." [39] It will be seen later that the rail carriers individually would restrict their liability by inserting various clauses in their bills.

This lack of uniformity, which is difficult to visualize today, placed a decided burden upon shippers, because the contractual terms of the respective bills of lading of each carrier had to be

---

[36] See, Hotchkiss, E. W.: *A Manual on the Law of Bills of Lading and Contracts of Shipment,* Ronald Press, New York, 1928.

[37] Braden, *op. cit.,* pp. 3–4.

[38] Information furnished by Mr. A. E. Greene, Jr., former Vice President—Traffic & Sales, The Mason & Dixon Lines, Kingsport, Tennessee, July 7, 1953. Tariff authority: Item 24310, *National Motor Freight Classification No. A-1;* Southern Motor Carriers Rate Conference Tariff 504, Item 17100, Column A and Item 1, Supplement 1.

[39] Wilson, G. L.: *Industrial Traffic Management,* The Traffic Service Corporation, Washington, 1949, p. 37.

scrutinized in order to know exactly the varying provisions thereof. It is understandable that those conditions caused confusion, controversy, and considerable litigation.

The railroads themselves first advocated uniformity in their bills of lading. At a conference of railroad executives in 1890, a uniform bill was prepared for use by all railroads in the country; but there developed so much opposition to the proposed new document by various commercial interests that efforts for its adoption were abandoned. Two years later, in 1892, commercial organizations were unsuccessful in their efforts to have the carriers agree to a simple bill which carried no terms and conditions. In 1904, following complaints of the Illinois Manufacturers Association and others, the Interstate Commerce Commission instituted an inquiry on the subject. After numerous hearings, a joint committee composed of representatives of both carriers and shippers submitted another new bill to the Commission in 1907, with the unprecedented request that the Commission approve and direct its adoption. The Commission, however, could not prescribe the proposed bill for required use by the carriers because, at the time, it did not have authority under the Interstate Commerce Act to issue such an order; but it is significant the Commission recommended its voluntary adoption as of September 1, 1908. The carriers in the South refused and, instead, established what was known as the "standard bill of lading," which meant the proposed new bill did not become the uniform bill of lading for use by all carriers throughout the country.[40]

In the meantime, Congress had enacted the Carmack Amendment[41] in 1906 to the Interstate Commerce Act. Essentially, it related to carrier liability; but it was the first attempt at federal regulation of bills of lading. Among other things, it required carriers subject to the Act to issue a bill of lading to a shipper. The terms and conditions of the bill in use today were not prescribed at that time.

By that part of the Mann-Elkins Act of 1910 which has since been incorporated into Section 1, Paragraph 6, of the Interstate Commerce Act, the Interstate Commerce Commission for the first time believed it had been given jurisdiction over bills of lading with authority to prescribe the form and content thereof; and, in 1912, it launched an investigation which consumed seven years but which culminated in an order prescribing the first uniform bill of lading.

---

[40] Braden, *op. cit.*, pp. 6–8; also, *In the Matter of Bills of Lading*, 14 I.C.C. 346, 1908.

[41] Named for the Tennesssee Senator who introduced it.

24

The intent of the Commission's investigation, which included the form, substance, and practices of the carriers regarding issuance of bills, was to bring "the carriers and the shippers of the whole country into uniformity with respect to the forms of bills of lading and to reduce the number that were then in existence. The purpose was also to see that nothing was placed in the bill of lading that was unlawful. . . . The Commission being bound by law, its purpose in this investigation was to endeavor to make the bill of lading conform to the law, and one for universal usage." [42]

Before the Commission had completed its exhaustive investigation, Congress enacted the two Cummins Amendments [43] of 1915 and 1916 which corrected some of the enforcement problems of the earlier Carmack Amendment pertaining to the limitation of carrier liability. For the present, discussion of liability provisions of the bill of lading will be postponed, although it should be kept in mind that the fixing of liability of a carrier was one of the fundamental purposes of legislation.

On the heels of the Cummins Amendments, the Pomerene Bills of Lading Act [44] was passed by Congress in 1916, and it became effective January 1, 1917. This Act is the real basis for the regulation of bills of lading, nothwithstanding that it did not specify terms and conditions. The Act differentiated between different kinds of bills and, essentially, clarified the liability provisions.

Both the Cummins Amendments and the Pomerene Act were brought into the considerations of the Commission in the bill of lading investigation which had been started in 1912. Further hearings were held. Finally, the Commission issued its order requiring adoption of the new uniform bill by *all* domestic carriers subject to the Act on or before August 18, 1919. [45] This was the first ruling of the Commission in which bills of lading forms and content were prescribed.

The order was enjoined by action of coastwise water carriers in the famous Alaska Steamship Company case [46] on the grounds that the Commission had exceeded its authority in prescribing a bill of lading in which water carriers, when participating in joint rail-water rates on a through bill of lading, were subjected to the same liability provisions of the Act as were rail carriers. Before the Supreme Court ruled on the Commission's appeal, the noteworthy

[42] Braden, *op. cit.*, p. 15.
[43] Named after the Senator from Iowa.
[44] Named after the Senator from Ohio.
[45] *In the Matter of Bills of Lading*, 52 I.C.C. 671, 1919.
[46] *Alaska Steamship Company v. United States*, 259 Fed. 713, 1919.

Transportation Act of 1920 had been passed by Congress which, among many other things, positively gave the Commission the power to prescribe the form and establish uniformity of bills of lading of carriers subject to the Act. However, the water carriers had convinced Congress of their position, for there was written into Section 20, Paragraph 11, of the Act recognition of the restricted liability of water carriers.[47] Hence, in the dramatic words of Professor Van Metre, "The water carriers had won their point and did not endeavor to challenge the validity of the new bill of lading or question the right of the Commission to prescribe it." [48]

Following passage of the Transportation Act of 1920, the Commission prescribed a uniform bill of lading which became effective in 1922; [49] but included therein was, and still is, Section 9 of the contract terms and conditions, printed on the back, which recognizes the limited liability of water carriers. Since that time, overland carriers in the United States have used the uniform bill and, although there have been a few slight modifications since 1922, "there have been no changes of a fundamental nature." [50]

The Uniform Bill of Lading. The Commission has never prescribed a uniform bill of lading for motor carriers; but Section 219 of the Interstate Commerce Act requires issuance of a bill of lading by motor carriers subject to the Act in exactly the same manner as railroads; likewise, there are comparable provisions in the Act applicable to all carriers engaged in domestic interstate commerce. In its first order on the subject pertaining to motor carriers, dated March 25, 1936, the Commission ordered motor carriers to provide appropriate bill of lading forms, "the contents and provisions of which must be just and reasonable. The responsibility for including any unlawful conditions or provisions . . . rests with the carriers." [51] Another order of the Commission in 1946 specified certain information to be shown on the bill. A few motor carriers use the rail bills, but the majority use the ones formulated by the American Trucking Associations, Inc., and presented in the *National Motor Freight Classification*, which are almost identical to the rail bills

[47] The Paragraph states in unquestioned language: "Provided, that if the loss, damage, or injury occurs while the property is in the custody of a carrier by water the liability of such carrier shall be determined by the bill of lading of the carrier by water and by and under the laws and regulations applicable to transportation by water, and the liability of the initial or delivering carrier shall be the same as that of such carrier by water."
[48] Van Metre, *op. cit.*, pp. 183–184.
[49] *In the Matter of Bills of Lading*, 65 I.C.C. 357, 1922.
[50] Van Metre, *op. cit.*, p. 184.
[51] *Receipts and Bills of Lading*, Interstate Commerce Commission, Washington, 1936.

prescribed by the Commission.[52] There are some slight differences in the terms and conditions of the respective motor and rail bills, but they are relatively unimportant.[53]

It should be observed that the Civil Aeronautics Board has not prescribed a uniform bill of lading for air carriers. In general, the airlines adhere to uniformity in what they term their "airbills," but the contractual provisions thereof are different from those of carriers subject to the Interstate Commerce Act. Likewise, there is no prescribed uniformity of the bills of lading of ocean carriers engaged in foreign trade. Also, the Interstate Commerce Commission has not prescribed a uniform bill of lading for pipe line companies, but the pipe lines issue a document which serves the same general purpose of the uniform domestic bill of lading.[54]

In effect, therefore, complete uniformity of domestic bills of lading has been achieved. No longer is a shipper subjected to the confusion and nuisance of having to determine the provisions of the bill of lading of each individual carrier he may employ. He can ship his goods with the positive assurance that the contract of carriage is settled and cannot be changed on the spur of the moment by any carrier nor at the behest of a competitive shipper. He can ship his goods without fear of any unreasonable discriminatory action growing out of the use of the bill of lading.

The advantages of complete uniformity have been beneficial to both shippers and carriers. In addition to establishing a common basis for carrier liability and shipper responsibility, it eliminates any possibility of unjust discrimination, it clarifies the position and duties of connecting carriers in a "joint" route, and it enables the shipping public to be certain that all commercial transactions will be handled in the same manner according to law. After half a century of controversy and litigation, the matter is now settled.

As has been stated above, the uniform bill of lading prescribed by the Interstate Commerce Commission for rail carriers is practically the same as that used by motor carriers. Two sizes are authorized, known respectively as the "full" and the "short" forms. The full-sized form must be printed on paper 8½ by 11 inches; the short-form, 8½ by 7¼ inches. On the back of the full-sized form are printed the contract terms and conditions of the bill. These terms and conditions do not appear on the short-form, although, when

---

[52] See, Miller, *op. cit.,* pp. 11–12.

[53] Colton, R. C.: *Practical Handbook of Industrial Traffic Management,* Second Edition, Funk & Wagnalls Company, New York, 1953, p. 11.

[54] Bryan, L. A.: *Traffic Management in Industry,* The Dryden Press, New York, 1953, p. 113.

signing the document, "the shipper acknowledges his acquaintance with these terms and accepts them as fully as if they were explicitly stated." [55] The information contained on the face of both the full and short forms has been illustrated earlier in this chapter in the section on the general functions of the bill of lading. In addition, however, are spaces at the bottom of both for the respective signatures of shipper and carrier, or their agents, *viz.:*

```
.....................Shipper .....................Agent
Per........................ Per........................
Permanent post office address of shipper..................
```

Furthermore, there is what is known as an "alternative" form for optional use with the so-called "standard" forms above mentioned. It provides space for more detailed information pertaining to the shipment, C.O.D. charges, and the equipment in which it is being transported.[56]

Although carriers subject to the Interstate Commerce Act are required to "issue a receipt or bill of lading," [57] it is common practice for the carriers to furnish shippers with an adequate supply of the full-sized form, at the top of which is usually printed the name of the individual carrier. The short form, however, is printed and provided by the shipper for his own use, and usually it carries the name of the firm at the top. As was stated earlier, the terms and conditions of the bill are omitted from the short form, but there is a statement on its face which refers to them. The short form is acceptable to both rail and motor carriers, and its use by shippers is highly recommended.[58] Many industrial traffic departments serially number their bills of lading for easy identification and reference purposes, and exclusive use of their own printed forms facilitates this desirable practice. Also, it is common practice for many industrial traffic departments to print the description of articles frequently shipped in the proper space on the face of the short form and thereby reduce clerical expense of securing and inserting that necessary information when preparing each bill of lading, as well as eliminating the ever possible opportunity for error. Use of the short form was authorized in 1949 as the result of demands by shippers for a bill of lading which would be interchangeable for use by rail, motor and water carriers.[59]

---

[55] Van Metre, *op. cit.*, p. 188.
[56] See, *Uniform Freight Classification, No. 2*, Consolidated Classification Committee, Chicago, effective December 10, 1953, p. 167.
[57] Interstate Commerce Act, Sections 20 (11), 219, 413.
[58] Colton, *op. cit.*, pp. 11–13.
[59] Knorst, *op. cit.*, p. 316.

It is worthy of mention that the Interstate Commerce Act prohibits disclosure of information contained in a bill of lading to unauthorized persons, "which information may be used to the detriment or prejudice of such shipper or consignee, or which may improperly disclose his business transactions to a competitor." Likewise, it is unlawful for anyone "to solicit or knowingly receive any such information which may be so used." [60]

---

[60] Interstate Commerce Act, Sections 15 (11), 222 (e), 317 (f), 421 (f).

Chapter 3

SHIPPING DOCUMENTS—
Part II

THE BILL OF LADING (CONTINUED)

Bill of Lading Rules. There are a number of shipping rules which have been promulgated by the carriers and approved by the Interstate Commerce Commission which have the same force as law and are binding upon both carriers and shippers. They supplement the terms and conditions of the uniform bill of lading contract. Since some of these rules pertain directly to bills of lading, they will be included in this discussion at the appropriate time. They appear in publications entitled the *Uniform Freight Classification* and the *National Motor Freight Classification*. For convenience, those publications will be referred to simply as the Rail Classification and the Motor Classification, respectively. The former is applicable to railroads, most domestic water carriers, and a few motor carriers; the latter, exclusively to motor carriers.

An important rule pertains to articles shipped on the uniform bill of lading. Under the law, as previously mentioned in Chapter 2, a common carrier is required to issue a bill of lading for each shipment, at which time the carrier enters into a contract with the shipper to perform certain transportation services. Likewise, the rates, fares, and charges of domestic common carriers must be published in tariffs in a manner prescribed by the Interstate Commerce Commission or the Civil Aeronautics Board. The freight rates of rail, motor, and the majority of inland water carriers, so published in the numerous tariffs, are subject to the provisions of either the Rail or Motor Classifications, a point which should be kept in mind at all times. The rates contained in tariffs are considered by the carriers to be "reduced" rates and they are conditioned upon use of the uniform bill of lading. In other words, rates published in tariffs apply only when the uniform bill of lading is employed.

Rule No. 1 of both the Rail and Motor Classifications provides that, in the absence of advice to the contrary, it is understood by the shipper that his shipment will be transported under the terms and conditions of the uniform bill, and that the so-called "reduced" rate will apply. Virtually all traffic moves on one of the prescribed uniform bills, except government freight, and the term "reduced" rate is a misnomer since it applies to practically every shipment.

However, a paragraph of Rule No. 1 makes it possible for a consignor not to comply with the prescribed bill of lading. The rule in both Classifications requires that if a shipper wishes not to accept all the terms and conditions on the uniform bill, he must notify the carrier's agent at the time the goods are offered for shipment. A shipper may elect to ship his goods under the common law, which places greater responsibility upon the carrier than the terms and conditions of the uniform bill of lading. It is extremely rare that a shipper should make this choice, but, nevertheless, he has that privilege. If he does, he must so indicate on the face of the bill of lading in language prescribed in Rule No. 1 of both Classifications. The freight rate on the shipment will be ten percent higher than the rate charged for property shipped subject to all the terms and conditions of the uniform bill. The provision of the ten percent higher rate is justified because it is a fundamental principle of law that a carrier may not restrict its liability without giving the shipper a corresponding advantage. It follows, therefore, that since the carrier's liability is greater under the common law than under the terms and conditions of the bill of lading contract, a lower or "reduced" rate is reasonable for shipments covered by the uniform bill of lading.

At this point, the confusion which must arise in the reader's mind is appreciated; but again he is reminded of the comment in Chapter 1 that an analysis of traffic management is comparable to a circle in that certain matters of necessity are injected into a discussion before there has been opportunity to explain them. For the moment, then, the reader is asked to accept as being true that the liability of a carrier under the common law is greater than under the terms and conditions of the uniform bill of lading.

Preparation of the Bill of Lading. Careful preparation of the bill of lading is a most important responsibility of all shippers. It should be accurate, legible, and complete in every detail; otherwise, there can arise unnecessary increases in shipping costs. The slightest mistake could prove expensive, such as, in the name or address of the consignee, the destination, route, description of the shipment. Absolute accuracy cannot be overemphasized. If in doubt regarding any individual entry on the bill, the safest policy is to seek advice from a commercial traffic organization[1] or from a carrier. The local terminal manager or agent of a carrier usually is glad to assist the occasional or uninitiated shipper in proper preparation of this most essential document. Inevitably, a mistake, whether caused by ignorance or otherwise, will prove costly.[2]

Professor Wilson lists the following points which always should be observed in preparing a bill of lading: [3]

1. That the shipping instructions are complete in all details.
2. That the name of only one shipper, consignee, and destination appear in the billing.
3. That the goods be accurately and completely described.
4. That trade names or other specialized descriptions be avoided and the goods described in the terms used in the classification or tariff governing.
5. That the number and description of containers are correct.
6. That the box makers' certificates be indicated, where required.
7. That the weights are accurate.
8. That the proper route and proper delivering carrier are inserted.
9. That junction points are shown when the goods are to move via certain interchange points—that is, over a "joint" route.
10. That the rate and route indicated are correct and reconcile with each other.
11. That the bills are properly dated.
12. That the writing or typing is clear, legible, and permanent.
13. That any alterations or corrections in the bills are signed by the initial carrier's agent before the goods are shipped.

It should be understood that a separate bill of lading must be prepared for each shipment. A shipment has been defined as "property which is transported on one bill of lading, from one shipper,

---

[1] Traffic Consultants or Traffic Management Services are available in many cities.

[2] The writer personally is familiar with the handling of a shipment which was to have moved from Washington, D. C., to Charleston, S. C. Apparently, the individual who prepared the bill of lading was more familiar with Charleston, West Virginia, than Charleston, South Carolina; or, possibly, the salesman omitted the state after the city in his shipping instructions. To add to the confusion, no complete route or delivering carrier was shown on the bill, only the originating carrier. It so happened, the originating carrier served Washington and Charleston, South Carolina, but not Charleston, West Virginia, which indicated the shipper, by force of habit or otherwise, indicated West Virginia instead of South Carolina. Of course, the shipment moved to the West Virginia city, and upon arrival the carrier was unable to locate the named consignee or his address. The consignor was notified, and the error discovered. The shipment then was sent to Charleston, South Carolina. Not only was the shipper required to pay the additional freight charges to cover movement of the goods from Washington to Charleston, West Virginia, to Charleston, South Carolina, plus incidental costs involved, but also, and of possible greater significance in the long run, the annoyance of the shipper's South Carolina customer may have resulted in loss of future business.

[3] Wilson, G. L.: *Industrial Traffic Management*, The Traffic Service Corporation, Washington, 1949, p. 45.

from one point of origin, on the same day, to one receiver, at one destination."[4] The quantity or volume of the goods being shipped is immaterial. One single shipment may require several railroad cars or motor truck trailers. Although not required by law, it is good practice for the shipper to prepare a separate bill for each unit of carrier equipment. At least, it is a cooperative gesture to the carrier in that it assists the carrier in the preparation and handling of its shipping papers on a per-car or per-trailer basis. Likewise, it positively identifies the contents of each car or trailer which could be of subsequent help to the consignee in arranging for unloading, or for tracing, or for other purposes, where specific information is needed as to exactly what part of an entire shipment moved in a particular car or trailer. Obviously, when a large shipment is billed separately according to the individual unit of carrier equipment, it then becomes a number of separate shipments; and care should be exercised in loading to be certain each unit of equipment contains at least the minimum tonnage to justify the carload or truckload rate.

Delivery of a shipment is facilitated by showing the complete address of the consignee on the bill of lading. Likewise, the address of the consignor, in the space provided therefor at the bottom of the bill, is desirable so that the carrier may know where to contact the shipper quickly for any reason which may arise, such as, refusal of the consignee to accept the shipment, inability to deliver, correction of an error, and others.

It was stated earlier that there may be only one consignee at one address shown on the bill of lading. An exception to this stipulation is allowed in one of the shipping rules of railroads which provide that a shipment consigned to one point with the consignee's address or instructions to notify the consignee or some other party, at another point, is permitted only under the following conditions: [5]

When the consignee or party to notify or advise is located at a river landing or other point inaccessible to carrier's deliveries; or

When the consignee or party to notify or advise is located at a prepay station or on a rural free delivery route or in the interior, in which cases the shipment must be consigned to an adjacent open office designated by the shipper; or

When the destination station and consignee's post office address adjacent to such station are differently named.

This rule does not prohibit showing the point or points at which shipments are to be stopped in transit for partial loading or unloading when

[4] See Chapter 1, above.
[5] *Uniform Freight Classification No. 2*, Rule 7, Section 1, p. 127.

such partial loading or unloading is specifically authorized by the carriers' tariffs applicable to such shipments.

Another exception is that there may be more than one consignee, but only at one destination, to receive parts of a single carload shipment. This is known as "split deliveries," wherein delivery is made by the carrier to two or more persons at the one destination. This service must be authorized in the carrier's tariff.[6] The Interstate Commerce Commission has held that, in view of the extra expense to the carriers in effecting delivery of split shipments, a special charge for the service is "not unreasonable."[7]

Usually, the consignor loads carload and truckload shipments, and the consignee unloads them; and the carrier neither supervises nor participates in the operations. Under such circumstances, the carrier is authorized to insert the notation "Shipper's Load & Count," on the face of the bill, which means the shipper is responsible for the manner in which the freight was loaded and the contents of the car or trailer. The Bills of Lading Act provides that this notation "or other words of like purport indicate that the goods were loaded by the shipper and the description of them made by him; and if such statement be true, the carrier shall not be liable for damages caused by the improper loading or by the nonreceipt or by the misdescription of the goods described in the bill of lading."[8] Excerpts from two court decisions quoted in Miller clarify the situation. In 1936, "Where 'shipper's load and count' appears on the bill of lading, and in fact, the goods were improperly loaded, the shipper is liable for the loss." In 1946, "The rule seems to be clear that when a fully loaded car is delivered to the railroad, the railroad company is responsible only for such defects as may be discoverable by such visual inspection as it is able to make, and it is not responsible for imperfect packing or other carelessness on the part of the shipper."[9]

If a shipper desires to forward a shipment C.O.D., meaning "collection on delivery," he may do so by making proper notation on the bill of lading and by complying with specific rules which have been prescribed by the carriers. Unless the "alternative" form of bill of lading is used, which provides space for C.O.D. data, there must appear on the face of the usual bill of lading, the following: amount

[6] *Ibid.*, Rule 14, Section 2 (c), p. 131.
[7] *Houston Milling Co. v. Agwilines, Inc., et al.*, 231 I.C.C. 312, 1939.
[8] Bills of Lading Act, Sec. 21.
[9] Miller, J. M.: *Law of Freight Loss and Damage Claims*, William C. Brown Company, Dubuque, 1953, pp. 222, 231.

to be collected on delivery, the C.O.D. collection charge of the carrier, name and address of the shipper or party to whom remittance is to be made by the carrier after collection from the consignee. The carriers publish their charges for providing C.O.D. service, the fee increasing with the amount to be collected.[10]

The weight of the shipment, the route over which it is to move, and the applicable freight rate should be shown in the spaces provided for each on the face of the bill.

On the side of the uniform straight and order bills of lading used by both rail and motor carriers, there appears the following:

> Subject to Section 7 of conditions, if this shipment is to be delivered to the consignee without recourse on the consignor, the consignor shall sign the following statement:
> The carrier shall not make delivery of this shipment without payment of freight and all other lawful charges.
>
> . . . .
> (Signature of Consignor)

The above is known as the "non-recourse" clause. If, for any reason, the shipper does not wish the consignee to gain possession of the shipment until all charges have been paid, he signs the directive to the carrier which is self-explanatory. The shipper is thereby relieved of liability for freight charges. If the clause is not signed by the shipper, he is liable for all lawful charges of the carrier.[11]

Below the "non-recourse" clause are spaces to indicate whether the charges are to be prepaid and, if so, the amount received by the carrier to apply in prepayment accompanied by the signature of the carrier's agent. The latter, therefore, serves as a receipt to the shipper for the sum paid to the carrier.

In preparing the bill of lading, it is of utmost importance that the articles being shipped are described in the technical language of the published Classifications. When it is realized that it is extremely rare for carrier employees actually to see or inspect the contents of a package, or a carload or truckload shipment, the importance of proper description of the shipment should be apparent. The carrier employee who rates a shipment is dependent entirely upon the information shown on his copy of the shipping order, which, as explained, usually is a carbon copy of the bill of lading. If the description is wrong, it is highly probable the rate assessed by the carrier will be higher than that which is applicable to the article

---

[10] See, *National Motor Freight Classification No. A-2*, Rule 31, pp. 166-A–167-A.

[11] Wilson, G. L.: *Industrial Traffic Management, op. cit.*, pp. 153–154.

itself; but, since the carrier's personnel must be guided by the description shown on the bill of lading, there is no other alternative than to apply the rate which is applicable to a shipment in the manner in which it is described on the bill. Since the lawful freight rate applies to the article actually transported, the description contained in the bill of lading is not controlling in the final analysis.[12] Later, after completion of the shipment, if the shipper or consignee finds the article was described incorrectly and a lower rate than the one assessed applies to the true description, the owner of the goods may recover the difference between the higher and the lower rate from the carrier upon presentation of adequate proof and necessary supporting papers for the claim. However, if the shipper is ignorant of the correct description of his shipment, he will not know the difference and he will have paid a higher rate, thereby unnecessarily increasing his shipping costs.

It is obvious, therefore, that all shippers should be familiar with the official descriptions of the items being shipped, not only to insure application of the proper rate, but also to avoid violation of the Interstate Commerce Act. Any person who willfully falsifies a description for the purpose of obtaining a lower freight rate than the lawful applicable rate "shall be deemed guilty of a misdemeanor" and, upon conviction, is subject to a fine of $5,000 or imprisonment of two years, or both, for each offense.[13] Rule No. 2 of both the Rail and Motor Classifications specifies descriptions should conform with those of the respective Classifications. Also, carriers may inspect the contents of individual packages or entire shipments to determine the actual character of the property, and if the description as shown on the bill of lading is found to be incorrect, "freight charges *must* be collected according to proper description." [14]

Bills of lading are prepared in manifold and, usually, by typewriter. There are at least three copies. The original, or No. 1 copy, is signed by the carrier's agent and returned to the consignor who, as a general rule, sends it by mail to the consignee. A notable exception is in the case of an "order" bill, which is described later. The No. 2 copy is the shipping order, discussed earlier in this chapter. It is signed by the shipper and retained by the carrier. It is the basis for the preparation of other carrier documents pertaining to the

---

[12] *Penn Facing Mills Co. v. Ann Arbor Railroad Co.*, 182 I.C.C. 614, 1932.
[13] Interstate Commerce Act, Sections 10 (2) (3), 222 (c), 317 (b) (c), 421 (b) (c).
[14] *Uniform Freight Classification No. 1*, Rule 2, p. 121; *National Motor Freight Classification No. A-2*, Rule 2, p. 156-A.

shipment. The No. 3 copy is known as the "memorandum copy." It bears no signatures and, usually, it is kept by the consignor for his permanent record. In recent years, a fourth copy has been added to the rail documents, which is the No. 1-A copy. This combination of documents is known as the "Unit Bill of Lading." Its use is not compulsory, but it has been recommended by both the Association of American Railroads and the National Industrial Traffic League. The No. 1-A copy bears no signatures. Actually, it becomes the railroad's waybill [15] and thereby relieves the carrier of having to prepare its waybill from information contained in the No. 2 copy of the bill of lading. Not only is its use cooperative on the part of shippers, but also it eliminates all possibility of error in transcribing data from the shipping order to the waybill. Currently, the Transportation Committee on Practices & Procedures, within the American Trucking Associations, Inc., has under consideration a proposal for the adoption of a combination bill of lading-freight bill, which goes further than the railroad document in that the proposed motor freight bill is prepared at the same time as the bill of lading.

Of course, a shipper may prepare any number of additional copies of the bill of lading that he may desire for his own use. In foreign trade, usually a minimum of five copies of the ocean bill of lading are required. [16]

Issuance of the Bill of Lading. The Interstate Commerce Act stipulates that all carriers engaged in interstate commerce subject to the Act "shall issue a receipt or bill of lading" for all property received by them for transportation. [17] It will be observed it is the duty of the carrier to issue the bill of lading, not the shipper. *Issuance* should be distinguished from *preparation*. In practically all cases, the bill of lading is prepared—that is, the bill of lading form is filled out—by the shipper; but mere preparation of the document does not constitute legal issuance. Technically, therefore, issuance occurs only when the bill of lading has been signed by the carrier's agent.

Only the date on which a bill of lading actually is issued may be shown on it. If a bill is pre-dated or post-dated with the intention of benefitting from a change in the effective date of a tariff, or for any other reason, it is considered a misdemeanor and the person responsible subjects himself to criminal prosecution which carries

---

[15] See, p. 10 above.
[16] Colton, R. C.: *Practical Handbook of Industrial Traffic Management,* Second Edition, Funk & Wagnalls Company, New York, 1953, p. 216.
[17] Interstate Commerce Act, Sections 20 (11), 219, 305 (a), 413.

a heavy penalty upon conviction.[18] Carriers require their agents to date bills of lading as of the same day they are issued.

After a bill of lading has been issued, the Bills of Lading Act specifies that "any alteration, addition, or erasure in a bill" shall have no effect unless authorized in writing or endorsed on the bill by the issuing carrier, "and the bill shall be enforceable according to its original tenor."[19] There is a similar provision in Section 10 of the terms and conditions of the uniform bills. Hence, it is illegal for a shipper to make any change or correction in the bill of lading after it has been signed by the carrier's agent; but if any alteration is made, it has no effect whatsoever for the carrier must follow the instructions and otherwise comply with the bill as originally issued. When a change is desired in any item on the bill after its issuance, the shipper either should request its cancellation and prepare a new bill, or arrange for the carrier to issue an "exchange" bill of lading which is described in the next chapter.

Bill of Lading Contract Terms & Conditions. The terms and conditions of the uniform domestic bill of lading constitute the contract of carriage; hence, their significance to both shipper and carrier should be obvious. It behooves all traffic personnel to become familiar with them. They are printed on the back of the respective forms. When signing the shipping order, the shipper agrees to their provisions; and the carrier is bound when its agent signs the original copy of the bill of lading.

These terms and conditions were prescribed by the Interstate Commerce Commission under authority vested in the Commission by the Transportation Act of 1920; therefore, they have the same force as law. They cannot be changed in any way by independent action of a carrier or shipper.

Since, however, these provisions of the bill of lading contract relate almost exclusively to liability aspects, they will not be treated in this book.

Kinds of Bills of Lading. There are two broad categories of bills of lading. They are either "straight" or "order." A bill cannot be both straight and order at the same time. Statutory foundation in the United States lies in the Bills of Lading Act of 1916, which was mentioned in the last chapter. Notwithstanding that the Act affects every interstate common carrier, it is a piece of legislation entirely separate and distinct from the Interstate Commerce Act.

Section 1 of the Bills of Lading Act stipulates that the bills of

---

[18] Interstate Commerce Act, Sections 10 (3), 222 (c), 317 (c), 421 (c).
[19] Bills of Lading Act, Section 13.

lading of every common carrier engaged in interstate commerce "shall be governed by this Act." [20] Sections 2 and 3, respectively, define straight and order bills in the following language:

A bill in which it is stated that the goods are consigned or destined to a specified person is a straight bill.

A bill in which it is stated that the goods are consigned or destined to the order of any person named in such bill is an order bill.

A person is defined as, "an individual, firm, copartnership, corporation, company, association, or joint-stock association; and includes a trustee, receiver, assignee, or personal representative thereof." [21]

The essential difference between the two kinds of bills of lading is that a straight bill is not negotiable, whereas an order bill, when properly endorsed, is negotiable.

Straight Bill of Lading. The straight bill of lading is the one in most common and frequent use. It provides the most simple means of making a shipment directly from one person to another. It is always printed on white paper.

The usual procedure is for the bill to be prepared by the shipper who should show complete and accurate information in the proper spaces. The carrier retains the No. 2 copy—that is, the shipping order—which has been signed by the shipper. The carrier's representative signs the No. 1 copy, and returns the No. 1 and No. 3 copies to the shipper. The shipper usually sends the No. 1 copy to the consignee and retains the No. 3 copy for his permanent record of the shipment. If the Unit Bill of Lading combination is used, the carrier retains the No. 1-A copy as its waybill.

The law requires that the word or words "nonnegotiable" or "not negotiable" be plainly inserted upon the face of the bill.[22] Upon reference to any uniform straight bill there will be found at the top, immediately under the name of the carrier or shipping firm and above the receipt provisions, the following: [23]

---

[20] The complete text of Section 1 follows: "That of lading issued by any common carrier for the transportation of goods in any Territory of the United States, or the District of Columbia, or from a place in a State to a place in a foreign country, or from a place in one State to a place in another State, or from a place in one State to a place in the same State through another State or foreign country, shall be governed by this Act."

[21] Interstate Commerce Act, Section 1 (3) (a).

[22] Bills of Lading Act, Section 6.

[23] See, *Uniform Freight Classification No. 2*, p. 164; and *National Motor Freight Classification No. A-2*, p. 170-A.

Title to goods represented by a straight bill may be transferred to a third party, when accompanied by an agreement, by mere delivery of the bill to him. The person who thus acquired title has the right to notify the carrier as to disposition of the shipment, but such notification must be to a representative of the carrier "the actual or apparent scope of whose duties includes action upon such notification," and the carrier is entitled to sufficient time "with the exercise of reasonable diligence" in which to communicate with the person in actual possession of the goods.[24]

Surrender of a straight bill of lading by the consignee to the delivering carrier is not required; however, as mentioned earlier, if the consignee is unknown to the carrier's representative, mere presentation of the bill serves as adequate identification. It will be recalled if a carrier delivers a shipment to the wrong person, the carrier becomes fully liable for the loss sustained by the true consignee.

Order Bill of Lading. Since goods moving on an order bill are shipped "to the order of" a named person or firm, it is a negotiable document. It can be bought and sold by endorsement and delivery, and its value is equal to that of the goods it covers. Therefore, it demands much greater care and respect than a straight bill. Plainly printed on the face of the uniform domestic order bill of lading in bold type are the words,[25]

UNIFORM ORDER BILL OF LADING

To further distinguish the two bills apart, and thereby lead to immediate and easy identification of each, the original order bill always is printed on yellow paper with the copies on blue paper, in contrast to all copies of the straight bill being on white paper.

Frequently, a shipment covered by an order bill is consigned to the order of the shipper himself, with instructions to the carrier to notify the person who ultimately is to receive the shipment after its arrival at destination. That part of the face of an order bill pertaining to the consignee differs from that of a straight bill, illustrated above, as follows:[26]

---

[24] Bills of Lading Act, Sections 29 and 32.
[25] See, *Uniform Freight Classification No. 2,* p. 170; and *National Motor Freight Classification No. A-2,* p. 173-A.
[26] *Ibid.* p. 170 and 173-A.

```
Consigned to ORDER of...............................
Destination..........State of..........County of........
Notify .............................................
At............State of............County of...........
Route .............................................
Delivering Carrier......(for rail) Car Initial....Car No.....
                       (for motor) Vehicle...... No......
```

With the order bill, the name of the person to whose order the shipment is consigned must appear in the space following the words "ORDER of;" otherwise, its issuance is prohibited.[27] On the back of the original copy is a space for endorsements above the printed terms and conditions of the bill.

Use of the Order Bill of Lading. The order bill of lading is prepared and issued in exactly the same manner as a straight bill; but similarity ceases with return of the No. 1 copy to the shipper, except that the shipper retains the No. 3 copy for his files. The No. 1 copy, *always* printed on yellow paper, is the original and it alone is the negotiable document. The blue copies are not negotiable.

To the original yellow copy, after having been issued by the carrier, signed by the carrier's agent, and returned to the shipper, is attached a draft drawn on the purchaser of the shipment in an amount equal to the selling price of the goods. Usually, "order" shipments move on the basis of freight charges collect; but if those charges are prepaid, they can be added to the selling price of the goods on the draft, depending upon the contract of sale. The shipper takes the original bill and the attached draft to his local bank. It is good practice for the shipper to endorse the original bill "to the order of" his bank, thereby being assured that the bank also will be forced to endorse the bill in order to pass title.[28] The bank retains both documents and credits the amount of the draft to the shipper, less the bank's handling charges. Hence, the shipper receives payment for the goods immediately.

The bank, through normal channels, forwards the two documents to its correspondent bank located in the city of the buyer of the shipment. The bank at the point of destination notifies the buyer of the arrival of the papers. The buyer makes his financial arrangements to meet the amount of the draft, by cash or credit, and upon payment thereof the same original copy of the bill of lading is turned over to him by the bank. The bank at point of origin is credited with the amount of the draft in accordance with usual banking procedures.

---

[27] *Ibid.*, Rule 7, Section 2, p. 127; and Rule 7, Section 2, p. 162-A.
[28] See, Miller, *op. cit.*, p. 57.

At this point, the buyer for the first time has acquired title to the shipment—that is, he secures title only after the bank has surrendered the original order bill of lading to him, and, of course, a bank would hesitate in so doing unless the amount of the draft had been paid or suitable security for the extension of credit had been submitted and accepted. Should the buyer refuse or fail to pick up the original order bill of lading from the bank for any reason, the documents are returned by the correspondent bank to the bank at point of origin, where the shipper is required to redeem the draft to repossess the original bill, title remains with the shipper, and he is liable to the carrier for all lawful charges which may have accrued. Under such circumstances, which admittedly are rare, the shipper would endeavor to sell the goods to another buyer and renegotiate the bill of lading. It is probable, rather than the documents being returned to the shipper's bank, the shipper would arrange for the papers to be sent directly by the first correspondent bank to the city at which the new buyer is located, which would necessitate further instructions to the carrier as to the new party to be notified and destination of the shipment. Let it be assumed, however, the original buyer promptly secured the original order bill from the first mentioned correspondent bank.

In the meantime, the shipment will have been moving from origin to destination as specified in the shipping order. Since the shipping order is a carbon copy of the original order bill of lading, it will be on blue paper and will show it is an "order notify" shipment. The blue paper alone is a danger signal to the carrier, for immediately the carrier knows the shipment must not be delivered to the consignee in the same manner as an ordinary shipment moving on a straight bill. So, upon arrival of the shipment at destination, accompanied by its waybill, the carrier holds it. The carrier's agent notifies the person so named in the bill that his goods have arrived, instead of effecting what might be considered automatic or immediate delivery. The buyer, then, endorses the original copy of the bill of lading he has secured previously from the bank and surrenders it to the carrier's agent, whereupon the shipment is delivered to him. The bill is cancelled by the carrier to prevent possible subsequent use, and it is placed in the carrier's files. The important point is that the carrier may not deliver a shipment covered by an order bill of lading until the original copy of the bill has been endorsed by the ultimate receiver of the shipment and surrendered to the carrier. The carrier retains the document; it is not returned to the consignee. This places a grave responsibility upon the carrier for lawful delivery. If the carrier delivers such a shipment to some one other than the last endorsee on the back of the order bill, the carrier is liable to the last endorsee for wrongful delivery. In view of the negotiable aspects of the order bill of lading, the document can be sold by one person to another any number of times, each transaction necessitating endorsement of the new buyer on the back of the bill. The carrier is bound to deliver the goods covered by the bill to the person who last endorsed the document. Should the carrier deliver the shipment without acquiring and cancelling the original endorsed bill, the carrier is "liable for failure to deliver the goods to anyone who for value and in good faith purchases such bill, whether such purchaser acquired title to the bill before or after the delivery of the goods by the carrier." [29] However, this requirement does not apply under the following circumstances: (1) delivery compelled by legal process, (2) sale of the goods by the carrier to satisfy its lien for applicable charges, (3) sale of the goods by the carrier if unclaimed, or (4) sale of the goods by the carrier because they are perishable or hazardous.[30]

Proper endorsement of an order bill of lading is when it is endorsed on the back in the space provided for that purpose by the person to whose order the bill is issued. Usually, an order bill is issued to the order of the shipper, with instructions to the carrier to notify some other party at destination who, normally, will be the ultimate consignee. In such instances, the shipper is required to endorse the bill at the time he negotiates it at his local bank. Sometimes he may endorse it to the order of the bank; or it may be endorsed "in blank," which means the shipper merely signs his name in the space for endorsements on the back of the bill, without specifying some other party. It is analogous to the endorsement of a bank check, and it may be transferred many times to any number of persons upon their respective endorsements before it passes into the hands of the person who actually demands delivery of the goods by the carrier.

It can be seen that use of the order bill of lading gives the shipper a tremendous advantage over use of a straight bill. The order bill is widely employed in both domestic and foreign commerce. Not only does title to the shipment remain with the consignor until the original bill is secured by the buyer at destination, which gives the consignor the right to do as he chooses with the shipment, but also it enables the shipper to secure the invoice value of the goods im-

---

[29] Bills of Lading Act, Section 11.
[30] *Ibid.*, Section 26.

mediately. It is a form of security which keeps the shipper's funds from being tied-up awaiting delivery and subsequent payment for the goods. It is more desirable than utilizing C.O.D. services, because the shipper secures his funds at once, whereas remittance of a C.O.D. is not made until after the sum has been collected from the consignee after delivery of the goods at destination. Furthermore, the carrier's C.O.D. collection charges are considerably higher than the nominal discount rates of banks. The negotiable features of the order bill give it definite advantages to the shipper, but added responsibility to the carrier.

One serious objection to the order bill is the time element. There are occasions when a shipment reaches its destination before sufficient time has elapsed for the documents to pass through normal channels, whereby the original endorsed bill of lading is not available for surrender to the carrier at destination upon or before arrival of the goods. It is for this reason that C.O.D. services are utilized for domestic shipments moving by air, the Railway Express Agency, and parcel post. In fact, those modes of transportation will not accept "order" shipments. Where distances are relatively long, it is advantageous to employ the order bill for shipments by motor carrier; but even then, it should be remembered one of the inherent characteristics and advantages of motor carrier service is its speed in delivery.

Although the order bill is authorized for general use by motor carriers, and it is employed by many certificated truck lines, there are some motor carriers which will not accept "order" shipments, or otherwise restrict use of the order bill to specified destinations or to points served by the carrier issuing the bill. In 1953, the Interstate Commerce Commission ruled a motor carrier may prohibit complete use of the order bill; but if the order bill is issued for some shipments, its use must be available for all, which means the carrier may not specify certain destination points to which "order" shipments will be accepted and refuse to issue order bills to other destinations. In the same proceeding, the Commission found that in many instances "order" shipments by motor carrier arrived at destination before the ultimate consignee could secure possession of the original copy of the order bill, which placed a burden on the carrier when it attempted to effect delivery. Such shipments would be taken to the consignee's place of business in the normal procedure of delivering other freight to other consignees, but in the absence of the original bill properly endorsed being available for surrender to the carrier's driver, the shipment had to be hauled back to the

44

carrier's terminal, unloaded, stored, rehandled, and redelivered at a future date when the bill of lading became available. "This presented a hindrance in handling other shipments which were in the same vehicle for delivery or which were to be picked up before the vehicle returned to the terminal." Further expense and operating difficulties were found in the handling of "order" shipments on local or peddle runs when the bill was not available for surrender. To partially cover the extra expense incurred by such instances, a few motor carriers had published in applicable tariffs a special charge to be assessed on all "order" shipments; but the Commission found that general practice to be unlawful and ordered its discontinuance. However, the Commission held that in instances where extra expense was incurred by the carrier in its attempts to deliver and otherwise handle "order" shipments, "the additional amounts for extra service should be charged to the individual shipments which entail the additional expense." The Commission further stated: "The defendants (that is, the carriers) have no duty to set up a special practice for the delivery of 'order' shipments. They have a right to expect order bills to be on hand for their collection upon tender of delivery, and to make reasonably compensatory charges for redelivery and storage when the vendee (that is, the consignee) is unable to accept delivery. If, as it appears, and the defendants claim, that their present charges for these services are less than compensatory, they should increase them so that they will yield a reasonable profit."[31]

Because of the time element, it can be concluded that a shipper should not employ an order bill of lading when it is impractical for the original copy of the bill to be in the hands of the ultimate consignee prior to the time the shipment will have arrived at destination and be available for delivery.

An exception to the rule of requiring surrender of an order bill to the agent of the delivering carrier occurs with an import shipment from a foreign country "in bond" which is covered by an order bill of lading. On such an occasion, the order bill, properly endorsed, is turned over to the United States Collector of Customs who, in turn, will issue a certificate to the person who had deposited the original order bill or, in lieu thereof, a bond of indemnity. The carrier at the domestic point of destination will deliver the shipment to the consignee upon surrender of the customs certificate.[32]

---

[31] *Southeast Shippers Association v. Associated Transport, Inc., et al.*, I.C.C. No. MC-C-1177, decided March 16, 1953.

[32] *The Freight Traffic Red Book*, Traffic Publishing Company, New York, 1950 Edition, p. 370

The Bills of Lading Act prohibits attachment by garnishment or otherwise of a shipment covered by an order bill of lading while in the possession of a carrier, "unless the bill be first surrendered to the carrier or its negotiation enjoined." Under no circumstances may the carrier be compelled to deliver such a shipment "until the bill is surrendered to him or impounded by the court." [33] The Act further provides that a creditor is entitled to injunction proceedings through the courts against a debtor who owns an order bill by attaching the bill to satisfy a claim against the debtor.[34]

Finally, the question can arise as to disposition of an "order" shipment by a carrier when the original endorsed order bill of lading cannot be produced by the lawful owner of the goods who is entitled to their possession. There are occasions where the bill has been lost, destroyed, delayed in transmission between banks, or even stolen. A special rule of the carriers takes care of such situations. A carrier is authorized to deliver an "order" shipment without surrender of the original bill properly endorsed when the following conditions are met: [35]

1. The party legally entitled to receive the shipment must submit to the carrier in writing a statement that he is lawfully entitled to possession of the goods and the circumstances surrounding his inability to produce the original document.

2. As a substitute for the original order bill of lading properly endorsed, he must present to the carrier security in the form of either currency or a certified or cashier's check in an amount equal to 125 per cent of the invoice value of the shipment, a specific bond of indemnity equal to twice the invoice value, a blanket bond of indemnity with surety, or an open-end bond of indemnity.[36] A cash deposit will be refunded upon surrender of the original bill of lading properly endorsed or if a bond of indemnity is given to the carrier.

The law does not specify the time in which a cash deposit may be returned to the depositor, nor a fixed date for cancellation or ex-

---

[33] Bills of Lading Act, Section 23.

[34] Ibid., Section 24.

[35] See, Uniform Freight Classification No. 2, Rule 7, Section 3, p. 127; and National Motor Freight Classification No. A-2, Rule 7, Section 4, p. 162-A.

[36] As explained in the Rules, a specific bond protects delivery of a single shipment. A blanket bond may be used repeatedly until cancelled; but if the original bill properly endorsed is not surrendered to the carrier within five days immediately following delivery of the shipment, exclusive of Saturdays, Sundays and bank holidays, further delivery of shipments under the bond will cease. An open-end bond may be used repeatedly until cancelled, but it applies separately to each shipment; and it further provides that unless the original bill properly endorsed is not surrendered within five days, as above, the liability of the surety is doubled.

piration of a bond. The statute of limitations for filing a claim against a carrier is nine months from date of delivery of the shipment, or nine months from the time delivery should have been accomplished; and if the claim is rejected by the carrier, two years and one day thereafter for institution of suit against the carrier. Hence, the deposit may be refunded and the bond cancelled at the end of nine months if no claim has been made; or if claim has been disallowed by the carrier, two years and one day from the date of rejection.

It might appear that these requirements are unduly rigid, but when the unusual responsibility of the carrier is appreciated, they are not unreasonable. They protect the carrier and the true owner of the goods from fraud. For instance, if the true owner loses the original bill and it is found by an unauthorized party, or if there is a case of outright theft of the bill, the unauthorized person merely has to forge the endorsement, present it to the carrier, and receive the goods; but if the true owner has complied with the requirements described above, the carrier is forewarned and, in fact, prohibited from delivery to anyone else.

Summary of Order B/L. Some of the special features of an order bill of lading may be summarized, as follows:

1. The original, No. 1, copy always is printed on yellow paper; the No. 2 and No. 3 copies, on blue paper.

2. It must contain the name and address of the party to be notified.

3. It is a negotiable document when properly endorsed which is acceptable for credit, and which may be sold and re-sold to any number of persons. However, *only* the original yellow copy, properly endorsed, is negotiable.

4. The original endorsed copy must be surrendered to the carrier prior to delivery of the shipment which it covers, otherwise the carrier is liable to the true owner. The carrier delivers the goods to the last endorsee. Some carriers hold their agents responsible for their loss if delivery is effected without surrender of the original document.

5. If the owner of the bill is unable to produce it, he may secure his shipment by depositing cash or posting bond with the carrier, as explained above. Also, a court of competent jurisdiction may order delivery in the absence of surrendering the original bill upon proof of its loss, theft, etc., "and upon the giving of a bond, with sufficient surety, to be approved by the court." [37]

---

[37] Bills of Lading Act, Section 14.

6. An order bill may not specify delivery and notification at a point or station where the carrier has no agent. These points are known as "non-agency" or "prepay" stations, in contrast to an "open" station. Such rail stations may be determined upon reference to a publication entitled, *Official List of Open and Prepay Stations*.

7. Order bills covering shipments anywhere in continental United States may not be issued in parts or sets covering portions of a shipment—that is, there may not be more than one bill covering a single shipment. The penalty against a carrier for violation is that it "shall be liable for failure to deliver the goods described therein to anyone who purchases a part for value in good faith, even though the purchase be after the delivery of the goods by the carrier to a holder of one of the other parts." If more than one order bill is issued, the word "duplicate" must be shown plainly on the faces of all copies except the first one, and failure of the carrier to do so makes it liable. The restrictions do not apply to "order" shipments to Alaska, Panama, Puerto Rico, Hawaii, or foreign countries.[38]

8. Goods covered by an order bill may not be attached by garnishment or otherwise while in possession of the carrier, unless the original bill is surrendered to the carrier or its negotiation enjoined. "The carrier shall in no case be compelled to deliver the actual possession of the goods until the bill is surrendered to him or impounded by the court." [39]

9. A person who negotiates an order bill warrants that the bill is genuine, that he has a legal right to transfer it, that he has knowledge of no fact which would impair the validity or worth of the bill, that he has the right to transfer title to the goods, and that the goods are merchantable or fit for a particular purpose.[40]

10. Endorsement of a bill does not make the endorser liable for any failure of the carrier or previous endorsers to fulfill their respective obligations.[41]

---

[38] Bills of Lading Act, Sections 4 and 5.
[39] *Ibid.*, Section 23.
[40] *Ibid.*, Section 34.
[41] *Ibid.*, Section 35.

Chapter 4

SHIPPING DOCUMENTS—
Part III

MISCELLANEOUS

Although the uniform domestic straight and order bills of lading described in the last two chapters are basic shipping documents, there are other types of bills in common use in the United States. Those with which the industrial traffic manager and individual shipper should be familiar are, the following:

Exchange Bill of Lading
Uniform Live Stock Contract
Ocean Bill of Lading
Through Export Bill of Lading
Government Bill of Lading
Express Receipt
Airbill
Pipeline Contract

Exchange Bill of Lading. As its name implies, an exchange bill of lading is one which is issued in exchange or in substitution of another. The shipment involved must be in the possession of the carrier which issues the exchange bill. When issued, the information contained in the original prior document for which it is being exchanged is considered as being a part of the exchange bill "as fully as if the same were written" on it.[1] The following statement must appear on the face of all exchange bills:

This bill of lading is issued in exchange for receipt or bill of lading No..... issued at..... on the......day of.....19....
By the...........................Company
...........................Agent

Uniform Live Stock Contract. Realizing that the transportation of live animals involves problems which are different and more exacting than those incident to the shipment of ordinary freight, the

---

[1] Section 8 of Contract Terms & Conditions of the Bill of Lading.

Interstate Commerce Commission prescribed the uniform live stock contract in 1922, along with the uniform domestic bills of lading.[2] It is not used by motor carriers. It is a special document essentially for domestic rail and water carriers used exclusively for livestock. Live animals and live poultry may be shipped only on this unique type of bill of lading. As Colton states, livestock is a "very special commodity." [3]

The live stock contract always is straight. It can never be an order bill. The distinguishing feature of the document is the distinction between "ordinary live stock" and "other than ordinary live stock." The terms are defined in two separate declarations which appear on the face of the live stock contract and read, as follows: [4]

ORDINARY LIVE STOCK

Ordinary live stock means all cattle, swine, sheep, goats, horses, and mules, except such as are chiefly valuable for breeding, racing, show purposes, or other special uses. On shipments of ordinary live stock no declaration of value shall be made by the shipper, nor shall any values be entered on this bill of lading.

I (We) declare the shipment covered by this bill of lading to be ordinary live stock.

. . . .
Shipper

OTHER THAN ORDINARY LIVE STOCK

On shipments of live stock chiefly valuable for breeding, racing, show purposes, or other special uses, different rates of freight are in effect dependent on the valuation placed thereon by the shipper; which valuation may be the basic value as stated in the classification, at which the lowest freight rate applies, or it may be any higher valuation up to actual value, in which event the freight rate will be higher by the amount prescribed in the tariffs or classifications. Such declared or agreed values shall be entered in the column provided therefor in this bill of lading, and in no event shall the carrier be liable for any amount in excess of such valuation.

I (We) declare the shipment covered by this bill of lading to be other than ordinary live stock, and of the value herein declared, or agreed upon, and entered.

. . . .
Shipper

---

[2] See, Chapter 2, above.
[3] Colton, R. C.: *Practical Handbook of Industrial Traffic Management*, Second Edition, Funk & Wagnalls Company, New York, 1953, p. 16.
[4] *Uniform Freight Classification No. 2*, Official Classification Committee, Chicago, effective December 10, 1953, p. 183.

There follows below, on the face of the document, spaces for the number and description of the animals, declared value of the shipper, weight, and the freight rate.

The shipper is required to execute one of the above declarations. If he signs the one for "ordinary live stock," no statement of value is inserted. If he signs the one for "other than ordinary live stock," he states the value in the space provided; but should he refuse to declare the value of such live stock, the shipment will not be accepted by the carrier. If the shipment consists of both "ordinary" and "other than ordinary" live stock, both declarations are executed, but values are declared only for the latter. These distinctions are essential because the freight rates, as published in applicable tariffs, are based upon the two categories.

The printed Classification of the railroads states the base value for different kinds of animals, *viz.:* [5]

STANDARD OR BASIC VALUES:

Kind of Stock	Values per Head
Each horse or pony (gelding, mare or stallion), burro donkey, mule, jack or jenny	$150.00
Each buffalo	100.00
Each colt under one year old	75.00
Each ox, bull or steer	75.00
Each cow	50.00
Each calf, 6 months old or under	20.00
Each hog	15.00
Each sheep	5.00
Each goat	5.00

If the declared value is higher than the above values, the freight rate is increased in accordance with tariff provisions. Hence, the freight rate on "other than ordinary live stock" depends upon the value declared by the shipper. In no instance will animals valued at more than $1,500.00 per head be accepted for shipment by railroad freight service.[6] Usually, animals of exceptionally high value are shipped by Railway Express Agency or by private motor carrier, although some move by commercial air carrier.

Railroads assume very little responsibility under the terms and conditions of the uniform live stock contract, unless caused by their negligence. Under no conditions is a carrier liable for an amount greater than that declared by the shipper.

If a shipment of live stock is accompanied by a caretaker, as is

---

[5] *Ibid.*, Item 26465, p. 348.
[6] *Ibid.*, Item 26475, p. 348.

frequently the case, a supplementary contract is required which practically relieves the carrier of all liability in the event of injury.[7]

Ocean Bill of Lading. For convenience, discussion of the ocean bill of lading will be subdivided between foreign and domestic services.

1. FOREIGN SERVICES. In striking contrast to the uniform domestic bills of lading, there is no required uniformity among all ocean carriers in their bills. "The terms of the contract vary among countries, carrying lines, and trades."[8] This is caused largely by the competitive situation arising from vessels of many nations plying the various ocean routes. The very nature of international trade, together with the conflicting interests of different maritime countries, have prevented success in achieving complete uniformity. The United States, of course, has no jurisdiction over foreign steamship companies and, therefore, cannot enforce any semblance of uniformity in the use of shipping documents by all ocean carriers. Since ocean carriers engaged in foreign trade are not subject to the Interstate Commerce Act, the Interstate Commerce Commission may not prescribe a uniform bill.

The Harter Act of 1893 provided for the issuance of bills of lading by water carriers, and the Shipping Act of 1916 contained somewhat comparable provisions. It is interesting to observe that under the Harter Act, if the carrier refuses to issue a bill of lading upon demand of the shipper, the carrier is liable to a fine of $2,000; *but,* when the fine is collected, one-half goes to the injured party and the other half to the United States Government![9] The Carriage of Goods by Sea Act of 1936 is more forceful in language regarding bills of lading. It put into law, and thereby governed vessels flying the flag of the United States, what is known as the Hague Rules and, later, the Brussels Rules, one of the purposes of which was to

---

[7] The contract reads: "In consideration of the carriage of the undersigned upon a freight train or vessel in charge of the live stock mentioned in the within contract, whether with or without charge for such carriage, each one of the undersigned severally hereby voluntarily assumes all risk of accident or damage to his person or property, and hereby releases and discharges each and every carrier from every claim, liability, or demand of any kind for or on account of any personal injury or damage of any kind sustained by him, unless caused by the negligence of such carrier or any of its employees; and agrees that whenever he shall leave the caboose and pass over or along the cars or track he will do so at his own risk of personal injury, except where the negligence of the carrier proximately contributes thereto, and that no carrier shall be required to stop or start its train or caboose cars at or from the depot or platforms, or to furnish light for his accommodation or safety."

[8] Bryan, L. A.: *Traffic Management in Industry,* The Dryden Press, New York, 1953, p. 99.

[9] Wilson, G. L.: *Industrial Traffic Management,* The Traffic Service Corporation, Washington, 1949, p. 42.

52

achieve world-wide uniformity in ocean bills of lading. Most of the leading maritime nations of the world have adopted those Rules.[10] The liability of ocean carriers for loss and damage to shipments is most restricted. It is because of the limited liability and, under certain circumstances, complete exemption from liability, that the great marine insurance business has developed.

Unlike domestic carriers, the usual practice is for the ocean carrier to prepare the bill of lading and send a copy to the shipper for his signature. Furthermore, in the absence of some special credit arrangement, executed export ocean bills are not surrendered to shippers until all freight charges have been paid to the steamship company.[11] The ocean bill may be either straight or order. Also, there are two types, known, respectively, as the "received for shipment" and the "on board" bills of lading. The former is nothing more than a receipt, acknowledging that the freight has been received at the steamship company's dock. The "on board" bill is what may be considered as the true bill of lading, for it is not signed and, therefore, not technically issued, until the shipment actually is loaded on the vessel.[12]

The ocean bill is much larger in size than the uniform domestic document and, as indicated above, its terms and conditions greatly restrict the liability of the ocean carrier. Commercial practices and requirements of foreign governments determine the number of copies of the document, but five copies is the minimum. Generally, more copies are required by South American countries than those of Europe and the Orient. Shipments into Haiti, for example, require eight copies.[13]

In passing, it should be mentioned that a number of documents, in addition to the ocean bill of lading, are necessary in international trade, such as: marine insurance certificate or policy, consular invoice, shipper's export declaration, certificate of origin, and the commercial invoice which describes the shipment in more or less detail.[14]

2. DOMESTIC SERVICES. Competition of foreign vessels does not exist in domestic commerce. An Act adopted by Congress in 1817

---

[10] Bryan, *op. cit.*, p. 100.

[11] Colton, *op. cit.*, pp. 16, 216–217.

[12] Johnson, E. R., Huebner, G. G., and Wilson, G. L.: *Transportation, Economic Principles and Practices*, D. Appleton-Century Company, New York, 1940, p. 429.

[13] United States Department of Commerce: *Uniform Through Bills of Lading*, Government Printing Office, Washington, 1928, pp. 34–35.

[14] Huebner, G. G., and Kramer, R. L.: *Foreign Trade*, D. Appleton-Century Company, New York, 1935, pp. 397–398.

gave to American vessels a complete monopoly of the domestic water trade of the United States.[15] Since 1817, foreign ships have been barred from engaging in transportation services between any two or more ports of the United States, including those located on the inland waterways and the Great Lakes. In 1898, this exclusion of foreign vessels was extended to include the insular possessions of the United States, as Puerto Rico and Hawaii.[16]

A foreign ship may call at any number of United States' ports to pick up or discharge cargo and passengers for or from foreign points, but it may not pick up at one United States port and discharge the same shipment at another United States port. For a simple illustration, a foreign ship may operate from New York to Havana, Cuba, and then proceed to New Orleans, but it may not discharge at New Orleans any shipment which originated at New York or the interior of the United States. On the other hand, an American ship operating over exactly the same route may handle New York–New Orleans traffic, and discharge and pick up at Havana; and the rates, tariffs, and bills of lading covering the New York–New Orleans traffic are within the scope of the Interstate Commerce Act, but the Interstate Commerce Commission has no jurisdiction over the New York–Havana nor over the Havana–New Orleans traffic. This situation is mentioned so that it will be understood all common carrier port-to-port water domestic commerce is subject to regulation by the federal government.

Provisions concerning the issuance of bills of lading by domestic water carriers are contained in Part III of the Interstate Commerce Act, Section 305 (a); but no uniform bill has been prescribed by the Commission. Most domestic water carriers still operate under the liberal liability terms of the old Harter Act.[17] Since liability is so slight, the shipper should cover his shipments with adequate marine insurance. As with foreign services, the liability of domestic water carriers is far less than that of the domestic overland carriers. For instance, all carriers subject to the Act *except* water carriers "shall be liable to the lawful holder thereof (that is, the bill of lading) for any loss, damage, or injury . . . and no contract, receipt, rule, regulation, or other limitation of any character whatsoever shall exempt such common carrier . . . from the liability hereby imposed; and

[15] Johnson, E. R.: *Government Regulation of Transportation,* D. Appleton-Century Company, New York, 1938, pp. 372–374.
[16] Wilson, G. L.: *Miscellaneous Transportation and Rates,* The Traffic Service Corporation, Washington, 1943, p. 11.
[17] Van Metre, T. W.: *Industrial Traffic Management,* McGraw-Hill Book Company, New York, 1953, p. 238.

any such common carrier . . . shall be liable . . . for the full actual loss, damage or injury to such property." [18]

Intercoastal steamship lines use a bill of lading which is comparable to that of the foreign service companies. They may be straight or order, and they contain considerably more detailed information than the uniform domestic bill, such as: date the vessel is due at a port, the amount of insurance to be issued, the voyage number, direction of the voyage, port of discharge and ultimate destination of the shipment, shipper's declaration of the goods, and others.[19] Also, they carry a long list of conditions which are printed on the back.

Coastwise carriers,[20] generally, have adopted the uniform domestic bill of lading. Possibly, the reason therefor is the close relationship which always has existed between coastwise and rail carriers.[21] However, marine insurance is not included in most instances in the port-to-port rates of coastwise carriers.[22] Domestic water carriers participating with rail and motor carriers in joint rates are required to use the uniform domestic bill prescribed by the Interstate Commerce Commission.

It is well to understand that a section of the contract terms and conditions of the uniform bill of lading makes specific reference to and defines the limited liability of water carriers. This section, therefore, makes the uniform bill just as satisfactory for use by domestic water carriers as by rail and motor carriers. However, some domestic water carriers participating in joint rail-water services provide in their tariffs that they assume the same full liability of the rail carriers, and under such circumstances the provisions for limited liability of water carriers do not apply.

Common carriers by water on the Great Lakes and inland waterways use the uniform bill of lading, and it is customary for their rates to include marine insurance.[23] However, a paragraph of Rule No. 1 in both the Rail and Motor Classifications states, "The cost of

---

[18] Interstate Commerce Act, Sections 20 (11), 219, 413.

[19] Wilson, G. L.: *Freight Shipping Documents, Routing and Claims,* The Traffic Service Corporation, Washington, 1942, p. 43.

[20] Coastwise water carriers are those which operate between ports of the Atlantic, Gulf, and Pacific, respectively, and between Atlantic and Gulf ports; Intercoastal carriers are those which operate between the Atlantic and the Pacific and between Gulf and Pacific ports, or domestic water traffic moving through the Panama Canal, thus: Boston to Charleston, New York to New Orleans, Seattle to San Francisco are Coastwise; New York to San Francisco, New Orleans to San Francisco are Intercoastal.

[21] For an excellent discussion, see, Joubert, W. H.: *Southern Freight Rates in Transition,* University of Florida Press, Gainesville, 1949.

[22] Wilson, G. L.: *Miscellaneous Transportation and Rates, op. cit.,* p. 14.

[23] *Ibid.,* p. 59.

insurance against marine risk will not be assumed by carriers unless specifically provided for in tariffs." [24] Hence, domestic water carriers participating in the Rail and Motor Classifications do not provide marine insurance as a part of the freight rate, unless it is covered in a tariff. In the absence of a specific statement in applicable tariffs that the water carrier will furnish marine insurance, the industrial traffic manager should make his own arrangements for insurance protection against marine perils.[25] When large quantities, particularly commodities in bulk, are to be shipped by water carrier, it is common practice for an industrial traffic manager to charter a vessel on a contract basis, in which event no bill of lading is required.

From a regulatory standpoint, water carriers do not include the extensive car ferry services on Lake Michigan by both the Chesapeake & Ohio Railway and the Ann Arbor Railroad, the car ferry operations of the Nashville, Chattanooga & St. Louis Railway on the Tennessee River, and the many car floats in New York harbor. Such services performed by or on behalf of railroads are considered the same as railroad services and, therefore, they are subject to the same bill of lading requirements as rail carriers.

Through Export Bill of Lading. A novel expedient for the convenience of inland shippers of export freight in carload or truckload quantities is the through export bill of lading. Prescribed by the Interstate Commerce Commission in 1922, it is a document which covers an export shipment from an interior point in the United States to a foreign port of a country nonadjacent to the United States. It combines the separate contracts of carriage of the domestic carrier and the ocean carrier, respectively. Its use, therefore, eliminates billing the shipment from origin to port of debarkation, the services of an agent or foreign freight forwarder at the port to receive the goods from the domestic carrier and arrange for their delivery to the ocean carrier, and rebilling or issuance of a separate ocean bill of lading by the steamship company.

Authority of the Commission to prescribe the bill was a new provision inserted into the Transportation Act of 1920. It was in what was then Section 25 of the Interstate Commerce Act, but it was repealed by the Transportation Act of 1940. The purpose of the 1920 action was to encourage the export trade and to promote the Amer-

---

[24] *Uniform Freight Classification No. 2*, p. 124; and *National Motor Freight Classification No. A-2*, p. 156-A.

[25] Glasgow, C. C., Jr., and Gifford, G. L.: *An Analysis of Motor Carrier Tariffs*, The University of Tennessee, Knoxville, 1952, p. 24.

ican merchant marine, its use being restricted to ships flying the flag of the United States. It required the domestic railroads to perform services far beyond their former duties, and it is doubtful if it yielded them comparable benefits. The bill is authorized by both rail and motor carriers; but its use was suspended early during World War II and, in 1955, it had not been restored.

The through export bill of lading is not a "joint" bill in any sense of the term, and it should not be confused with joint rates and joint routes applicable to domestic commerce. Under the through export bill, the domestic carrier's rates and liability are in no way connected with those of the ocean carrier. Both are entirely separate and distinct, for the inland and ocean carriers are severally, not jointly, responsible. There are three parts of the bill, namely:

Part I covers movement of the goods from point of origin in the interior to delivery to the vessel at the port and, hence, it is similar to the uniform domestic bill of lading. It contains additional conditions pertaining to the domestic carrier's liability, in that it is specifically stated the domestic carrier shall not be liable after the shipment has been delivered to the next carrier thereby eliminating joint responsibility with the ocean carrier. Part II is applicable to the ocean carrier and covers the shipment from the time it is received at the American port of export until delivery at the foreign port, and it, too, states the ocean carrier shall not be liable after the shipment has been delivered to another carrier for further movement beyond the port of discharge. Part III has to do with the transportation service after delivery by the steamship company at port of discharge until delivery at the ultimate destination beyond that port, and "the property shall be subject exclusively to all conditions of the carrier or carriers completing the transit." At the end of a long list of conditions is space for the respective signatures of both shipper and agent of the originating carrier. Under the latter there is printed, "On behalf of carriers severally but not jointly." [26] There has been infrequent use of Part III. In general, shipments move from the port of discharge to final destination on the documents of the foreign carrier as separate shipments.

The uniform export bill of lading may be either straight or order, and it is applicable only for export shipments moving in American vessels to only those foreign countries which are shown in the tariffs of the domestic carrier.

An industrial traffic manager at an inland point desiring to use

---

[26] *Uniform Freight Classification No. 2,* pp. 177–182; and, *National Motor Freight Classification No. A-2,* pp. 176-A–181-A.

this bill for an export shipment will request the local agent of the domestic carrier to arrange for reservation of the necessary space on a vessel, secure the ocean freight rate and any additional port or terminal charges, and issue the bill of lading. The bill, however, is not issued by the local agent until space on a particular vessel is confirmed by the steamship company and until all necessary papers are in order, such as, the consular invoice, shipper's export declaration, etc. The shipper pays the originating carrier both the domestic and ocean charges, but he does not receive a separate ocean bill of lading. The domestic carrier then transports the shipment to the port where it is delivered to the pier at which the vessel on which space has been reserved is berthed. Possible storage and transfer charges at the port are eliminated; and since the goods remain in the custody of the domestic carrier until delivery to the vessel, possibility for loss or pilferage is minimized.[27]

There are a number of advantages to the American shipper located at an interior point in the use of the through export bill of lading, such as: (1) in most instances, the freight rate from point of origin to the port is lower than the normal rate on a strictly domestic shipment; (2) the inland domestic haul is exempt from the three percent federal transportation tax on freight shipments; (3) such shipments are not subject to domestic embargoes; (4) inland exporters are able to quote "C.I.F." [28] prices to their foreign customers; (5) services of a middleman and accompanying charges at a port are eliminated; (6) if it is an order bill, the shipper may secure his funds immediately upon delivery of the shipment to the domestic carrier at point of origin.[29] Some of the objections to the document are, as follows: (1) many foreign customers are not familiar with it and do not know how to use it; (2) foreign buyers must give permission to its use in arranging letters of credit; (3) where consular visas are required, issuance of the bill is delayed unless an interior consular office is available; (4) C.I.F. prices may be quoted without use of the through export bill of lading; (5) it is difficult to establish responsibility for loss or damage, as each carrier is liable severally and not jointly; (6) most letters of credit call for an "on board" bill of lading issued by the ocean carrier; (7) a railroad or motor carrier may favor a particular ocean carrier which utilizes its port facilities;

[27] Colton, *op. cit.*, pp. 217–226; also, Knorst, W. J.: *Transportation and Traffic Management*, Vol. 1, Fourth Edition, College of Advanced Traffic, Chicago, 1952, pp. 317–319.

[28] "C.I.F." is the abbreviation for "cost, insurance, and freight."

[29] See p. 40, above.

(8) some banks and marine insurance companies are opposed to the use of the through export bill of lading.[30]

Government Bill of Lading. A special document which covers the shipment of goods of the federal government is the government bill of lading. It was prescribed by the Comptroller General of the United States and became effective in 1943.[31] It is acceptable by all common carriers and it is required for the shipment of government-owned property, including material and supplies of the armed forces. The federal government, of course, is not subject to the Interstate Commerce Act; therefore, many of the terms and conditions of the uniform bills of lading do not apply to shipments moving on the government bill of lading. In general, the provisions of the contract of carriage are the same.

There are a number of features wherein the government bill of lading differs from the uniform bills of lading. The former contains three divisions which contain its conditions, instructions for preparation and use, and administrative directions. Since it covers exclusively property owned by the federal government, no problem concerning title to the shipment is involved.

There are five copies of the government bill, the original being printed on white paper, the shipping order on salmon paper, the memorandum copy on yellow paper, and the others on white paper. It is prepared by the agency or department of the government initiating a shipment. Most purchases of the federal government are on the basis of f.o.b. origin.[32] If a shipment is made from a government installation, such as a supply depot, the government bill of lading is prepared by the shipping agency at that point. However, when a shipment of government freight originates in private industry, or by an individual purveyor, the government bill is prepared by the government agency which has ordered the goods and is sent to the shipper who, in turn, surrenders it to the agent of the carrier at point of origin. In instances where there would be delay in forwarding a shipment awaiting receipt of the government bill, the freight may move on a uniform straight bill of lading; but, upon arrival at destination, the uniform bill is exchanged for a government bill which is prepared by the government agency receiving the goods.

Unlike the uniform bills, the original government bill of lading

---

[30] See, Huebner & Kramer, *op. cit.*, p. 655.
[31] *The Freight Traffic Red Book,* Traffic Publishing Company, New York, 1955 Edition, p. 270.
[32] Colton, *op. cit.*, p. 14.

is surrendered by the shipper of government freight to the carrier at point of origin. It is retained by the carrier, not the consignor! Upon delivery of the shipment at destination, the consignee signs a receipt in a space provided therefor on the government bill, which is evidence of completion of the transportation service by the carrier. Then, the carrier submits the bill to the government for payment of all applicable charges. Hence, government freight moves collect and it is never prepaid. There is no non-recourse clause on the face of the government bill, nor is there space to show prepaid freight charges.

The form of the government bill does not adhere to the general form of the uniform bill; but, of course, spaces are provided to show full information regarding consignor, consignee, route, description of the shipment, etc. Detailed instructions for its preparation and handling are printed on the back. The bills are numbered serially, and the office of the federal government in which they are prepared is held accountable for all bills issued to it. The consignee, whomever he may be, should never pay the freight charges on shipments governed by a government bill of lading, for the carrier is paid for its services directly by the appropriate accounting office of the federal government. One of the conditions of the government bill reads, as follows: "Prepayment may not be required by the carriers nor may payment be collected from consignees, but only through vouchers on government forms through authorized government accounting offices."

Express Receipt. The Railway Express Agency, Inc., is the only operating express company in the United States. The document issued by the Agency to cover express shipments is the express receipt. It serves exactly the same purpose as the bill of lading. The uniform express receipt is non-negotiable, but C.O.D. service is available. There are two forms: one for a prepaid shipment, the other for a shipment where the express charges are collect. Like the uniform bill of lading, the uniform express receipt was prescribed by the Interstate Commerce Commission and its provisions, too, are binding upon the shipper, the carrier, and the consignee.[33] For shipments of live animals, a special live stock receipt is required.

It is well to note at this time that a shipper shows on the express receipt the declared value of his shipment, and express rates increase with the higher declared values by about fifteen cents per $100 additional value. The liability of the Express Agency for loss or damage is not more than $50 for any shipment weighing up to 100

---

[33] Bryan, *op. cit.,* p. 102.

pounds, or 50 cents a pound actual weight if over 100 pounds, unless a higher valuation is declared by the shipper on the express receipt.

For shipments moving by air express, the Railway Express Agency issues an Air Service Uniform Express Receipt, commonly known simply as an "air express receipt." It serves the same purpose as the other express receipt, it is nonnegotiable, and it may cover either a prepaid or collect shipment.

Airbill. Shipments moving by air freight, not to be confused with air express, are covered by a document called the "airbill." No uniform airbill has been prescribed by the Civil Aeronautics Board, but, in practice, the air carriers have adopted uniformity.

The airbill serves the same purpose as the bill of lading. In many respects, it is comparable to the express receipt in that the declared value of a shipment must be shown. It is nonnegotiable, but C.O.D. service is available. The airbill specifies if the shipment is to be picked up at the consignor's place of business, at the airline's city terminal, or at the airport, and if delivery is to be effected at the destination airport or city proper.[34]

Pipe Line Contract. There is no prescribed bill of lading for pipe line shipments. Pipe line companies issue a contract which covers the products to be transported, and it serves the same general purpose of a bill of lading.

It should be understood that pipe line transportation is practical and economical only when performed on a large scale. Unlike other modes of transportation where the weight of a shipment is a governing factor, with pipe lines the measure of a shipment is in terms of barrels. There is no such thing as a less-than-truckload or a carload shipment by pipe line. Instead, there has been developed what is known as a "minimum tender," which is the smallest quantity of oil or petroleum products which will be accepted by a pipe line company for transportation. These minimum tenders vary from 1,000 to 100,000 barrels, although the tariffs of many pipe lines contain provisions for the accommodation of small shippers who are unable to meet the minimum tenders.[35]

Unlike the practice of preparing the shipping order as a carbon copy of the uniform domestic bill of lading, a pipe line "Notice of Shipment" is a separate document, one of which is reproduced below:

---

[34] Wilson, G. L., & Bryan, L. A.: *Air Transportation,* Prentice-Hall, New York, 1949, pp. 333–336.
[35] Wilson, G. L.: *Miscellaneous Transportation and Rates, op. cit.,* pp. 114–115.

NOTICE OF SHIPMENT
Not Negotiable

Shipment No.   1391
Date   May 15, 1953

Shipper   Skelly Oil Company
Will offer to the Phillips Pipe Line Company a shipment
To originate at   Borger, Texas
And be available for inspection on   June 1, 1953
The shipment to consist of:

    Quantity   91,000 barrels
    Grade   W
    Specifications   13#

Shipment to be transported to terminal points as designated below:

Terminal Points	Quantity	Consignee
Kansas City	91,000 barrels	Skelly Oil Company

Any over or under barrelage to be applied to the following terminal
   and consignee   Kansas City (Skelly)
Transportation and loading and billing charges, in accordance with
the tariffs, shall be prepaid by the consignor at the point of origin.
All subsequent charges in accordance with the tariffs shall be paid
the consignee and such payment guaranteed by the consignor.

Accepted:
Date_____Time_____

<u>   Skelly Oil Company   </u>   Phillips Pipe Line Company
          Shipper

By_____   By_____

A typical Tender of Shipment, which serves the same purpose as
a bill of lading, is a nonnegotiable document which is prepared in
quadruplicate and reads, as follows: [36]

TENDER OF SHIPMENT

Pipe Line Order No._____

Shipper's No._____
_____ 19____

PHILLIPS PIPE LINE COMPANY

Shipment is hereby tendered at_____
To be delivered to_____
of____ thousand barrels of 42 gallons each of____ crude petroleum oil
and____   "   " " " " |" "____ "   "   "
                       Joint)
Subject to rate and regulations in_____Local) Tariff No._____
   which are filed and posted according to law.
      Accepted:

PHILLIPS PIPE LINE COMPANY

_____
             (Shipper's Name)
By_____
Date_____   _____
                (Address)

---

[36] Information furnished by Mr. M. E. Foster, President, Phillips Pipe Line
Company, Bartlesville, Oklahoma, July 13, 1953.

62

In addition to the several types of bills of lading, there remain four other shipping documents which are of direct concern to the industrial traffic manager, namely: the arrival notice, the freight bill, the delivery receipt, and the indemnity bond.

Arrival Notice. Unless a shipment is to be delivered directly to the consignee, the carrier's agent at point of destination will notify the consignee that his shipment has arrived. This notification is an official document known as the "arrival notice." It contains full information concerning the shipment, and it informs the consignee that the shipment is available for delivery to him upon payment of freight charges, if any. The arrival notice is sent by United States Mail, and the postmark thereon determines the official time of notification. In numerous instances, local arrangements may be in effect whereby information of a shipment's arrival is extended by telephone; but in such cases, the carrier's agent may supplement the oral advice by mailing the official arrival notice.

The arrival notice is important for a number of reasons. It serves the obvious purpose of informing the consignee that his freight has arrived at the local depot of the carrier. This can be of considerable significance if the consignee has no facilities of his own at which or with which to unload a carload or truckload shipment, and particularly if the shipment is covered by an order bill of lading. In case of the latter, it will be recalled the freight will not be delivered until the original copy of the order bill, properly endorsed, is surrendered to the carrier. If the consignee had made no inquiry of the carrier, without the arrival notice there would be no way for him to know his shipment was available for delivery to him.

The arrival notice serves notice on the consignee as to the time in which he has to secure his shipment from the carrier's depot. A penalty charge is assessed if a shipment is not removed from carrier's property within a stated period of time called "free time." If the freight is left on the carrier's premises, the charge for the extra time after free time is known as "storage." If a shipment is not unloaded from a railroad freight car within the specified time, the charge for detention of the car beyond free time is known as "demurrage." In addition to the extra expense to the consignee, there is a vast difference in the extent of the carrier's liability for loss or damage after the expiration of free time. The arrival notice indicates the beginning of free time for unloading carload freight or for removal of the freight from the carrier's premises. Hence, by strict observance of the free time as shown by the arrival notice, an industrial traffic manager can save his firm considerable expense. Likewise, the reduced liability of the carrier after free time could be of significance.

Freight Bill. Like any other business enterprise, carriers render statements to their customers for services rendered; but, as has been pointed out previously, carriers operate on a cash basis. While arrangements may be made for extension of credit for the convenience of some shippers and consignees so that there need not be the necessity for actual payment of all applicable charges at the time of delivery of freight, the periods of time in which the carriers' freight bills must be paid are limited. The extension of credit for thirty days or longer, which is routine in many businesses, does not exist in the transportation industry of the United States. Likewise, the common practice of allowing two percent discount for payment of a bill within ten days does not apply to American carriers. The only customer of the carriers to whom unlimited credit is extended, both as to amount and time of payment, is the federal government for shipments moving on government bills of lading.

On a prepay shipment, where the consignor pays the freight rate at the time of shipment, the carrier's agent at point of origin presents a freight bill to the shipper on which is acknowledgment for the sum paid. Hence, it serves as a receipt for payment of charges. A freight bill is not issued at point of origin if the shipment moves on the basis of freight charges to be collected by the carrier from the consignee.

At destination of a shipment, the carrier's agent is required to present a freight bill to the consignee, regardless of whether the shipment is prepaid or collect. If completely prepaid, of course, there is no collection by the carrier. If collect, or if any charges for any service whatsoever have accrued since departure of the shipment from point of origin, the consignee is required to pay all such charges. Upon payment of the amount specified by the freight bill, acknowledgment thereof is made by the carrier's agent and, hence, the bill serves as a receipt for the consignee.

The freight bill contains complete information concerning the shipment. In addition to listing in detail all the charges involved, including the obnoxious transportation tax, the freight bill describes the shipment, names of consignor and consignee, route, and other data taken from the original shipping order and waybill. The freight bill is identified by a number, preceded by the letters "P R O" which mean "progressive" as the bills are numbered consecutively from the first of each month by the issuing agent or station. If the shipment has been forwarded on a C.O.D. basis, the freight bill will show the amount to be collected from the consignee, together with the carrier's extra charge for performing the C.O.D. service.

In addition to being a document of record showing the prices of all carrier services performed for a given shipment, the paid freight bill is a receipt. It is evidence that the owner of the shipment has complied with his part of the bill of lading contract by the payment of all lawful charges. This evidence is of vital importance in the event a claim subsequently is filed against the carrier. The original paid freight bill is a basic document in support of a claim, and it must be presented when filing claim against a carrier for overcharge, loss, or damage.

In practice, the carriers prepare the freight bill in manifold. Carbon copies are used for the arrival notice and copy thereof for the carrier's record, delivery receipt, memorandum for the carrier's cashier and for accounting purposes, station record of the shipment, and for other purposes as may be desired by the carrier.

As long as human beings are engaged in the preparation of the various shipping documents and in the handling of freight shipments, honest errors are bound to occur. The consignee may have misdescribed the shipment on the bill of lading, resulting in a higher rate being assessed than would apply to the correct description. The carrier's rating clerk or the shipper himself may have used an incorrect rate. There could have been a mistake in the weight of the shipment. Figures in the rate or weight, or both, might have been transposed. The wrong tariff may have been used. Many, many things can occur by honest error which alter the charges shown on the freight bill. Professor Wilson has summarized some of the sources of error, as follows: [37]

1. Mathematical errors in extending charges.
2. Transposition of figures in charge columns.
3. Incorrect total charges due to the addition of an extra digit.
4. Incorrect shipping points when different rates apply from the different points.
5. Incorrect shipping dates, when rates change upon dates just prior to shipment.
6. Disagreements between shipping and billing dates, in cases where rate changes have occurred between these dates.
7. Incorrect car numbers due to the transfer of the goods from one car to another which may effect charges by higher carload minima applying to larger cars.
8. Junction rebilling errors, when incorrect advance charges are carried forward.
9. Incorrect weights at which the freight is billed.
10. Application of incorrect tariffs.

---

[37] Wilson, G. L.: *Industrial Traffic Management, op. cit.*, pp. 123–124.

11. Misdescription of articles, resulting in higher rates than are lawfully applicable.
12. Transposition of figures in the weight or rate columns.
13. Incorrect description of containers.
14. Erroneous assessment of penalty ratings for improper containers.
15. Incorrect delivery arrangements that result in extra cartage charges.
16. Mistake in number of packages.
17. Failure to credit prepayments or partial prepayments.
18. Incorrect additions of special charges that should have been absorbed in rates, or failure to absorb charges properly absorbed.
19. Failure of carriers to protect lowest rated routes.
20. Incorrect or improper addition of charges of connecting carriers.
21. Charges at combinations of local rates higher than through rates properly applicable.
22. Charges based on through rates higher than lawful aggregate of intermediate rates.
23. Use of actual weights in place of authorized estimated weights.
24. Failure to allow for dunnage and bracing provided for in tariffs.
25. Unauthorized higher rates for shorter than for longer hauls over same line or route in same direction or same traffic without fourth section relief.
26. Failure to absorb proper amounts out of the line-haul rates for switching or spotting as provided for by absorption tariffs.
27. Errors in routes resulting in higher charges.

It is the unquestioned responsibility of the industrial traffic manager to have in his organization qualified personnel to scrutinize each and every freight bill with meticulous care in search of errors. If an overcharge is discovered, the industry is entitled to a refund from the carrier and, upon presentation of the facts and necessary supporting papers for the claim within the statutory period of nine months, reimbursement will be made. Likewise, if an undercharge is found, it is the moral as well as the legal obligation of the industrial traffic manager to reimburse the carrier. There is only one lawful rate on any shipment and that one rate is the one to be applied, and it alone!

Delivery Receipt. When a shipment is delivered, the consignee signs a delivery receipt which, usually, is a carbon copy of the freight bill. It is retained by the carrier as evidence of its having fulfilled the contract of carriage contained in the bill of lading.

The delivery receipt contains a statement to the effect that the goods covered thereby were received by the consignee in apparent good order. If there is evidence of damage or shortage at the time of delivery, the consignee makes an appropriate notation on the receipt, and the carrier's representative signs a similar notation on the freight bill. The primary purpose of a receipt is to provide a written statement of facts which existed at the time of its execution. A delivery receipt showing that a shipment was received by the consignee in apparent good condition is only *prima facie* evidence thereof. The facts which obtained at the time of delivery, although determined at a later date and regardless of statements on the delivery receipt itself, are what govern.[38]

Some consignees erroneously believe they are protecting themselves when they accept delivery of a shipment by inserting on the delivery receipt such notations, as: "subject to further check," "received subject to recount," "subject to our count, weight, and inspection," and others. Such endorsements serve no useful purpose, and, in fact, they should not be accepted by the carrier. If, at some future date following physical delivery, shortage or damage is discovered, after the consignee has had reasonable time in which to unpack and inspect the shipment, convincing evidence will show that the data contained on the delivery receipt was in error, and "the effect of the receipt will be modified to reflect the true conditions. It is upon this theory, for example, that carriers honor claims for concealed loss and damage although a 'clear' receipt was obtained at time of delivery. . . . It would appear that there could be little doubt that a so-called receipt bearing the notation 'received subject to later count and inspection,' or other vague general notation, would in fact not constitute a bona fide receipt which a carrier would have to accept when making tender of delivery." Continuing, John M. Miller states: [39]

The use of qualified delivery receipts is usually for the sole attempted purpose of "covering-up" inefficiency at the receiving point. Their use is a constant encouragement for dishonesty on the part of the consignee's employees. Instances have been cited where material has been taken directly from the receiving docks direct to production departments, without proper records, and claim later asserted against the delivering carrier solely as a result of carelessness on part of consignee's employees developed as a result of using qualified receipts. . . . There are few things more absurd than a delivery receipt for one or two pieces of merchandise boldly signed by the consignee as "received subject to recount."

In summary, there are two documents involved when freight is delivered to the consignee by a carrier, *viz.:* (1) the freight bill which is signed by the carrier's representative and retained by the consignee; (2) the delivery receipt which is signed by the consignee, or his representative, and retained by the carrier.

---

[38] Miller, J. M.: *Law of Freight Loss and Damage Claims,* William C. Brown Company, Dubuque, 1953, pp. 164–166.

[39] *Ibid.,* pp. 165–166.

Indemnity Bond. It will be recalled from the discussion of the order bill of lading that if the original copy of the bill is not available for surrender to the carrier, the shipment may be delivered to the consignee upon his execution of an indemnity bond.

In addition to its use in connection with an order bill, the indemnity bond may serve as identification of a consignee for shipments moving on a straight bill of lading. The carrier is bound to deliver a shipment to the consignee specified in the bill of lading. If the consignee is known personally to the agent of the delivering carrier, normally there is no problem in effecting delivery. However, when the consignee is not known by the carrier's agent, or if he is unable to furnish adequate identification, or if he is unable to produce the bill of lading to identify himself as the person to receive the shipment, then the carrier may insist upon execution of an indemnity bond to protect itself from possible fraud or incorrect delivery. A thief could present himself to the carrier's agent and represent himself to be the person named as consignee in the bill of lading. If the carrier proceeded to deliver the freight to him on the sole basis of his statement and subsequently the true consignee appeared, identified himself, and lawfully demanded delivery of his goods, the carrier would be liable to the rightful owner for the value of the shipment. It can be understood, therefore, that a carrier is justified in requiring the indemnity bond under certain conditions.

Another use of the indemnity bond relates to claims. Although claims are discussed later, the original bill of lading and the paid freight bill are required as supporting papers to a claim. If neither can be produced by the claimant, the indemnity bond will suffice. Again, it serves as protection to the carrier.

Chapter 5

CLASSIFICATION—
Part I

The heart of a traffic department is its rate section; but before there can be an understanding of rates themselves, a knowledge of classification is essential. Classification is the initial step in rate-making; it is the basis for determining the actual rates on thousands of shipments, and it is the cornerstone of rate structures.

A diligent effort has been made to present this subject in as simple a manner as possible. At the beginning, no attempt is made to explain, nor justify, nor even mention the many exceptions to the Classification that exist, for to do so would only add confusion to a complex situation. Likewise, commodity rates will be ignored. As the reader pursues the study of traffic, an appreciation of the significance of classification will become apparent; and the application of exceptions, class, commodity, and other tariffs may be more readily understood.

Matters pertaining to classification are published in volumes which, for the present, will be referred to as the *Classification*. There is no single Classification applicable to goods which are shipped by all modes of transportation with the result that all common carriers of the United States do not subscribe to one and the same Classification. In the interest of brevity, the Classification used by railroads will be referred to as the Rail Classification; that by motor carriers, the Motor Classification; and so on.

Introductory. In Chapter 1, classification was defined as the grouping of commodities into a limited number of classes, or groups, for the application of rates.[1] Hence, classification is the segregation of goods possessing more or less similar characteristics into specified categories. Rates are applied to those categories or groups, and the necessity for making a separate rate for each individual article is

---

[1] See, p. 4, above.

eliminated. The primary purpose of the process is simplification in rate determination. The result is that hundreds of different articles are placed in the same group, which is known as a *class;* and each class into which the various articles are grouped is assigned a rating. The word "rating" must not be confused with the word "rate." Although closely related, there is a distinct difference in meaning. As the Interstate Commerce Commission stated in 1901, "The fixing of a classification determines the relation of rates, not the rate itself . . . (and) a plain distinction exists between fixing a rate and determining a relation in rates." [2]

A most precise explanation of classification has been devised by Joseph C. Colquitt, former Chairman of the motor carriers' National Classification Board, which was published in one of a series of copyrighted articles in *Transport Topics* which were edited by Fred G. Freund, Secretary of the National Traffic Committee and Director of the Traffic Department of the American Trucking Associations, Inc., as follows: [3]

What is classification? In its broadest sense freight classification is a relation. It is an economical and practical method of equitably distributing freight charges on, and applying them to, articles of commerce offered for transportation by rail, express, and motor service.

In its narrower sense, it is a relative distribution, governed by various elements (which are described later in Chapter 7), of all such articles into numbered or lettered classes, otherwise known as ratings, for the purpose of determining conveniently what is the measure of the rate from point A to point B in cents per 100 pounds on a given article packed in a certain form . . . (It is) the arrangement of the several articles of commerce under different heads, as pupils in a school may be arranged in classes for recitations . . .

At this point, it is advisable to distinguish between a *rating* and a *rate*. Although closely related, the meaning of each is different and often, interpretation of the two terms is confused. It is incorrect to use the words interchangeably. As the Interstate Commerce Commission stated over half a century ago, "The fixing of a classification determines the relation of rates, not the rate itself . . . (and) a plain distinction exists between fixing a rate and determining a relation in rates." [4] Hundreds of different articles are placed in a given group known as a *class*. There are several classes and each is assigned a rating; therefore, there is a relative relationship among the

---

[2] *The Hatters' Furs Case,* 9 I.C.C. 79 (86), 1901.
[3] Colquitt, J. C.: *The Act and Development of Freight Classification,* National Motor Freight Classification Association, Inc., Washington, 1956, p. 1.
[4] *The Hatters' Furs Case,* 9 I.C.C. 79 (86), 1901.

classes, and a rating is the designation of a class. The assignment of articles to classes is a vital part of the classification process. A rate, on the other hand, is the price of a carrier for providing a stipulated transportation service. A rate refers only to the amount of money in dollars and cents charged for hauling goods from one designated place to another. Hence, carriers derive their income from rates, whereas a rating is the indicator of what the rate shall be on a particular commodity. If the rate on a particular commodity yields a carrier an amount which is much higher than the income derived from some other comparable commodity, then the rating, not the rate, should be reduced, and vice versa. On the other hand, if carrier revenues *as a whole* are too low, the remedy lies in read-justment of the rates. "Classifications are not the correct media for remedying inequalities in territorial rate levels, which should be accomplished by modifying the rates themselves." [5]

Classes are identified in the published Classifications in two ways, viz.: (1) by a numbered or lettered class, as first class, second class, or class A, class B, etc.; or (2) by a figure, as 80, 37½, or 125, and so on. First class and class 100 are the same and both are the bases of all the other classes which are percentages of the basic first class or class 100 rating. For example, second class is 85 percent of first class and, therefore, a rating of second class means 85 percent of the first class *rate* applies to the particular shipment involved. Likewise, class 125 means 125 percent of the first class rate is applicable. The classes into which articles are grouped will be explained later.

The rating of each class is different in that each class bears a different percentage relationship to first class. Generally, high valued freight carries a higher percentage of the first class rating than low-valued freight. The higher the rating, the greater the amount of the freight rate.

Prior to 1952, the classes were first class, second class, third class, etc. Except for a Classification used by certain motor carriers in New England, first class *always* is the base, or one hundred percent; and the other classes are percentages of first class. Hence, the rating of any commodity may be considered as its percentage of first class, or its percentage relationship to first class, unless the commodity under consideration happens to be allocated to first class. Since 1952, the system of identification by first class or second class, etc., has been abandoned generally in the territory east of the Rocky Mountains for the more simple plan of showing a number which

---

[5] Class Rate Investigation, 1939, 262 I.C.C. 447 (509), 1945.

itself is the percentage relationship to the base 100 percent. As stated above, first class is always 100 percent. Second class is 85 percent, third class is 70 percent, and so on; but under the new system, the rating is shown as the percentage figure itself. There is no longer a first, second, or third class. Instead, an article which would have been assigned to first class is now rated simply as 100; the former second class, as 85; etc.

The question may well be asked: why bother with the old system of classification ratings when it has been supplanted by a new system? There are a number of reasons. In the first place, in order to understand the new system, a sound knowledge of the old is essential. Secondly, the new method does *not* apply on a completely national basis for all shipments and under all conditions. The old system still is effective for the vast area of the United States west of the Rocky Mountains, for some types of transcontinental traffic, on certain shipments moving generally between points west of the Mississippi River, and the current issue of the railroads' *Uniform Freight Classification No. 2*, which became effective December 10, 1953, states at page 514 that ratings on certain articles "will not apply on traffic moving between or destined to points in" several specified states east of the Mississippi River. Therefore, the old system must be used for certain traffic. Thirdly, and this feature will be discussed in greater detail later, there still exist many "Exceptions" to the old system in the East and South, which means the old system governs such shipments as are covered by those "Exceptions."

Because of this overlapping, at the present time the old method of classification continues in use for certain types of traffic and in specified geographical areas; therefore, familiarity with both the old and the new systems is essential, and the new method may be considered as being supplementary to the old. Undoubtedly, with the passing of years, the old will be entirely superseded by the new, for the ultimate objective of the Interstate Commerce Commission is complete uniformity of classification for the nation as a whole. To add to the confusion, it should be mentioned in passing that still a third method of classification is used by motor carriers in the New England states, and the Railway Express Agency, Inc., has its own method of classification, both of which will be explained later.

Following the process of assigning articles to different classes, a rate is determined for first class or class 100, which means the price is the same for shipping all articles in a given class between the same points by the same kind of transportation service. To illustrate, if the first class rate from "here" to "yonder" is $1.00 per hundred pounds by ABC Truck Line or XYZ Railroad, then the rate of $1.00 applies to all articles that carry a rating of first class or class 100. Technically expressed, for identical transportation services the *rate* for all articles of the same *rating* is the same between the same points.

For example, for shipments moving by railroad under the old method of classification in carload quantities, corn degerminators, adding machines, weather vanes, sheet music, pecan cracking machines, embroidery hoops, dry alligator hides, bananas, fried pork skins, artificial Christmas trees, automatic cigar cutters, eye glass cases, and hundreds of other items are placed in third class.[6] Since third class is 70 percent of first class, if the first class rate were $1.00, the price for shipping all the articles grouped in third class between two given points would be 70 percent of $1.00, or 70 cents. Under the new system of classification, all the articles which formerly were "rated" third class do not necessarily carry the equivalent third class rating of 70 percent of the base 100, or first class, rating. Public hearings which were conducted throughout the country prior to 1952 developed factual information which lead the carriers to change some ratings while others remained the same. The new system continued the rating of 70, which is the same percentage relationship of old third class, for all the articles mentioned above, except: corn degerminators and embroidery hoops were increased to Class 85, and pecan cracking machines were decreased to Class 45.[7]

Continuing the illustration further, there are some commodities which are assigned to a rating higher than first class. Thus, under both the old and the new systems of classification, less-than-carload and less-than-truckload shipments of airplane wings, fur hats, hobby horses, and others carry a rating of double first class and Class 200, respectively; and airplane pontoons are four times first class or Class 400.[8]

Classification, the grouping of commodities into a limited number

---

[6] *Consolidated Freight Classification No. 20*, Consolidated Classification Committee, Chicago, effective October 15, 1951, Items 27820, 27605, 45479, 33100, 30055, 24175, 23940, 19255, 18712, 14665, 14440, 9615; *National Motor Freight Classification No. 10*, American Trucking Associations, Inc., Washington, effective August 13, 1949, Items 56570, 59160, 96710, 70370, 63930, 52310, 51830, 41850, 40570, 31720, 31310, 20530.

[7] *Uniform Freight Classification No. 2*, Consolidated Classification Committee, Chicago, effective December 10, 1953, same item numbers as above; *National Motor Freight Classification No. A-1*, American Trucking Associations, Inc., Washington, effective June 10, 1952, same item numbers as above.

[8] *Consolidated Freight Classification No. 20* and *Uniform Freight Classification No. 2, op. cit.*, Items 1380, 23815, 20755, 1315; *National Motor Freight Classification No. 10* and *No. A-1, op. cit.*, Items 2950, 51490, 45130, 2730.

of classes, therefore, establishes the rating of each of those various commodities; and freight rates are applied to those several ratings. As the Supreme Court of the United States said many years ago, "Classification in carrier rate-making practice is grouping—the associating in a designated list commodities which . . . may justly and conveniently be given similar rates." [9] As was mentioned earlier, it must be kept in mind that a classification rating is *not* the freight rate itself. The rating designates the class to which an article is assigned. The rate, which is the price of the carrier in dollars and/or cents for performing the service of transportation, is determined from the classification rating. Again, to quote Mr. Colquitt: [10]

The rates for the different classes or, technically speaking, the class rates, are separately published in what are known as class rate tariffs, which show therein to what classification each tariff is subject. In short, the class rate tariffs are the expression in cents per one hundred pounds of the classified ratings found in the Classifications. Classification is to class rates what equity is to statutory law—flexibility as compared to rigidity. . . . classification of freight is a logical and natural development, the idea, of course, primarily being a plan of convenience and simplification as well as a fair method of distribution of freight charges on all articles.

Throughout its long and distinguished existence, the Interstate Commerce Commission has commented frequently on classification, some of which are presented below.[11] Classification is of such funda-

[9] *Director General v. Viscose Company,* 254 U. S. 498 (500), 1921.
[10] Colquitt, *op. cit.,* p. 14.
[11] "Classification in its nature must be a compromise."—*Proctor & Gamble Company v. Cincinnati, H & D Railroad Company,* 3 I.C.C. 131 (137), 1889.
"No classification can be so minute as to conform to the different varieties and conditions of traffic. To separate different grades of densities of the same articles into different classes with varying rates, even if it could be accomplished, would go far to defeat the real purpose of classification."—*Planters Compress Company v. Cleveland, Cincinnati, Chicago & St. Louis Railway Company,* 11 I.C.C. 382 (405), 1905.
"A rating accorded a particular commodity may not be determined alone by the yardstick, the scales, and the dollar. At best, it (classification) is but a grouping . . ."—*Forest City Freight Bureau v. Ann Arbor Railroad Company,* 18 I.C.C. 205, 1910.
"Classification is an art or a science in itself. A classification is a universal tariff from which the schedules of individual carriers should not depart except in cases demanded by special conditions."—*Investigation & Suspension Docket 76,* 25 I.C.C. 442 (453), 1912.
"Classification is intended to offer a standardization of rate relationships."—*Rates on Lumber and Lumber Products,* 52 I.C.C. 598 (604), 1919.
"Classification is largely a matter of comparison of all commodities that move as freight and the assignment of ratings such that each shall bear its fair share of the transportation burden."—*Classification of Canned Goods,* 98 I.C.C. 166 (176), 1925.
"For each group of commodities as thus classified, carriers must establish a class rate, which rate, likewise under normal conditions of transportation, must be reasonable for application to all the commodities in that class."—*Barshi & Son v. Baltimore & Ohio Railroad Company,* 155 I.C.C. 350 (351), 1929.

74

mental importance to rate-making that a thorough understanding of its basic principles cannot be overemphasized.

Necessity for Classification. Classification of freight is the primary basis for rate construction. Another reason for classification is simplification. It is much easier to determine the rate applicable to a particular class which embraces a large number of commodities than to have a heterogeneous mass of individual rates for each commodity. Since it is impractical, if not impossible, to make and publish a separate rate for each article, the process of freight classification has been developed.

A third reason for freight classification is that it is an easy and convenient guide to shippers and carriers alike. The data are printed in accordance with requirements of the Interstate Commerce Commission and they are available to anyone. Accurate application of the provisions contained in the published volumes to the proper tariffs, which will be described later,[12] enables a shipper to ascertain the amount he must pay for transportation services; and, at the same time, makes it possible for him to determine the shipping costs of his competitors.

The published Classification used by railroads [13] contains over 30,-000 items describing various commodities which are shipped daily in the commerce of the United States, and there is an unknown number of other articles of a semifabricated nature which do not have a specific classification identification by name. As of October 1, 1953, there were 57,130 railroad stations in the United States, 9,011 in Canada, and 2,377 in Mexico, making a total of 68,518 stations between which freight may be shipped by railroad on one bill of lading.[14] It should be understood that this figure does not mean there are 68,518 different cities and towns, because hundreds of places are served by more than one railroad, each railroad usually having its own facilities, and frequently an individual railroad operates more than one depot in many of the larger cities; but it does show the colossal possibilities for movements of freight by railroad alone, together with the complexities involved in determining fair and reasonable rates for all articles of commerce between all those stations. Furthermore, there are thousands of "blind sidings" and industrial spurs to and from which rail shipments are made.

Motor carriers serve virtually every city, town, and hamlet, as well as intermediate points. The exact number of places is not

---

[12] See, p. 143, below.

[13] *Uniform Freight Classification No. 2, op. cit.,* pp. 187–451.

[14] Information furnished by A. P. Leland, Agent, *Official List of Open and Prepay Stations,* Station List Publishing Company, St. Louis, in letter dated February 4, 1954.

known; but there are several times the number served by motor carriers than by railroads. It has been reported that in the State of Tennessee there are over 2,000 communities, including 30 county seats, and 14 entire counties that have no rail service and are dependent upon motor carriers.[15]

To the huge number of points to and from which freight is moved by railroads and common carrier motor trucks must be added the stations served by other modes of transportation. Since, under the laws of the land, rates must be determined and published by all types of common carriers for all articles that comprise the commerce of the nation, an extremely complicated situation is apparent.

Attempt to visualize citizens in each of the thousands of communities in the United States shipping numerous and diverse commodities in varying quantities to persons and factories at other places! It is not an academic problem, because, actually, it occurs just about every day of the year. There must be an established price for those thousands of daily transportation transactions. It has been pointed out earlier that these prices of common carriers must be the same for all persons and that they must be published in duly authorized and approved documents known as "tariffs." Now, continue the mental picture of there being published a separate rate for each of the thousands of articles to and from each of the thousands of communities by each of the thousands of individual carriers. Immediately, the impracticability of such a fantastic situation is obvious. Why, to make all those prices available to the public, as required by law, would necessitate numbers of huge buildings scattered over the country in which to house the tariffs alone, to say nothing of the personnel which would be required to man such fabulous establishments! And then, there would be a very serious question as to whether or not a prospective shipper could find the price of a particular service he desires, to say nothing of the inconvenience to both shippers and carriers. The answer to the dilemma is Classification.

Evolution of Classification. Classification is not a modern device with which to simplify rate-making and rate determination. The long-forgotten wagoner, creeping through the South Carolina swamps in the early 1700's over the "Old State Road" from Charleston into the interior, and in Pennsylvania over the "Lancaster Pike" from Philadelphia, who decided that "light" goods would be hauled at a higher rate per hundred pounds that "heavy" goods, was clas-

---

[15] Tennessee Motor Transport Association, *Tennessee Trucking Industry,* Nashville, 1952, pp. 24–25.

sifying his traffic. Admittedly simple and crude, nevertheless, it was classification of commodities for freight rate purposes.

Shortly after the turn of the nineteenth century, the Sheffield Canal, and a few years later in 1830, the Stockton & Darlington Railroad, both in England, grouped articles into five classes and assigned a specific rate to each class. For example, the canal company assessed a rate of two pence per ton-mile "for all coal, coke, charcoal, limestone, slag, sand arusa, sweep-washing waste, stones, slates, cord-wood, cinders, manure, bones for manure, turnips, carrots, and potatoes"; and the railroad levied a flat charge "for all goods, commodities and merchandise not before specified." In America, an inland water carrier on the Mississippi River announced in 1816, "from New Orleans to Louisville, 4½ cents per pound for heavy goods, and 6 cents for light." [16]

Historically, the early American railroads of over a century ago adopted the same principles of their predecessor wagon and canal companies by the simple method of distinguishing only between "heavy" and "light" articles in order to more evenly equalize the revenues derived from a carload of freight. There was no fixed rate per unit of weight as is the custom today; instead, articles of light weight were assessed a rate on the basis of cubic feet, and the rate for heavy shipments was determined by weight. The ancient charter of the old South Carolina Railroad in 1827 provided that rates would be one-half of the usual wagon charge.[17] Likewise, freight rates were proportioned according to an arbitrary mileage charge based upon length of haul. The rating itself was determined either by the weight of the shipment or by the space it occupied, the carrier reserving the right to employ the one which produced the greater revenue.[18] In passing, it is interesting to observe that this ancient dual space-weight system still is followed by ocean carriers and, in a modified form, by air carriers.

By 1848, most of the American railroads were segregating freight into groups and applying rates to those groups, and a few railroads even identified the groups by numbers.[19] In 1855, the South Carolina Railroad, today comprising most of the Charleston Division of the Southern Railway System but which in its day (1833) was the long-

---

[16] Colquitt, *op. cit.*, p. 2.
[17] Ripley, W. Z.: *Railroads: Rates and Regulation*, Longmans, Green & Company, New York, 1923, pp. 306–307.
[18] Cushman, F. M.: *Transportation for Management*, Prentice-Hall, New York, 1953, p. 162.
[19] Healy, K. T.: *Economics of Transportation in America*, Ronald Press, New York, 1940, p. 203.

est railroad in the world,[20] issued a combination classification and tariff of rates which provided for four classes and listed some 300 articles. It typified the "primitive" traffic conditions of the times, but, nevertheless, established four classes. It is interesting to observe that first class, among other commodities, included such incongruous articles as ladies' bonnets, pianos, and tea; "but it is evident that rough classification according to weight, value, use and service was being attempted" and it was "far more elaborate than those commonly used at the time." [21] At about the same time, the Louisville & Nashville Railroad had established three classes, first class being based upon bulk, second class on weight, and third class for live stock. It was reported that in Illinois, the Classification was printed on the back of the bill of lading and consumed only a part of the page.[22]

In 1859, the Baltimore & Ohio Railroad, which has the distinction of being the first common carrier railroad in the United States,[23] established a classification in which 342 articles were assigned to four classes which were identified as "first class," "second class," etc.; and it is interesting to note that this early publication provided that, "All articles not weighing 500 pounds or more, shall pay first class rates, though they may be named in a lower class, but not more than 500 pounds would pay under the class in which they are named." [24] Shortly thereafter, in 1864, the Michigan Southern & Northern Indiana Railroad, now a part of the New York Central System extending between Chicago, Toledo, and Detroit, published in pamphlet form a "Revised Classification of Articles" which contained four classes under which all articles were listed alphabetically instead of under generic headings as is the modern procedure.[25] In 1866, the Georgia Railroad grouped some 500 commodities into nine classes.[26] Many other individual railroad classifications appeared, but those mentioned above serve "as well authenticated examples" of the development of classification and "the intimate relation" thereof to the commerce of America.[27]

During the late 1850's, a definite percentage relationship between classes began to be established, thereby originating the modern

[20] Way, William, Jr.: *The Clinchfield Railroad,* University of North Carolina Press, Chapel Hill, 1932, p. 15.
[21] Ripley, *op. cit.,* p. 307.
[22] *Ibid.,* p. 308.
[23] Hungenford, Edward: *The Story of the Baltimore and Ohio Railroad,* G. P. Putnam's Sons, New York, 1928, p. 1.
[24] Colquitt, *op. cit.,* p. 4.
[25] Colquitt, *op. cit.,* p. 5.
[26] Colquitt, *op. cit.,* pp. 4–5.
[27] Colquitt, *op. cit.,* pp. 5–6.

system of classification. A typical classification of the times made first class the base 100 percent rating in the same manner as ratings are recognized today, thus: second class was 80 percent of first class, third class was 67 percent, and fourth class was 50 percent.[28] The present day concept of classification had been born.

The immortal Professor William Z. Ripley, of Harvard University, summarizes the situation which existed during the 1870's, as follows: [29]

. . . Denver, for example, under the Western Classification enjoys no carload rates, while competitors at San Francisco have a large number . . . All sorts of details, covering relatively unimportant differences in conditions of carriage, bill of lading contracts, marking and packing, led to constant confusion and annoyance, especially in cases of shipment from one classification territory to another. An eastern shipper of iron bolts, having in mind that a gunny sack is equivalent to a box or barrel in the East, orders a small shipment in a bag to a far western point. He finds that bolts in bags under the rules of Western Classification, are specially enumerated only for carload lots, and that he must pay a rate one class higher for such shipment than if contained in a barrel, box or keg. This difference in classification may more than absorb his profit . . . Only in a customs tariff of the United States would one expect to find any such complexity as is discoverable in railway documents of this sort. . . . Not only the increasing refinement of commerce, but the technical nomenclature or trade jargon, necessary for the specific and accurate description of so many thousands of articles, have conspired to render these documents extremely cumbersome in the absence of a general revision and simplification.

By the middle of the 1870's, more and more attention was being directed to classification matters, but in a disorganized way. Data pertaining to classification were printed in separate pamphlets entirely distinct from the publications containing the actual rates. A greater number of commodities were being included in the classes, more detailed descriptions of articles began to appear, more elaborate shipping rules were being created, and additional classes were established. In general, however, each individual railroad continued to issue its own classification for its own purposes and which applied only to traffic moving over its line. "The classification business was, in short, in extraordinary disorder." [30]

There existed no semblance of standardization in the allocation of articles to particular classes, in the percentage relationships of the classes, nor in the actual freight rates themselves which were ap-

[28] Healy, *op. cit.,* p. 203.
[29] Ripley, *op. cit.,* pp. 312–313.
[30] Colquitt, *op. cit.,* pp. 6–7.

plied to those class ratings. Each individual railroad had its own system of classification which was designed to meet its needs in accordance with the ideas of its management. Consequently, "there was soon a muddle of classifications." [31] Furthermore, there was no cooperative action on the part of individual carriers until well after the Civil War to accomplish the rudimentary elements of uniformity which exist today. It should be remembered that each railroad was what is considered now as being a "short line," its management was composed of highly individualistic persons, and there were few, if any, "joint" through rates which characterize the modern method of shipping freight over the lines of a number of carriers for long distances. The automatic manner in which freight cars and, more recently, truck trailers are interchanged among carriers today to facilitate the through movement of shipments was unknown, and standardization of railroad gauge was not accomplished until about 1886.[32]

In the evolution of classification, one early railroad established five classes: heavy goods, light goods, case goods, logs, and whiskey.[33] It is reported that in the 1880's, one railroad alone had nine different classifications in effect at the same time; [34] and that there were 138 different classifications in the East.[35] Some lines used one classification for traffic moving in one direction and another classification for goods being shipped in the opposite direction.[36] The complexity of those early shipping conditions must have been intolerable, for it must have been most difficult, and frequently impossible, for both carrier representatives and shippers to determine exactly what amount the price for transportation would be, particularly on long-haul shipments moving over several railroads.

As the economy of the United States expanded, more and more articles of varying kinds were tendered to the railroads and steamship lines for shipment. Likewise, distances of shipments increased. The nation's railroad net-work consisted of a hodgepodge of short lines each having its own system of classification with the resulting confusion to shippers. For example, the through rail route of the

[31] Colquitt, op. cit., p. 6.
[32] Henry, R. S.: This Fascinating Railroad Business, Third Edition, Bobbs-Merrill Publishing Company, Indianapolis, 1946, p. 37.
[33] Bigham, T. C., & Roberts, M. J.: Transportation, McGraw-Hill Book Company, New York, 1952, p. 390.
[34] Knorst, W. J.: Transportation and Traffic Management, Vol. 1, College of Advanced Traffic, Chicago, 1947, p. 73.
[35] Daggett, Stuart: Principles of Inland Transportation, Third Edition, Harper & Brothers, New York, 1941, p. 339.
[36] Colquitt, op. cit., p. 6.

present day Atlantic Coast Line Railroad from Richmond, Virginia, to Jacksonville, Florida, consisted of no less than eight different companies, as follows: [37]

Richmond to Petersburg—Richmond & Petersburg Railroad (completed, 1838)

Petersburg to Weldon—Petersburg Railroad (completed, 1834)

Weldon to Wilmington—Wilmington & Weldon Railroad (completed, 1840)

Wilmington to Florence—Wilmington & Manchester Railroad (completed, 1854)

Florence to Charleston—Northeastern Railroad of South Carolina (completed, 1857)

Charleston to Savannah—Charleston & Savannah Railroad (completed, 1860)

Savannah to Waycross—Savannah, Albany & Gulf Railroad (completed, 1858)

Waycross to Jacksonville—Waycross & Florida Railroad

Concurrently as distances of shipments increased, necessitating the use of more separate railroads, and as the variety of commodities being shipped expanded, a greater number of classes appeared in the all too numerous classifications; and special rules were adopted by the railroads with more or less elaborate specifications for packing and other transportation characteristics. Shipping conditions became more complicated.

The extensive authority over classification matters granted by law to the Interstate Commerce Commission today did not exist in the original Act to Regulate Commerce of 1887. The word "classification" was not mentioned in that statute, but Section 6 thereof required the carriers (that is, the railroads) to file and publish "schedules." [38] As Ripley states, "the anomaly existed for many years, therefore, of a grant of power intended to regulate freight rates, which, at the same time, omitted provision for control over a fundamentally important element in their make-up." [39] However, the Commission assumed it had jurisdiction over classification matters and, despite doubts of the United States Department of Justice, acted upon complaints of shippers "without protest even from the carriers themselves." [40] It was not until 1910 that Congress recognized the vital importance of freight classification, and subsequent amendments to the Interstate Commerce Act have given complete

[37] Dozier, H. D.: *A History of the Atlantic Coast Line Railroad,* Houghton Mifflin Company, New York, 1920, Chs. III, IV, VII.

[38] Colquitt, *op. cit.,* p. 18.

[39] Ripley, *op. cit.,* p. 301.

[40] *Ibid.,* p. 301.

authority to the Commission. Nevertheless, the right to initiate ratings and other phases of classification has always remained with the carriers themselves, and shippers are required to consider them "as lawful until they have been declared unlawful by the Commission." [41]

Recognition of the distinction between carload and less-than-carload shipments had been slow. In the East, for example, in 1877 only 24 articles were accorded the lower carload rating. Just before passage of the original Act in 1887, however, the eastern railroads suddenly increased the number of carload ratings to about 900, "provoking a storm of protest from eastern shippers who resented this advantage accorded to jobbers in the West and South, because it enabled the latter to buy their supplies directly at wholesale." [42]

One of the earliest attempts at some semblance of regional uniformity with which to relieve the chaotic conditions of the times was in the South. The Southern Railway & Steamship Association, a cooperative organization embracing 40 railroads and 29 coastwise steamship companies, had been established primarily to increase the direct flow of traffic between the South and the Golden West for the particular benefit of its membership, and to curb carrier competition. It determined the financial destiny of most southern carriers, and it ruled transportation affairs with an iron, and sometimes ruthless hand; but it succeeded in bringing considerable stability to freight rates in the South. Strangely, it was not pressure from either the shipping public or regulatory bodies, but the necessity of self-preservation which caused the railroads in the South to take the first important step towards classification uniformity. Among other things, the Association was authorized to prepare a Classification which, when adopted by the member lines, would be applied exclusively on all competitive traffic. Thus was born the Southern Classification. Issue No. 1 became effective April 15, 1876, and embraced 910 articles, of which only 41 were assigned carload ratings! [43] By 1878, uniform Classification for the entire Southern Territory consisted of ten classes, six numbered 1 to 6 and four lettered B, C, D, F; and by 1886, the Classification contained 1,250 items which, in its day, was a meritorious achievement.[44] Since that time, there "has been a single uniform Classification for the whole

---

[41] *Bell Potato Chip Company v. Aberdeen Truck Line,* 43 M.C.C. 337 (341), 1944.

[42] Ripley, *op. cit.,* p. 310.

[43] An address by Robert E. Boyle, Jr., Chairman, Southern Classification Committee, before the Southeast Shippers Conference, Atlanta, October 10, 1946.

[44] Joubert, W. H.: *Southern Freight Rates in Transition,* University of Florida Press, Gainesville, 1949, pp. 50–53.

Southern Territory" in place of the chaos which had existed before.[45]

In 1887, the eastern carriers banded together and established a uniform Classification for all railroads east of Chicago and north of the Ohio and Potomac rivers. It was followed in 1889 by uniformity on the part of the western railroads.[46]

Thus, there developed three distinct Classifications which were applicable independently in the East, South, and West, respectively. The geographical areas covered by each became known as Classification Territories, the one in the East being named Official Territory. The word "Official" is misleading for it implies that the other Classifications either are not authoritative or are subservient to it, which definitely is not the case. Each of the three Classifications contained a different number of classes, each had its own ratings of commodities and rules applicable to shipments which frequently differed among the three territories, and each was a separate publication. At least, uniformity on a regional basis had been attained. Shipper and carrier representatives had to refer only to a maximum of three volumes, if the shipment were to move in all three territories, in contrast to a different Classification for each carrier participating in a movement.

For a long time, the three major Classifications applied essentially to interstate shipments, for many states continued to require the use of their own Classifications for strictly intrastate traffic. All the state Classifications, however, have disappeared except the Illinois Classification.[47]

Classification Territories. Geographical location of the three major classification territories are, roughly, as follows: [48]

Official Territory: north and east of the Potomac and Ohio rivers, east of the Mississippi and Illinois rivers (that is, a line between Chicago and St. Louis), and east of Lake Michigan.

Southern Territory: south of the Potomac and Ohio rivers, and east of the Mississippi River.

Western Territory: west of the Mississippi and Illinois rivers, and west of Lake Michigan.

As was mentioned above, one state maintains its own Classifica-

[45] Ripley, W. Z.: *Railway Problems,* Revised Edition, Ginn & Company, Boston, 1913, p. 141.

[46] Knorst, *op. cit.,* p. 74.

[47] Van Metre, T. H.: *Industrial Traffic Management,* McGraw-Hill Book Company, New York, 1953, p. 44.

[48] For a detailed description of the boundaries of the classification territories, the reader is referred to *The Freight Traffic Red Book,* Traffic Publishing Company, New York.

tion: Illinois. It applies to intrastate traffic in Illinois and to some interstate movements to and from border points in adjoining states. Justification for its continued existence is questionable.

Technically, there is no *exact* geographical boundary of the classification territories. Points on or near the borders overlap. To illustrate: Cairo, Illinois, geographically is located in both Official and Illinois Territories; but the classification applicable to traffic moving into or out of Cairo could be either of the four, depending entirely upon the direction. Thus, if the shipment were moving to Denver, the Western Classification would apply; if to Atlanta, the Southern Classification; if to Buffalo, the Official Classification; and if to Chicago, the Illinois Classification. Furthermore, when a through rate is published between two points located in different territories, it is common practice for the Classification of only one named territory to apply, such as: a Philadelphia–New Orleans through rate might be governed by the Classification of Southern Territory; a Dallas–Boston rate, by Official Territory. In general, shipments moving from one territory to another are governed by the Classification of the destination territory; [49] but the applicable tariff will indicate which Classification to use.

The Consolidated Classification. Another progressive step occurred in 1919 when, for the first time, all three of the major territorial Classifications were published in a single volume. Differences in the Classifications had become burdensome to shippers of interterritorial traffic and, following an investigation, the combined single volume was ordered by the Interstate Commerce Commission.[50] It contains complete uniformity in every respect with the sole exception of the ratings, although many ratings were made uniform. It was recognized that industrial and transportation conditions, traffic density, carrier costs, etc., differed in varying degrees among the three major territories and, therefore, complete uniformity of ratings was found to be impractical. The title of the volume is the *Consolidated Freight Classification,* published periodically by the Consolidated Classification Committee, with headquarters at 202 Union Station Building, Chicago. It has become the "Bible" of the traffic manager. The first issue became effective December 30, 1919. A total of twenty volumes have appeared, the last one, "No. 20," becoming effective October 15, 1951. The Illinois Classification has been included in the *Consolidated Freight Classification* since 1933.[51]

---

[49] Cushman, *op. cit.,* p. 168.
[50] *Consolidated Freight Classification Case,* 54 I.C.C. 1, 1919.
[51] Van Metre, *op. cit.,* p. 44.

The Consolidated Freight Classification contains the ratings of Official, Southern, Western, and Illinois Territories, respectively. As was explained in the first section of this chapter, each individual rating is identified by a class which may be either a number or a letter, first class is the basis of 100 percent of the first class rate that is published in the applicable tariffs, and all specified classes, except first class, are a fixed percentage of first class. There are 7 numbered classes in Official Territory, 12 numbered classes in Southern Territory, 5 numbered and 5 lettered classes in Western Territory, and 7 numbered and 5 lettered classes in Illinois Territory. In addition, there are 7 other classes in the four territories which provide for a percentage that is higher than first class, such as, one and a half times first class, double first class, etc. These percentage relationships will be explained in detail later; but for the present, it should be understood that all the classes are not the same among the four territories and that there are both numbered and lettered classes in two of the territories.

Uniform ratings were omitted for the following reasons: [52]

1. Adoption of uniform ratings would require a reprinting of all tariffs and a revision of rate schedules, necessitating a tremendous expenditure of time and money;
2. The changes necessitated by uniform ratings would upset commercial conditions and result in the destruction in many instances of long-established business, and the only method of offsetting this disarrangement of business conditions would be the issuance of many exceptions to the classifications and of commodity tariffs, which would defeat the desired uniformity.[53]

Therefore, since its inception, the *Consolidated Freight Classification* has been uniform except as to ratings.

---

[52] Memorandum of Conference on Uniform Classification (mimeo.), Washington, February 25, 1918, at which the following participated: J. E. Williams, Chairman, Uniform Classification Committee; J. C. Colquitt and G. M. Grosland, of the Interstate Commerce Commission; R. C. Wright, Assistant Director, Division of Traffic, United States Railroad Commission. Interstate Commerce Commission, file 11342-A.

[53] Exceptions and commodity rates are described later. See p. 185, below.

Chapter 6

CLASSIFICATION—
Part II

The Uniform Classification. In 1945, the Interstate Commerce Commission ordered the railroads to eliminate the differences in territorial ratings in order to achieve absolute uniformity throughout the country. Originally, complete uniformity was to have been applicable to the entire United States; but subsequently, the Commission found it would cause severe repercussions on the resulting rates in the far West, and uniformity was directed for the area generally east of the Rocky Mountains. The basis for the order was that the Commission had found the existing non-uniform classification ratings were unreasonable, resulting in undue preference in violation of the Interstate Commerce Act, and that the only means by which the discriminatory conditions could be corrected was by a uniform system of classification. The Commission had determined that a "just, fair, and reasonable" uniform classification should be adopted by the railroads, that the existing numbered and lettered classes be abolished and in their stead thirty classes or ratings be adopted which would be numbered according to their respective percentages of Class 100, and that the new Class 100 would replace first class as the basis.[1] It is to be observed that the Commission's order was directed to the railroads, not the motor carriers; therefore, at the outset, uniform ratings were required only in the Rail Classification. No comparable directive was issued to motor freight carriers, but the motor carriers voluntarily assumed the task and responsibility to adopt uniform ratings in the Motor Classification.[2]

It should not be assumed that classification uniformity is a recent

---

[1] Docket No. 28300, *Class Rate Investigation,* 1939, 262 I.C.C. 447 (510–511), 1945. (There were several different I.C.C. reports under this Docket and, hereafter references thereto will cite the particular volume of I.C.C. Reports.)

[2] Letter from F. G. Freund, Director, Traffic Department, American Trucking Associations, Inc., Washington, dated April 5, 1954.

86

undertaking. Actually, there had been actual demand for uniformity since about 1870.[3]

Prior to passage of the original 1887 Act there had been submitted to Congress in 1886, after extensive hearings during the two preceding years, a most comprehensive report of a committee headed by Senator Shelby M. Cullom which has since been commonly known as the "Cullom Report." It listed under eighteen separate headings, "The Causes of Complaint against the Railroad System as Stated by the Cullom Committee," one of which was, as follows: [4]

No. 14. That the differences in the classifications in use in various parts of the country, and sometimes for shipments over the same roads in different directions, are a fruitful source of misunderstandings, and are often made a means of extortion.

It will be recalled from the preceding chapter that the 1887 Act contained no provisions concerning classification *per se*.[5] Efforts of the Interstate Commerce Commission to achieve uniformity have been long and arduous. After passage of the original Act, the newly created Commission, in its first annual report to Congress, emphasized the necessity for a single Classification to apply to the entire country, and this stand for uniformity has continued in subsequent annual reports.[6] There followed in 1888 and 1889 considerable discussion in Congress concerning proposals that the railroads be required to establish a uniform Classification, but there was no legislation. Railroad officials, representing what was to become the three grand classification territories, actually prepared a uniform Classification which was to have become effective in 1890, but its adoption was blocked by what is now the New York Central Railroad. "This first abortive attempt reflected the mutual jealousies of competing roads," wrote Professor Ripley, "as well as the difficulties of suiting a single classification to the variety of local conditions existing throughout the country . . . The absolute refusal of New York Central & Hudson River (Railroad) to accede to this plan (of uni-

---

[3] An address by Robert E. Boyle, Jr., Chairman, Southern Classification Committee, before the Southeast Shippers Conference, Atlanta, October 10, 1946.

[4] Board of Investigation & Research: *Report on Rate-Making and Rate-Publishing Procedures of Railroad, Motor, and Water Carriers*, 78th Congress, 1st Session, House Document No. 363, Government Printing Office, Washington, 1944, p. 91.

[5] See p. 81, above.

[6] "Policy of the Interstate Commerce Commission with respect to, and their efforts to promote, Unification of Classifications," (mimeo.), Southern Freight Tariff Bureau, Atlanta, 1945.

formity) prevented its acceptance. Apparently too many special or commodity rates were in force upon its line, in order to hold its powerful clients in markets all over the country, to make it practicable to adopt the scheme." Subsequent efforts to achieve uniformity were centered around an attempt to merge Western and Official Classifications, "but the same jealous regard of local interests in each territory, especially with reference to the treatment of carload ratings, once more proved an insuperable obstacle." [7] In the meantime, pressure for a uniform classification had been expressed by the Interstate Commerce Commission itself, various groups of shippers' interests, several of the state regulatory commissions, and even by a number of railroads. In no less than 33 annual reports to Congress had the Commission urged classification uniformity.[8]

At the annual convention of State Railroad Commissioners in 1896, it was found "that unless uniform classification of freight is secured within a reasonable time by voluntary action of the railroads themselves, the necessary legislation should be asked of Congress requiring its adoption." The convention went on to recommend that the carriers appoint a committee to study and prepare such a Classification, rather than having one made for them and prescribed by the Interstate Commerce Commission. It is interesting to observe that this convention, almost sixty years ago, went on record in stating the following two points should always be kept in mind in framing a Classification: (1) "that equal justice should be done all shippers and discriminations prevented in every form," and (2) "that the revenues of the companies (railroads) should be preserved so that the money honestly and judiciously invested will receive a proper return on investment." Earlier in the same year, the National Board of Trade had adopted a memorial to Congress urging adoption of legislation which would require the Interstate Commerce Commission to prepare and publish a uniform Classification "on or before October 1, 1896," and such a resolution was introduced in the Senate by Senator Cullom.[9]

In 1897, the Commission requested Congress to grant it authority to require a uniform Classification, but, again, there was no action. It was not until 1910 that the Commission was authorized to prescribe "reasonable" classification of articles. In 1912, however, the

---

[7] Ripley, W. Z.: *Railroads: Rates and Regulation,* Longsmans, Green & Company, New York, 1923, p. 338.

[8] Boyle, *op. cit.,* pp. 1–2.

[9] Letter from Ira B. Mills, Chairman, Committee on Uniform Classification, National Convention of Railroad Commissioners at Washington, addressed to "The Railroad Traffic Managers and Freight Associations of the United States," dated November 1, 1896.

Senate unanimously adopted a bill requiring establishment of classification uniformity, but it failed to pass the House.[10]

In the meantime, a Committee on Uniform Classification had been created by the National Association of Railroad Commissioners. Its Chairman, Ira B. Mills, of the Railroad & Warehouse Commission of the State of Minnesota, rendered a report at the annual meeting of the Association in 1906 after canvassing opinions of various railroad traffic officers and shippers.[11] The result was a movement to have Congress invest "the Interstate Commerce Commission with sufficient authority to make a Universal Classification that would be good on Interstate Commerce to and from any point in the United States"; [12] but it was reported that "many traffic officers of high standing are of the opinion that uniformity in classification is next to impossible." [13] Numerous meetings were held throughout the country at which classification uniformity was discussed, but, for many years, there was no positive action.[14]

---

[10] Board of Investigation & Research, *op. cit.*, pp. 8–11.

[11] Letter from I. B. Mills, State of Minnesota, Railroad & Warehouse Commission, to H. F. Smith, Traffic Manager, The Nashville, Chattanooga & St. Louis Railway, Nashville, dated, St. Paul, February 19, 1906.

[12] Letter from P. W. Coyle, Commissioner, Freight Bureau of the Business Men's League of St. Louis, to P. G. McGovern, Chairman, Southern Classification Committee, Atlanta, dated, St. Louis, October 16, 1906.

[13] Letter from L. Green, Freight Traffic Manager, Southern Railway Company, to M. P. Washburn, Chairman, "S.E.M.V.A.," Louisville, dated Washington, November 27, 1906.

[14] The following chronological summary portrays interest in the question of classification uniformity, the information having been secured from the files of the Southern Classification Committee through the courtesy of its Chairman, R. E. Boyle, Jr.:

February 5, 1907. The Chairman of the Western Classification Committee requested the Chairman of the other territorial committees "to appoint a permanent Committee to compile a Uniform Classification."

April 5, 1907. The Chairman of Official Classification Committee informed the Chairman of Western Classification Committee that members of the Official Committee "unanimously favor early action looking towards preparation and establishment of a Uniform Classification to govern the entire territory of the United States.

May 13, 1907. A committee was appointed to represent Southern Territory.

August 2, 1907. Representatives of the three classification committees met in New York City, at which the following recommendation was adopted: "That in the opinion of the representatives present, a Uniform Classification is highly desirable and that immediate measures looking towards the preparation of such a Classification be taken."

January 1, 1908. The three territorial committees, having become known as the General Committee on Uniform Classification, convened in Chicago. A permanent full-time organization, with headquarters in Chicago, was established later in the year.

December 1, 1909. The General Committee on Uniform Classification submitted to the territorial committees for action, its adoption and recommendations of uniform classification rules, descriptions of articles, package requirements, and minimum carload weights.

November 1, 1912. Adoption and publication of the recommendations of the

As late as 1912, the Commission called attention to the multiplicity of individual Classifications and condemned them as being "a public evil." [15] To meet the incessant and pressing demands of the Commission, a General Committee on Uniform Classification had been established by the railroads, and by 1917 some progress had been manifested in the three major classification territories. In Official Territory, 87 percent of the recommendations of the Uniform Committee had been accepted, and the *Official Classification* was uniform to the extent of 81 percent. In the South, 72 percent of the recommendations were in force, and *Southern Classification* was 73 percent uniform. In the West, 91 percent of the recommendations had been adopted, and *Western Classification* was uniform by 87 percent.[16] The initial issue of the "Consolidated" Classification in 1919 represented attainment of the first step towards national uniformity. In recognition of that great accomplishment by the railroads of the country, the Commission stated: [17]

The Consolidated Classification is the result of effort toward uniformity extending over a long term of years, and since uniform rules and descrip-

---

General Committee "on an intensive scale" in *Southern Classification* No. 39.

September 18–28, 1917. Conference of representatives of the three territorial classification committees and of the Interstate Commerce Commission in Washington, at which a "large number" of items which theretofore had been non-uniform were adjusted to uniform bases.

October 1, 1917. The Secretary of the Interstate Commerce Commission reported that Western Territory had accepted more of the recommendations of the General Committee on Uniform Classification than had the other two territories, with Official Territory being "not far behind," and he admonished the Southern Classification Committee to handle more promptly the recommendations of the Uniform Committee, "some of which have never even been docketed."

November 16, 1917. The Secretary of the Interstate Commerce Commission wrote each of the territorial committee chairmen in part, as follows: "The several classification committees do not appear to have a uniform method of figuring their percentage of uniformity. . . . Owing to the different methods of numbering and printing items in the three Classifications, it is impossible to arrive at a precisely correct check and one that will represent in each case the exact situation as to the status of uniformity. . . . As a matter of fact, the Uniform Committee is itself not consistent. . . . It is therefore suggested that this is a matter to which the classification committees should give serious consideration and this is to request that the question be taken under advisement as early as practicable."

July 30, 1918. The Uniform Committee was abolished by order of the Director General of Railroads.

December 30, 1919. The first issue of the *Consolidated Freight Classification* became effective.

May 30, 1952. The first issue of the *Uniform Freight Classification* became effective.

[15] *Western Classification Case,* 25 I.C.C. 442, 1912.

[16] *Thirty-first Annual Report of the Interstate Commerce Commission,* Government Printing Office, Washington, 1917.

[17] *Consolidated Classification Case,* 54 I.C.C. 1 (3), 1919.

tions are necessary before uniformity in ratings is possible, it marks an important step toward a Uniform Classification.

But, continued the Commission, "there was no concerted effort (by the carriers' committee) to make the ratings uniform."[18] It is interesting to observe that the Commission, in 1919, recommended adoption of ten numbered classes for all territories with uniform percentage relationships which was rejected by the carriers,[19] but which came to be the basis for the system of ratings prescribed by the Commission for Southern Territory in 1925.[20] Through the years, the Commission has continued its fight for uniformity and has been unceasing in its efforts to keep the subject before all interested parties.[21] Finally, the new "Uniform" Classification shows the result of a program "which has been followed since 1886."[22]

In supporting the ideals of classification uniformity many years ago, Professor Ripley commented:[23]

The present threefold territorial division of the country, for the purposes of classification, naturally affords all sorts of possibilities in the way of veiled discrimination, not merely as between persons but as affecting the interests of different competing markets. Not only is there liability to confusion, but the way is paved for all sorts of favoritism. Whenever shipment is made from one classification territory to another, it is always possible to adjust the rates with a view to local advantage. For instance, one of the principal causes for complaint in the South is the advantage which Nashville, Tennessee enjoys through having all of its rates from eastern and northern centers made upon the Official Classification. Inasmuch as the rates under the Southern Classification are considerably higher, this operates to place other competing cities in the South under a distinct disability in competition with Nashville. It is possible, therefore, for the Louisville & Nashville (Railroad) by this means to build up one com-

---

[18] *Ibid.*, p. 4.
[19] *Ibid.*, p. 11.
[20] *Southern Class Rate Investigation*, 100 I.C.C. 513, 1925.
[21] "For years we have endeavored to promote uniformity in Classifications. Except for unification of rules and commodity descriptions, the progress in that direction has not been encouraging." (*Consolidated Southwestern Cases*, 123 I.C.C. 203 (398), 1925.)
"One of the beneficial results of these extensive investigations . . . should be the hastening of the much-desired uniformity of ratings." (*Western Trunk-Line Class Rates*, 164 I.C.C. 1 (217), 1930.)
"Further study of the subject of classification uniformity and the experience which we have gained in recent years in fixing class rates make it increasingly apparent that . . . such unification can not be fully extended to embrace the Official Classification unless and until there is a closer alignment of the basic rate structures, as between Official Territory and the other sections of the country, than it has so far been found practicable to accomplish." (*Forty-fifth Annual Report of the Interstate Commerce Commission*, Government Printing Office, Washington, 1931, p. 67.)
[22] Board of Investigation & Research, *op. cit.*, p. 11.
[23] Ripley, *op. cit.*, pp. 341–343.

munity at the expense of another . . . Again rates from New York to Memphis and New Orleans are made upon the Official Classification, by whatever route; while to intermediate points . . . they go on the rates prescribed by Southern Classification, which are considerably higher . . . One of the principal advantages, therefore, from the unification of the three systems now existing, would be the possibility of readjusting not only definitely, but also equitably, the conflicting interests of various shippers and communities now tied up by these local arrangements.

Professor Ripley recognized, however, the difficulties of attaining absolute classification uniformity, such as: (1) it would tend to increase the number of exceptions or commodity rates, "Whenever the uniform classification was at variance with local interests"; (2) it would necessitate a complete revision and overhauling of tariffs in order to yield the carriers satisfactory returns; (3) many old rates of long standing would be abolished; (4) new schedule of rates would have to be determined; and, (5) "the magnitude of such a task can be scarcely appreciated." [24]

Shortly before the Commission's investigation, a study prepared under the direction of the Honorable J. Haden Alldredge, at the time Principal Transportation Economist of the Tennessee Valley Authority at Knoxville and later to become an Interstate Commerce Commissioner, pointed out the need for "establishment of a uniform principle for making interterritorial freight rates." [25] A supplemental report developed that first class rates for comparable distances from points in the South and from points west of the Mississippi River to points in Official Territory "are in all instances higher than the first-class rates from Canadian and Official Territory origins to destinations in Official Territory." [26] A third report concluded, "that the existing system of regionalized rates is contrary to the broad public interest in that it arbitrarily disturbs equality of economic opportunity, promotes unbalanced national development, and interferes with the wise and efficient use of resources." [27] Added impetus to national uniformity occurred especially in the South, culminating in the Southern Governors' Case of 1939,[28] and in the provision of the

[24] *Ibid.*, pp. 346–348.
[25] Tennessee Valley Authority: *The Interterritorial Freight Rate Problem of the United States,* 75th Congress, 1st Session, House Document No. 264, Government Printing Office, Washington, 1937, p. ix.
[26] Tennessee Valley Authority: *Supplemental Phases of the Interterritorial Freight Rate Problem of the United States,* 76th Congress, 1st Session, House Document No. 271, Government Printing Office, Washington, 1939, p. 8.
[27] Tennessee Valley Authority: *Regionalized Freight Rates: Barrier to National Productiveness,* 78th Congress, 1st Session, House Document No. 137, Government Printing Office, Washington, 1943, p. 60.
[28] *Southern Governors' Case,* 235 I.C.C. 255, 1939.

Transportation Act of 1940 clarifying the Commission's power to remove regional discriminations and the mandate directing the Commission to investigate intra- and interterritorial rates in general.[29]

The "ultimate findings" of the Commission in 1945 were, in part, as follows: [30]

1. That the present Official, Illinois, Southern, and Western classifications, insofar as the ratings named therein are concerned, as a whole, are, and for the future will be unjust and unreasonable, in violation of Section 1 (4) and (6) of the Act.

2. That the several classifications named in finding 1 (above), insofar as the ratings therein are concerned, as a whole, because of the substantial number of differences in such ratings that now exist, result, and will result in the future, in undue and unreasonable preference, advantage, prejudice, and disadvantage as between shippers and receivers of freight in interstate commerce and as between classification territories, in violation of Section 3 (1) of the Act.

3. That in the assignment of commodities to various classes in the classification, in order that the classification may be just, fair, and reasonable, it is essential not only that the grouping of analogous articles and those possessing similar transportation characteristics, according to the accepted principles of classification recognized by us, shall be observed, but it is essential that there be maintained scales of class rates, providing different rates for the several classes of property, which shall bear a just and reasonable relation for the various classes each with the others. . . .

4. That it is impossible, without a basic unity in classification ratings throughout the country, to maintain a just and reasonable relation between the class rates on commodities . . . or as between competing commodities moving at class rates.

5. That it is entirely feasible for the respondents (railroads) to establish, observe, and enforce classifications . . . which shall be uniform. . . .

6. That it is not intended that the foregoing findings with respect to uniformity shall prevent the making of exceptional classification ratings when required either by the provision of the Interstate Commerce Act or for commercial or competitive reasons, provided such exceptional ratings may be justified individually upon their own merits. . . .

7. . . . the classification pattern . . . (of) Official Territory . . . (should be the basis).

8. That it is just, fair, and reasonable that a uniform classification should be established which should contain: (a) classes, intermediate between the several classes in the official classification . . . ; (b) the present regular classes which are multiples of class 1 (class 100); and (c) additional classes for commodities which should take lower ratings than the lowest class in the official classification. . . .

---

[29] *The Interstate Commerce Act,* Revised to November 1, 1951, Government Printing Office, Washington, 1951, Section 3 (1), (1b), p. 18, Section 5 (b) of Transportation Act of 1940.

[30] Docket No. 28300, *op. cit.,* 262 I.C.C. 447, 1945.

9. That substantial uniformity exists in classifications as to descriptions of articles and carload minimum weights.

The primary objectives of the Commission's order were, (1) to eliminate discriminatory ratings where they were found to exist, and (2) to simplify the process of rate determination. This revolutionary decision pertaining to classification is known as "Docket No. 28310." Its companion, pertaining to the new rates to be applied to the new system of classification, is "Docket No. 28300." Since matters covered by the two dockets are so closely interrelated, hearings on both were conducted simultaneously and the orders of the Commission pertaining to both were handed down together.

Again, the reader's attention is called to the distinction between a rating and a rate which was described earlier.[81] Pending adoption of the new uniform classification, the Commission authorized an "interim" adjustment of rates, as well as a number of subsequent general rate increases, which, of course, were based on the old "Consolidated" Classification, and the Commission recognized that "a considerable lapse of time inevitably must occur before a uniform classification of freight could be devised." [82] Appropriate tariffs covering the "interim" adjustments were issued, but their effectiveness was temporarily delayed by suits opposing the Commission's action brought by "certain northern and New England States, and also by a number of western railroads," [83] contending that the rate increases were contrary to the principles of uniformity on which the increases were based.[84] The Supreme Court of the United States sustained the Commission's findings that class rates within the South and in the territory, roughly, between the Mississippi River and Rocky Mountains,[85] and from those territories to Official Territory, "are generally much higher, article for article, than the rates within Official Territory," and that the Commission's findings were "abundantly supported by the evidence." [86] Carriers in Official and Southern Territories complied, but those in the West did not accept the findings "and complied with them only under compulsion." [87] In the words of the Commission, "it is important to bear in mind that the scales of first-class rates . . . were each designated on the assump-

---

[81] See, p. 74, above.
[82] Docket No. 28300, *op. cit.*, 281 I.C.C. 213 (216), 1951.
[83] *Ibid.*, p. 216.
[84] *Ibid.*, p. 225.
[85] The two rate areas involved are named Southwestern and Western Trunk Line Territories.
[86] *New York v. United States,* 331 U. S. 284, 1947.
[87] Docket No. 28300, *op. cit.*, 281 I.C.C. 213 (236), 1951.

tion that they will be applied to a new and uniform classification . . ." [38]

The memorable investigation was inaugurated in 1939; but the proceedings were interrupted by World War II and they were not resumed until after the war. More than forty public hearings were conducted throughout the country, and innumerable briefs were filed with the Commission. Many carriers, shippers, and shippers' organizations vigorously opposed complete uniformity, while other shippers, organizations, and interested groups, including the Southern Governors' Rate Conference, actively advocated uniform ratings. There was strenuous opposition by southern railroads who contended uniformity would be detrimental both to the carriers and to their customers; but, when the order was issued by the Commission, the railroads "promptly made it known that they would accept this decision and do every possible thing to make it work." [39]

Obviously, where ratings on a given commodity were different in all classification territories, either increases or decreases of the former ratings were necessary in order to secure a single uniform rating applicable throughout all territories. In the absence of appropriate territorial adjustments of the freight rates themselves, and assuming the unrealistic continuance of an inelastic demand for transportation services, a higher rating will increase both carrier revenues and shippers' costs, and vice versa. However, it was not the intention of the Commission that the new uniform ratings should be the means of unduly increasing carrier revenues nor "to require large reductions (in ratings) with resulting losses of carriers' revenues as the method of achieving uniformity of classification." [40] In its 1952 report, the Commission stated that "there may be an over-all slight increase in the less-than-carload ratings, and a smaller decrease in carload ratings, but these increases and reductions are less than the spread between the classes set up, and changes are inevitable in any comprehensive revision." [41] The new rates which were determined and published by the carriers to apply to the new classification amounted to "substantial reductions in all territories . . . , except within Official Territory where the basic rates are slightly increased in some instances and slightly reduced in others." [42] In pass-

---

[38] *Ibid.*, p. 220.
[39] Boyle, R. E., Jr.: "What Do I.C.C. '28300 & 28310' Rate Changes Mean to Shippers and Carriers in the Southeast," as published in *Proceedings: The First Annual Southeastern Transportation Clinic,* Atlanta Division, University of Georgia, Atlanta, 1952, pp. 12–13.
[40] Docket No. 28300, *op. cit.*, 286 I.C.C. 171 (174), 1952.
[41] *Ibid.*, p. 174.
[42] *Ibid.*, p. 174.

ing, it is interesting to observe that the new rates which were pro-
tested by certain parties "are precisely those (rates) which the
Commission had found lawful . . . after full hearing, judicial review thereof, and further hearing." [43]

Over 400 protests of ratings directed against some 1,450 classification items were filed with the Commission.[44] The essential reasons
of those who opposed uniformity were competition, variations in the
resulting territorial rate levels, and the kinds of traffic that would
move. The Commission made public its report on uniformity on
July 31, 1951. In a statement explaining this unprecedented action,
the Secretary of the Commission, W. P. Bartel, stated, in part, in a
copyrighted story in *Traffic World:* [45]

"The Interstate Commerce Commission today issued two reports,
adopted July 26, 1951, in the long-litigated Consolidated Freight Classification and Class Rate cases. Both reports in these companion cases were
under the name of Commissioner Clyde B. Aitchison, and adoption by
the Commission were unanimous, with Commissioner Richard F. Mitchell
participating.

"In the country-wide classification case, the Commission ordered the
railroads to file within four months a new uniform classification of
freight. . . .

"The two complementary proceedings (Classification and the applicable scale of rates) have been strongly litigated before the Commission
and in the federal courts, because so wide-spread in scope and affecting
highly competitive commercial and sectional interests. The original decision of the Commission in 1945 was made in the two cases combined. It
found that the existing freight classifications and the applicable class
rates, then widely differing in the eastern (or official), southern, and
western rate territories, caused unjust discrimination forbidden by the
Interstate Commerce Act, which should be cured by applying to a new
nation-wide uniform classification a uniform class rate scale within the
official, southern, western trunkline, and the southwestern rate territories.
Rates in the Mountain-Pacific group and on transcontinental traffic were
not in the class rate case, but now are under investigation. . . .

"In the classification case, meantime, the Commission instituted a
'notice of proposed rule making'. . . Citing its original findings of an
unlawful situation in the maintenance of three diverse classifications, and
reaffirming them, it points to the statutory duty of the carriers to file and
maintain lawful classifications, and requires them within four months to
file the uniform classification as required by law and in fulfillment of their
promise of full cooperation. The report indicates that a continued but
limited use of the existing classifications may be required during the readjustment period, and in the far west and transcontinentally. . . .

---

[43] *Ibid.*, p. 176.
[44] *Ibid.*, pp. 172–173.
[45] *Traffic World*, The Traffic Service Corporation, Washington, August 4,
1951, pp. 24–27.

"The present duty of the respondents under the act is clear: they should proceed without further delay to complete, publish, file, and put in force the just and reasonable uniform classification of freight which we have found is necessary to clear away unjust and undue preferences and prejudices under section 3(1) of the Act. Their duty is spelled out in section 1(4), which was amended after this proceeding was begun, so as to include the classification of through routed traffic, section 6(1) and (3). Our authority under section 15(1) to determine what individual or joint classification the respondents shall be required to adopt and the practice or regulation to which they must conform, is perfectly clear and continuing. . . .

"We are not now passing on the propriety of any particular item in any of the classifications or in the proposed classification. All who may be concerned will have their rights preserved, whatever they are. It will apparently be necessary to continue in effect the existing Consolidated Classification and its supplements, pending adjustments and the ascertainment of reasonable rates in other territories, unless the carriers in the meantime themselves adjust their class rates to the new classification. Therefore, we do not now enter an order to cease and desist the use of the existing classifications."

The Uniform Freight Classification is the result of more than six years of diligent effort by classification experts, carrier traffic officers, and industrial traffic managers. The ratings of more than 10,000 articles were adjusted. In the dramatic words of R. E. Boyle, Jr., Vice-Chairman of the Southern Freight Association and Chairman of the Southern Classification Committee, "In scope of territory, the number of commodities affected, and the amount of revenue involved, these changes constitute the most extensive, certainly the most complex, and by far the most important freight rate revision ever undertaken." [46] In the final analysis, any such drastic revision affecting freight rates "is good or bad in the eyes of a shipper according to whether he pays more or less." [47] Likewise, it is good or bad in the eyes of a carrier according to the anticipated increase or decrease in revenues it will produce.

Although classification has never been an exact science, usually the revenues of carriers have been determined by adjustments in rates rather than by manipulating the Classification ratings. Here, the procedure was reversed, because the pattern of class rates was rigidly fixed by the Interstate Commerce Commission, and the Classification Committee was faced with the problem of fitting about 10,000 articles into the new class rate pattern. In accomplishing that colossal task, the carriers have attempted to build a Classi-

---

[46] Boyle, *op. cit.*, p. 12.
[47] *Ibid.*, p. 15.

fication which will realize the following: (1) to fairly and substantially preserve the carriers' revenues; (2) to establish just and reasonable rates for shippers; (3) to remove Exceptions from the Classification; (4) to disturb commodity rates as little as possible; and, (5) to create a Classification which will not set up discriminations but which will satisfy the demands of competition in all its forms—between articles, places, territories, shippers, and carriers.[48]

While the magnitude and complexity of the undertaking made it impossible to observe any fixed pattern, determination of ratings in the new uniform Classifications were influenced to a more or less extent by the following factors: [49]

1. Recognized classification principles were observed where exceptions were not involved.

2. Exceptions ratings within and between the several territories had a decided influence in arriving at the uniform ratings; in fact, existence of exceptions were often the controlling influence.

3. In some instances, the uniform ratings were arbitrarily fixed high enough so as not to do violence to, or disrupt, important rate adjustments. For example, carload ratings were fixed at a figure high enough not to interfere with the sensitive commodity rates on such articles as, fresh fruits and vegetables, grain and grain products, feed, salt, sugar, packing house products, and others. Generally, those articles move on commodity rates, so it would make little difference what the classification ratings are as long as the class rates are higher than the commodity rates.

4. Sometimes the territory of movement was a factor in determining the uniform rating. For example, creosote oil is produced predominantly in Official Territory and its greatest consumption is in Southern Territory. Generally it moves on commodity rates and it was necessary to maintain a competitive level of rates from all producing points. The uniform carload rating that was established comes nearest to the level of rates on which most of the traffic moved from the North to the South.

5. In determining less-than-carload ratings, special attention was directed to the cardinal principle that there should be an appropriate spread between carload and less-than-carload ratings.

6. "From beginning to end the ratings in uniform classification were designed to bring about the least disruption in present rates

---

[48] Boyle, an address in 1946, *op. cit.*, pp. 6–7.
[49] Interstate Commerce Commission, Docket No. 28310, "General Reply of Respondent Railroads to Protests and Requests for Suspension of Uniform Freight Classification No. 1, or Parts Thereof," Bureau of Information of the Eastern Railways, 1 Park Avenue, New York City, 1952, pp. 4–7.

on which the traffic moves, whether classification ratings, exceptions ratings or commodity rates." [50]

It is interesting to observe that the average of all less-than-carload ratings in the Consolidated Classification which was effective in 1950 and 1951 was 87.07 percent of the 100 percent first class rating, while the average in the first Uniform Classification which became effective in 1952 was 89.96 percent of first class. A comparison of carload ratings shows an average of 50.42 percent in the Consolidated Classification and 49.31 percent in the Uniform Classification. The following table shows the average percentage of reduction in class rates when the Uniform Classification became effective in 1952: [51]

Area	Percentage of Reduction
Between Southern & Official Territories	12.81
Between Southern & Southwestern Territories	26.38
Between Southern & Western Trunk Line Territories	20.70
Between Representative Western Points	21.57
Between Southwestern & Official Territories	19.72
Between Official & Western Trunk Line Territories	10.80
Within Official Territory	2.10
Within Southern Territory	16.22
Within Southwestern Territory	25.65

The strenuous and tedious task was achieved in the summer of 1952 when the railroads and the motor carriers published their new ratings on a single basis of application for the United States generally east of the Rocky Mountains.

It should be understood that absolute uniformity for the entire country has not been attained. At the present time, there exists a period of transition from the old to the new method of determining the rating of articles, which means both systems currently are in effect depending upon the geographical area in which the traffic is moving. Therefore, use of the two published volumes must be continued for application within their respective areas, although this does not mean to imply that both volumes could be applicable to a single shipment. Actually, at the present time there are five rail classifications in effect, namely: Official, Illinois, Southern, and Western, which, as has been stated, are included in the Consolidated Freight Classification; and the new *Uniform Freight Classification* is the fifth. In summary, the *Consolidated Classification* still

---

[50] *Ibid.*, p. 7.
[51] *Ibid.*, pp. 8–13.

applies to all traffic west of the Rocky Mountains, to transcontinental traffic, to some shipments generally west of the Mississippi River, to traffic moving intrastate in several states, and to specified traffic covered by Exceptions. Said the Interstate Commerce Commission in its 1951 order: [52]

It will apparently be necessary to continue in effect the existing Consolidated Classification and its supplements, pending adjustments and the ascertainment of reasonable rates in other territories . . . Therefore we do not now enter an order to cease and desist the use of the existing classifications.

With the passing of years, the *Consolidated Freight Classification,* with many of its ratings differing among the several territories, will become a thing of the past, respected and revered in the memory of many a traffic man; but it will be a long time before the Uniform Freight Classification completely supplants its predecessor. It is interesting to observe that the title page of the "Uniform" Classification lists the names of the respective publishing agents for each of the four territories which is indicative of the continued existence of those territories for classification purposes. The task of the carriers in accomplishing what has been done was a stupendous one. Unquestionably, uniform ratings for the country as a whole leads to greater simplicity in rate determination. To quote the distinguished Commissioner of the Georgia Public Service Commission, the Honorable Walter McDonald: "Because of the patch-work system of rates in effect before May 30, (1952), it had almost become impossible to determine rates accurately, but the new Classification and rate tariffs provide a clean-cut, simple method of determining rates and are a great boon to carriers and shippers alike." [53]

It has long been recognized that transportation and traffic conditions differ in different parts of the country. A particular commodity may be of great significance to carriers and to shippers in one territory, but of minor importance in other territories. Uniformity can cause the rating of a given article to be lowered in one territory with the result that the carriers in that area suffer a reduction in revenues, and vice versa. An industry may have enjoyed a lower rating on its product than a competing industry in another terri-

---

[52] Docket No. 28310, *Consolidated Freight Classification,* 281 I.C.C. 329 (339), 1951.
[53] McDonald, Walter: "What Do I.C.C. '28300 & 28310' Rate Change Mean to Shippers and Carriers in the Southeast," as published in *Proceedings: The First Annual Southeastern Transportation Clinic,* Atlanta Division, University of Georgia, Atlanta, 1952, p. 17.

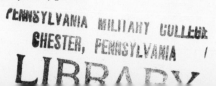

tory, and if uniformity raises the former's rating without a corresponding reduction in the freight rate itself, it will be placed at a competitive disadvantage in marketing its product. In its 1945 order, the Interstate Commerce Commission directed that these regional differences be reflected in the actual rates themselves rather than in the Classification—that is to say, that the territorial rates be changed as may be necessary to yield the carriers adequate and reasonable revenues under uniform ratings.[54]

Effectiveness of a uniform system of classification is entirely dependent upon a uniform scale of applicable rates. In other words, uniform ratings are worthless without uniformity in the application of rates to those ratings. This distinction may be vividly illustrated in the South where, if *no* change had been made in the level of rates under Docket No. 28300 to conform with the new uniform ratings in Docket No. 28310, the class rates themselves in Southern Territory would be an average of 39 percent higher than in Official Territory! [55] Although the goal of the Commission is complete uniformity throughout the entire United States, it should not be assumed the three major classification territories will disappear. Undoubtedly, they will continue to exist well into the future for rate-making purposes.

The new uniform class ratings, together with considerable essential data, applicable to practically all railroads, domestic water carriers, freight forwarders, and a few motor carriers, appear in the *Uniform Freight Classification* which, like its predecessor, is published by the Consolidated Classification Committee.[56] There have been two issues, "No. 1" becoming effective May 30, 1952, and "No. 2" on December 10, 1953.

Motor Freight Classification. Classification of articles shipped by motor carriers has developed in a comparable manner to that of the railroads, except the former has been more rapid. The truck lines had the benefit of a century of railroad experience and "know how"; in fact, many of the persons who compiled the first comprehensive motor truck classification were recruited from the railroads. The pattern of classification had been established by the railroads. The problem was to adapt it to the motor carrier industry.

It will be recalled, the first federal law regulating interstate motor carriers was the Motor Carrier Act of 1935, which today is Part II

---

[54] Docket No. 28310, *op. cit.*
[55] Morton, Mignon: *The Complicated ABC's of Changes in Class Railroad Rates*, Industrial Research Series No. 10, University of Kansas Publications, University of Kansas, Lawrence, 1948, p. 76.
[56] See, p. 84, above.

of the Interstate Commerce Act.[57] Prior to 1935, there were numerous motor freight classifications throughout the country. Like the early railroads of the nineteenth century, each truck line had its own classification, or none at all, or merely the ancient distinction between "light" and "heavy" commodities. Some carriers established a unique refinement of the "light" and "heavy" distinction by rating shipments on the basis of the package, regardless of contents, whereas, of course, the article being shipped, not its container, is the proper determinant of classification. In some instances, certain truck lines adhered to the railroad Classification. Other motor carriers adopted the sea-going practice of "space-weight," whichever is the greater, and commonly known as "Ship's option."[58] This last method of classification has merit, for it recognizes the limited capacity of a motor vehicle and it is the basis of classification in the New England states.[59] Clearly, therefore, there was no semblance of uniformity in the classification of motor freight, and railroad history had been repeated in the motor carrier industry. Enactment of the Motor Carrier Act marked the beginning of the end of the hodgepodge of motor freight classifications, for, among other things, the Act required the motor carriers to publish classifications and tariffs in the same manner as railroads.

In the South, one of the first meetings of interested parties was held in Atlanta on August 16, 1935, to decide if a separate motor Classification should be adopted or if the motor carriers should conform to the railroad Classification. Subsequently, agreement was reached to adhere to the latter, "with changes necessary to meet motor truck operations."[60] One of the guiding minds behind the development of motor freight classification in the South has been W. M. Miller who for many years was General Manager, and since 1953 has been Executive Vice-President of the Southern Motor Carriers Rate Conference. In relating some of the events which transpired at the Atlanta meeting of 1935, Mr. Miller remarked in an address entitled, "The Relationship and Contrast between Motor Carrier and Rail Rates in Southern Territory:"[61]

There were many (persons) advising the carriers as to what they should do . . . A very influential traffic man in a forceful and convincing

---

[57] This was accomplished in 1942.
[58] Glasgow, C. C., Jr., & Gifford, G. L.: *An Analysis of Motor Carrier Tariffs,* The University of Tennessee, Knoxville, 1952, pp. 6–7.
[59] See, p. 132, below.
[60] Way, William, Jr., Ed.: *Proceedings, Industrial Traffic Conference,* The University of Tennessee, Knoxville, 1951, p. 59.
[61] *Ibid.,* pp. 60–61.

manner, pointed out to the motor carriers how they might avoid the pit-falls of a complicated rate structure, such as the railroads had . . . He mentioned the fact that the railroads had made a mistake in developing their rate structure by groups and regions and that the motor carriers should build a national structure free from territorial breaks, and that there should be one national classification and one basic rate structure for the country as a whole.

Note particularly the recommendation back in 1935 that there be *one national* classification!

In the meantime, a national committee had been created by the newly organized American Trucking Associations, Inc. One of its commendable endeavors was that "any . . . classification adopted should be so simple in construction that anyone who can read or write can readily understand it." Another belief of the committee was that it would be difficult to substantiate a truck classification based on that of the railroads, whereas if the motor carrier industry established its own classification, "it would immediately improve its recognition as a mode of transportation." [62]

Hence, during the year 1935, there were two schools of thought: one was to adopt the railroad Classification; the other, to establish a separate Classification for motor carriers.

The motor carriers "were faced with a bewildering situation which had to be met by a certain date" in conformity with require-ments of the 1935 Act. The national committee decided that the only way "to meet the exigencies of the situation" was to prepare and issue one Classification to replace the numerous individual car-rier Classifications which were in effect, and to adhere to the general format of the Rail Classification. From those deliberations and subsequent toil by members of the committee, there evolved the *National Motor Freight Classification,* published by the Ameri-can Trucking Associations, Inc., Washington, the first issue of which became effective April 1, 1936.[63] The original publication was in two volumes, one for less-than-truckload and the other for truck-load or volume shipments. With minor exceptions, it was the same as that of the railroads, including three columns of ratings for the three grand classification territories. The reasons for the similarity were: (1) to meet railroad competition; and (2) the time element in complying with the Act, because it was quicker and easier to utilize what the railroads had done.

Since 1936, there has been considerable refinement of the original

---

[62] *Ibid.,* pp. 61–62.
[63] Colquitt, *op. cit.,* p. 10.

publication and it has been condensed into one volume. Thirteen issues have appeared, "No. 13" having become effective July 7, 1955. Continuous effort has been exerted to adapt the method of railroad classification to motor carrier use. Today, there still exists considerable similarity of the ratings and other features. Likewise, the motor carriers recognize the three major classification territories, the boundaries of which are about the same. However, Official Territory of the railroads is known as Eastern Territory by the motor carriers. The following comment is informative: [64]

Insofar as ratings and descriptions are concerned, the present (motor) classification, when originally published in 1936, was a reproduction, almost in its entirety, of the railroad classification. This was considered a competitive necessity at the time. While some minor departures from the railroad classification have been made, the two classifications are still almost identical. They both fall far short of perfection, and in many instances are inconsistent with recognized and approved classification principles. This is particularly true in the case of ratings on light and bulky articles, which have a low weight density, and the motor carrier industry is finding it necessary to publish higher ratings on such articles in order to avoid direct revenue losses.

Following the "uniformity" order directed to the railroads by the Interstate Commerce Commission in Docket No. 28310, which was described in the preceding section, the motor carriers revised their existing Classification to conform with the *Uniform Freight Classification* of the railroads. The new uniform motor Classification is entitled, *National Motor Freight Classification No. A-1*, also published by the American Trucking Associations, Inc. The original issue was to have become effective June 10, 1952; but the effective date was postponed by thirty days.[65] The second issue, "No. A-2" became effective July 7, 1954.

It should be observed that all the motor truck lines of the country do not adhere to the *National Motor Freight Classification* and, therefore, it is not truly "national" in its application. True, a large majority of the motor carriers conform to it. The "No. 12" issue lists about 6,000 participating carriers,[66] and the new uniform issue, "No. A-1," lists 6,101.[67] The railroads' Uniform Classification "No. 2" shows about 400 motor carrier participants, most of which are railroad subsidiaries.[68]

---

[64] Middle Atlantic States Motor Carrier Conference, Inc.: *Construction and Interpretation of Freight Tariffs*, Washington, 1944, p. 16.

[65] Cushman, R. M.: *Transportation for Management*, Prentice-Hall, New York, 1953, p. 184.

[66] *National Motor Freight Classification No. 12, op. cit.*, pp. 3-A–81-A.

[67] *National Motor Freight Classification No. A-1, op. cit.*, pp. 3-A–76-A.

[68] *Uniform Freight Classification No. 2, op. cit.*, pp. 11–14.

Two separate Classifications were used in the New England states, the *Official Motor Freight Classification* and the *Coordinated Motor Freight Classification,* "in which two separate groups of motor common carriers participate," and "the ratings in both are substantially the same." [69] The New England motor carriers participated in the original *National Motor Freight Classification,* but after a short time they found it inadequate from a revenue producing standpoint. The *Coordinated Motor Freight Classification* was established in 1938 and there have been seven issues. "No. 7," which became effective January 8, 1954, lists 1,407 participating carriers.[70] It is published by the New England Rate Bureau, 262 Washington Street, Boston. There have been five issues of the *Official Motor Freight Classification,* "No. 5" having become effective January 19, 1952, with 601 listed participating carriers of which 226 were authorized to handle only intrastate traffic.[71]

Continuance of the separate New England Classifications has been advocated by various shipping interests and motor carriers in that area, except the carriers in Maine. The Interstate Commerce Commission has stated, "we find it is not unlawful for the New England respondents (carriers) to continue the use of their present type of classification." [72] On the other hand, the Commercial Motor Vehicle Association of Maine, composed of carriers in Maine, the Middle Atlantic States Motor Carrier Conference, representing carriers in Eastern Territory south and west of New England, the American Trucking Associations, Inc., and others, contend that the New England Classifications "should be brought in line with the national classification maintained throughout the rest of the country." [73]

Whether or not the few Mid-Western and the New England carriers will be forced into complying with the new uniform National Motor Freight Classification is questionable; but, if accomplished, a common classification will apply to all motor carriers throughout the nation. From the standpoint of the shipper of freight, simplicity and standardization of shipping procedures are always desirable. A step towards uniformity occurred in 1955 when the Eastern Motor Freight Conference was dissolved and its membership was trans-

---

[69] *Motor Carrier Rates in New England,* Ex Parte No. MC-22, 47 M.C.C. 657 (658), 1948.
[70] *Coordinated Motor Freight Classification No. 7,* The New England Motor Rate Bureau, Inc., Boston, effective January 8, 1954, pp. 3–27.
[71] *Official Motor Freight Classification No. 5,* Eastern Motor Freight Conference, Inc., West Hartford, effective January 19, 1952, pp. 3–14.
[72] *Motor Carrier Rates in New England, op. cit.,* p. 663.
[73] *Ibid.,* p. 660.

ferred to the New England Motor Rate Bureau.[74] The *Official* Motor Freight Classification ceased to exist as of June 1, 1955; [75] but the "Coordinated" Classification continues in effect for motor carriers of New England.

Express Classification. Prior to enactment by Congress of the original Interstate Commerce Act in 1887, there had been no classification of express traffic by the several express companies in the United States. Although express companies were not included in that Act, in 1887 the Adams Express Company issued a "Freight Classification and Index" which established what amounted to four classes, namely: "double merchandise, one and one-half merchandise, and three times merchandise," with "merchandise" being the basic class. Following a convention of superintendents of the several express companies in 1889, Classification No. 1 was adopted. It is most significant that this first Express Classification applied to traffic being handled by all the express companies throughout the United States and, therefore, it was truly a "uniform" classification in every sense of the word. Also, it is interesting to observe that "No. 1" was prepared by superintendents, who were, and are, operating and not traffic officials, for there was "no such thing as a Traffic Department at that time." The second issue in 1890, totaling eight pages, listed articles in alphabetical order with the respective ratings in a comparable manner to the present system. Express companies were brought under federal regulation by the Hepburn Act of 1906, and since that time Express Classifications have been published in accordance with requirements of the Interstate Commerce Commission. Between 1887 and 1906, sixteen issues had appeared, and "No. 17" became effective November 15, 1906. The former "merchandise" classes were abolished and replaced with the existing classes in 1914. At the same time, a "Directory of Express Stations" and a "Directory of Collection and Delivery Limits" were issued bearing Interstate Commerce Commission numbers A-3 and A-4 respectively; and the two publications still bear those original 1914 numbers, although several revisions have since been issued.[76]

There is only one express carrier in the United States today, the Railway Express Agency, Inc. It publishes its own Classification in accordance with rules of the Interstate Commerce Commission in

---

[74] *Transport Topics*, April 4, 1955, p. 18.

[75] Supplement No. 42 to *Official Motor Freight Classification No. 5*, MF-I.C.C. No. A-28, (cancelling *Official Motor Freight Classification No. 5* in full) Eastern Motor Freight Conference, West Hartford, Connecticut, issued December 2, 1954, effective June 1, 1955.

[76] Letter from L. R. Burke, General Traffic Manager, Railway Express Agency, Inc., New York City, dated March 8, 1954.

the same manner as railroads and motor carriers. It is absolutely uniform and much broader in scope than any other Classification, for it applies to express traffic moving between all points in continental United States, Alaska, Hawaii, and Canada.[77] The title of the document is the *Official Express Classification,* issued by the Agency itself at its main office in New York City. "No. 35," consisting of 79 pages, became effective May 20, 1952.

Air Classification. In striking contrast to other modes of transportation, there is no uniform classification of air freight. The air carriers have not published a common classification for air freight, notwithstanding that the Civil Aeronautics Board possesses the authority to require its issuance.[78] Such classification as there is, in general, is included in the air freight tariffs of the carriers. Suffice it to say, there is no single volume of air freight classification in which all the domestic air carriers participate.

[77] *Official Express Classification No. 35,* Railway Express Agency, Inc., New York, effective May 20, 1952, p. 2.
[78] Civil Aeronautics Act, Section 403.

Chapter 7

CLASSIFICATION—
Part III

Classification Ratings. It was stated in the preceding chapter that the thousands of commodities which are shipped throughout the United States are grouped into a limited number of *classes*, and a *rating* is assigned to each class. Furthermore, until 1952, the ratings in the three major classification territories were not uniform, and non-uniform ratings still exist in the far West and on certain types of traffic elsewhere in the country. It had been found that approximately 60 percent of all the rail ratings were the same in the three territories, and that about 13 percent were unlike in any two of the territories.[1] First, the ratings of the railroads will be presented.

In Official Territory, there are seven classes which were prescribed by the Interstate Commerce Commission in 1930, and which still remain in effect where the old Consolidated Classification has not been cancelled. Six of the classes are numbered "1" to "6," inclusive. The seventh is known as "Rule 26" class, referred to as Class "R26." Years ago, it was found the spread between third and fourth classes was too great, with the result that a new rule, or amendment, to the Classification of the railroads in Official Territory was adopted. It was called "Rule 26" and Class "R26" appears between third and fourth classes as one of the regular classes.[2]

In Southern Territory, the Interstate Commerce Commission prescribed twelve classes in 1925 which are numbered "1" to "12," inclusive.[3]

In Western Territory, there are five numbered and five lettered classes which were specified by order of the Commission in 1930. The classes are numbered "1" to "5" and "A" to "E," inclusive.[4]

---

[1] Morton, Mignon: *The Complicated ABC's of Changes in Class Railroad Rates*, Industrial Research Series No. 10, University of Kansas Publications, University of Kansas, Lawrence, 1948, p. 13.
[2] *Eastern Class Rate Investigation*, 164 I.C.C. 314, 1930.
[3] *Southern Class Rate Investigation*, 100 I.C.C. 513, 1925.
[4] *Western Trunk Line Class Rates*, 164 I.C.C. 1, 1930.

As has been previously explained, the rating of each class is a fixed percentage of first class, first class always being the base of 100 percent.[5] The percentage relationships of the different classes in each of the classification territories are outlined below:

OFFICIAL CLASSIFICATION TERRITORY

Class	1	2	3	R26	4	5	6
Percentage	100	85	70	55	50	35	27½

SOUTHERN CLASSIFICATION TERRITORY

Class	1	2	3	4	5	6	7	8	9	10	11	12
Percentage	100	85	70	55	45	40	35	30	25	22½	20	17½

WESTERN CLASSIFICATION TERRITORY

Class	1	2	3	4	A	5	B	C	D	E
Percentage	100	85	70	55	45	37½	32½	30	22½	17½

ILLINOIS CLASSIFICATION TERRITORY

Class	1	2	3	R26	4	A	5	B	6	C	D	E
Percentage	100	85	70	55	50	40	35	32½	27½	27½	22½	20

The following table shows the percentage relationships of the regular class designations to first class rates as published in applicable tariffs for the four classification territories: [6]

Percent of First Class	Official Territory	Southern Territory	Western Territory	Illinois Territory
100	1	1	1	1 (class)
85	2	2	2	2
70	3	3	3	3
55	R26	4	4	R26
50	4	—	—	4
45	—	5	A	—
40	—	6	—	A
37½	—	—	5	—
35	5	7	—	5
32½	—	—	B	B
30	—	8	C	—
27½	6	—	—	6 & C
25	—	9	—	—
22½	—	10	D	D
20	—	11	—	E
17½	—	12	E	—

From the above, it will be seen the percentage relationships of the first four classes in all territories, including Class Rule 26 in

---

[5] See, pp. 71–72, above.
[6] Docket No. 28300, *Class Rate Investigation, 1939,* 262 I.C.C. 447 (467), 1945. (Tabulation of classes in Mountain-Pacific Territory, included in the I.C.C. report, has been intentionally deleted, for it can serve no useful purpose in this presentation.)

Official and Illinois Territories, are the same throughout the country. Thus, if the rating of a commodity were second class (Class 2), the rate applicable to its shipment anywhere in the United States would be 85 percent of the first class rate. Assuming the first class rate to be $1.00 per hundred pounds between two given points, the freight rate on all articles assigned to second class would be 85 cents per hundred pounds between those two points. It will also be observed that Classes 6 and C are the same in Illinois Territory.

The ratings or classes, as published in the Classifications, appear as bare numbers—1, 2, 3, 4, etc.—except for Western and Illinois Territories where there are both numbers and letters, and "R26" for Rule 26 Class in Official and Illinois Territories. Thus, the number "1" refers to first class, the number "5" to fifth class, the letter "B" to Class B, etc. It should be mentioned that formerly there was a Rule 25 Class in Official Territory which was 70 percent of first class, but it was replaced by Class 3.[7] The twelve consecutively numbered classes in Southern Territory may be considered the simplest manner of rating identification.

In addition to the regular classes, however, there are instances where certain articles are assigned ratings which differ from the established percentages of first class. For those commodities which are given rating less than first class, and somewhere between the fixed percentages of the recognized classes, the published Classifications will show a number, such as: 92½, 60, 37½, 16, 13, etc. Where such a number appears as the rating of a certain article, it means that that particular number is the percentage of first class itself. All-told, there are 16 of these intermediate variations in Official Territory, 14 in Southern Territory, and 12 in Western Territory,[8] which have the effect of increasing the number of classes accordingly. For example, in the Rail Classification, the number 37½ appears as the carload rating for vermiculite in Southern Territory, 37½ being between the regular sixth (40 percent of first class) and seventh (35 percent) classes. The rating on the same article in Official Territory is fifth class (35 percent) and fifth class in Western Territory (37½ percent).[9] Obviously, it must have been found that a rating of sixth class in Southern Territory (40 percent) was too high and that seventh class (35 percent) was too low and, therefore, vermiculite was granted a relationship of 37½ percent of first class. Likewise, the motor Classification shows a rating of Class 50 for less-than-truckload shipments of zinc ingots in Southern Terri-

[7] *Eastern Class Rate Investigation, op. cit.*
[8] Docket No. 28300, *op. cit.*, p. 468.
[9] *Consolidated Freight Classification No. 20, op. cit.*, Item 44622.

tory, which is between fourth and fifth classes. The rating of that commodity in Eastern Territory is fourth class (50 percent); therefore, the rating of Class 50 in Southern Territory puts it on a parity with the rating in Eastern Territory. The rating of the same article in Western Territory is fourth class, which is 55 percent of first class.[10] It should be mentioned that the percentages themselves are not the only factors involved in determining the amount of a rate. Prior to the Docket 28300 rate adjustment, there was considerable variation in the rate scale in each of the classification territories, and those variations still exist where the Uniform Classification is not effective. For example, the rate scale in Southern Territory was approximately 140 percent of the rate scale in Official Territory, and the Western Territory scale was fractionally higher than that of Southern Territory. Consequently, the percentages themselves would not necessarily mean that where 50 per cent was shown for two territories that the rate for the same distance would be the same.

Since 13 is the lowest percentage rating published in the Classifications, there can be no confusion with identification of the established class. A simple rule for interpreting a rating is: if the figure is 12 or below, it refers to the established class; if the figure is higher than 12, it refers to the actual percentage of first class.

Many articles are assigned ratings higher than first class. In such instances, some confusion might arise in the mind of the reader in interpreting the Classification because either the actual number of the percentage relationship to first class may be shown or, instead, there may be use of standard abbreviations which have been adopted. Concerning the former, upon reference to page 114, below, on which a page of the Motor Classification is reproduced, the less-than-truckload rating for Vending Machine Stands, item 87665, is shown as "110." When such a bare figure higher than 100 appears in the Rating Section, it indicates the rating is a percentage of first class which here would be 110 percent. The abbreviations which appear as ratings for articles higher than first class are, as follows: [11]

"$1\frac{1}{4}$" means.......one and one-fourth times first class (125%)
"$1\frac{1}{2}$"..............one and one-half times first class (150%)
"$1\frac{3}{4}$"..............one and three-fourths times first class (175%)
"D1"..............double first class (200%)
"$2\frac{1}{2}$t1"............two and one-half times first class (250%)
"3t1"..............three times first class (300%)
"$3\frac{1}{2}$t1"............three and one-half times first class (350%)
"4t1"..............four times first class (400%)
"5t1"..............five times first class (500%)

[10] *National Motor Freight Classification No. 12, op. cit.,* Item 98720.
[11] *Ibid.,* p. 1.

The percentage relationships of ratings in the Motor Classification are the same as in the rail publication, except as described below. Just as with the older railroad system of classification, the motor carriers have divided the United States into three grand territories for classification purposes. Their respective geographical areas are about the same. However, "Official" Territory of the Rail Classification is identified by the more realistic term "Eastern" Territory in the Motor Classification; and there is no separate Illinois Territory for motor carriers. Another difference is that there is no Rule 26 Class in the Motor Classification; instead, Class F in Eastern Territory is 55 percent of first class, and between third and fourth classes.[12] In other words, Class F for motor carriers is the same as Rule 26 Class for railroads. The percentage relationships in Eastern Territory for motor carriers, therefore, are, as follows:

EASTERN CLASSIFICATION TERRITORY

Class	1	2	3	F	4	5	6
Percentage	100	85	70	55	50	35	27½

The relationship of classes in Southern and Western Territories are the same as those of the Rail Classification presented on page 109, above, except there are no motor ratings with a percentage relationship below 27½.[13]

Page 259 of *National Motor Freight Classification No. 13*, effective July 7, 1955, is reproduced on the next page. Some abbreviations will be observed upon reference thereto. From item 87665, Vending Machine Stands, the letter "T" in a circle preceded the truckload rating of third class. The "Explanation of Abbreviations and Reference Marks" Section on page 1 of the Classification explains that the "T" indicates a truckload rating; [14] and the letter "w" before the minimum truckload weight for the same article refers to the minimum weight factor which is described later in Chapter 14.

It should be understood that the above explanation refers to the pre-uniform method of classification which is still effective in certain areas. Under the new uniform system, there is no distinction between the territories, nor are the classes identified by numbers or letters as heretofore. There are thirty-two classes stated in terms of

---

[12] Taff, C. A.: *Commercial Motor Transportation*, Revised Edition, Irwin, Chicago, 1955, p. 390.

[13] Item 14840 in *National Motor Freight Classification No. 13*, effective July 7, 1955, cement mixing compound, carries a rating of "6-7-5," or 27½ percent in Eastern Territory, 35 percent in Southern Territory, and 37½ percent in Western Territory.

[14] See, pp. 119–120, below.

percentages of the base 100 percent rate from a high of 500, to a low of 13 for railroads and 27½ for motor carriers, as follows: [15]

1.	Class	500	17.	Class	55
2.	"	400	18.	"	50
3.	"	300	19.	"	45
4.	"	250	20.	"	40
5.	"	200	21.	"	37½
6.	"	175	22.	"	35
7.	"	150	23.	"	32½
8.	"	125	24.	"	30
9.	"	110	25.	"	27½
10.	"	100	26.	"	25
11.	"	92½	27.	"	22½
12.	"	85	28.	"	20
13.	"	77½	29.	"	17½
14.	"	70	30.	"	16
15.	"	65	31.	"	14½
16.	"	60	32.	"	13

For illustrative purposes, the following articles have been selected at random from the new Motor Classification: less-than-truckload shipments of ping pong balls are Class 500,[16] certain kinds of lunch boxes are Class 400,[17] bees in hives are Class 300,[18] certain kinds of kitchen sinks with legs in place are Class 250,[19] and golf club bags are Class 200; [20] by rail, less-than-carload shipments of airplane pontoons are Class 400,[21] ivory billiard balls are Class 300,[22] camera lenses are Class 200,[23] and pea shellers are Class 150.[24] It is worthy of mention that in Docket No. 28310, the Interstate Commerce Commission proposed 30 classes; [25] but Classes 500 and 110, which were not included in the original order of the Commission, were added by the carriers.[26]

The simplicity of the new over the old system can be shown effectively, as follows: assume the pre-uniform method of classification is in effect, that a volume shipment of composition shoe soling is

---

[15] *Uniform Freight Classification No. 2* and *National Motor Freight Classification No. A-2, op. cit.*
[16] *National Motor Freight Classification No. A-2, op. cit.*, Item 4823.
[17] *Ibid.*, Item 12990.
[18] *Ibid.*, Item 9230.
[19] *Ibid.*, Item 78410.
[20] *Ibid.*, Item 5250.
[21] *Uniform Freight Classification No. 2, op. cit.*, Item 1315.
[22] *Ibid.*, Item 2290.
[23] *Ibid.*, Item 8850.
[24] *Ibid.*, Item 850.
[25] Docket No. 28310, *op. cit.*
[26] Uniform Rail and Motor Classifications, *op. cit.*

Item	ARTICLES	RATINGS LTL	RATINGS @Vol.	@ Vol.Min. Wt.-Lbs.
	STANDS—Continued:			
87660	Stands, NOI, other than Furniture:			
	SU, not nested nor interlaced, in packages	1½	2	10,000
	SU, interlaced or nested or KD, other than flat, in packages	1	3	16,000
	Flat, folded flat or KD flat, in packages	3	37½–5–45	30,000
87665	Vending Machine, sheet steel, in boxes or crates	110	Ⓣ3	Ⓝ14.4
87670	Starch, Arrowroot. See item 33465 for ratings dependent upon agreed or released value:			
	In containers in barrels or boxes	1	5–6–5	40,000
	In bulk in bags or barrels	3	5–6–5	40,000
87680	Starch, liquid, in barrels or boxes	F–4–4	Ⓒ5–Ⓕ7– Ⓒ5	Ⓝ40.6
87690	Starch, NOI, in bags, barrels, boxes or pails, see Note, item 87700	F–4–4	6–7–5	40,000
87700	Note—Ratings will also apply when in 5-ply multiple-wall paper bags, total basis weight for all walls not less than 230 pounds, net weight of contents not exceeding 140 pounds, or in 4-ply paper bags, total basis weight for all walls not less than 170 lbs., net weight of contents not exceeding 120 pounds.			
87710	Starch Substitutes, inedible, consisting of a physical mixture of starch made from grain or flour made from grain and chemical constituents, the chemical content not to exceed two per cent, in bags, barrels, boxes or pails, see Note, item 87700	F–4–4	6–7–5	40,000
87720	Starting cranks, internal combustion engine, in packages; also Vol., loose	F–4–4	5–7–5	30,000
87730	**STATIONERY:**			
87740	Book Mailing Corners, metal, paper covered, in boxes	1	3	20,000
87750	Calendars, NOI (including calendars with thermometers attached), Calendar Backs, Calendar Mounts, Date Pads or list finders, in boxes, or in inner containers in cloth bags	2	ⒹF–Ⓒ4– Ⓒ4	Ⓝ24.6
87760	Crayons, Artists', in boxes	1	3	20,000
87770	Crayons, School or Marking, in barrels or boxes	3	37½–6–5	36,000
87780	Desk pen sets (pens with or without gold or gold plated points and inkwells or bases), in boxes	1	1	AQ
87790	Erasers, NOI, in boxes	2	F–4–4	30,000
87800	Fasteners or Clips, paper, in boxes:			
	Metal, NOI, or steel, NOI	2	ⒹF–Ⓒ4– Ⓒ4	Ⓝ24.6
	Steel wire	3	Ⓒ4	Ⓒ24.6
87810	Ink Stands or Wells, Cut Glass, with or without bases or fittings, in barrels or boxes	1½	1	10,000
87820	Ink Stands or Wells, earthenware, in barrels or boxes	2	F–4–4	24,000
87830	Ink Stands or Wells, other than glass or earthenware, NOI, with or without bases or fittings, in barrels or boxes	1	3	20,000
87835	Pads, memorandum, desk, with metal or plastic holders, see Note, item 87836, in boxes	2	ⒹF–Ⓒ4– Ⓒ4	Ⓝ24.6
87836	Note—Ratings will also apply on shipments containing not to exceed one mechanical pencil for each pad.			
87840	Paper Weights, in barrels or boxes	2	F–4–4	24,000
87850	Parchment or Vellum, in boxes	1½	1	10,000
87860	Pen holders, Pen holder Sticks, Slate Pencils, Pencils, NOI, or Children's School Pencil or Pen holder Sets, in boxes	2	F–4–4	24,000
87870	Pen Points, steel, in boxes	1	3	20,000
87880	Pencil Leads, in boxes	1	3	30,000
87890	Ribbons, Inked, in boxes	1	3	24,000
87900	Staples, Stapling Machine, steel wire thinner than ⁵/₆₄ inch, in boxes	3	45–5–45	30,000
87910	Stationery, NOI, in boxes	1	3	20,000
87920	Tacks, Thumb, in barrels or boxes	2	F–4–4	24,000
87930	Stays or Steels, Corset or Dress steel, in barrels or boxes	2	4	30,000
87940	Stearic Acid, in bags, barrels or boxes	F–4–4	5–7–5	30,000
87950	Stearine, Animal, NOI, LTL, in bags, barrels or tubs; Vol., in bulk or in packages, also in tank trucks, see Rule 23	F–4–4	37½–37½–5	30,000
87960	Sterilizers, NOI:			
87990	Cabinet, in boxes or crates	1	2	16,000
88000	Other than cabinet, in boxes or crates, see Note, item 88001	2	Ⓣ40–Ⓒ3– Ⓒ3	Ⓝ24.6
88001	Note—Sterilizers, other than cabinet type, weighing 2,000 lbs. or more, may be shipped on skids, provided motors, gauges, valves and other accessories are protected by boxing or crating.			
88010	Stolons (Chopped Grass), in bags	D1	2	14,000
88020	Stone Stencil Compound (Paper, Glue and Glycerine combined, or Rubber and Glue combined, in sheet form), in boxes	2	4	36,000
88030	Stoppers, Bottle:			
88040	Aluminum, in barrels or boxes	1	3	20,000
88050	Bottle Stoppers, NOI, in bags, barrels or boxes	2	4	30,000
88060	Bottle, with Swab Attachments, in bags, barrels or boxes	2	4	24,000
88070	Cork and wood combined, in bags, barrels or boxes	2	F–4–4	24,000
88080	Glass, other than cut or ground, in barrels or boxes	3	5–6–5	30,000
88085	Plastic, in barrels or boxes	1	Ⓒ3	Ⓝ20.6
88090	Stoppers, Carboy, clay, in bags, see Note, item 88100, in barrels or boxes	4–50–4	5–6–5	36,000
88100	Note—Bags must be Grade A burlap bags with a five-ply Kraft paper bag liner.			
88105	Sticks or Stirrers, beverage, candy or ice cream, cellulose film, in boxes	3	Ⓒ5–Ⓒ7– Ⓒ5	Ⓝ30.6

to move by motor carrier from Boston to Dallas via Memphis, and that the first class, or 100 percent, rate is $1.00. Prior to the summer of 1952, the soling was rated fourth class in all territories for volume shipments.[27] Hence, in Eastern Territory, the freight rate would be

[27] *National Motor Freight Classification No. 10*, effective August 13, 1949, Item 12420.

based on 50 percent of the first class rate; in Southern and Western Territories, 55 percent. If there were no through rate published for the article, the total rate would be computed by adding together the respective rates applicable in each of the three territories, thus: from Boston to Roanoke, or at whatever point it crossed the territorial boundary, the rate would be on the basis of 50 percent; Roanoke to Memphis, on the basis of 55 percent; Memphis to Dallas, on the basis of 55 percent. In the absence of a through rate from Boston to Dallas, the respective percentage relationships in each territory would have to be considered, which necessitates an intimate knowledge of routes and the boundaries of the territories. Normally, however, where a shipment moves over a route where there is no one published rate applicable for the carrier or carriers involved, the lowest combination of rates will apply via whatever points they can be worked out, and this would be based upon the length of haul of each carrier and the application of the tariffs carrying the through rates of each participating carrier. It should be kept in mind that the rate tariffs are the governing factors in determining the classification territory applicable to a given movement. Where a combination of local rates is necessary, usually it is determined on the basis of the carrier's tariff rather than by interterritorial gateways.

To further illustrate, under the old system volume shipments of "Boston Baked Beans" [28] were rated 5-7-5—that is, fifth class in Eastern Territory, seventh class in Southern Territory, and fifth class in Western Territory.[29] In the absence of a through rate from Boston to Dallas via Memphis, and if the base rate were $1.00 as before, the total rate would be computed on the basis of 35 percent of the first class rate, in Eastern and Southern Territories, and 38 percent in Western Territory. If there were a through rate from Boston to Dallas, the tariff containing the through rate would state which one of the three Classifications governs, because only one Classification may apply to a single published through rate. Frequently, the Classification of the destination territory applies.[30]

Under the new system, composition shoe soling is rated as Class 37½,[31] which means, of course, the rate would be 37½ percent of the Class 100 rate all the way from Boston to Dallas, without regard

---

[28] Officially described in the Classification as, "Vegetables, canned or preserved, . . . pork and beans . . ." Item 41060, *Ibid.*
[29] *National Motor Freight Classification No. 10, op. cit.,* Item 41060.
[30] Cushman, F. M.: *Transportation for Management,* Prentice-Hall, Inc., New York, 1953, p. 168.
[31] *National Motor Freight Classification No. A-2, op. cit.,* Item 12420.

to the territorial boundaries. Likewise, the volume rating of "Boston Baked Beans," in the second illustration, is Class 35.[32]

There is a decidedly different method of applying ratings to motor freight in New England. As was stated earlier, the New England motor carriers generally do not participate in the *National Motor Freight Classification* of the American Trucking Associations, Inc., on traffic local to their territory,[33] which means that publication does not apply entirely in the area east of the Hudson River. Instead, they subscribe to the *Coordinated Motor Freight Classification*, which is applicable to traffic moving exclusively within New England Territory.[34] New England motor carriers subscribe to the *National Motor Freight Classification* on through traffic to and from points outside of the New England states.

Under the "Coordinated" Classification, there are five classes numbered 1 to 5, inclusive, and a sixth class designated as "Class 4 times 5"; but, there are ratings which go up to as high as eight times first class, which are shown in the Classification as "8t1," [35] with intermediate multiples of first class. In striking contrast to other systems of classification, a unique feature of the New England Motor Classification is that Class 5, *not* first class, is the base 100 percent rating. The percentage relationships of the classes as authorized by the Interstate Commerce Commission are, as follows: [36]

Class 5	100 percent
Class 4	120 percent
Class 3	150 percent
Class 2	200 percent
Class 1	300 percent
Class 4 times 5	400 percent

The independent Classification of the Railway Express Agency, Inc., contains four classes, three numbered 1 to 3 and a special "Money Classification." In addition, the Express Classification provides for a "pound" rate which bears a percentage relationship to first class, but the percentage relationship varies with the weight of the shipment. The Classification provides that where such rates are applicable, the rate per 100 pounds is multiplied by the number of pounds in the shipment, the product so obtained is divided by 100,

[32] *Ibid.*, Item 41060.
[33] See, pp. 104–105, above.
[34] *Motor Carrier Rates in New England*, Ex Parte No. MC-22, 47 M.C.C. 657, 1948.
[35] *Coordinated Motor Freight Classification No. 7*, New England Motor Freight Bureau, Boston, effective January 8, 1954, p. 120.
[36] *Motor Carrier Rates in New England, op. cit.*, p. 664.

and the resulting figure will be the rate. To illustrate: assume Pound Rates are applicable to a shipment weighing 75 pounds and that the normal published rate between the two points the shipment is to move is $2.84 per 100 pounds; then, the Pound Rate would be determined by multiplying 2.84 by 75 which gives a product of 213.00, and 213 divided by 100 is 2.13, resulting in a Pound Rate of $2.13 for the 75-pound shipment.[37]

The Money Classification of the Express Agency covers shipments of extraordinary value, such as, coin, paper currency, bullion, securities, negotiable instruments, etc., and the applicable rate is determined primarily by actual value of the particular shipment.[38]

First class in the Express Classification is the common 100 percent basic rating; but second and third classes definitely are influenced by the weight of a particular shipment. In general, for shipments weighing over ten pounds, Class 2 is 75 percent of first class. Class 3, however, does not bear a percentage relationship to first class; instead, the resulting rate is determined entirely by weight of the article assigned to third class, the basis being one cent per ounce, or fraction thereof, with a minimum charge of $1.50 per shipment. Similar to the other Classifications, there are multiples of first class with a maximum of eight times first class, exclusive of the Money Classification. All articles which are not assigned a specific rating are rated as first class; second class, in general, includes articles of food and drink, "except as otherwise provided"; and third class comprises special commodities on which the Express Agency restricts its liability to $10.00 per package.[39] There is further refinement of the first class rating dependent upon weight and applicable only between specified points, thus: a Class 1 shipment weighing from 300 to 1499 pounds is assigned a rating of 75 percent of first class; from 1500 to 2499 pounds, 70 percent; and over 2500 pounds, 65 percent.[40]

There are no separate classification ratings for air freight. In 1944, American Airlines established four distinct classes, but it was later abandoned in favor of the single-class system. At the present time, the only classification of air freight is on the space-weight basis.[41]

---

[37] *Official Express Classification No. 35, op. cit.,* Rule 1 (k), p. 20.
[38] *Ibid.,* pp. 74–79.
[39] *Ibid.,* pp. 20, 46.
[40] Railway Express Agency, Inc.: "Local & Joint Commodity Tariff applying on Miscellaneous Merchandise," issued by L. R. Burke, New York, I.C.C. No. 8048, effective December 4, 1953, p. 7.
[41] Locklin, D. P.: *Economics of Transportation,* Fourth Edition, Richard D. Irwin, Inc., Chicago, 1954, p. 817.

In summary, except for the Railway Express Agency's third class and money class, and the unique situation in New England for motor carriers, the classification *rating* is a percentage of the base 100 or first class *rate*. The ratings appear in the published Classifications; the rates, in tariffs. A rating is a bare figure without consideration of dollars and cents or units of any kind, for a rating is *not* a price for transportation service; but, a rating has a direct relationship to and a positive effect upon the price which the public pays for the shipment of commodities. A rating which is represented by a high number, as Class 85, means the resulting applicable freight rate will be higher than if it were accorded a lower number, as Class 60. The reverse, of course, would be true for the pre-uniform system of identifying ratings; for a high number, as Class 3 which is 70 percent of first class, results in a lower rate than a low number, as Class 2 which is 85 percent. The transportation price, the *rate*, is determined by use of the classification *rating*. The Class 100, or first class, rate between any two points is a fixed amount expressed in terms of dollars and/or cents per 100 pounds; and the actual sum paid to a carrier by a shipper varies directly in accordance with the rating which has been assigned in a published Classification to the particular article that is being shipped.

Large & Small Shipments. A distinctive feature of classification ratings is the differentiation between carload and less-than-carload shipments, and between truckload or volume and less-than-truckload shipments. For simplification in this section, carload and truckload shipments will be termed "large" shipments, and less-than-carload and less-than-truckload shipments will be referred to as "small" shipments. At this point, it is advisable to review the definitions in Chapter 1 of truckload, less-than-truckload, etc.[42]

Almost invariably, the rating of a large shipment is lower than that of a small shipment. Justification for the higher ratings of small shipments is on the basis of costs incurred by the carriers. In general, a large shipment is loaded by the consignor at his place of business, and it is unloaded by the consignee at his location. The consignor furnishes the necessary labor, lumber, and other materials with which to brace and block the shipment so that it will not be damaged enroute and be received by the consignee in good condition. If the shipment is by rail, the shipment moves through from point of origin to point of destination, regardless of the number of railroads in the route. Likewise, with the recent innovation of interchange of truck trailers between motor carriers, a truckload ship-

---

[42] See, p. 5, above.

ment loaded in one vehicle usually will go through to destination without rehandling at intermediate points.

In contrast, all the loading and unloading, blocking and bracing, of small shipments are performed by carriers at carrier expense, except for shipments of unusual size. For long distances and for origins or destinations at small stations, frequently the freight car or trailer containing a number of small shipments will not move through from origin to destination of the shipments; hence, contents of the carrier's piece of equipment must be removed at intermediate points, segregated as to destinations, and reloaded into other equipment. Every time a shipment is handled or re-handled by carrier personnel, both the carrier's costs and the susceptibility to damage increase.

The clerical costs per unit of weight are greater for small than for large shipments because each individual shipment must be "billed" which necessitates preparation by the carrier of the waybill, arrival notice, freight bill, and other papers.[43] In addition, the carrier has the expense of acquiring, maintaining, and manning station facilities, together with the costs of supervision and labor to load and stow small shipments in units of equipment at points of origin, and to unload and segregate the freight according to local addresses of consignees at points of destination. If all the l.t.l. shipments in one trailer weigh 200 pounds each, and 20,000 pounds are loaded into the trailer, obviously 100 "bills" must be prepared and 100 shipments must be handled and re-handled at both origin and destination, and possibly at intermediate points. In contrast, only one "bill" is necessary for a single truckload shipment which may weigh 40,000 or more pounds; and usually it is loaded by the consignor and unloaded by the consignee without cost to the carrier.

In summary, clerical costs of a carrier are about the same for a single large shipment of 50,000 pounds as for a small shipment of 200 pounds; and, generally, the former entails no handling costs whatsoever for the carrier. In some instances, clerical costs actually are less for the large shipment. Handling costs of a carrier increases directly with the number of small shipments, but comparable costs do not obtain for large shipments.

As was mentioned earlier, the terms "truckload" and "volume" are used interchangeably for motor freight, although the Motor Classification uses the word "volume" rather than "truckload." Actually, the term "truckload" is somewhat indefinite; and it should not be assumed that a "truckload" of freight necessarily must be loaded on

---

[43] See, Chapter 4, above.

one vehicle. Nowhere in the Classification is it stated that a truck-load must move on a single vehicle, for it depends upon operating condition of the individual carrier and the nature of the traffic whether or not a "truckload" shipment is forwarded on one or more vehicles. A pamphlet of the Middle Atlantic States Motor Carrier Conference explains the distinction in the following language: [44]

The Term "truckload quantity" implies a minimum weight not in excess of that which may be loaded into a truck of fair average cubical capacity (usually 1000 cubic feet), and the term "volume quantity" implies a minimum weight which may be in excess of a truckload quantity. The word "truckload" is commonly understood to mean a truck loaded to its full cubical capacity. The terms "truckload" and "volume" are given different meanings in different parts of the country, and are sometimes used interchangeably. However, in the absence of any tariff provision to the contrary, whether a minimum weight is designated as a "truckload" or "volume" minimum weight, it must be observed in the application of any rate subject thereto, regardless of the weight which may consume the entire truck cubical capacity.

In view of the clear distinction between large and small shipments, classification ratings differentiate between the two; the former usually carrying a lower rating than the latter. This means the price for transportation—the freight rate—is lower per 100 pounds for large shipments than for small shipments of the same commodity. The minimum weight which establishes a shipment to be entitled to a carload or truckload rating is set forth for each article in the respective published Classifications. However, a Classification, in some instances, may assign a rating to apply to "any quantity" of an article by weight, rather than specifying a fixed minimum weight for a carload or truckload shipment. In such cases, the letters "AQ" appear in the appropriate column of the publication instead of a number indicating the minimum weight. For example, "AQ" appears in both the Rail and Motor Classifications for blankets.[45]

Classification Factors. Classification of freight is the allocation of commodities to different ratings and, as has been described earlier, the ratings are expressed by bare numbers. The ratings, then, are graduated above or below, or including, the base 100 or first class rating, except for motor carriers in New England which will be ignored for the present; and the ratings reflect various charac-

---

[44] Middle Atlantic States Motor Carrier Conference, Inc.: *Construction and Interpretation of Freight Tariffs*, Washington, 1944, pp. 14–15.
[45] *Uniform Freight Classification No. 2, op. cit.*, Item 12600; *National Motor Freight Classification No. A-2, op. cit.*, Item 27080.

teristics of a shipment which are known as "classification factors." The basic theory of freight classification is that commodities which possess similar classification factors should be assigned to the same class and, therefore, have the same rating.

Grouping of the thousands of articles which move in daily commerce into particular classes constitutes a real problem which is far from academic. Since classification ratings are the bases for the actual amounts in dollars and cents paid by the public for the shipment of goods, the determination of ratings is a matter of vital concern to both carriers and shippers: to carriers, because their livelihood is dependent upon revenues derived from freight rates; to shippers, because freight rates comprise a potent cost of production and distribution. To decide the class into which each commodity shall be placed or to decide which commodities shall be assigned to the same class and, therefore, bear exactly the same rate for identical transportation service, involves many questions. Why, for example, is abrasive cloth, including sand paper, in carload or truckload lots, assigned to Class 37½ in both the Rail and Motor Classifications? [46] Why should not a rating of 35 or 40 apply? It will be the purpose of this section to present some of the more important factors which influence the determination of ratings.

Since the common carriers of the United States are privately owned and operated, it is natural that they, like other American industries, possess the urge to earn the greatest profit that is possible in a highly competitive market of transportation services. Therefore, it would seem logical for the carriers to place their classification ratings on a high level in order to realize greater profits from the increased yield of freight rates. All common carriers, however, are public utility industries and, as such, they have a positive obligation to the public of providing the vital service of transporting goods at reasonable and nonprejudicial prices. As a result, under the American system of transportation regulation, classification ratings are controlled by the Interstate Commerce Commission with a view to preventing unfair discriminations and practices. Upon the carriers rests the grave responsibility of allocating the thousands of articles to specified classes. Each article must be examined with great care and fairness to avoid any semblance of an arbitrary or discriminatory method of classification.

Although ratings are determined by carriers through their specialized committees or boards, shippers and the general public have the

---

[46] *Uniform Freight Classification No. 2, op. cit.,* Item 10; *National Motor Freight Classification No. A-2, op. cit.,* Item 20.

legal right to air their views to the carriers and to appeal carrier decisions to the state and federal regulatory bodies. Ratings on a great many articles have been established by the carriers as a direct result of representations of shippers. The following comment of Professor Frank M. Cushman, Director of Transportation & Traffic Management Institute at Northeastern University, is significant: [47]

Shippers have often complained about a classification rating given to their commodities by the carriers in the firm belief that the rating was applied arbitrarily or capriciously by the carriers, or perhaps with discrimination aforethought. Under ordinary circumstances, this complaint is entirely without justification.

"Originally in the internal railway and steamboat freight movement of the country" a century or more ago, the essential determinants of ratings were the intrinsic value of the article, the relative ease of loading and unloading (for in those days, the carrier loaded and unloaded freight), the weight-space factor, or whether the shipment was "dry goods or groceries." [48] In the South, during the 1840's the early railroads considered density of a shipment as the primary determinant of a rating, for light and bulky articles were rated by the cubic foot and denser items by the pound, the lowest ratings being assigned to such commodities as coal, iron, and manure, and the highest to bulky merchandise of light weight. During the period of from about 1880 to 1900, there was recognition of the distinction between carload and less-than-carload shipments by reduced ratings being introduced for the former. [49]

With the passing of time, there has been considerable refinement of the old methods of classification. Over a half-century ago, the Interstate Commerce Commission recognized that a number of elements entered into the determination of a rating. [50] Today, many

---

[47] Cushman, *op. cit.*, p. 190.

[48] Ringwalt, J. L.: *Development of Transportation Systems in the United States*, Railway World Office, Philadelphia, 1888, p. 282.

[49] Healy, K. T.: *Economics of Transportation in America*, Ronald Press, New York, 1940, pp. 203–206.

[50] "It is believed that the great mass of freight articles could be fairly grouped . . . in a single classification. They would take into account whether commodities were crude, rough, or finished; liquid or dry; knocked down or set up; loose or in bulk, nested or in boxes, or otherwise packed; if vegetables, whether green or dry, desiccated or evaporated; the market value and shippers' representations as to their character; the cost of service; length and direction of haul; the season and manner of shipment; the space occupied and weight; whether in carload or less than carload lots; the volume of annual shipments to be calculated on; the sort of car required, whether flat, gondola, box, tank, or special; whether ice or heat must be furnished; the speed of trains necessary for perishable or otherwise rush goods; the risk of handling, either to the goods themselves or other property; the weights, actual and estimated; the carrier's

122

features are considered in the allocation of a certain commodity to a specific class. The importance of each characteristic varies from article to article, so that it cannot be said that any one factor is more important than another. Instead, the relative importance of all features are considered as they apply to each article, one factor being given more weight for one article than for another. Because there is such a wide variety of commodities offered for shipment, in different stages of manufacture, with divergent kinds of containers, with different degrees of perishability, for widely varying distances, etc., there are hundreds of characteristics which may enter into the individual ratings of all those articles.

Professor Gilbert L. Gifford, formerly Chairman of the Transportation Division in the Atlanta Division of the University of Georgia, and Captain C. C. Glasgow, Jr., a former graduate student of Professor Gifford and the writer, have divided the several classification factors into three general categories, namely: (1) physical, (2) commercial, and (3) transportation.[51] A few items, and some explanatory comments, have been added to their presentation. The factors which enter into the determination of classification ratings are summarized below, the Glasgow & Gifford study being the basis.

Physical Factors. This group includes the nature or physical characteristics of an article and, essentially, it involves carrier liability, together with what is known as the value of the transportation service to the shipper.

At this point, an explanation of the term, "value of the service," may be advisable. It is a term employed by traffic men to indicate the demand of shippers for transportation service in response to existing or changes in ratings and the resultant prices of carriers for such services. It is comparable to what the economist labels as "elasticity of demand"; but, "by either name it adds up to the same thing." [52] It marks the highest rating on which traffic will move; for if the resulting freight rate is higher than the value of the service to the shipper, it is inevitable that he will not ship his goods. It is an individual matter as it pertains to the shipper of a particular article. It measures how much a particular transportation service is

risk or owner's release from damage or loss." *Seventeenth Annual Report of the Interstate Commerce Commission,* Government Printing Office, Washington, 1903.

[51] Glasgow, C. C., Jr., & Gifford, G. L.: *An Analysis of Motor Carrier Tariffs,* The University of Tennessee, Knoxville, 1952, pp. 16–18.

[52] Edwards, F. K.: *Transportation Costs and Freight Rates,* Association of Interstate Commerce Commission Practitioners, Washington, "Cost and Value of Service in Rate Making for Common Carriers," January, 1952, p. 83.

worth to a shipper in dollars and cents. However, it is not necessarily the actual rating itself or the actual amount of the freight rate; instead, it is that amount which he would pay rather than not ship his goods.[53] Hence, it represents what the economist would term as the "maximum demand price" of a shipper.

Since the elasticity of the respective demands for transportation services of all shippers of all commodities are far from being the same, different classification ratings have been devised which reflect, in part at least, those differences in the value of service. As Locklin explains: [54]

> At the outset, it is well to recognize that the demand for the transportation of a commodity and the demand for the commodity itself are two different but related things. They are related, in that anything which restricts the demand for a commodity restricts the demand for the transportation of that commodity. But the demand for the transportation of a commodity may be restricted without affecting the demand for the commodity itself.

Value of the service should not be confused with value of the shipment. Although in traffic matters there is a definite relationship between the two, each is different. The former refers to the transportation service performed by carriers; the latter, to some particular commodity itself. A relatively high rating of a high-valued article results in a freight rate which is higher than one obtained from a low rating; but the resultant high rate is a small proportion of the selling price of the high-valued article, in contrast to a low rating of a cheap commodity resulting in a rate which is a substantial part of its price. Therefore, even the resulting low rate on a low-valued commodity has much greater influence both upon its selling price and the consequent demand of the public for it than a high rate on high-valued articles. Consequently, relatively high ratings do not restrict shipments of high-valued goods nearly as much as they influence the geographical extent of markets for low-valued goods, which means value of service is much greater and more sensitive for shippers of low-valued commodities than for shippers of high-valued commodities. The former are able and willing to pay less than the latter for transportation service because the freight rate is a greater direct part of the former's costs of production and distribution than the latter's.

---

[53] Bigham, T. C., & Roberts, M. J.: *Transportation,* McGraw-Hill Book Company, New York, 1952, p. 354.
[54] Locklin, D. P., *op. cit.,* p. 151.

This situation is recognized by the carriers in rating determination, for they realize any action on their part which restricts the demand for an article itself, by an appreciable proportionate increase in its price, will reduce the demand of shippers of that article for transportation service. It is for this reason that there is such wide divergence among ratings and that "Exceptions," which will be explained later, have been adopted. Of course, no rating can be so low, regardless of the value of service and ultimate loss of traffic, that the applicable rate will produce revenue at least no less than the carrier's out-of-pocket costs of providing the service.[55] While value of service to the shipper constitutes the highest level of rates, costs to the carrier of furnishing the service represent the lowest level. In practically all instances, the rating of a particular article falls somewhere between the two extremes, depending entirely upon the influence of the other classification factors as they are applied to individual situations.

In general, the rating of an article varies directly with its value, not only because articles of high value can better absorb the higher rate resulting from a higher rating than low-valued articles but also the resulting higher rate includes the element of insurance for protection of the carrier in the event of loss or damage to such shipments. Since, in effect, common carriers are insurers of goods, there must be some slight excess in the revenues derived from rates over and above the fair return to which they are entitled, as a sort of reserve to take care of any loss or damage which might occur both to the article in question and to other shipments or carrier equipment. In determining a rating, carriers always keep in mind the amount they will have to pay in case of a claim and, of course, that sum varies directly with the value of the shipment. A carrier is entitled to a higher margin of profit *per se* on shipments which necessitate higher insurance coverage than on commodities requiring less protection. It is for this reason essentially, for example, that the rating of a carload of human hair is 200,[56] certain types of lamp shades [57] and fur goods is 100,[58] certain kinds of rugs is 150,[59] some explosives is 100,[60] eye glasses is 150; [61] in contrast to bulk

[55] Out-of-pocket costs are those direct costs of providing a service which would not have been incurred had the service not been performed.
[56] *Uniform Freight Classification No. 2, op. cit.,* Item 22355.
[57] *Ibid.,* Item 21455.
[58] *Ibid.,* Item 19455.
[59] *Ibid.,* Item 17955.
[60] *Ibid.,* Items 16345–16395.
[61] *Ibid.,* Item 15010.

sand being only 13,[62] soapstone 17½,[63] bulk stone 13,[64] peanut hulls 17½,[65] and so on.

Physical factors include the following:

1. Value of the article.
2. Susceptibility of the article to loss, damage, spoilage, or pilferage.
3. Differences in price of the shipment at origin and destination.
4. Dangerous character of the commodity.
5. Inherent qualities or defects in the article.

Commercial Factors. As the term implies, commercial factors relate to the commercial characteristics of the article which, also, involve the value of the article together with competitive influences, as:

1. Stage of manufacture of the goods—raw materials, semi-finished articles or parts, or finished products.
2. Number of shipments to be made over a period of time and frequency of movements.
3. Seasonal nature of the movement.
4. Competition of sources of supply, including possible new sources.
5. Competition of markets.
6. Competition among producers, manufacturers, or distributors.
7. Competition of commodities.
8. Competition of possible substitute commodities.
9. Competition among carriers.

An excellent illustration of the influence of competition of commodities is afforded by a relatively recent case before the Interstate Commerce Commission. For classification purposes, prior to 1934 inedible tallow had been included with edible tallow and lard in the "packing-house products" group. In that year, it was transferred to the "soap-stock" list as being competitive with soap stocks rather than with packing-house products. In the proceeding before the Commission, the complainant desired to replace inedible tallow in the "packing-house products" group on a showing of the usual classification factors *except* competition. Actually, inedible tallow encounters keen competition with every article in the "soap-stock" list, but practically no competition with articles in the "packing-

---

[62] *Ibid.,* Item 21950.
[63] *Ibid.,* Item 21988.
[64] *Ibid.,* Item 22063.
[65] *Ibid.,* Item 17330.

house products" list. Logically, the Commission ruled that no change was justified.[66]

Another interesting case on the same subject developed that ice-cream mix competes with dessert preparations rather than with whole-milk powder and dairy products.[67] In another case, the Commission gave consideration to the competitiveness of rubber battery insulating partitions and wooden battery partitions.[68]

Prior to the advent of the motor common carrier as a real inter-city competitor of the railroads, the railroad classification commit-tees were not so much concerned with competition among railroads as with competition between commodities. However, some consid-eration had to be given to railroad competition where interterritorial movements of commodities became involved. The Commission, in some of its early cases,[69] stated competition among carriers was a classification factor, because: (1) differences in the levels of rates in the rate territories, (2) differences in the number of classes in the major classification territories, and (3) variations in the percentage relationships of the lower classes to first class.[70]

With the rapid development of motor carriers, the railroads "finally became conscious of the fact that they were confronted with acute competition from this form of transportation." [71] This "con-sciousness" is well illustrated by the railroads in Southern Territory alone in 1940 having established some 3,500 exceptions on less-than-carload ratings which were lower than the comparable Classification ratings; [72] and whether right or wrong, the motor carriers in the South deemed it necessary to meet this competition by somewhat comparable action. Since that time, many of those exceptions have been worked into the new Uniform Classification,[73] but some were not. Roughly, passage of the Motor Carrier Act of 1935 marked the

[66] *Minneapolis Hide & Tallow Company v. Chicago & North Western Rail-way Company,* 258 I.C.C. 360, 1944.
[67] *Maple Island Farm, Inc., v. Chicago, St. Paul, Minneapolis & Omaha Rail-way Company,* 280 I.C.C. 344, 1951.
[68] *United States Rubber Company v. Associated Transport, Inc.,* 48 M.C.C. 6, 1948; see also, *Classifications—Synthetic Cloth or Sheeting, Woven,* 49 M.C.C. 334, 1949.
[69] Colquitt, *op. cit.,* p. 102—*Coxe Brothers & Company v. Lehigh Valley Railroad Company,* 3 ICR 460, 1891. *Alason S. Page v. Delaware Lackawanna & Western Railroad Company, et al.,* 6 ICR 148, 1894. *National Hay Associa-tion v. Lake Shore & Michigan Southern Railroad Company, et al.,* 9 ICR 264, 1902. *Western Classification Case,* 25 I.C.C. 442, 1912. *Hires Condensed Milk Company v. Pennsylvania Railroad Company,* 38 I.C.C. 441, 1916. *General Gas Light Company v. Alabama Great Southern Railroad Company,* 83 I.C.C. 361, 1923.
[70] Colquitt, *op. cit.,* p. 103.
[71] *Ibid.*
[72] *Class Rate Investigation,* 1939, 262 I.C.C. 447 (477), 1945.
[73] See, p. 195, below.

127

beginning when classification makers have recognized the positive influence of competition between rail and motor carriers. The fact that exactly the same rating is assigned to so many articles in both Classifications can hardly be considered as coincidental! In its famous Docket 28300 report in 1945, the Commission recognized that "competition between agencies of transportation" had affected the policies of classification committees.[74] In another case, the Commission commented: [75]

Where necessary, railroad rates have been very freely reduced to meet competition. It is frequently urged, especially by shippers, that motor carrier rates should be based principally on cost of service, and that this is necessary, if the shipping public is to have the benefit of what he calls the "inherent advantages" of motor transportation. It requires no great penetration, however, to perceive that such a method of making motor carrier rates cannot produce satisfactory results so far as earnings are concerned, unless the rates of competitors are constructed in a similar manner. Without such limits on competition, the *rates of competitors* [76] are bound to gravitate together.

In a later motor carrier case, the Commission added: [77]

Competition between the various forms of transportation is beneficial to carriers and shippers so long as it does not result in wasteful practices bringing about a deterioration of service and casting a burden on non-competitive traffic.

Transportation Factors. To a large extent, this group determines the cost to the carrier of performing transportation and supplementary services. Carrier costs are increased when special facilities are required to load and unload certain kinds of shipments, to provide refrigeration or heat for perishables, to furnish unusual precautions against damage. Since the available space within or upon any piece of carrier equipment is limited to a fixed number of cubic feet, whether it be a railroad car, truck trailer, barge, ship, or airplane, the density of all shipments is a matter of prime consideration. Weight being the common unit of freight rates, it is understandable that density of an article influences carrier costs and carrier revenues. A ton of feathers requires much more space to be transported in a piece of equipment than a ton of lead; or, conversely, a box car or truck trailer can accommodate far greater tonnage of lead than

---

[74] *Class Rate Investigation, 1939 op. cit.,* p. 485.
[75] Ex Parte No. MC-21, *Central Territory Motor Carrier Rates,* 8.M.C.C. 233 (249), 1938.
[76] Italics supplied.
[77] Ex Parte No. MC-22, *Motor Carrier Rates in New England,* 47 M.C.C. 657 (663), 1948.

feathers. Light weight and bulky shipments commonly are referred to as "balloon-freight." Many shipments are of irregular shape which results in loss of space in the carrier's vehicle without a corresponding increase in weight. Therefore, "balloon freight" is allocated a higher rating than an article of relatively high density which occupies a smaller amount of space in relation to weight. Thus, the rating of a truckload of ordinary feathers of less than 4 pounds per cubic foot is Class 300,[78] Holly wreaths is 200,[79] parachutes is 70,[80] but the rating of lead ingots is only 35,[81] iron bars is 35,[82] steel plate is 35,[83] and cement compound is 35,[84] to mention a few.

The transportation factors follow:

1. Weight of the article in proportion to the space it occupies.

2. Type of package in which the article is packed for shipment.

3. Nature of the article, whether liquid or dry.

4. Manner in which the goods are shipped, whether loose, packaged, or in bulk.

5. Type of carrier equipment (vehicle) required to transport the goods.

6. Frequency of shipments.

7. Quantity of goods offered in single shipments.

8. Risk.

9. Necessity for special or incidental services, as protection against heat and cold.

10. Speed with which goods must be transported.

11. Danger of damage to other freight.

12. Danger of damage to carrier's equipment and other property.

13. Extra handling services or precautions which may be necessary.

14. Seasonal, monthly, or weekly variations in shipments.

15. Local, state, and federal regulations.

16. Special considerations, as, to aid in the development of a new industry, to expand marketing area of an article and thereby increase traffic volume in the future.

A review of the many decisions of the Interstate Commerce Commission will show that since the very first year of its existence,[85] it

[78] *National Motor Freight Classification No. A-2, op. cit.*, Item 36810.
[79] *Ibid.*, Item 35320.
[80] *Ibid.*, Item 77110.
[81] *Ibid.*, Item 56640.
[82] *Ibid.*, Item 54020.
[83] *Ibid.*, Item 54870.
[84] *Ibid.*, Item 20970.
[85] *James Pyle & Sons v. East Tennessee, Virginia & Georgia Railroad Company*, 1 I.C.R. 465, 1888.

has been consistent in holding that no one factor has been controlling in framing a classification.[86] Also, in a number of motor carrier cases, the Commission has emphasized that the rating or rate of an article cannot be based upon the use to which the article is put. In one proceeding, synthetic resin articles were used by the consignee in the manufacture of fuse boxes; and they were claimed to be electric switch parts in order to benefit from a 5th instead of a 3rd class rating. The Commission said: [87]

Complainant argues that as a fuse is a device for breaking an electrical circuit, it should be classified as a switch. With this contention we do not agree. In determining the use to which an article is put, primary consideration should be given to the generally accepted or primary use. A fuse is generally considered a protective device and not a switch. The mere fact that it also breaks an electric circuit in performing its function as a protective device does not make it a switch or circuit breaker.

For ratings to be made dependent upon the use to which a product is put after it has been sold would cause hardship to many shippers and would constitute a basis of classification which the Commission has refused to sanction.[88]

It should be obvious that segregation of the thousands of articles into a limited number of classes is no simple task. Careful consideration of the factors outlined above, not in a theoretical or academic manner, but from a most practical point of view, leads to the rating of an article and, hence, determines the actual rate in dollars and cents which the traffic will bear. If the rating is too high and above the value of the service to the shipper, the commodity will not move, and carrier and shipper alike lose revenue; if too low, so that the revenue derived therefrom by the carrier is less than the cost of producing the service, the carrier will be operating at a loss, it will not earn the fair return to which it is entitled, its service will deteriorate, and total costs of the shipper will increase to the detriment of both shipper and carrier.

No specific rule or formula has been established on which to base the relative importance each classification factor should bear to the others, nor to the weight to be placed on each factor in determining a precise rating. Each article is considered on its own merits. While

---

[86] Colquitt, *op. cit.*, p. 78.

[87] Colquitt, *op. cit.*, p. 94—*Federal Electric Products Company v. Salter's Express Company, Inc.*, 52 M.C.C. 473 (475), 1951. See also, *Airplane Engines between Points in the Southwest*, 43 M.C.C. 242, 1944; *Glen L. Martin Company v. W. T. Cowan, Inc.*, 44 M.C.C. 726, 1945; *Ratings on Aluminum Articles*, 46 M.C.C. 397, 1946; *Ranger Joe, Inc. v. Biter's Transfer Company, Inc.*, 54 M.C.C. 587, 1952.

[88] Colquitt, *op. cit.*, p. 93.

all the factors do not enter into each and every rating, many of them must be considered to assure equitable treatment to both shippers and carriers. Regardless of the mode of transportation, the underlying principles behind the determination of classification ratings are the same. Inasmuch as classification is the initial step in rate-making, it is no coincidence that those same principles, in general, govern the determination of both ratings and the actual rates themselves. The treatment the factors receive must be left to the good judgment of the classification committees, whose members possess the highly technical knowledge and experience which enable them to allocate ratings in a constructive and impartial manner on the basis of the actual facts submitted to them pertaining to individual cases.

Chapter 8

CLASSIFICATION—
Part IV

Classification Factors in New England. It will be recalled, the New England motor carriers do not participate in the *National Motor Freight Classification*, except for interterritorial hauls for which through rates are published; and that a separate Classification is published which is applicable generally to motor truck shipments east of the Hudson River and between the metropolitan New York City area and points in New England. According to Cushman, the objectives of the New England system are two-fold, namely: (1) to produce adequate revenues for the carriers, and (2) to classify freight in a nondiscriminatory manner for the benefit of a shipper. Of course, these same principles are basic to the "standard" Rail, Motor, and Express Classifications, and they have long been recognized by the Interstate Commerce Commission in carrying out the requirements of the Interstate Commerce Act; but, the system used to achieve those purposes are different in New England and, therefore, they are worthy of separate consideration. The objectives are said to have been attained in New England with "laudible success" and "shippers supported the classification proposals with remarkable unanimity." [1]

Costs are of predominating influence in the determination of New England motor carrier ratings, although competition by railroads and the Railway Express Agency is recognized and is reflected in lower ratings on commodities subject to such competition. [2] In general, density of an article is the primary consideration so that maximum revenue may be realized by the motor carriers from transporting any kind of freight, regardless of it being "balloon" or "heavy," to the capacity of the vehicle. The result is that "whether

---

[1] Cushman, F. M.: *Transportation for Management*, Prentice-Hall, New York, 1953, p. 210.
[2] *Motor Carrier Rates in New England*, Ex Parte No. MC-22, 47 I.C.C. 657 (661, 676) 1948.

the carrier hauls 1st class freight, 3rd class freight, or 5th class freight, his revenue per vehicle load will remain substantially constant.[3]

With this great recognition of density as the all-important factor, a rule in the New England Classification specifies the minimum shipping weight per cubic foot for each class, as follows: [4]

DENSITY (POUNDS PER CUBIC FOOT) MUST BE	WHERE RATING IS:
0 to 5 1	(300 percent)
5 to 10 2	(200 percent)
10 to 15 3	(150 percent)
15 to 20 4	(120 percent)
20 or over....................5	(100 percent)

Therefore, a shipment normally rated Class 4 but which weighs only 12 pounds per cubic foot would have to move at the higher rating of Class 3, thus: knives are rated Class 4,[5] but if the package of knives has a density of 12 pounds per cubic foot instead of the allowed minimum of 15 pounds for Class 4, the shipment would be classified under the third class rating. A most distinctive feature of the New England Classifications is that there is no differentiation whatsoever between truckload and less-than-truckload shipments.

Of secondary importance in the allocation of ratings by the New England motor carriers is the factor of value of the shipment, but "upon which a lesser degree of importance is placed." [6] Carrier liability for loss or damage to freight, with the resulting necessity for financial reimbursement to the owner, requires that intrinsic value of the article also be considered; hence, just as with the "standard" Classifications, high-valued commodities are assigned to high ratings.

The ideal of any carrier, of course, is to secure maximum and consistent revenues from the freight handled in each unit of equipment. That is what the New England motor carriers have attempted to accomplish through their unique system of classification which is designed to assure a carrier of constant revenues from each truck load of freight, regardless of the density of the individual shipments which may be included in a single trailer load. The system is said to have the distinct advantage of a carrier actively soliciting ship-

---

[3] Cushman, *op. cit.*, p. 209.
[4] *Coordinated Motor Freight Classification No. 7*, New England Motor Freight Bureau, Boston, effective January 8, 1954, Rule 22, p. 111.
[5] *Ibid.*, Item 20835.
[6] Cushman, *op. cit.*, p. 208.

ments of "balloon" freight on an equal basis with "heavy" freight, whereas if there were not comparable revenue to be derived from the "balloon" category, the carrier would concentrate on the movement of the higher-paying "heavy" freight, which, of course, would be detrimental to the interests of shippers of low-density commodities. Without this equalization of revenue-producing ratings, it is contented that a carrier would devote its efforts to securing traffic which would yield the greatest revenues, and the carrier would tend to move the "light" freight only when space became available in its units of equipment. It is just as important to the producer and distributor of "balloon" freight to have his products moved promptly as it is for a shipper of "heavy" commodities, and the revenue-producing aspects of each to the carrier definitely should not influence it in performing its obligations as a common carrier to all shippers who desire and are willing and able to pay for its services. As Cushman dramatically states: [7]

Although the common carrier is duty bound to transport all freight at all times, unscrupulous carriers are known to discriminate against the shippers of low-density freight whenever possible. Obviously, if the carrier has the choice of moving a vehicleload of high revenue-bearing freight in contrast to a vehicleload of low-revenue bearing freight, he will naturally devote his equipment and facilities to the solicitation and transportation of the former and will ignore the latter. Thus the carrier who is finally forced to take the low-density freight is discriminated against as well as the shipper of that freight, who customarily finds his commodity continually "awaiting available equipment," which if the carrier has his way will never become available.

The above quotation is a serious indictment against the carriers. Professor Cushman is a traffic consultant of high reputation in Boston and, unquestionably, he possesses intimate knowledge of transportation conditions in New England. Possibly, although unstated, it was due to the intolerable conditions mentioned by Professor Cushman that New England "shippers supported the classification proposals with remarkable unanimity." [8]

True, any privately owned and operated business enterprise, such as a railroad or a motor carrier, is imbued with the profit motive; but, essentially for protection of the shipping public, there are state and federal laws on the statute books which are designed to prevent the flagrant discriminatory practices indicated above. A flour mill, a wholesaler, a textile plant, a mine, a furniture factory, a steel mill,

---

[7] *Ibid.*, p. 209.
[8] See, p. 132, above.

and practically any kind of private industry, *except* common carriers and other public utilities, may do just about as they please in selling their respective products to the American public. They can choose their customers and divide their markets at will, within the limits of federal anti-trust legislation which outlaws conspiracy and collaboration in restraint of trade. It is granted there are some unscrupulous carrier managements, not restricted exclusively to motor carriers as may be implied, which are prone to discriminate against shippers of low-rated articles; but it is hoped enforcement of the law will overtake them. For the most part, however, and certainly for the respectable and conscientious managements, there exists full realization of and compliance with the public utility responsibility of a common carrier to serve all shippers indiscriminately in accordance with the accepted and recognized responsibilities of a common carrier. While, unquestionably, a carrier would *prefer* to accept only high-rated commodities, it is doubted that any respectable carrier deliberately would force low-rated articles to be subjected to unreasonable delay. The shipper of low-grade freight is just as much a customer of a carrier as the shipper of high-grade freight; and the carrier so recognizes him and solicits his traffic, particularly because frequently that low-grade freight will fill out a train load or a truck load of other merchandise and thereby enable the carrier to more fully utilize its equipment and facilities, all of which adds to greater profit. It should be understood that *any* revenue, as long as it is above so-called "out-of-pocket" costs,[9] contributes its share to the overhead costs of the carrier and, therefore, a carrier is foolish to shun any kind of traffic which will increase its total volume and thereby reduce the excess capacity which characterizes the transportation industry.

It was mentioned earlier [10] that New England motor ratings are influenced primarily by density. The Interstate Commerce Commission, in its investigation of the New England situation, took cognizance of elaborate cost studies which had been conducted by the carriers in that area.[11] There can be no doubt that costs of providing transportation service by a carrier must be considered in establishing the ratings upon which freight rates are based; and, generally, it is recognized by transportation economists that a carrier's cost of

---

[9] A simple explanation of "out-of-pocket" costs are those costs which would not have been incurred by a carrier in providing a particular service had the service not been performed. They fall within the general category of "operating expenses," but they do not include all the operating expenses of a carrier.

[10] See, pp. 132–133, above.

[11] *Motor Carrier Rates in New England, op. cit.,* p. 659.

service is the minimum below which no rate should be set.[12] As the eminent John R. Turney has stated: [13]

> The use of cost in ratemaking is as dangerous as it is essential. Cost is an indispensable servant but a ruthless master . . . The proper function of cost is as a shield to protect the carrier against losses and the shipper against extortion which may result from ill-advised ratemaking. Full cost should mark the bottom which any carrier may be compelled, or generally be permitted to charge.

As was presented in the preceding section, many factors in addition to carrier costs enter into the final determination of a rating, for as Gilbert J. Parr, former Director of Cost & Research of the Waterman Steamship Company, commented in summarizing the role of costs in ratemaking, "in order to make the costs as useful as possible, it is necessary to supplement them with economic data dealing with the volume of movement, the value of the commodity, market and carrier competition, and the effect which the rate itself may have upon the movement of the traffic and the carrier's earnings." [14] To make costs the predominating determinant of a rating is to ignore the very practical aspect of the trite but true expression, "a rate which the traffic will bear." In 1912, the Interstate Commerce Commission reported: [15]

> To be sure costs do not determine rates (or ratings); yet most rates have within them as a constituent the element of cost . . . What weight shall be given to that element as compared with all the other elements entering into a particular rate . . . is a matter to be decided in each individual case. Questions regarding the calculation of the cost of service and the weight to be given such cost suggest controversies which are as old as the railway itself.

Any system of accounts reflects what has happened in the past,

---

[12] Bigham, T. C., & Roberts, M. J.: *Transportation*, McGraw-Hill Book Company, New York, 1952, p. 353; Daggett, Stuart: *Principles of Inland Transportation*, Third Edition, Harper & Brothers, New York, 1941, p. 336; Fair, M. L., & Williams, E. W., Jr.: *Economics of Transportation*, Harper & Brothers, New York, 1950, p. 366; Healy, K. T.: *Economics of Transportation in America*, Ronald Press, New York, 1940, p. 209; Locklin, D. P.: *Economics of Transportation*, Fourth Edition, Richard D. Irwin, Inc., Chicago, 1954, p. 158; Johnson, E. R.: *American Railway Transportation*, D. Appleton & Company, New York, 1910, p. 271; Van Metre, T. W.: *Transportation in the United States*, Foundation Press, Chicago, 1939, p. 279; Westmeyer, R. E.: *Economics of Transportation*, Prentice-Hall, New York, 1952, p. 233; Wilson, G. L.: *Elements of Transportation Economics*, Simmons-Boardman Publishing Corporation, New York, 1950, p. 47.

[13] Turney, J. R.: *Use of Cost in Ratemaking*, Association of Interstate Commerce Commission Practitioners, *op. cit.*, p. 75.

[14] Parr, G. J.: *Cost Finding in Rate Cases*, Association of Interstate Commerce Commission Practitioners, *op. cit.*, p. 92.

[15] *Boioleau v. Pittsburgh & Lake Erie Railroad Company*, 22 I.C.C. 640 (652), 1912.

for an accurate statistical statement of costs, although unquestionably valuable for many purposes, can only show what has already transpired. Simply stated, accounting and cost records are historical records. Ratings, and the resulting freight rates which produce revenue to carriers, are projected into the future. Carrier costs are far from constant and, particularly in the motor carrier industry, vary from year to year, month to month, and even day to day in direct relation to the volume of tonnage hauled. As Professor Locklin states, "carrier cost depends upon the volume of traffic, and the volume of traffic depends upon the rate charged." [16] Therefore, from a very practical standpoint, past costs cannot be considered as the sole criterion for ratings which will produce revenues from rates in the future. Continuing, Locklin says: "If cost apportionments, for instance, result in rates greater than the most profitable rate, the railroad will lose by charging that rate. If the cost allocation should give the most profitable rate, it would be the result of pure chance. The advocates of cost apportionments argue that their method is the only 'scientific' way of making rates, but nothing could be more unscientific than an attempt to base rates on cost in disregard of the conditions of demand." [17]

Admirable as cost studies are, costs cannot be the primary basis of rating and rate determination. This, definitely is not intended to reflect discredit on cost studies, because the importance thereof is well recognized; but it should be understood that other factors besides carrier costs enter into ratemaking. To quote the distinguished Interstate Commerce Commissioner, the Honorable J. Haden Alldredge: "The Interstate Commerce Commission (has) stated that cost has never been out of mind even though it has not always been in sight . . . Primarily because of the expense involved, the carriers have never kept their books in accordance with routine cost-accounting principles. Of necessity, therefore, all cost computations are the result of special studies." [18]

Furthermore, the existence of joint costs in all modes of transportation make it impossible to accurately allocate each element of costs to each item of traffic that is moved. Although historical events may be used as a most valuable guide for prognostications of the future, the determination of ratings and the resulting freight rates is for the purpose of producing future revenues to the carriers. "It should be remembered . . . that the obtainable costs are always

[16] Locklin, *op. cit.*, p. 161.
[17] *Ibid.*, p. 161.
[18] Alldredge, J. H.: *Cost Utilization in Ratemaking for Common Carriers*, Association of Interstate Commerce Commission Practitioners, *op. cit.*, p. 19.

historic costs," which "means that however exact and precise a cost computation may be for current purposes, it can only serve an estimate for the future." [19] Just as the accident experience of a motor carrier last year influences the price of its insurance premium for next year, last year's costs must be given some weight in deciding what next year's rates should be; but, because of the American system of federal regulation, carrier ratings and rates do not fluctuate automatically and immediately with changes in the business cycle and in general price levels. Hence, if past costs were high and those costs are used as the exclusive basis for arriving at ratings to be applied in the future, the resulting rates may be so high as to exceed the value of the transportation service to shippers, in which event inevitably there will be a decline in traffic volume and accompanying reduction in carrier earnings. As Bigham and Roberts state: [20]

Under a cost standard, the rates on articles of low value relative to bulk and weight would have to be raised, while the rates on goods of high value would need to be lowered. Such a readjustment would be undesirable, for it would reduce the total volume of traffic, force the average unit cost upward, and in some cases make it impossible for (carriers) to operate. Shipments of articles of high value would increase, but the increase would be more than offset by a decrease in the movement of low-class articles.

This situation was recognized by the Interstate Commerce Commission in two of its earliest decisions handed down in 1888 when, in one, the Commission said: [21]

It may cost no more to carry a box of silk weighing 100 pounds than a bale of refuse rags of like weight; but the charge will perhaps be several times as great, and the carrier justifies the discrimination by showing that equal rates on both would put transportation of the less valuable article out of the question. Like discriminations are made everywhere; property is classified with a purpose, among other things, to make the most valuable kinds pay most largely for the service performed.

In the other case, the Commission reported: [22]

The element of cost of service which may at one period have been recognized as controlling in fixing rates has long ceased to be regarded as the sole or the most important factor for that purpose. The value of the service with respect to the articles carried, the volume of business, and the conditions and force of competition are justly considered to have controlling weight in determining the charges for transportation.

[19] *Ibid.*, p. 23.
[20] Bigham & Roberts, *op. cit.*, p. 351.
[21] *Rice v. Louisville & Nashville Railroad Company*, 1 I.C.C. 722 (739), 1888.
[22] *Boston Chamber of Commerce v. Lake Shore & Michigan Southern Railway Company*, 1 I.C.C. 754 (761), 1888.

Although it has been suggested that "cost of service is the proper measure of reasonableness" [23] of ratings, all the classification factors must be considered to a more or less degree along with costs in determining ratings which will move the traffic at an over-all profit to the carrier. Regardless of the most elaborate and detailed cost studies which may be undertaken, the age-old slogan, "what the traffic will bear," is of predominating influence. As long ago as 1848, the early railroad attempts at classification of freight not only gave some consideration to costs by recognition of the density of shipments, "but also according to what each particular commodity might be made to pay." [24]

Definitely, it should not be inferred that carrier costs should be relegated to a minor or insignificant factor in rating determination; to the contrary, each individual rating should reflect a rate which will yield the carrier revenue above its costs of providing a particular service or under special circumstances, at least equal to its "out-of-pocket" costs, although the Interstate Commerce Commission has said, "rates yielding merely out-of-pocket costs have been condemned as being less than reasonable minima." [25] At the other extreme, if a rating results in a rate which is greater than the value of the service to the shipper, obviously the shipper will not purchase the transportation service.[26] He either will forego shipment of his commodity or choose a competitive mode of transportation, and the original carrier under consideration loses the traffic with resulting decrease of available capacity and decrease in earnings. As Locklin points out, in defining value of service as the highest rate which "can be levied without preventing a shipment from moving," the upper limit of a rating "is determined by no one factor." [27]

On the other hand, such a classification system based primarily upon carrier costs often will result in rates on some commodities being less than the value of service; but with a different system, as that employed by the "standard" methods of classification, it is possible to increase rates on those commodities and thereby offset the lower earnings derived from low-valued freight. If the value of service is great, the higher rate will not result in a proportionate decrease in traffic; and, therefore, revenues will either be the same or higher in the aggregate, excess facilities and equipment capacity will be utilized, and, from the standpoint of the industrial traffic

---

[23] Van Metre, *op. cit.*, p. 261.
[24] Healy, *op. cit.*, p. 203.
[25] *Class Rate Investigation*, 1939, 262 I.C.C. 447 (693), 1945.
[26] See, pp. 123–124, above.
[27] Locklin, *op. cit.*, p. 154.

manager and shippers in general, a greater volume of diversified articles will be enabled to move. In the final analysis, determination of ratings which will move the greatest volume of traffic at a reasonable profit to the carrier is the ultimate objective of both carrier management and regulatory bodies.

Any cost analysis is influenced both by the analyzer and the purpose to be achieved. The economist is interested mainly in the long range effect of costs on prices under varying assumed competitive conditions. The cost accountant is concerned with ascertaining the different items of expense which consitute the total costs of doing business as a guide to management in its price determination, production schedules, distribution and advertising policies, etc. The classification expert, by considering all the classification factors mentioned earlier to a more or less degree depending upon the particular article of commerce involved, endeavors to establish ratings on commodities which as a whole will produce rates to yield adequate revenues in the future, to cover all costs, and give a fair return to the carriers within the realms of reasonableness as prescribed by law.

Although the above objective is what the New England motor carriers have attempted to accomplish by their unique system of classification, one of the more common measures of operating efficiency does not substantiate that they have been entirely successful. This is the "operating ratio." [28] It is of value only when comparing carriers of a single type; that is to say, comparison of the respective operating ratios of airlines with railroads, or railroads with motor carriers, or even household goods motor carriers with regular route common motor carriers of general commodities, would be meaningless because of the lack of homogeneity in accounting practices and the wide variance in the different kinds of carrier costs according to the mode of transportation and type of operation. For instance, railroads are characterized by high fixed costs in contrast to the high proportion of operating expenses of motor carriers; also, railroads consider depreciation as an operating expense while motor carriers do not.[29] It is recognized that the relationship of operating

---

[28] The operating ratio of a carrier is the percent of its operating revenues used to meet its operating expenses. It shows the number of cents spent by a carrier in a fixed accounting period to earn one dollar. It is the ratio of operating expenses to operating revenues, thus: if a carrier's operating expenses are $9,000,000 and its operating revenues are $10,000,000, the operating ratio is determined by dividing the former by the latter and multiplying by 100, which, in this case, would give an operating ratio of 90.

[29] Bigham & Roberts, *op. cit.*, p. 125. Depreciation expense is not included in the group of accounts entitled "Operation and Maintenance Expenses" under

140

revenues to operating expenses, as expressed by the operating ratio, is influenced by many variables other than the revenues derived from freight rates; and the ability of management to keep costs in line with income, particularly the day to day operating expenses, is reflected in the operating ratio just as are the earnings which vary with volume of traffic. The geographical location of one motor carrier's operating authority (that is, its "rights") frequently is superior to that of another carrier in the same general area, with resulting differences in both operating expenses and income. Also, restrictive state laws pertaining to maximum lengths and weights, whether a carrier handles predominantly interline or strictly single-line or local traffic, the policies of individual managements, and other factors, influence the operating ratio. Therefore, the relatively unfavorable operating ratio of the New England motor carriers may be caused by factors other than their system of determining classification ratings; but, unquestionably, the income derived from rates based on any system of classification is certain to have a profound, although not necessarily exclusive, effect on the operating ratio. Insofar as a particular type of carrier is concerned, the operating ratio is an excellent means of comparing the operating efficiency of carriers within a specified group.

Comparison of the operating ratio of motor carriers in New England with those in other parts of the country which conform to the "standard" methods of classification reveals that the net earnings of the former group is below the national average. For the year 1954, the average operating ratio of 903 reporting Class I [30] intercity common motor carriers of general commodities for the entire country was 96.9, with the 116 reporting New England carriers having the highest of 98.2 of any other geographical region except the Midwestern; likewise, Class I local carriers in New England had an average operating ratio of 99.7 in contrast to the national average of 96.5. The following table [31] shows the operation ratios of intercity Class I motor carriers of general commodities by regions for the years 1950 to 1954, inclusive.

It is difficult to understand the practicability of the dual classifica-

---

the Uniform System of Accounts prescribed for motor carriers by the Interstate Commerce Commission. Although depreciation is not treated as an operation expense in profit and loss statements prescribed by the Commission, it definitely is treated as an operation expense in cost finding procedures of the Commission, which is as it should be.

[30] A Class I motor carrier, as designated by the Interstate Commerce Commission, is one whose gross revenues are $200,000 or more a year.

[31] Trinc's, *5-Year Red Book,* Transport Research, Inc., Washington, 1955, pp. ii–iii.

tions which existed in New England until 1955, notwithstanding that the New England method has been reported to be "the sounder

Region	No. Carriers Reporting	1950	1951	1952	1953	1954
New England	116	94.3	97.5	95.1	97.8	98.2
Middle Atlantic	205	93.7	95.7	96.0	96.5	97.6
Central	242	93.3	95.4	94.7	96.4	97.1
Southern	112	92.9	94.6	95.0	95.9	96.4
Northwestern	40	93.9	98.4	96.5	96.7	97.0
Midwestern	59	94.7	96.7	96.9	96.2	100.2
Southwestern	48	90.8	94.4	95.7	96.0	95.8
Rocky Mountain	24	85.6	88.9	93.3	92.1	92.2
Pacific	57	91.7	93.6	94.9	95.2	95.2
Entire Country	903	92.9	95.2	95.2	96.1	96.9

of the two methods of classifying motor freight 'from the standpoint of abstract reason.'" [32] As long as two separately published Classifications of motor freight were effective on local traffic in the same territory, especially in such a relatively small geographical area as New England, it would seem that there could be no unanimity in shipping costs, and there was certain to be some confusion in ascertaining the cheapest applicable rate. However, the former *Official Motor Freight Classification* was discontinued in 1955. A large number of interterritorial motor carriers do not participate in the remaining "Coordinated" Classification and, instead, subscribe to the National Motor Freight Classification, which means that traffic handled by those carriers is subject to the provisions of the "National." Such conditions are not conducive to sound transportation policies nor to uniform shipping practices. Notwithstanding numerous investigations of the situation by the Interstate Commerce Commission,[33] the practicability and ultimate advantages to both carriers and shippers of continuation of the New England system is questioned; and it is believed the position of the American Trucking Associations, Inc., and others, that "the classification in New England should be brought in line with the National Classification maintained throughout the rest of the country," [34] is well taken. Until

[32] Locklin, *op. cit.*, Third Edition, p. 687.
[33] *Motor Carrier Rates in New England*, Ex Parte No. MC-22: 8 M.C.C. 549, 1937; 9 M.C.C. 737, 1938; 10 M.C.C. 157, 522, 581, 1938; 11 M.C.C. 325, 1939; 12 M.C.C. 417, 1939; 16 M.C.C. 499, 1939; 18 M.C.C. 79, 1939; 19 M.C.C. 471, 777, 1939; 21 M.C.C. 373, 1940; 22 M.C.C. 705, 1940; 23 M.C.C. 361, 389, 1940; 24 M.C.C. 213, 423, 723, 1940; 26 M.C.C. 195, 623, 689, 783, 1940; 27 M.C.C. 1, 1941; 28 M.C.C. 31, 355, 537, 1941; 29 M.C.C. 9, 1941; 30 M.C.C. 143, 151, 209, 455, 1941; 31 M.C.C. 207, 418, 503, 1941; 32 M.C.C. 220, 1942; 47 M.C.C. 657, 1948.
[34] *Ibid.*, 47 M.C.C. 657 (660), 1948.

such time as New England motor carriers, with the concurrence of New England shippers, agree to participate in the *National Motor Freight Classification* and discontinue their provincial Classification, there can be no absolute nation-wide uniformity in motor freight classification. One of the two existing systems must give way to the other, and adoption of the Classification of the American Trucking Associations, Inc., would appear the more desirable.

Express Classification Factors. In general, ratings of articles transported by the Railway Express Agency, Inc., are determined by the same factors which influence the "standard" Rail and Motor Classifications. There is one decided distinction, however, for there is no differentiation between carload and less-than-carload shipments in the ratings of the Express Classification. Express traffic consists predominately of small shipments and, therefore, the need for carload ratings is not nearly as great as for railroads and motor carriers. Provisions for carload shipments are contained in certain rules of the Express Classification and, in occasional instances, in the description of an article; but, generally, special "commodity" rates are authorized for large quantities. Where the dimensions or weight of a shipment assigned to first class require the use of a separate car, a rating of 95 percent of first class is applicable with a minimum of 12,000 pounds, "except as otherwise provided." For an article rated second class, the charge is based on actual weight of the shipment with a minimum of 12,000 pounds, except that the minimum weight for a refrigerator car is 15,000 pounds.[35]

Relationship of Classification to Tariffs. Since the published Classifications show only a bare figure which is the rating of a commodity, reference to another source is necessary in order to determine the price itself for the transportation service. That other source is a *Tariff*. Hence, at least two distinct publications must be consulted in order to determine the actual freight rate of an article between any two points, namely: the Classification and the Tariff. Earlier, a tariff was defined as, "a publication setting forth the rates, fares, and charges of a carrier . . ."[36] Therefore, a tariff is comparable to the price list of a carrier or a group of carriers. It states the freight rates in terms of dollars and/or cents; but it does not mention any commodity by name, such descriptions falling within the compass of the Classification. There are many different kinds of tariffs, some of which will be described later; but, for the present,

---

[35] *Official Express Classification No. 35,* Railway Express Agency, Inc., New York, effective May 20, 1952, p. 27.

[36] See, p. 4, above.

their application will be restricted to use of the Classification when only the ratings are used.

Insofar as determining what the amount will be for shipping a particular article is concerned, the proper Classification must be used in connection with the applicable tariff. Over fifty years ago, the Interstate Commerce Commission reported to Congress in the following language: [37]

Classification is the basis of freight rates. When an article is presented for shipment the classification is examined and the rate upon the article is determined by the class to which it is assigned. The classification and the tariff of rates are interdependent. Classification is a means of making a rate. It fulfills no purpose in itself. The tariff is the necessary complement of the classification. The one is useless without the other.

The classifications . . . do not contain any rates, but provide the class or rating which articles mentioned therein shall take, the individual carriers publishing and filing the tariffs which name the rates for the various classes of freight provided for in the classifications, and specifically referring to the particular classification by which the rates are to be governed.

Later, in 1912, the Commission stated: [38]

Classification is an art or a science in itself. Having completed a new classification . . . , each carrier can readjust its rates on the basis of that classification in such a manner as to preserve its existing revenues. Classification and rates and revenues should be kept entirely separate.

From the above it should be clear that after the rating of an article has been determined in a Classification, the rate itself is found by consulting the applicable tariff. To illustrate: assume there is a shipment of 25,000 pounds of baled broom corn to move by motor carrier from Knoxville to New York City. The Motor Classification shows that 20,000 pounds of that commodity constitute the minimum weight for application of the volume rate and, therefore, the volume rate applies to the shipment of 25,000 pounds. The Motor Classification further shows that a volume shipment of broom corn carries a rating of Class 45. If it were a less-than-truckload shipment weighing 10,000 pounds, the rating would be Class 85.[39] After having determined proper ratings and the volume minimum weight from the published Classification, the next step is to consult the applicable tariff which, in this case, is one published by the Southern Motor Carriers Rate Conference designated as No. 504.[40] That tariff shows

<hr>

[37] *Sixteenth Annual Report of the Interstate Commerce Commission,* Government Printing Office, Washington, 1902.

[38] *Western Classification Case,* 25 I.C.C. 442 (453), 1912.

[39] *National Motor Freight Classification No. A-2, op. cit.,* Item 14450.

[40] *Eastern-Southern Class Tariff,* SMCRC (Southern Motor Carriers Rate Conference) No. 504, MF-ICC 614, Supplement No. 1, effective April 15, 1953.

the first class, or 100 percent rate, is $3.34 per hundred pounds. Since the shipment of broom corn is assigned to Class 45, the rate is 45 percent of $3.34, or $1.51 per 100 pounds on a truckload basis. Therefore, the rate on the 25,000 pounds is determined by multiplying $1.51 by 250, which is $377.50. Furthermore, the three percent federal transportation tax must be included! The additional three percent of $377.50 is $11.34, which amount goes into the Treasury of the United States, making a total charge of $388.84 for shipping the 25,000 pounds of baled broom corn from Knoxville to New York by any of the three certificated motor carriers providing direct service between those two cities.[41]

It should be obvious, therefore, that a Classification and the applicable Tariff are two interdependent publications which complement each other. One is useless without the other. Both publications "are indispensable in the transportation business because only in them can be found the most convenient, practicable, efficient and economical way of establishing rates for application on many thousands of articles . . ." [42] The Tariffs of the carriers are governed by the ratings and rules contained in some particular published Classification named by the Tariff, which makes the Classification the basic document in the application of freight rates.

The rating published in a Classification and a rate published in a Tariff are binding upon both carrier and shipper. Tariffs published under the rules and regulations of the Interstate Commerce Commission, Civil Aeronautics Board, and state commissions, and filed with the appropriate regulatory body, have the same force as law. They contain the legal rate which is applicable to all users of the service and which the carriers must apply in like manner to all concerned.[43] Failure to comply with the rates or other provisions of a Classification or tariff is a violation of law. Hence, it is essential that a shipper possesses a sound knowledge of those portions of a Classification and Tariffs which affect his business. Since the contents of those publications are public information and since there is nothing secret about them, ignorance thereof is no excuse. Usually, ignorance will be expensive and result in increased shipping costs. To carry the above illustration of the shipment of broom corn a step further:

Assume the shipper has no knowledge of the Classification, nor

---

[41] The three certificated motor carriers are: Associated Transport, Inc., Mason & Dixon Lines, and Super Service Motor Freight Company.
[42] Middle Atlantic States Motor Carrier Conference, Inc.: *Construction and Interpretation of Freight Tariffs*, Washington, 1944, p. 15.
[43] See, Chapter 15.

does he wish to consult it. Upon inquiry, he might be told by the carrier the first class rate from Knoxville to New York City is $3.44, including the federal tax; and without further investigation he pays that amount for the 25,000 pound shipment, totaling $860.00, which is $471.16 above the legal applicable rate. Of course, there are the moral and legal obligations of the carrier to refund him the excess $471.16; but since the shipper was ignorant of the Classification, there is the probability that he was ignorant of other shipping procedures, such as, description of the shipment which will be discussed later, with the result that the carrier could not know there had been an unintentional error. Ignorance of one sort frequently leads to ignorance of another, the final result being that the shipper does not know when he is paying more than the legal applicable rate. The point is, if the shipper does not know what he is doing, he will not know when he is paying too much; and he will not know he has the right to demand a refund for the excess he has paid nor the amount of the refund to which he is entitled.

A thorough knowledge of the relationship of a Classification to the applicable tariff is a necessity for effective rate determination.

Format of the Classification. The style and shape of the published Classifications are the results of experience and regulation. They have grown from a single sheet affair to volumes of several hundreds of pages. The original Act to Regulate Commerce of 1887 marked the beginning of jurisdiction by the Interstate Commerce Commission. Since that time, the Commission has prescribed regulations pertaining to the Classification used by railroads, and comparable rules for motor carriers were issued shortly after passage of the Motor Carrier Act of 1935.[44]

One of the problems confronting the framers of the first Motor Classification in 1935 was whether to show truckload ratings for each item or to list only less-than-truckload ratings. Establishment of truckload ratings was complicated by weight restrictions of various states, and "a hundred and one" other complications were encountered. Finally, at a meeting of the predecessor of the present National Classification Committee on Sunday, December 8, 1935, a motion was unanimously adopted to issue the Classification under the name of the "National Motor Freight Classification," which was done and the first issue became effective April 1, 1936. The initial issue was in two separate volumes, one for volume and the other for less-than-truckload ratings. The two parts were consolidated into a single volume with issue No. 2, effective December 24, 1936. Until

[44] Colquitt, *op. cit.*, p. 29.

publication of issue No. 9 in 1937, the Classification contained two columns of commodity descriptions. The broader single column now used overcomes the prior objections of confusion and excessive use of space.[45]

Regulations covering the format of Classifications are contained in publications of the Commission entitled "Tariff Circulars," which will be explained later.[46] For the present, suffice it to say that such minute details are specified as, the size of each page, quality of paper, printer's type, "a margin not less than five-eighths of an inch," the requirement that tables of figures "be ruled from top to bottom," and many others.[47] These rules of the Commission are published by it under authority delegated by the Interstate Commerce Act,[48] and, therefore, they have the same force as law.

The published Classifications are numbered serially. Prior to the publication of uniform ratings in 1952, there had been twenty issues of the Rail Classification and twelve of the National Motor Classification; and they were identified by the number being included in the respective titles, as follows: *Consolidated Freight Classification No. 20*, and *National Motor Freight Classification No. 12*. There have been thirty-five issues of the *Official Express Classification*, seven of the *Coordinated Motor Freight Classification*, and five of the *Official Motor Freight Classification*; the last two, as was previously mentioned, being restricted to the New England area. Since 1952, there have been two issues of the railroads' *Uniform Freight Classification*, the "No. 2" becoming effective December 10, 1953. The uniform motor publication is entitled *National Motor Freight Classification No. A-1*, and it was issued on May 6, 1952, to become effective June 10, 1952; and "No. A-2" became effective July 7, 1954. Each section of the Classification contains data which is vital to carriers and shippers alike, each serves a positive and useful purpose, and each facilitates the use of other sections. For the present, discussion will be restricted to the "standard" Rail and Motor Classifications, both of which are most similar.

Classification Contents. The published Classifications contain a wealth of information. In addition to the ratings which have been mentioned, the publications provide the rules which govern the shipment of freight, terminology in technical traffic language for

---

[45] Colquitt, *op. cit.*, p. 35.
[46] See Chapter 15, pp. 305–306.
[47] Interstate Commerce Commission: *Tariff Circular No. 20*, effective October 1, 1928, Government Printing Office, Washington; and, Interstate Commerce Commission, *Tariff Circular MF No. 3*, effective April 1, 1941, Government Printing Office, Washington.
[48] Interstate Commerce Act, Sections 6 (6), 217 (a), 306 (b), 405 (b).

descriptions of shipments, packing requirements, and other matters. Literal compliance therewith will result in lowest expenditures for transportation services. It can be readily understood, however, that "to the uninitiated a Classification looks like a cross between an encyclopedia and a dining car menu." [49] The immortal Professor William Z. Ripley, of Harvard University, once stated: "Imagine the Encyclopedia Britannica, a Chicago mail-order catalogue, and a United States protective tariff law blended in a single volume, and you have a freight classification as it exists in the United States." [50]

Although the physical composition of the Rail and Motor Classifications are the same, except, as previously noted, the New England Motor Classification does not differentiate between truckload and less-than-truckload shipments; there are essential differences in their content as to ratings, minimum weights, and rules. Truckload minimum weights range from 10,000 to around 30,000 pounds, whereas rail carload minima range from about 24,000 to 60,000 pounds. Of course, exceptions can be found to this broad average. The difference is attributed to the physical capacity of the transporting unit. A standard railroad box car has a capacity of up to 3,925 cubic feet with a load limit of 100,000 to 120,000 pounds; whereas the capacity of truck trailers vary from about 1,000 to 3,200 cubic feet, and the load limit is dependent upon the weight laws of the respective states in which the trailer is operated. The wide variance of weight laws among the several states is a positive detriment to motor carriers in accomplishing full utilization of their equipment and, consequently, to shippers by the higher operating costs being reflected in motor carrier freight rates.

Contents of the Classifications are, as follows:

1. Title page or front cover.
2. Regulatory bodies with whom copies are filed.
3. Table of contents.
4. Names of members of the classification committee or board.
5. Participating carriers.
6. Index to rules.
7. Index to articles.
8. Shipping rules.
9. Reproduction of bills of lading forms.
10. Explanation of abbreviations and symbols.
11. Descriptions and ratings of articles.
12. Package descriptions (in rail only).

---

[49] Colquitt, *op. cit.*, p. 1.
[50] Ripley, W. Z.: *Railroads: Rates and Regulation*, Longmans, Green & Company, New York, 1923, p. 297.

Those of the above which are self explanatory by their titles will be omitted from the following discussion.

There are reproduced on the next several pages the title pages of different Classifications. The reader should examine them with great care, for future references will be made to them.

For I. C. C., C. T. C. and State Commission Nos. and Cancellations, See Page 2.

UNIFORM FREIGHT CLASSIFICATION No. 2

RATINGS, RULES AND REGULATIONS

APPLICABLE TO

FREIGHT TRAFFIC COVERED BY TARIFFS GOVERNED BY THE UNIFORM FREIGHT CLASSIFICATION, AS SUCH TARIFFS MAY SPECIFY.

ISSUED OCTOBER 12, 1953　　　　**EFFECTIVE DECEMBER 10, 1953**

W. S. FLINT,
Agent for lines in
Official Classification
One Park Ave. at 33rd St.,
NEW YORK (16), N. Y.

A. H. CARSON,
Alternate Agent for lines in
Southern Classification
101 Marietta Street,
ATLANTA (3), GA.

R. G. RAASCH,
Agent for lines in
Illinois Classification
236 Union Station,
CHICAGO (6), ILL.

GEO. H. DUMAS,
Agent for lines in
Western Classification
202 Union Station,
CHICAGO (6), ILL.

82,000　　　　(Edw. Keogh Ptg. Co., Chicago—19480)

A. C. C. No. 5
Arkansas No. 7
P. U. C. Colo. No. 5
Conn. P. U. C.-MF No. 7
F. R. C. No. 7
G. P. S. C. No. 7
P. U. C. Ida. No. 5
MF-Ill. C. C. No. 7
P. S. C. I. No. TR-7
Ia. C. C. No. 7
K. C. C. No. 5
L. P. S. C. No. 7
Me. P. U. C. No. 7
M. P. U. B. Man. No. 6
MF-P. S. C. Md. No. 7
M. D. P. U. No. 7
M. P. S. C. No. 7
M. R. C. No. 5
M. C. No. 7
P. S. C. Mo. No. 7
Mont. R. C. No. 5
N. S. R. C. No. 5

P. S. C. N. No. 5
N. H. P. S. C. No. 7
P. U. C. N. J. No. 7
S. C. O. N. M. No. 5
N. C. U. C. No. 6
N. D. P. S. C. No. 5
P. U. C. O. No. 7
♦O. C. Okla. No. 5
P. U. C. Ore. No. 5
Freight Pa. P. U. C. No. 7
P. T. C. B. No. 7
P. S. C. S. C. No. 7
S. D. P. U. C. No. 5
P. U. C. T. No. 7
R. C. T. No. 5
P. S. C. U. No. 5
V. P. S. C. No. 7
MF-V. C. C. No. 7
WN. T. No. 5
MF-P. S. C.-W. Va. No. 6
♦P. S. C. Wisc. No. 5
Wyo. P. S. C. No. 5

MF-I. C. C. No. 7
F. M. B. No. 5
(For cancellations, see page 2-A)

(For State cancellations, see page 2-A)

♦—Volume and Truckload ratings not applicable. See Page 2-A for application.

AMERICAN TRUCKING ASSOCIATIONS, INC., AGENT

National Motor Freight Classification No. 13

Applies on Freight Traffic covered by tariffs

Subject to EAST-SOUTH-WEST Ratings

As such tariffs may provide.

ISSUED MAY 7, 1955   **EFFECTIVE JULY 7, 1955**
(Except as otherwise provided herein)

ISSUED BY
F. G. FREUND, Issuing Officer
1424 SIXTEENTH STREET, N. W.
WASHINGTON 6, D. C.

Ⓐ   (4808)   (Printed in U. S. A.)

A. P. S. C. No. 6
Arkansas No. 6
Conn. P. U. C.-MF No. 6
F. R. C. No. 6
G. P. S. C. No. 6
MF-Ill. C. C. No. 6
P. S. C. I. No. TR-6
Ia. C. C. No. 6
KY. D. M. T. No. 5
L. P. S. C. No. 6
Me. P. U. C. No. 6
M. P. U. B. Man. No. 5
MF-P. S. C. Md. No. 6
M. D. P. U. No. 6
(For State cancellations, see page 2-A)

M. P. S. C. No. 6
M. C. No. 6
P. S. C. Mo. No. 6
N. H. P. S. C. No. 6
P. U. C. N. J. No. 6
P. S. C.-N. Y.-MT No. 5
P. U. C. O. No. 6
Freight Pa. P. U. C. No. 6
P. T C. B. No. 6
P. S. C. S. C. No. 6
P. U. C. T. No. 6
V. P. S. C. No. 6
MF-V. C. C. No. 6

MF-I. C. C. No. 6
F. M. B. No. 3
(For cancellations, see page 2-A)

AMERICAN TRUCKING ASSOCIATIONS, INC., AGENT

National Motor Freight Classification No. A-2

NAMING

UNIFORM RATINGS, RULES AND REGULATIONS
(except as noted)

APPLYING ON

FREIGHT TRAFFIC COVERED BY TARIFFS GOVERNED BY THIS CLASSIFICATION AS SUCH TARIFFS MAY PROVIDE

ISSUED MAY 14, 1954　　　　　　　**EFFECTIVE JULY 7, 1954**

ISSUED BY
F. G. FREUND, Issuing Officer
1424 SIXTEENTH STREET, N. W.
WASHINGTON 6, D. C.

(2971)　　　(Printed in U. S. A.)

I. C. C. No. 7950.
U. S. M. C. No. 12.
C. T. C. No. 2603.

CANCELS
I. C. C. No. 7600.
ME—I. C. C. No. 6860.
U. S. M. C. No. 9.
C. T. C. No. 2575.

(Except Items Nos. 1320-A, 1325-A.
2126, 2130-A, 2135-A, 2145-A, 2155-A,
2160-A, under Suspension in I. and S.
Docket No. 5762 and Items Nos. 1421,
1951, 2492, under Suspension in I,
and S. Docket No. 5795.)

	Cancels No.		Cancels No.		Cancels No.
Ariz. C. C. No. 163	199	P. S. C. Md. No. 325	398	P. U. C. O. No. 167	109
Ark. P. S. C. No. 151	136	Mass. D. P. U. No. 387	353	P. U. C. Ore. No. 254	206
Colo. P. U. C. No. 177	163	M. P. S. C. No. 300	382	Pa. P. U. C. No. 467	435
Conn. P. U. C. No. 174	154	P. S. C. Mo. No. 219	200	R. I. P. U. C. No. 137	122
Del. No. 192	166	P. S. C. Nev. No. 146	133	Tenn. R. & P. U. C. No. 367	384
L. R. C. No. 260	237	N. H. P. U. C. No. 199	178	P. S. C. Utah No. 108	94
P. S. C. I. No. TR 114	68	P. U. C. N. J. No. 276	290	Vt. P. S. C. No. 208	197
Ia. S. C. C. No. 173	156	N. M. C. C. No. 190	174	WN. T. No. 221	198
S. C. C. Kans. No. 174	163	P. S. C. N. Y. No. 505	463	P. S. W. Va. No. 204	185
K. R. C. No. 404	381	N. C. U. C. No. 383	368	P. S. C. Wis. No. 217	197
L. P. S. C. No. 156	146	Ohio No. 575	510	Wyo. P. S. C. No. 148	136
Me. P. U. C. No. 166	173				

Railway Express Agency

INCORPORATED

In Connection With

ALGOMA CENTRAL AND HUDSON BAY RAILWAY COMPANY (Express Department)
CANADIAN NATIONAL RAILWAYS (Express Department)
CANADIAN PACIFIC EXPRESS COMPANY
NORTHERN ALBERTA RAILWAYS (Express Department)

OFFICIAL
EXPRESS CLASSIFICATION
No. 35

Applying on Express Traffic covered by Tariffs issued subject thereto.

ON INTERSTATE AND INTRASTATE TRAFFIC.

AN ADDITIONAL CHARGE OF SIX (6) CENTS PER LESS CARLOAD SHIPMENT OF ONE OR MORE PACKAGES OR PIECES shall be added to the total of all other applicable charges on shipments rated First-Class and Multiples thereof and Second-Class herein and in Exceptions to Official Express Classification, I. C. C. No. 7850, C. T. C. No. 2590, Supplements thereto and subsequent issues thereof.

Rates, Rules and Charges published in this Classification will also apply as local express-motor rates, rules or charges applicable wholly over the lines of one or more of the following Companies, viz.: Railway Express Agency, Incorporated, Canadian National Railways (Express Department) and Canadian Pacific Express Company, for transportation within the United States by such Express Companies wholly by motor vehicle or partly by rail or water and partly by motor vehicle.

This tariff contains joint express-motor rates with motor common carriers and between points served by such carriers listed in MOTOR CARRIER SECTION of Joint Directory of Express Stations, I. C. C. No. A-3, Supplements thereto and subsequent issues thereof.

MASSACHUSETTS INTRASTATE TRAFFIC.

Rates, Rules and Regulations shown herein will apply on traffic transported over routes authorized under Regular Route Common Carrier Certificate Number 290, Issued by the Department of Public Utilities, Commonwealth of Massachusetts.

MICHIGAN INTRASTATE TRAFFIC.

Rates, Rules and Regulations shown herein will apply on traffic transported over Motor Truck Routes as published and filed in "Directory of Motor Truck Routes," M. P. S. C. No. 280, Supplements thereto and subsequent issues thereof.

NEW YORK INTRASTATE TRAFFIC.

This tariff contains joint rates with motor common carriers and between points served by such carriers listed in Directory of MOTOR CARRIERS, P. S. C. N. Y. No. 504, Supplements thereto and subsequent issues thereof.

OHIO INTRASTATE TRAFFIC.

Rates, Rules and Regulations shown herein will apply on traffic transported over Motor Truck Routes, as published and filed in "Directory of Motor Truck Routes," P. U. C. O. No. 166, Supplements thereto and subsequent issues thereof.

ISSUED APRIL 11, 1952.   **EFFECTIVE MAY 20, 1952.**

Date Received... .. ..1952.

Issued by

C. F. MESSENKOPF,
General Traffic Manager,
Railway Express Agency, Inc.
New York 17, N. Y.

L. R. BURKE,
Traffic Manager,
Railway Express Agency, Inc.
219 E. 42nd Street,
New York 17, N. Y.

Printed in U.S.A.   (M-54894)

CONN. PUC-MF-No. A-56
M. D. P. U. No. A-76   R. I. D. P. U. No. A-63   MF - I. C. C. No. A-143
N. H. P. U. C. No. A-58   V. P. S. C. No. A-48   I. C. C. - F. F. No. A-6
(For Cancellations, see page 2)   (For Cancellations, see page 2)   (For Cancellations; see page 2)

THE NEW ENGLAND MOTOR RATE BUREAU, INC.
AGENT

COORDINATED MOTOR FREIGHT
CLASSIFICATION No. 7

(Cancels Coordinated Motor Freight Classification No. 6)

CONTAINING

RATINGS, RULES AND REGULATIONS

APPLICABLE TO

**FREIGHT TRAFFIC COVERED BY TARIFFS GOVERNED BY THE
COORDINATED MOTOR FREIGHT CLASSIFICATION,
AS SUCH TARIFFS MAY SPECIFY**

ISSUED DECEMBER 5, 1953   EFFECTIVE JANUARY 8, 1954

Issued by
T. J. MOONEY, Chief of Tariff Bureau
262 Washington Street
Boston 8, Mass.

154

Chapter 9

CLASSIFICATION—
Part V

CLASSIFICATION CONTENTS (CONTINUED)

1. TITLE PAGE (FRONT COVER). There have been reproduced in the preceding pages copies of front covers of several
published Classifications. The reader is urged to examine them with
meticulous care. The title page of each Classification always shows
its name and serial number in bold type in about the center of the
page.

At the top of the cover is the Interstate Commerce Commission
number assigned to the publication by the issuing officer for identification purposes and required by the Commission, or a notation
showing where the number may be found. There are also identifying
file numbers of state commissions. This data must appear in detail.
Thus, at the top of the cover of the Motor Classification, on page
152 herein, appears the number, "MF-I.C.C. No. 6," which indicates
the identification number assigned to the publication is number 6,
the "MF" being an abbreviation for "Motor Freight." At the left
on the top part of the same cover will be found a series of letters and
numbers which are explained inside the front cover. The series be-
gins with "A.P.S.C. No. 6," the abbreviation for the Alabama Service Commission, which means the contents of the Classification apply to intrastate traffic in the State of Alabama.

It will be observed the front cover makes reference to, "tariffs
governed by this Classification." The relationship of a Classification
to a Tariff was pointed out earlier.[1] Before provisions of a Classification can be applied to any Tariff, that Tariff must refer specifically
to the Classification. Thus, the Tariff of the Southern Motor Carriers Rate Conference referred to on pages 144–145 above, carries
the following statement: [2]

---

[1] See, pp. 143–145, above.
[2] *Eastern-Southern Class Tariff*, SMCRC No. 504, MF-ICC 614, Supplement No. 1, effective April 15, 1953.

This tariff is governed, except as otherwise provided herein, by the following described publications and by supplements thereto and subsequent issues thereof:

    (a) National Motor Freight Classification No. A-1 ....
    (b) Explosives and Dangerous Articles Tariff No. 7 ....
           (and others)

The above again demonstrates that in rate determination, neither the Classification nor the applicable Tariff is workable without the other.

Furthermore, the title page shows the name or names of the agent(s) who publishes the Classification in behalf of the carriers. On the Rail Classification, the names and addresses of four men appear who are the respective agents for carriers in Official, Southern, Western, and Illinois Classification Territories. The members of the four classification committees are listed inside the front cover. The Motor Classification likewise carries the name of its issuing officer, F. G. Freund, on the face and the names of members of the motor classification board inside the front cover.

Of utmost importance is the effective date, which is in bold type towards the bottom of the title page. A shipment made before the effective date is governed by the preceding Classification. The effective date must not be confused with the issuing date because the latter merely shows the date on which it was issued and thereby made available for public inspection. The Hepburn Act of 1906 amended the Interstate Commerce Act by requiring a minimum of thirty days' notice for any change in a Classification or Tariff, unless a shorter period of time is authorized by the Commission to meet some emergency situation.[3] The issuing date, therefore, constitutes the extending of "notice" as required by the Act; and, upon reference to the front covers of Classifications reproduced on the preceding pages, it will be found that a period of more than thirty days between the respective "issued" and "effective" dates is applicable to each. The practical importance of the effective date cannot be overemphasized from the standpoint of both shipper and carrier personnel. Since, under the law, carriers are required to apply the correct rate, use of an out-of-date publication by a carrier's employee could cause a serious error for which the carrier would be held responsible. Therefore, all parties concerned should observe and be governed by the effective date whenever a new issue is received.

Inside the front cover of the Rail and on page 3 of the Motor Clas-

---

[3] Interstate Commerce Act, Sections 6 (3), 217 (c), 306 (d), 405 (d).

156

sifications there is a Cancellation Notice, which is self explanatory. For example, the Notice in *Uniform Freight Classification No. 2* reads: "Items in Uniform Freight Classification No. 1 not brought forward herein are cancelled. Ratings otherwise provided in this Classification apply." [4] Also, there is a Table of Contents showing the subject of all information contained in the publication.

2. PARTICIPATING CARRIERS. In general, railroads, freight forwarders, and domestic water carriers subscribe to the Rail Classification; and most of the motor carriers which comply with it are railroad subsidiaries. The Motor Classification is for motor carriers only,[5] except that a rail or water carrier must participate in the motor Classification when either applies the motor carrier rates on joint interline traffic. It will be observed that a number of railroad and steamship companies participate in *National Motor Freight Classification No. A-2* which indicates they participate in joint traffic with motor carriers.

The list of participating carriers is of vital importance. It should be examined to determine whether or not it includes the carrier, or carriers, selected to handle a shipment. If the name of the carrier so selected is listed, it means the carrier conforms with and is legally bound to observe the provisions of the Classification. It should be understood that the carrier listed as participating in a Classification does not necessarily mean all of them participate in joint rates with each other; instead, the respective tariffs of those carriers are subject to the Classification. If a carrier chosen by a shipper is not listed, then the Classification does not apply and the shipment is not governed thereby. In such a case, a carrier either will have a Classification of its own, or it participates in some other Classification with another group of carriers. If the shipper is determined to use the services of that particular carrier, he should consult the Classification which is applicable. The Interstate Commerce Act required all carriers subject to the Act, "to establish, observe, and enforce just and reasonable classifications of property for transportation, with reference to which rates, tariffs, regulations, or practices are or may be made or prescribed." [6]

3. INDEX TO ARTICLES. Articles which may be offered for shipment are identified by numbers and are termed "items." The Index lists

---

[4] *Uniform Freight Classification No. 2*, Consolidated Classification Committee, Chicago, effective December 10, 1953, p. 2.

[5] A carrier may not agree to all parts of the Classification in which it participates, in which event an "Exception" is published. Exceptions are discussed later. For the present, it will be assumed a participating carrier complies with all phases of the Classification.

[6] Interstate Commerce Act, Sections 1 (6), 216 (a), 305 (a), 404 (a).

articles in alphabetical order and shows the item number assigned to each. It enables the user of the Classification to find quickly and easily the item number of the commodity to be shipped. After the item number is determined, the user will turn to the section of the Classification entitled "Ratings of Articles" where detailed information will be found.

Reference to the Index is essential for accuracy because *all* articles in the ratings section are not listed in alphabetical order; instead, they are listed according to generic headings or groups, and the ratings appear in numerical order by the item number assigned to each article by the Index. Thus, in the Rail Classification ordinary mops are found in the rating section under the general grouping of "Brooms, Brushes, or Mops," the "B" in "Brooms" being the alphabetical indicator instead of the "M" in "Mops"; but in the alphabetical Index, "mops" immediately follow "moose hides." [7] Likewise, in the Motor Classification, ice cream is in the rating section under the "Dairy Products" group; but in the Index, "ice cream" is listed immediately after "ice breaking machines." [8]

It should be observed that trade names do not appear in a Classification. For example, the word "Victrola" is common to every household—rather, it was common a generation ago! There is no item termed "Victrolas"; instead, it comes under the heading of "Talking Machines." [9] Likewise, the well-known Shredded Wheat Biscuit is shipped as a "cereal food preparation." [10]

4. SHIPPING RULES. The rules prescribed in the Classifications govern the shipment of freight. They state the basic regulations and conformity therewith leads to good shipping practices.

The subject matter covered by each rule is shown in the Index to Rules. For example, if a shipper desires to know the requirements for a collect on delivery (c.o.d.) shipment, he will find reference to rule 31 on pages 166-A and 167-A of *National Motor Freight Classification No. A-2*. Merely upon turning to the pages indicated, he will find complete and detailed information concerning the subject in question. [11]

These rules have been devised from time to time to assist the carriers in the conduct of their business, and to enumerate certain re-

---

[7] *Uniform Freight Classification No. 2, op. cit.*, p. 77.
[8] *National Motor Freight Classification No. A-1*, American Trucking Associations, Inc., effective June 10, 1952, p. 108-A.
[9] *Ibid.*, Item 88380.
[10] *Ibid.*, Item 21100.
[11] *National Motor Freight Classification No. A-2, op. cit.*, pp. 154-A & 155-A.

sponsibilities of both shippers and carriers. Hence, they define the relationships which exist between carrier and shipper. They establish a uniform code of procedures. They set forth the conditions under which the carriers will provide the service of transportation, and certain privileges of both carriers and shippers.

The several rules will be discussed in later chapters.[12]

5. DESCRIPTION & RATINGS OF ARTICLES. The Ratings Section is the "meat" of the published Classifications. Since the subject requires considerable explanation, which would unduly increase the scope of this section, it will be presented separately.

Description & Ratings of Articles. The Ratings Section of a Classification contains in highly technical traffic language exactly the proper terminology to be used in describing a shipment on the bill of lading. In addition, it shows the rating of each article on the basis of carload or truckload and less-than-carload or less-than-truckload, and the minimum weight of carload or truckload shipments. For the present, the discussion will be restricted to the "standard" Rail and Motor Classifications.

The utmost importance of ratings cannot be overemphasized in order to unequivocally stress that they are the foundation of freight rates and, therefore, they are the basis of both shipping costs to industry and revenues to carriers. As Cushman states in no uncertain terms, "proper determination of the classification rating of a given commodity is a fundamental and vitally important procedure." [13] Closely associated with the ratings is application of the rules as they apply to certain shipments and under certain circumstances, so that the rules always must be kept in mind in interpreting the proper rating of a particular shipment.

Likewise, since abbreviations are used throughout the Ratings Section, reference should be made to the section on abbreviations to clarify the meaning of any symbol or abbreviation which is not understood. For example, the symbol "KD" means "knocked down"; and invariably a "knocked down" shipment takes a lower rating on the same article than a "set up" shipment, the abbreviation for which is "SU." The reason for the distinction is that a "KD" shipment occupies less space in the carrier's vehicle than if it were "set up." To illustrate, in both the Motor and Rail Classifications the less-than-truckload and less-than-carload rating for children's bi-

---

[12] See, Chapters 11–14.
[13] Cushman, F. M.: *Transportation for Management*, Prentice-Hall, Inc., New York, 1953, p. 236.

cycles is Class 200 when "set up," but Class 100 when "knocked down." [14]

Another abbreviation which appears frequently in the Ratings Section of the rail classification is, "NOIBN." As a result of years of usage, a word has been coined from the abbreviation, pronounced "noy-bin." The letters represent, "not otherwise indexed by name," which means it is a "catch-all" for any article in the same general category which is not specifically identified in a description. Since a description containing a "NOIBN" qualification can cover just about anything of a similar nature which is not "spelled out" in the Ratings Section, usually a higher rating is applied to a "NOIBN" shipment than to a defined commodity. To illustrate, the first appearance of "NOIBN" in the Rail Classification is in the subdivision pertaining to advertising matter. The Ratings Section provides a rating of 150 for less-than-carload shipments of advertising displays "NOIBN"; [15] but if such advertising matter is made of paper or paperboard, and so described on the bill of lading, the rating is $77\frac{1}{2}$.[16] Therefore, if a shipper had a l.c.l. shipment of paper advertising matter, if he did not so specify and apply the Class $77\frac{1}{2}$ rating, it is highly probable the railroad billing clerk, in the absence of specific information on the bill of lading, would assess the Class 150 rating. Furthermore, the experienced shipper will know there is a rule in both the Rail and Motor Classifications which permits advertising material to accompany a shipment at the same rating as the primary shipment itself and thereby save himself the higher rate applicable to advertising matter *per se*.[17] Motor carriers have adopted an abbreviated identification, "NOI," which is defined as, "not more specifically described herein." [18]

A shipper always should remember that when he describes his shipment on the bill of lading in exactly the same technical language as the item provides in the Classification, he is assured of the proper freight rate. A simple illustration is the distinction between asphalt composition shingles and aluminum shingles for roofing purposes. In the Motor Classification, the volume rating for the asphalt shingles is Class 35; [19] for aluminum shingles, Class 50.[20] Assume the

---

[14] *National Motor Freight Classification No. A-2, op. cit.*, Item 92520; *Uniform Freight Classification No. 2, op. cit.*, Item 43420.

[15] *Uniform Freight Classification No. 2, op. cit.*, Item 295.

[16] *Ibid.*, Item 235.

[17] *Ibid.*, Rule 45, p. 157; *National Motor Freight Classification No. A-2, op. cit.*, Rule 28, p. 166-A.

[18] *National Motor Freight Classification No. A-2, op. cit.*, p. 1.

[19] *Ibid.*, Item 83660, p. 236.

[20] *Ibid.*, Item 83595.

shipment consists of asphalt shingles. If the description on the bill of lading shows only "shingles," the carrier's rating clerk has no way of knowing what kind of shingles are being shipped and, in the absence of further information, the chances are that he will use the higher rating. Hence, in this instance, failure to describe the shipment in an accurate manner and in the language of the Classification results in the shipper paying a higher freight rate than would have been the case had he observed the literal description of the Classification.

It should be understood that the carriers' employees who prepare the bills in their best judgment determine which of several possible ratings of a shipment shall be used for the application of rates; and they rarely, if ever, actually see the article itself. Particularly is this true for carload and truckload shipments, where the consignor loads the freight and prepares the bill of lading. Hence, carrier employees generally must depend entirely upon the description shown on the bill of lading for their rating of shipments. Ignorance or carlessness on the part of the consignor usually will cause an unnecessary increase in his shipping costs by reason of a higher rating being assessed by carrier personnel. An honest error through ignorance or otherwise is one thing; but willful misdescription of a shipment with the intent to secure a lower rating and a resulting lower freight rate is something else, and it is punishable by fine and/or imprisonment upon conviction of violating the Interstate Commerce Act.[21] The above examples refer to honest errors, not intent to defraud.

It is well to remember that the manner in which a manufacturer describes his shipment on the bill of lading fixes the identity of the article for rating purposes, and description of his products for sales purposes also determine their identity for transportation purposes.[22] A leading case on the subject involved the rating of a product labeled "Dextri-maltose." Is it a "maltose" or a "prepared food"? Maltose carries a less-than-truckload and less-than-carload rating of Class 70, while Class 85 is assigned to prepared food n.o.i. in both the motor and rail Classifications.[23] Prior to 1927, the labels on the product contained the descriptive words "malt sugar," and the rates were based on the higher rating applicable to maltose. Subsequently, the term "malt sugar" was omitted resulting in rates then

---

[21] Interstate Commerce Act, Sections 10 (2) & (3), 222 (c), 317 (b) & (c), 421 (b) & (c).
[22] Colquitt, *op. cit.*, p. 96.
[23] *National Motor Freight Classification No. A-2, op. cit.*, Item 40290, p. 115, and Item 39880, p. 114; *Uniform Freight Classification No. 2, op. cit.*, Item 18595, p. 298, and Item 18425, p. 297.

being based on the lower rating of Class 70. The new label also showed the chemical analysis of the article and the purpose for its use. Nowhere on the label was there anything to indicate that the product was a specially prepared maltose. The Commission ruled for the producer, authorizing the lower Class 70 rating.[24]

A subsequent proceeding involving the same producer as in the above case further demonstrates the importance of proper descriptions as well as the highly technical nature of classification language. The second case concerned products labeled as, "Boilable Protein Milk," "Powdered Whole Milk," "Powdered Lactic Acid Milk," and others. Now, the question was whether the articles took the Class 70 rating of "Prepared Food, n.o.i.," which the producer had won in the earlier case, or the higher Class 85 rating assigned to l.t.l. and l.c.l. shipments of "Milk Food, other than Malted Milk, other than Liquid."[25] Said the Commission: [26]

Complainant's own testimony is that it primarily is an "infant diet manufacturer" and it is obvious that the impression conveyed to the consuming public through the printed matter appearing on the can labels is that the commodities in question are infant foods. We have frequently found that the description of a commodity for sales purposes also fixes its identity for transportation purposes. If a manufacturer finds it advantageous to describe his product in a manner calculated to give purchasers the impression that it is a different and higher-grade article than it actually is, he cannot consistently complain if the carriers accept that description as a basis for collecting freight charges.

It is the nature of the article itself, not the use to which it may be put, which governs the freight rate. "A commodity may come within two tariff descriptions such as 'soda ash' and 'cleaning compounds' on which different rates are maintained. If it is shipped and sold as the higher-rated commodity, cleaning compounds, the higher rates are applicable."[27]

An interesting case involved the billing of a shipment of hosiery handled by a motor carrier. The shipper contended that the description on the bill of lading that the shipment consisted of silk hosiery was in error and should have been a mixture of cotton and silk thereby resulting in a lower rate. It was developed that the toes and

---

[24] *Mead Johnson & Company v. Atlantic Coast Line Railroad Company*, 168 I.C.C. 157, 1930.

[25] *National Motor Freight Classification No. A-2, op. cit.*, Item 40390, p. 116; *Uniform Freight Classification No. 2, op. cit.*, Item 18635, p. 299.

[26] *Mead Johnson & Company v. Atlantic Coast Line Railroad Company*, 171 I.C.C. 5, 1930.

[27] *J. B. Ford Company v. Michigan Central Railroad Company*, 19 I.C.C. 507, 1910.

heels of the hose were reinforced with cotton and that the tops were of cotton; hence, the article could not be termed a "Mixture" of cotton and silk because hosiery so constructed is commonly designated as "silk hosiery." Furthermore, it was found the product was advertised and sold as "pure silk" bearing the trade designation of "Maid-o-Silk." In ruling for the carrier, the Commission held: [28]

> The Commission has frequently found that a manufacturer's description of an article for sales purposes fixes its identity also for transportation purposes. If a manufacturer finds it advantageous to describe his product in a manner calculated to give purchasers the impression that it is a different and higher-grade article than it actually is, he cannot consistently complain if the carriers accept that description as a basis for collecting freight charges. . . . We conclude that the articles were properly described as silk hosiery.

The initial step in determining the official technical description and rating of a shipment is to consult the alphabetical Index of Articles, the page numbers of which appear in the Table of Contents of the Classification. Each individual article is assigned a number known as the "item" number, and the item numbers appear in numerical order in the Ratings Section. Therefore, after ascertaining the item number of a particular commodity from the Index of Articles, one turns to the Ratings Section where the same item number identifies the shipment both as to its official description and its rating. There are occasions where more than one rating will be listed for a single commodity, depending upon the manner in which it is prepared for shipment or on the basis of what is known as "released value." [29] For illustrative purposes, two articles will be considered for shipment by motor freight on a less-than-truckload basis, wheeled weeders and glassware. The item for wheeled weeders [30] has three ratings which are described in the Motor Classification, as follows:

1210 Weeders, wheeled:
    SU, in boxes or crates............ (l.t.l. rating) ... 150
    SU, loose........................ (l.t.l. rating) ... 200
    KD, in packages................. (l.t.l. rating) ... 77½

In contrast, the item for glassware [31] contains ratings dependent upon value in relation to weight as follows:

---

[28] *The May Department Stores Company, Famous Barr Division v. Service Lines, Inc.*, 34 M.C.C. 773 (775), 1942.
[29] Under a "released value," the shipper specifies the value of his shipment.
[30] *National Motor Freight Classification No. A-2, op. cit.*, Item 1210.
[31] *Ibid.*, Item 46520.

46520 Glassware, NOI, in barrels or boxes.................
    Actual value not exceeding 25 cents per lb. (l.t.l. rating)..   70
    Actual value exceeding 25 cents per lb., but not exceeding
      75 cents per lb....................................   85
    Actual value exceeding 75 cents per lb., but not exceeding
      $1.50 per lb.. 100
    Actual value exceeding $1.50 per lb., but not exceeding
      $3.00 per lb.. 150
    Actual value exceeding $3.00 per lb., but not exceeding
      $4.50 per lb.. 200
    If actual value exceeds $4.50 per lb., or if shipper declines
      to declare value—NOT TAKEN

Originally, articles were not listed according to commercial groups as is the existing practice; instead, all commodities were shown under the particular class to which they were assigned. Thus, those articles which were rated first class were all listed under the general heading of "First Class"; those carrying a rating of second class were listed under "Second Class"; and so on. Some of the early Classifications showed articles in strictly alphabetical order.[32]

A page of the Ratings Section contains data pertaining to many different articles. As was stated in the preceding section, each article is identified by an "Item Number"; and the respective item numbers are listed in numerical order, *not* alphabetically according to the name of the commodity. Reading from left to right, first there is the item number itself, in a column listing all the item numbers numerically, entitled, "Item"; then, there follows a description of the article in technical traffic nomenclature regarding the article itself and, usually, specific requirements as to its packaging or other manner of shipment; and, finally, three columns of figures, viz.: in the motor classification, the first column shows the rating of the article as a less-than-truckload shipment, the second column gives the truckload or volume rating of the article, and a number in the third column indicates the minimum weight expressed in terms of pounds on which the more favorable volume rating applies. The distinction between less-than-truckload and volume or truckload *must* be kept in mind, for the former (l.t.l.) usually, but not always, carries a higher rating and a resulting higher freight rate than the latter (t.l.). The basis for determining whether a shipment moves on a less-than-truckload rating or on a volume rating is the minimum weight shown in the "Volume Minimum Weight" column. The reader is again reminded that exactly the same method of interpret-

---

[32] Colquitt, *op. cit.*, p. 64.

ing the Motor Classification applies to the Rail Classification, the only essential differences being in nomenclature.

However, a notable exception to the statement that less-than-truckload ratings are higher than volume ratings, occurs when the letters "AQ" appear in the column for volume minimum weights instead of a number indicating weight. "AQ" is the abbreviation for "Any Quantity," meaning there is no volume minimum weight applicable to the particular article. In those instances, there is no distinction between less-than-truckload and truckload (or less-than-carload and carload), and the ratings will be found to be the same for both regardless of the volume or weight. To illustrate, "AQ" ratings are assigned to various individual items under the general heading of "Cloth, Dry Goods, or Fabrics." [33]

First, the pre-uniform rail system of classification will be presented, it being understood that the "old" method is still applicable to certain articles and in some parts of the country.[34] Afterwards, the "new" uniform system will be described. For illustrative purposes page 413 of *Consolidated Freight Classification No. 20* is reproduced on the following page, and the reader should refer to it throughout the ensuing explanation. It is also recommended that the reader review the identification of classification ratings which were presented earlier on page 109.

At the top of the reproduced page, on the right, are the numbers "41295–41510," which serve as a supplementary index for they indicate that items 41295 to 41510, inclusive, appear on that particular page thereby facilitating use of the Classification when searching for a certain item. Exactly the same applies to the Motor Classification; but, for reasons unknown to the writer, the supplementary index is omitted from the pages of the Ratings Section of the Express Classification.

The first item of the reproduced page of the Rail Classification is Item 41295, an article with which former generations were most intimately associated, but probably, unknown to most young people today: corset stays. The description specifies that this commodity must be shipped "in barrels or boxes"; otherwise, it will not be accepted by the carrier, because there is provision for no other method of packaging, for shipment loose or in bulk. Continuing across from left to right, the reader finds the number "2" in the column for less-

---

[33] *Uniform Freight Classification No. 2, op. cit.,* Item 12725; *National Motor Freight Classification No. A-2,* Items 26970–27740, not inclusive.
[34] See, pp. 70–72, above.

than-carload ratings. That single figure means the l.c.l. rating of corset stays is second class, or Class 2, throughout the entire country. The figure in the next column indicates that 30,000 pounds constitute the minimum weight for application of a carload rating. The final number, "4," in the carload ratings column, shows the article

CONSOLIDATED FREIGHT CLASSIFICATION NUMBER 20 41295–41510

Item	ARTICLES	Less Carload Ratings	Carload Minimum (Pounds)	Carload Ratings
41295	Stays or steels, corset or dress, steel, in barrels or boxes	2	30,000	4
41300	Stearic acid, in bags, barrels, boxes or package 822	R26–4–4	30,000	5–7–5
41305	Stearine, animal, noibn, LCL, in bags, barrels or tubs; CL, in bulk or in packages; also in tank cars, Rule 35	R26–4–4	30,000	37½–37½–5
41310	Steel wool and soap combined in same inner container,i n cartons in boxes	2	24,000R	4
41320	Sterilizers, noibn, cabinet, in boxes or crates	1	16,000R	2
41325	Sterilizers, noibn, other than cabinet, in boxes or crates	2	24,000R	40–3–3
41330	Stolons (chopped grass), in bags	D1	14,000R	2
41335	Stone stencil compound (paper, glue and glycerine combined, or rubber and glue combined, in sheet form), in boxes	2	36,000	4
41340	Stoppers, bottle:			
41345	Aluminum, in barrels or boxes	1	20,000R	3
41350	Bottle stoppers, noibn, in bags, barrels or boxes	2	30,000	4
41355	Bottle, with swab attachments, in bags, barrels or boxes	2	24,000R	4
41360	Cork and wood combined, in bags, barrels or boxes	2	24,000R	R26–4–4
41365	Glass, other than cut or ground, in barrels or boxes	3	30,000	5–6–5
41370	Stoppers, carboy, clay, in bags, barrels or boxes	4–50–4	36,000	5–6–5
41375	Straps, leather, imitation leather or webbing, fitted with buckles, hooks or other fastenings, noibn, in barrels, boxes or crates	1	20,000R	3
41379	Straw, from threshed grain or rice, in machine pressed bales	1–3–4–3	20,000R	5–C–9–C
41380	Straw goods, noibn, in boxes	1	20,000R	3
41385	Straw pulp, in bags, barrels or boxes	4–50–4	36,000	6–8–C
41390	Straws, drinking, in boxes, or in package 841	1	16,000R	3
41395	Stretchers or stretcher frames, artists':			
	SU, in boxes or crates	1	20,000R	3
	KD, in boxes or crates	3	30,000	45–5–A
41397	Stretchers, curtain, aluminum, in packages	1	20,000R	3
41398	Stretchers, curtain, steel rod, in boxes	3	30,000	37½–6–5
41399	Stretchers, curtain, wooden or steel and wood combined, or steel other than steel rod, KD, in packages	3	20,000R	4–50–4
41400	Sugar cane, in packages; also CL, loose	1–3–6–3	30,000	5–B–32½–B
41405	Sugar clarifier compound, noibn, dry, in bags or barrels	3	36,000	5–6–5
41410	Sugar clarifier compound, noibn, liquid or paste, in barrels	3	30,000	5–6–5
41412	Sugar of milk, crude, in bags or barrels	3	36,000	5–6–5
41413	Sugar of milk, refined, in barrels or boxes	2	30,000	4
41415	Sugar or syrup evaporator furnaces, without pans:			
	With legs or rockers attached, loose or in packages	1	15,000R	3–5–3
	Without legs or rockers, or legs or rockers detached, loose or in packages	2	15,000R	3–5–3
41420	Sugar or syrup evaporator furnaces, kettles or pans, in mixed CL with cane mills	....	24,000R	40–6–A
41425	Sugar or syrup evaporator kettles, iron, loose or in packages	3	24,000R	40–5–A
41430	Sugar or syrup evaporator pans, copper or copper lined:			
	Tops and bottoms protected by wooden strips not less than ½x2¼ inches, not more than 7 inches apart on bottom and 18 inches apart on top	1½	15,000R	3–4–3
	In boxes or crates	2	15,000R	3–4–3
41435	Sugar or syrup evaporator pans, sheet steel:			
	Tops and bottoms protected by wooden strips not less than ½x2¼ inches, not more than 7 inches apart on bottom and 18 inches apart on top	1	15,000R	3–5–3
	LCL, in boxes or crates; CL, in packages or loose, braced in car	2	15,000R	3–5–3
41437	Sulphate black liquor skimmings (not acidified or otherwise processed), in barrels; also CL, in tank cars, Rule 35	4–50–4	40,000	25–10–D
41440	Sulphur (brimstone), LCL, in bags, barrels or boxes; CL, in bulk or in packages or in tank cars, Rule 35	4–50–4	40,000	6–8–C
41445	Sulphur candles or strips, in barrels or boxes	3	30,000	5–6–5
41450	Sumac, ground, in bags, barrels or boxes	3–4–3	30,000	5–6–5
41455	Sumac leaves:			
	In bags, or in bales not machine pressed	2	20,000R	5–4–4
	In machine pressed bales	3	20,000R	5–4–4
41457	Sunflower seed, roasted, salted, in boxes	2	36,000	R26–4–4
41460	Sunflower seed hulls:			
	In bags or barrels	3–4–3	30,000	5–B–10–B
	LCL, in machine pressed bales; CL, n bulk or in packages	4	30,000	5–B–10–B
41465	Superphosphate (acid phosphate), ammoniated, LCL, in bags or barrels, or in package 41; CL, in bulk or in packages	4–50–4	40,000	6–32½–B
41470	Superphosphate (acid phosphate), other than ammoniated, LCL, in bags or barrels, or in package 41; CL, in bulk or in packages	4–50–4	40,000	6–E–11–E
41472	Suspensions, droppable airplane fuel tank, wood and steel combined, KD, in packages	3	36,000	5–37½–5
41473	Syenite, crude or ground, in 5-ply paper bags; CL, in bulk or in packages	4–50–4	40,000	6–8–C
41475	Tables, steam, or steam tables and warming closets combined:			
	SU, legs attached or detached, in boxes or crates	1	20,000R	3
	Completely KD, in boxes or crates	2	24,000R	R26–4–4
41480	Tags or lables, cloth or cloth and paper or zinc combined, in boxes	2	24,000R	R26–4–4
41482	Talc, pigmented, in barrels	R26–4–4	40,000	30–8–C
41490	Talking machine operating and sound mechanism assemblies or turntables, in boxes	2	30,000	4
41495	Talking machine parts, noibn, or needles, in barrels or boxes	1	20,000R	3
41500	Talking machine record carrying cases, in boxes or crates	1	20,000R	3
41505	Talking machine record compound, powdered or in sheets, in barrels or boxes; also CL, in wheeled steel containers	3	40,000	37½–6–5
41510	Talking machine record shaving machines, in boxes or crates	1	24,000R	R26–5–A

For explanation of abbreviations, characters and ratings, see page 179; for packages, see pages 437 to 478.

418

is rated fourth class. The significance of the above illustration is that a single number in either the l.c.l. or c.l. column, regardless of the commodity, means that that particular one rating is applicable everywhere in the United States without distinction to the classification territories. Hence, the lone number "2" in the l.c.l. rating column means that Class 2, or 85 percent of first class,[85] is applicable to all l.c.l. shipments of corset stays whether they be in Official, Southern, Western, or Illinois Territory.

The next item on the page, stearic acid, Item 41300, appears complicated, for a series of three separate numbers appear in both the l.c.l. and c.l. ratings columns. Where three numbers, or symbols in lieu of numbers, are shown in a rating column, reading from left to right the first is the rating for Official Territory, the second is for Southern Territory, and the third is for Western Territory. So, for stearic acid, the l.c.l. ratings of "R26–4–4" refer to Rule 26 Class in Official Territory, fourth class in Southern Territory, and fourth class in Western Territory. The carload ratings of "5–7–5" indicate fifth class in Official Territory, seventh class in Southern Territory, and fifth class in Western Territory. As has been explained, the amount of the freight rate itself for a shipment of stearic acid between any two points would be determined by applying the percentage relationship of the classification rating to the first class rate as published in the applicable tariff. Without consideration of those relationships, the bare numbers "5–7–5" would give the appearance of a wide spread in the carload ratings on the article in the South; but, upon reference to the table on page 109, it will be discovered that Class 5 in Official Territory and Class 7 in Southern Territory are exactly the same percentage of first class, 35 percent, while Class 5 in Western Territory is 37½ percent.

The third article on the page, Item 41305, animal stearine, presents a different method of describing ratings in the l.c.l. column: "37½–37½–5." Actually, the ratings of this article on both l.c.l. and c.l. bases are exactly the same percentage of first class and, therefore, they are uniform; but, the casual observer of those ratings might not realize their similarity when the actual rates are applied. The "37½" indicates the percentage itself of first class, there being no established numbered class in either Official or Southern Territory bearing a percentage relationship of 37½. This situation was explained earlier; and if further clarification is needed, pages 109 and 110 should be consulted.

The fourth item, 41310, steel wool and soap combined, presents

[85] See, pp. 71–72, above.

still a different situation by the letter "R" being inserted in the carload minimum weight column, "24,000 R." This is a symbol of great importance which demands further inquiry. The "R" is a warning that one of the shipping rules contained in the published Classification, specifically Rule 34, applies to the particular shipment. Although Rule 34 will be discussed in a later chapter,[36] suffice it to say for the present that Rule 34 establishes a basis of carload minimum weights which vary directly with the size of the freight car ordered by the shipper. In general, Rule 34 is made applicable to carload shipments of less than 30,000 pounds; hence, when a minimum carload weight below 30,000 pounds is shown in the Classification, the letter "R" usually accompanies it. However, there are exceptions to this general statement, as: "R" is absent from the minimum weight of 20,000 pounds for a carload shipment of live snails.[37] Whenever the letter "R" appears with a carload minimum weight, direct reference to Rule 34 is imperative.

Continuing down the reproduced page of the Classification, it will be observed there are four series of symbols for the ratings of straw, Item 41379. The l.c.l. ratings are, "1–3–4–3"; the carload, "5–C–9–C." This means a separate rating is applicable in all four territories and specifically recognizes Illinois Classification Territory. Interpretation of four ratings in either the l.c.l. or c.l. column is, reading from left to right, that the first is for Official Classification, the second is for Illinois Classification, the third is for Southern Classification, and the fourth is for Western Classification. Hence, for l.c.l. shipment of the article under consideration, the ratings would be first class in Official Territory, third class in Illinois Territory, fourth class in Southern Territory, and third class in Western Territory. The identification of classes, and their respective percentage relationships, under the Illinois Classification was presented earlier;[38] but where three instead of four ratings are listed, the ratings for Illinois Territory are the same as those for Official Territory.[39] It should be observed that Illinois Territory is not recognized as a separate classification territory for motor carriers and, therefore, Illinois Territory is not included in the Ratings Section of the *National Motor Freight Classification.*

At the bottom of the reproduced page, and of all pages in Ratings Section of both the Rail and Motor Classifications, attention of the reader is directed to where he may find an explanation of "abbrevia-

---

[36] See, p. 277, below.
[37] *Consolidated Freight Classification No. 20, op. cit.,* Item 40855.
[38] See, p. 109, above.
[39] *Consolidated Freight Classification No. 20, op. cit.,* p. 179.

tions, characters, and ratings." Without exception, one should refer to the explanation of any symbol which may appear with the description of an article to be shipped, when the meaning thereof is not understood.

The "new" uniform system of classification adheres to all the physical features of the "old" published volume except in the ratings column. It will be recalled the differentiation between territories was abandoned in order to obtain uniformity in ratings, and there was adopted the method of showing the actual percentage relationships of ratings to the base Class 100 (first class) in lieu of the former numbered or lettered classes.[40] For illustrative purposes, page 427 of *Uniform Freight Classification No. 2* is reproduced on the next page, for it contains most of the same articles shown in the previous reproduction from *Consolidated Freight Classification No. 20* on page 166 above. It will be observed that corset stays, Item 41295, are rated "85" and "55" for less-than-carload and carload shipments, respectively; stearic acid, Item 41300, "65" and 37½"; and so on. A comparison between the "old" and the "new" classification systems of the respective percentage relationships to first class (Class 100) for a few of the articles included on the two reproduced pages is summarized in the following table:

		"Old" System Territory			"New" System
		Official	Southern	Western	Non-Territorial
Item	Article	lcl cl	lcl cl	lcl cl	lcl cl
41295	Corset Stays	85–50	85–55	85–55	85–55
41300	Stearic Acid	55–35	55–35	55–38	65–37½
41305	Stearine	55–37½	55–37½	55–38	65–37½
41379	Straw, etc.	100–35	55–25	70–27½	65–32½
41385	Straw Pulp	50–27½	50–30	55–27½	60–30
41400	Sugar Cane	100–35	40–32½	70–32½	70–32½
41457	Sunflower Seed	85–55	85–55	85–55	65–40

Package Descriptions. In the Rail Classification some 60 pages are devoted to detailed packing specifications which are used in connection with the section on Description of Articles. In some instances, the packaging requirements or the type of container to be used are provided concurrently with the description of the article; in other cases, there appears a package number which necessitates reference to the section on Package Descriptions. For example: it will be observed upon reference to the preceding page, on which is

---

[40] See, p. 86, above.

reproduced a page of *Uniform Freight Classification No. 2,* that Item 41390, drinking straws, contains the requirement that the article be shipped "in boxes, or in package 841." Reference to Package No. 841 in the Package Descriptions section reveals that the shipment be "In fibre boxes meeting requirements of Rule 41 for

UNIFORM FREIGHT CLASSIFICATION NUMBER 2 41280–41473

Item	ARTICLES	Less Carload Ratings	Carload Minimum (Pounds)	Carload Ratings
	STATIONERY—Concluded:			
41280	Staples, stapling machine, steel wire thinner than 3/32 inch, in boxes	70	30,000	45
41285	Stationery, noibn, in boxes	100	20,000R	70
41290	Tacks, thumb, in barrels or boxes	85	24,000R	55
★ 41293	Staurolite residue (residue material produced in the mining of ilmenite ore), LCL, in bags, barrels or boxes; also CL in bulk or in packages	60	50,000	27½
41295	Stays or steels, corset or dress, steel, in barrels or boxes	85	30,000	55
41300	Stearic acid, in bags, barrels, boxes or package 822	65	30,000	37½
41305	Stearine, animal, noibn, LCL, in bags, barrels or tubs; CL, in bulk or in packages; also in tank cars, Rule 35	65	30,000	37½
41310	Steel wool and soap combined, in same inner container, in cartons in boxes	100	24,000R	55
41320	Sterilizers, noibn, cabinet, in boxes or crates	100	24,000R	55
41325	Sterilizers, noibn, other than cabinet, in boxes or crates	85	24,000R	55
41330	Stolons (chopped grass), in bags	200	14,000R	85
41335	Stone stencil compound (paper, glue and glycerine combined, or rubber and glue combined, in sheet form), in boxes	85	36,000	55
41340	Stoppers, bottle:			
41345	Aluminum, in barrels or boxes	100	20,000R	70
41350	Bottle stoppers, noibn, in bags, barrels or boxes	85	30,000	55
41355	Bottle, with swab attachments, in bags, barrels or boxes	85	24,000R	55
41360	Cork and wood combined, in bags, barrels or boxes	85	24,000R	55
41365	Glass, other than cut or ground, in barrels or boxes	70	30,000	27½
41370	Stoppers, carboy, clay, in bags, barrels or boxes	70	36,000	37½
41375	Straps, leather, imitation leather or webbing, fitted with buckles, hooks or other fastenings, noibn, in barrels, boxes or crates	100	20,000R	70
41379	Straw, from threshed grain or rice, in machine pressed bales	65	24,000R	32½
41380	Straw goods, noibn, in boxes	100	20,000R	70
41385	Straw pulp, in bags, barrels or boxes	60	36,000	30
41390	Straws, drinking, in boxes, or in package 841	100	16,000R	70
41395	Stretchers or stretcher frames, artists':			
	SU, in boxes or crates	100	20,000R	70
	KD, in boxes or crates	70	30,000	45
41397	Stretchers, curtain, aluminum, in packages	100	20,000R	70
41398	Stretchers, curtain, steel rod, in boxes	70	30,000	40
41399	Stretchers, curtain, wooden or steel and wood combined, or steel other than steel rod, KD, in packages	77½	30,000	50
41400	Sugar cane, in packages; also CL, loose	70	30,000	32½
41405	Sugar clarifier compound, noibn, dry, in bags or barrels	70	36,000	37½
41410	Sugar clarifier compound, noibn, liquid or paste, in barrels	70	30,000	40
41412	Sugar of milk, crude, in bags or barrels	70	36,000	37½
41413	Sugar of milk, refined, in barrels or boxes	85	30,000	45
41415	Sugar or syrup evaporator furnaces, without pans:			
	With legs or rockers attached, loose or in packages	100	20,000R	45
	Without legs or rockers, or legs or rockers detached, loose or in packages	85	20,000R	45
41425	Sugar or syrup evaporator kettles, iron, loose or in packages	70	24,000R	45
41430	Sugar or syrup evaporator pans, copper or copper lined:			
	Tops and bottoms protected by wooden strips not less than ½x2¼ inches, not more than 7 inches apart on bottom and 18 inches apart on top	150	20,000R	45
	In boxes or crates	85	20,000R	45
41433	Sugar or syrup evaporator pans, sheet steel:			
	Tops and bottoms protected by wooden strips not less than ½x2¼ inches, not more than 7 inches apart on bottom and 18 inches apart on top	100	20,000R	45
	LCL, in boxes or crates; CL, in packages or loose, braced in car	85	20,000R	45
41435	Suitcase half sections, unfinished, glass fibre and synthetic resin combined, nested, in boxes	100	24,000R	55
41436	Sulphate black liquor skimmings, dried, ground or not ground (not acidified or otherwise processed), in bags or barrels	55	40,000	22½
41437	Sulphate black liquor skimmings, not acidified or otherwise processed, liquid, in barrels; also CL, in tank cars, Rule 35	50	50,000	20
41440	Sulphur (brimstone):			
	Other than crude, LCL, in bags, barrels or boxes; CL, in bulk or in packages or in tank cars, Rule 35	60	40,000	27½
	Crude (not ground or not refined), LCL, in bags, barrels or boxes; CL, in bulk or in packages or in tank cars, Rule 35	50	80,000	17½
41445	Sulphur candles or strips, in barrels or boxes	70	36,000	37½
41450	Sumac, ground, in bags, barrels or boxes	65	36,000	30
41455	Sumac leaves:			
	In bags, or in bales not machine pressed	100	20,000R	55
	In machine pressed bales	70	30,000	35
41457	Sunflower seed, roasted, salted, in boxes	65	36,000	40
41460	Sunflower seed hulls:			
	In bags or barrels	70	30,000	32½
	LCL, in machine pressed bales; CL, in bulk or in packages	65	30,000	32½
⊕ 41465	Superphosphate (acid phosphate), ammoniated, LCL, in bags or barrels, or in package 41; CL, in bulk or in packages	50	40,000	20
⊕ 41470	Superphosphate (acid phosphate), other than ammoniated, LCL, in bags or barrels, or in package 41; CL, in bulk or in packages	50	40,000	20
41472	Suspensions, droppable airplane fuel tank, wood and steel combined, KD, in packages	70	36,000	37½
41473	Syenite, crude or ground, in 5-ply paper bags; CL, in bulk or in packages	50	60,000	20

For explanation of abbreviations, numbers and reference marks, see pages 186 and 514; for packages, see pages 452 to 514.

boxes testing not less than 200 lbs., except that dimensions must not exceed 90 united inches." [41] Rule 41 is one of the shipping rules which is discussed later.

The Package Description Section contains a complete list of every conceivable kind of shipping container with most detailed specifications regarding type, size, capacity, strength, material with which constructed, etc. Each individual package is assigned a number and the descriptions are listed in numerical order. The section is divided into 24 subsections under the following headings, which illustrate the detailed nature of authorized shipping containers: [42]

Bags	Cans	Cylinders	Rolls
Bales	Carriers	Drums	Trunks
Baskets	In Cars	Hampers	Tubes
Boxes	Cartons	Loose	Tubs
Bundles	Cases	Packages	Wrapped
Cabinets	Crates	Pails	Miscellaneous

Classification Committees. Both the rail and motor carriers have created their respective committees to which have been delegated the responsibility of handling classification matters. The nature of the work of these committees is so specialized and so important to both carriers and shippers it is imperative that membership be composed of capable and honest individuals who are thoroughly familiar with the technical aspects of classification. Unquestionably, the carriers have been most diligent in naming highly qualified men to these responsible posts. A simple, but significant, statement of a recognized authority, R. C. Colton, formerly General Traffic Manager of Radio Corporation of America and currently Vice President of Lukes Brothers Company, Inc., is: "The members of these Committees are men of good judgment with a wealth of experience in this particular field. It is difficult for the average person fully to appreciate the time, effort, patience and clear thinking that is necessary to compile a freight classification." [43]

These committees perform a number of functions directly affecting the industrial traffic manager. When the latter desires a change in a rating, establishment of a new description, or any other related matter, he petitions the appropriate committee; it investigates and hands down its decision. Frequently, a committee may act as arbitrator between carrier and shipper.

---

[41] *Uniform Freight Classification No. 2,* Consolidated Classification Committee, Chicago, effective December 10, 1953, p. 486.
[42] *Ibid.,* pp. 452–514.
[43] Colton, R. C.: *Practical Handbook of Industrial Traffic Management,* Second Edition, Funk & Wagnalls Company, New York, 1953, p. 41.

Although much of the work of the committees is performed on an informal basis by correspondence or conference, frequently proper adjudication of matters necessitates public hearings in which both carriers and shippers may participate and submit evidence. The preparation of such evidence and the convincing manner by which it is presented is a most important responsibility of the industrial traffic manager. In order that all interested persons may be informed of the time and place of a hearing and the matter to be investigated, the committees periodically publish and distribute a document known as a "Docket."

A person desiring any change in an existing Classification submits his proposal to the appropriate classification committee on a special "Application for Change in Classification" form, to which may be attached photographs or other exhibits in substantiation thereof. The completed form furnishes the name of the article, the materials from which it is made, uses of the commodity, the kind of packages or method of shipment, dimensions of the packages, gross weight, weight per cubic foot, value per pound, and other pertinent information. The form also shows the present Classification in which the article appears, together with the existing ratings, and the proposed description and ratings, if any. Of particular importance is a complete explanation of the desired change or addition. The data thus provided are assembled and printed in the Docket, showing both the present and proposed situations. The front cover shows the Classification or Classifications involved, the Docket number, date of issuance, the date and place at which public hearings will be conducted, the name and address of the committee member to whom proposals should be sent, and the names of members of the classification committee or committees. Thus, Docket No. 161 of the Uniform, Official, Southern, Western, and Illinois Classification Committees, issued February 13, 1954, announced the respective dates and places of hearings during March, 1954, and it consisted of a volume of 55 pages.

The purposes of public hearings are to enable the committee to secure additional information to that contained in the original application, and to enable shippers both to know about the proposals and to be given the opportunity to express their wishes in connection therewith. Following completion of hearings, the committees review the facts and submit their recommendations to the appropriate Executive Committee in the case of railroads, or to the National Traffic Committee for motor carriers, both of which are described later.[44] If a Classification Committee's recommendations are approved, the applicant and other interested parties are so informed; and the proposal is published in the next issue of the Classification or Supplement.[45]

If a proposal is rejected, the applicant, if he desires, may resubmit the matter to the Classification Committee with additional supporting information. If that, too, is rejected, the next step is to file a complaint with the Interstate Commerce Commission; and if that fails, the matter may be brought before a court of proper jurisdiction, with the decision of the Supreme Court of the United States on an appeal from the lower court being the final action.[46]

The printed Dockets are distributed by the Classification Committees to subscribers. They are reported in both the daily and weekly issues of *Traffic World,* published by the Traffic Service Corporation, Washington. Clearly, it is incumbent upon the industrial traffic manager to examine with care the copy of each Docket as it is received by him; and if a matter for consideration by a classification committee relates to his business, definitely he should attend, or be represented at, the hearing to protect the interests of his firm. Furthermore, the opportunity for cooperation with other industrial traffic managers concerning matters of common interest, together with cooperation with carriers, is apparent. By enlisting aid and support to a carrier in a proceeding against another carrier or group of carriers, particularly when the industrial traffic manager does business with the former, naturally that particular carrier will exert every effort to assist him with his shipping problems which may arise in the future. The old adage, "you scratch my back and I'll scratch yours," is well demonstrated in such situations.

The enormous and responsible task of assembling, analyzing, and adjudicating all phases of information and testimony for presentation in the published Classifications, in the detailed manner prescribed by the Interstate Commerce Commission, is performed by the respective classification committees. The work of the national motor and rail committees will now be briefly considered.

(1) THE RAIL CLASSIFICATION. There are four major classification committees representing the railroads, namely: the Consolidated,

---
[44] See, pp. 173–179, below.
[45] Letter from A. H. Carson, member, Southern Classification Committee, to J. L. Frye, Assistant Professor of Transportation, The University of Tennessee, Knoxville, dated April 5, 1954.
[46] Colton, *op. cit.,* pp. 52–53.

Official, Southern, and Western. While mention has been made of Illinois Classification Territory which, too, has a committee, its application is restricted to a relatively small geographical area and it will not be included here.

Membership of the Consolidated Classification Committee consists of the respective chairman of the Official, Southern, Western, and Illinois committees, the Chairman of the Illinois Classification Committee having been admitted to membership in 1933.[47] The original Consolidated Committee of Official, Southern, and Western committee chairmen, was established January 1, 1919, by order of the Director General of Railroads, who, at the time, was operating the railroads of the United States in behalf of the federal government in World War I.[48] It coordinates the work of the territorial committees regarding classification matters. It publishes both the "Consolidated" and the "Uniform" Classifications, and its Chairman serves as the agent for all participating carriers in issuing and filing the published volumes in accordance with requirements of the Interstate Commerce Commission and of state regulatory bodies. It has been practice of long standing for the Chairman of the Western Classification Committee to serve without additional compensation as Chairman of the Consolidated Classification Committee.[49]

The work of the Consolidated Classification Committee is under the nominal supervision of an Executive Committee on Consolidated Classification. It is composed of fifteen members, five from each of the respective Executive Committees of Official, Southern, and Western Classification Committees.[50] This committee has jurisdiction over matters pertaining to organization, salaries, and expenses of the Consolidated Committee; and it is charged with reconciling differences which arise between the three major territories. The duties of the Consolidated Committee may be summarized, as follows: [51]

1. Publish and issue the "Consolidated" and "Uniform" Classifications, proofs of which shall be submitted to the territorial committees for examination and approval before printing.

---

[47] Van Metre, T. W.: *Industrial Traffic Management,* McGraw-Hill Book Company, New York, 1953, p. 44.

[48] United States Railroad Administration, Division of Traffic, Circular No. 6, Washington, January 30, 1919.

[49] Letter to the author from R. E. Boyle, Jr., Chairman, Southern Classification Committee, and Vice-Chairman, Southern Freight Association, Atlanta, dated April 23, 1954.

[50] See, pp. 174–177, below.

[51] "Organization of Consolidated Classification Committee" (mimeo.), Southern Classification Committee, Atlanta, 1945, pp. 11–14.

2. Maintain uniformity in rules, descriptions, and minimum weights.

3. Prepare Dockets of petitions submitted by carriers and the shipping public. The charge to the public for copies of Dockets shall be fixed by the Committee.

4. Conduct public hearings as may be warranted, the Interstate Commerce Commission and State Commissions to be invited to be represented.

5. The Chairman of the territory in which a hearing is conducted shall conduct the meeting.

6. In event of territorial disagreement regarding any matter, the Chairman of the Consolidated Committee shall submit a statement thereof to the Executive Committee.

7. When formal complaints before the Interstate Commerce Commission or State Commissions do not include all territories, nevertheless the Chairman of each territorial committee shall intervene and testify as may be necessary to preserve the revenues of the carriers.

8. The sales price of each published Classification shall be determined by the Consolidated Committee. Free distribution is prohibited, except as provided by regulations of regulatory bodies.

9. Expenses of the Committee, other than those pertaining to printing and distribution of the Classifications and Supplements, shall be borne equally by the three territorial committees.

The territorial committees possess independent jurisdiction in their respective geographical areas, and they cooperate with each other on matters involving two or more territories. For many years, membership was composed of traffic officers of various railroads who divided their time and energy between the committee and their respective companies. With the expansion of classification affairs and responsibilities, it was found that no individual could perform efficiently in the dual capacity of committee member and railroad officer. Further, "the requests of large shippers for classification changes were sometimes granted in an effort to obtain or hold the traffic of such shippers. The divorcement of classification committees from solicitation influences and the continuous devotion of members to the problems of freight classification brought higher standards of skill and accumulated knowledge to bear on these problems." Today, as will be described later,[52] members of the territorial classification committees are named by an Executive Committee composed of railroad traffic executives, and they are on a

---

[52] See, pp. 176–177, below.

full-time basis without financial dependency upon any single rail-road company.[53] This is a wise policy because classification committee work requires concentrated study and the exercise of impartial judgment to serve the best interests of both carriers and shippers. The committee members are compensated directly by the territorial association which, in turn, is financially supported by assessments to the member carriers based upon mileage. The Official Classification Committee consists of four members, including the Chairman; the Southern and Western Classification Committees are composed of three members each, including the Chairman.[54]

The organization and functions of the Southern Classification Committee will serve to illustrate operations of the other territorial committees. Membership is available to all transportation companies operating in Southern Territory which adhere to the Classification of the Southern Committee. Prior to adoption of the "Consolidated" Classification in 1919, the publication applicable to carriers in the South was the *Southern Freight Classification;* and, upon reference to reproduction of the front cover of "Consolidated" Classification No. 20 on page 149, it will be observed that *Consolidated Freight Classification No. 20* includes, among others, *Southern Classification No. 63.* At the present time, membership in the Southern Committee consists of railroads, coastwise steamship companies, freight forwarders and a few motor carriers which, in general, are railroad subsidiaries.[55] Expenses of the organization are borne by the member lines prorated on the basis of the mileage of each.[56]

Organization of the Southern Classification Committee consists of: (1) a General Committee, (2) an Executive Committee, (3) the Classification Committee, and (4) the Classification Committee Chairman. Robert E. Boyle, Jr., is the Chairman, with headquarters in Atlanta.

The entire membership constitutes the General Committee. The chief traffic officer of each member line designates a person in his organization to serve on this committee, and the majority in attendance at a meeting governs the proceedings.

---

[53] Board of Investigation & Research: *Report on Rate-Making and Rate-Publishing Procedures of Railroad. Motor, and Water Carriers,* House Document No. 363, 78th Congress, 1st Session, Government Printing Office, Washington, 1944, pp. 35–38.

[54] Letter from Boyle, *op. cit.*

[55] *Consolidated Freight Classification No. 20,* Consolidated Classification Committee, Chicago, effective October 15, 1951, pp. 7–26.

[56] The ensuing explanation of the Southern Classification Committee has been summarized from: "Articles of Association" (mimeo.), Southern Classification Committee, Atlanta, June 11, 1938.

The Executive Committee consists of eleven persons, each of whom must be the chief traffic officer of a member line. They are elected by the chief traffic officers of all the member lines at a general membership meeting called for the purpose of electing members of the Executive Committee. It determines by a two-thirds majority vote the carriers which will be admitted to membership in the Classification Committee. It assumes general control of the affairs of the organization and formulates and directs its policy. Except for election of new members, unanimous action of those present at a meeting is required for adoption of all matters brought before it. The Executive Committee elects the Chairman of the Classification Committee.

The Classification Committee itself is composed of three members, including the Chairman, who are elected by unanimous vote of the Executive Committee and who devote their full time and energies to classification affairs. As was stated earlier, this committee handles all matters pertaining to freight classification; it has jurisdiction over all cases before regulatory bodies involving classification, and it may be required to perform such other duties as may be designated by the Executive Committee.

Decisions of the Classification Committee are determined by majority vote, two thirds of the membership constituting a quorum. Its recommendations are required to be submitted in writing to individual members of the General Committee. Unless a member of the latter committee requests the Classification Committee to withhold publication of its recommendations and to furnish additional information to substantiate its conclusions within ten days, the recommendations are considered to be approved. However, if any General Committee member is not satisfied with a recommendation and subsequent explanation thereof, he may refer it to the Executive Committee for consideration, in which event he must furnish full information in support of his appeal to the Chairman of the Classification Committee within ten days.

All actions of the Classification Committee are subject to the separate and independent approval or disapproval of the rate-making officers of the member lines. Any member line may appeal a decision within ten days to what is known as the Traffic Executive Association of Southern Territory; and, pending action, the matter involved may not be published in the Classification. Also, a member line may take independent action on any matter with which it disagrees with the findings of a committee. Likewise, the Chairman of the Executive Committee may appeal any action of his committee to the same Association if he believes the action is detrimental to the interests of Southern carriers as a whole.

(2) THE MOTOR CLASSIFICATION. Unlike the railroads' plan, motor carriers do not have separate committees representing the several classification territories. Instead, matters pertaining to classification of motor freight are handled by one organization whose activities are nation-wide in scope. It is the National Classification Board with headquarters in Washington, D. C. Membership of the Board consists of four persons who are appointed by the National Traffic Committee of the American Trucking Associations, Inc., and who devote their full time and energies to its affairs. The salaries of board members are paid directly by the American Trucking Associations, Inc.; but activities of the Board and the salaries of other personnel are financed by the motor carriers through payment of fees for participation and listing in the published Classification.[57]

The National Traffic Committee is an autonomous body answerable only to the carriers participating in the published Classification who have signed what is known as the National Motor Freight Traffic Agreement of the American Trucking Associations, Inc. This committee is composed of one hundred persons, there being at least one member from each state and the District of Columbia. Representation from a given state and the District of Columbia is determined annually in accordance with the participating fees received from carriers in each state and the District during the previous fiscal year. Any officer, owner or full-time employee both of motor carrier who is a party to the Agreement and of an organization which publishes tariffs for the account of such carriers is eligible for membership on the committee. Election of members is by ballot which is mailed to all parties to the Agreement by the Secretary on June 1 of each year; and the committee elects its officers at the first meeting following the annual election.[58]

The number of representatives by states on the Committee for the July election in 1954, based on fees paid by carriers in the respective states for participation in the National Motor Freight Classification during the 1952-53 fiscal year, is shown in the following table: [59]

---

[57] Letter from F. G. Freund, Director, Traffic Department, American Trucking Associations, Inc., Washington, dated June 26, 1953.

[58] "Agreement and Rules Relating to Procedure for the Joint Consideration and Handling of Classification Ratings, Rules and Regulations and Other National Traffic Problems of General Concern to Common Carriers by Motor Vehicle," American Trucking Associations, Inc., Washington, undated, pp. 1-6.

[59] Transport Topics, American Trucking Associations, Inc., Washington, April 5, 1954, p. 14.

Alabama 1	Louisiana 1	Ohio 8
Arizona 1	Maine 1	Oklahoma 1
Arkansas 1	Maryland 1	Oregon 1
California 3	Massachusetts 2	Pennsylvania ... 7
Colorado 1	Michigan 4	Rhode Island ... 1
Connecticut 1	Minnesota 1	South Carolina .. 1
Delaware 1	Mississippi 1	South Dakota ... 1
District of Columbia 1	Missouri 5	Tennessee 1
Florida 1	Montana 1	Texas 3
Georgia 1	Nebraska 1	Utah 1
Idaho 1	Nevada 1	Vermont 1
Illinois 7	New Hampshire ... 1	Virginia 2
Indiana 4	New Jersey 5	Washington 1
Iowa 1	New Mexico 1	West Virginia .. 1
Kansas 1	New York 9	Wisconsin 2
Kentucky 1	North Carolina 3	Wyoming 1
	North Dakota 1	

The National Classification Board conducts public hearings as may be necessary; and it handles proposals for changes in descriptions of articles, minimum truckload weights, packing requirements, ratings, rules, and other matters pertaining to motor freight classification. The Board instructs the publishing agent regarding changes to appear in the published Classification.

Chapter 10

CLASSIFICATION—
Part VI

Classification Publication. The rail Classification is issued, published, and filed in the name of an individual who serves as agent for and holds powers of attorney from all carriers participating therein.

There is a striking contrast in the agency relationships of the motor Classification. Instead of the agent being an individual, the agent for the motor Classification is a corporation, namely: the American Trucking Associations, Inc. This means that since the Association is the agent of the National Motor Freight Classification, the powers of attorney are issued in favor of ATA. This system has a definite advantage because of the indeterminate life of a corporation. Originally, the motor carriers followed the same practice as the railroads; but it was changed for very practical considerations. Some years ago, an individual died while he was serving as the individual agent of the motor carriers which necessitated the securing of new powers of attorney from some 10,000 different carriers. Today, if the issuing officer should withdraw from the organization, it would not be necessary to secure new powers of attorney from all the participating carriers because they have been issued in favor of the corporation.

Application of the Classification of the Railway Express Agency, Inc., is restricted to traffic handled by that company.

The issuing agents of Classifications from whom copies may be obtained at nominal cost are, as follows:

Official Freight Classification: W. S. Flint, Agent for lines in Official Classification, 1 Park Avenue, New York (16), New York.
Southern Freight Classification: A. H. Carson, Alternate Agent for lines in Southern Classification, 101 Marietta Street, Atlanta (3), Georgia.
Western Freight Classification: G. H. Dumas, Agent for lines in Western Classification, 202 Union Station, Chicago (6), Illinois.

Illinois Freight Classification: R. G. Raasch, Agent for lines in Illinois Classification, 236 Union Station, Chicago (6), Illinois.

Consolidated Freight Classification: Messrs. Flint, Carson, Dumas, and Raasch, as above, Mr. Dumas being Chairman.

Uniform Freight Classification: Messrs. Flint, Carson, Dumas, and Raasch, as above, Mr. Dumas being Chairman.

National Motor Freight Classification: F. G. Freund, Issuing Officer, 1424 Sixteenth Street, N. W., Washington (6), D. C.

Coordinated Motor Freight Classification: T. J. Mooney, Chief of Traffic Bureau, 262 Washington Street, Boston (8), Masschusetts.

Official Express Classification: L. R. Burke, Traffic Manager, Railway Express Agency, Inc., 219 East 42nd Street, New York (17), New York.

The size, shape, style, and other details of publication are prescribed by the Interstate Commerce Commission. Such minute phases as the size of each page, quality of paper, printer's type, "a margin of not less than five-eighths of an inch," the requirement that tables of figures "be ruled from top to bottom," format of the title page, and other details are included in the Commission's requirements. Also, the name, title, and address of the person issuing a Classification must appear "near the bottom of the title page." Even uniform abbreviations and symbols are stipulated.[1]

Mere issuance and publication of a Classification pertaining to interstate commerce in a single bound volume are not the final answers to classification matters; rather, they are just the beginning! To complicate matters and add to the complexities with which the shipper is faced, the printed Classifications are augmented by what are known as "Supplements" and "Exceptions," which, probably, the reader will assume contribute greater cloudiness to the already murky waters. Yet, they serve a positive purpose; and at least an introductory explanation is essential.

Supplements to Classification. The published volumes of both the Rail and Motor Classifications are reissued at irregular intervals. During the interim period between publication dates, necessity for changes, additions, and/or deletions arise, which are symbolic of the dynamic and non-static nature of the transportation industry. Rather than undergo the expense of printing and distributing an entirely new issue of a Classification in order to publish and make known to the public (as required by law) a correction or change which has been adopted, the less expensive expedient of printing and distributing only as many pages as may be necessary to cover

---

[1] *Tariff Circular No. 20,* Interstate Commerce Commission, Washington, effective October 1, 1928; and *Tariff Circular MF No. 3,* Interstate Commerce Commission, Washington, effective April 1, 1941.

the changes has been devised. Such supplemental data are made available to both carriers and shippers, and they are legally filed with the Interstate Commerce Commission and state regulatory bodies in accordance with their respective regulations, in separate publications knowns as "Supplements."

Sometimes, these various sorts of changes and corrections are most simple, or they may be voluminous necessitating many printed pages. To illustrate: Supplement No. 1 to *National Motor Freight Classification No. A-1,* issued on June 2, 1952, was a one-page document which merely postponed the effective date of the new Classification from June 10, to July 10, 1952. Supplement No. 2 to the same Classification changed the ratings of a few articles and established a new item which was numbered 1936, "Post Hole Augers or Diggers, KD." Immediately preceding the item number in the supplement will be found the symbol indicating that it is a new number, an asterisk (*). In contrast to the two short examples mentioned above, Supplement No. 27 to *Consolidated Freight Classification No. 20,* effective September 15, 1953, is a document of 83 pages.

Supplements are serially numbered, and the number of each appears at the top of the front page together with reference to the Classification which it supplements. On succeeding pages are reproduced the title pages of Supplement No. 1 to the Motor Classification "No. A-1" and of Supplement No. 6 to the Rail Uniform Classification "No. 2."

Sometimes, a new supplement will contain all the changes which were incorporated in previous Supplements, in which event appropriate explanation thereof will be found on the title page. However, when the front cover does not contain such a statement, it is necessary that the person checking the document refer to all previous Supplements to ascertain whether or not there has been any change in the item under consideration. For example, on the title page of the reproduced Motor Supplement No. 1 is the statement, "Supplement No. 1 contains all changes." Obviously, since that one was the first Supplement, there could be no other to which to refer. Supplement No. 2 to the same Classification, which is not reproduced herein, carries no mention of the previous supplement and, therefore, reference to Supplement No. 1 would be necessary. Had the change in Supplement No. 1 been incorporated in No. 2, then the phrase, "contains all changes," would have appeared on the face of No. 2, and reference to No. 1 would not be necessary. Or, the cover of No. 2 might have contained the statement, "Cancels Supplement No. 1," which is self explanatory.

The reproduced title page of the Rail Supplement No. 6 shows that it "Cancels Supplements 1, 2, 4, and 5," and that "Supplements

---

POSTPONEMENT SUPPLEMENT

Supplement No. 1
(Supplement No. 1 contains all changes.)

To

A. P. S. C. No. 3	P. S. C. Mo. No. 3	
Conn. P. U. C.-MF No. 3	N. H. P. S. C. No. 3	
F. R. C. No. 3	P. U. C. N. J. No. 3	**MF-I. C. C. No. 3**
G. P. S. C. No. 3	N. C. U. C. No. 3	
Ill. C. C. No. 3	P. U. C. O. No. 3	
P. S. C. I. No. TR-3	Freight Pa. P. U. C. No. 3	
L. P. S. C. No. 3	P. T. C. B. No. 3	
Me. P. U. C. No. 3	P. S. C. S. C. No. 3	
M. P. U. B. Man. No. 3	P. U. C. T. No. 3	
MF-P. S. C. Md. No. 3	V. P. S. C. No. 3	
M. D. P. U. No. 3	MF-V. C. C. No. 3	
M. P. S. C. No. 3	MF-P. S. C.-W. Va. No. 3	
M. C. No. 3		

AMERICAN TRUCKING ASSOCIATIONS, INC., AGENT

Supplement No. 1
(Supplement No. 1 contains all changes.)

To

National Motor Freight Classification No. A-1

NAMING

UNIFORM RATINGS, RULES AND REGULATIONS
(except as noted)

APPLYING ON

FREIGHT TRAFFIC COVERED BY TARIFFS GOVERNED BY THIS CLASSIFICATION, AS SUCH TARIFFS MAY PROVIDE

POSTPONEMENT NOTICE

Refer to title page of original classification and change that portion now reading "**EFFECTIVE JUNE 10, 1952**" to read "**EFFECTIVE JULY 10, 1952**".

ISSUED JUNE 2, 1952   **EFFECTIVE JUNE 10, 1952**

Issued on one day's notice under authority of special permission of the Interstate Commerce Commission No. M-79110, dated May 22, 1952.

(For state authorities, see page 2.)

ISSUED BY

F. G. FREUND, Issuing Officer
1424 SIXTEENTH STREET, N. W.
WASHINGTON 6, D. C.

Copyright, 1952, by American Trucking Associations, Inc.

Ⓐ   (9610)   (Printed in U. S. A.)

For I. C. C., C. T. C. and State Commission Nos., See Page 2.

SUPPLEMENT 6

TO

UNIFORM FREIGHT CLASSIFICATION 2

Cancels Supplements 1, 2, 4 and 5

Supplements 3 and 6 contain all changes.

RATINGS, RULES AND REGULATIONS

APPLICABLE TO

FREIGHT TRAFFIC COVERED BY TARIFFS GOVERNED BY THE UNIFORM
FREIGHT CLASSIFICATION, AS SUCH TARIFFS MAY SPECIFY.

ISSUED JANUARY 29, 1954   **EFFECTIVE MARCH 10, 1954**

(Except as otherwise provided herein)

W. S. FLINT,	A. H. CARSON,	R. G. RAASCH,	GEO. H. DUMAS,
Agent for lines in Official Classification	Alternate Agent for lines in Southern Classification	Agent for lines in Illinois Classification	Agent for lines in Western Classification
One Park Ave. at 33rd St., NEW YORK (16), N. Y.	101 Marietta Street, ATLANTA (3), GA.	236 Union Station, CHICAGO (6), ILL.	202 Union Station, CHICAGO (6), ILL.

(Edw. Keogh Ptg. Co., Chicago—20870)   46,000   Copyright, 1953, by Geo. H. Dumas

3 and 6 contain all changes." Here, reference need only be made to Nos. 3 and 6, and Nos. 1, 2, 4, and 5 may be ignored because the data contained in the latter group of supplements have been included in Nos. 3 and 6. The most recently issued supplement will show all previous supplements by their respective numbers which continue to be effective. The information contained in a supplement

cancels the same part of the basic Classification and, hence, a supplement takes precedence over the Classification.

To insure accuracy, all supplements should be filed with or attached to the Classification to which they refer. Binders may be secured for this purpose. The supplements should be examined before the Classification itself in order to ascertain if there has been any change in the matter under consideration. A good practice to follow is, immediately upon receipt of a supplement, examine it and make a pencil notation in the Classification itself at the exact point or points which are changed by the supplement, and reference to the number of the supplement. If this procedure is always followed, chances of an error when looking up something are minimized; and it will save time by eliminating the necessity of checking through each supplement every time reference is made to the Classification itself.

The format of a supplement is exactly the same as that of the basic Classification. After an irregular period of time, a new Classification is issued in which is incorporated all the changes and corrections contained in the supplements to the previous Classification and which, of course, cancels the former supplements and the older Classification. Rules of the Interstate Commerce Commission, in its respective *Tariff Circulars,* are detailed as to the number of supplements which may be issued for any one basic publication; but the Commission has granted special authority to permit supplements to aggregate up to fifty percent of the number of pages in the basic Classification.[2]

Classification Exceptions. Another phase of classification is the exception, commonly known as "Classification Exceptions" or "Exceptions to the Classification" which are published in an "Exceptions Tariff." It is these exceptions that add to the complexity of rate determination and, in the words of the Interstate Commerce Commission, "verge on the edge of incomprehensibility."[3] Although freight rates on most articles are based on the ratings contained in the published classifications, it does not necessarily follow that *all* commodities move on rates based on the classification ratings. With the greater flexibility of the new uniform Classifications by establishment of an increased number of classes, there should be a substantial reduction in the necessity for exceptions in the future. However, as was mentioned earlier,[4] many exceptions to the pre-uniform

---

[2] Letter from F. G. Freund, *op. cit.*

[3] Docket No. 28300, *Class Rate Investigation,* 1939, 281 I.C.C. 213 (286), 1951.

[4] See, pp. 71–72, above.

Classifications continue in effect, which means the old Classifications still apply to the situations involved and will continue to apply until the exceptions are canceled.

Before attempting to explain the significance of exceptions, it is advisable to clarify the confusion that exists in some instances in distinguishing between an exception rating and a change made in a supplement to the Classification. Broadly speaking, an exception may affect only a single carrier or a group of carriers that may apply the exception to application of some phase of the governing Classification in a single territory. It provides for something different from the requirements contained in the basic Classification than is applicable to all other carriers as a whole throughout the country. In contrast, a change in any particular rating or description contained in a supplement to the Classification is applicable to all carriers which participate in the Classification. Hence, an exception is not of an "interim" nature, as is a supplement pending re-issue of the Classification which it supplements. Unlike a supplement, an exception is *not* included in the following issue of the Classification. An exception absolutely supersedes the "unexcepted" provision or provisions of the basic Classification. Obviously, however, any exception which might be accepted by all carriers on a nation-wide basis would lead to appropriate revision of the published Classification.

According to the Interstate Commerce Commission, some of the reasons for establishment of exceptions are, competition between carriers, convenience and expedition in publishing, to restrict application of some particular rate and rule, to remove or reduce the amount of differences between class rates and between small quantity (l.c.l. and l.t.l.) and large (c.l. and t.l.) shipments, and to provide a quicker method for railroads to comply with the Long and Short Haul Clause of the Interstate Commerce Act. "The volume of traffic in all territories which moves under rates subject to exception ratings greatly surpasses that subject to the classification ratings." [5]

There is reproduced below an excerpt from South Exception Tariff No. 3-E, issued by the Southern Motor Carriers Rate Conference, which changed the truckload or volume rating of one particular article when transported only by the seven motor carriers named therein and under the conditions so specified. At the time, December, 1952, *National Motor Freight Classification No. 11* was effective; and it provided a rating of Class 6 (40 percent of first

---

[5] Docket No. 28300, *op. cit.*, 262 I.C.C. 447 (477), 1945.

SECTION 1—GENERAL EXCEPTIONS
(For application, see Page 53 of tariff)

EXCEPTIONS TO RATINGS OF GOVERNING CLASSIFICATION

ITEM	CAN-CELS ITEM	ARTICLES	RATINGS		VOL. MIN. WT.-LBS.
			LTL	VOL.	
31010½-A	31010½ (Sup. 63)	Covers, Fillers, Partitions or Wrappers, for packing, fibreboard, pulpboard or strawboard, flat, KD flat or folded flat, in packages (see Note A below) (Auth. Dkt. 061-76):			
		Corrugated_____	_____	27½Z	24,000
		Other than corrugated_____	_____	27½Z	30,000

Note A—Applicable only as follows:
    Via Akers Motor Lines, Incorporated, on traffic handled direct, and then only in connection with "other than corrugated", vol min wt 30,000 lbs.
    Via Alabama Highway Express, Inc., on traffic handled direct.
    Via Gordons Transports, Inc., on traffic handled direct from New Orleans, La. and Mobile, Ala. to points served direct.
    Via Great Southern Trucking Co., on traffic handled direct.
    Via Lewis and Holmes Motor Freight Corp. (See Note B).
    Via Lowther Trucking Co., J. Wesley Lowther, d/b/a, on traffic handled direct.
    Via Mason & Dixon Lines, Inc., The, on traffic handled direct.
Note B—When via Lewis and Holmes Motor Freight Corp., applicable only between points shown in SMCRC Tariff 2-F (South Group Guide), MF-ICC 425, as being served by that line direct and then only when entire transportation is via that line.

class) in Southern Territory, which was continued in Classification "No. 12" and Class 40 is assigned in the uniform "No. A-1"; and the same article was accorded an exception rating of 27½ percent of first class by railroads in Southern Territory for carload quantities. Hence, there existed a difference of 12½ percentage points between the two modes of transportation in the South and, other things being equal or in the absence of some particular extenuating circumstance, shippers of the commodity would employ the less expensive service of railroads. In order to compete with the lower, and more attractive to shippers, rating of the railroads and thereby participate in the movement of the traffic, the seven named motor carriers published a reduction in the rating from the equivalent of 40 percent (sixth class) to 27½ percent, which was granted.[6] Undoubtedly, those seven motor carriers had determined that they could handle the particular commodity at something better than out-of-pocket costs; and those carriers must have reasoned that a reduced income was better than no revenue at all, which is illustrative of the over-capacity characteristic of the transportation industry. In this case, the sole reason for lowering a rating was to meet competition of a different mode of transportation by those particular carriers who were in a position to render competitive services in one geographical area. Essentially because of volume, the revenue producing qualities of the article were attractive to those carriers, and the lower resulting freight rate will not only be of direct benefit to the shipper but also to the carriers in the future for it will tend to stimulate greater production. Obviously, the change had no affect on other motor carriers; but, in order to protect their revenues from

[6] Letter from W. M. Miller, Executive Vice President, Southern Motor Carriers Rate Conference, Atlanta, July 15, 1953.

occasional or irregular shipments in other parts of the country, the higher rating has been maintained in the Classification.

For years, the carriers have employed the use of exceptions to meet some traffic situation not covered to their shippers' satisfaction in the basic Classification. For example, a single carrier, or a group of carriers in a given geographical area smaller than a classification territory, may be enjoying an unusually heavy volume of traffic of some particular commodity; whereas, the tonnage of the same commodity moved by carriers in other parts of the country may be much less. Assume the article is assigned to Class 55 in the published Classification. The carrier, or group of carriers, hauling a large quantity of the commodity may feel justified in giving it a rating of 45. So, an exception will be issued, specifying the carrier or carriers, or the area, or the points between which the commodity will be transported at Class 45 instead of at Class 55 as stated in the Classification.

The reason for an exception is to meet some particular or unusual situation in the movement of a certain item of traffic. One of the principal causes is competition between different modes of transportation in their respective efforts to "control" the movement of a particular commodity.[7] To illustrate: an exception to the Rail Classification may be issued to provide for a lower rating or lower minimum carload weight on some article which produces attractive revenue or moves in large quantities in a certain area to meet a comparable rating or minimum weight published by the motor carriers. Since heavy shipments of the article involved may be restricted to a relatively small section of the country, railroads elsewhere would not condone the reduction nor would they agree to the change in the basic Classification which would affect all carriers everywhere. On the other hand, the reduction or change in the provisions of the Classification would be of profound significance both to rail carriers and shippers in the area under consideration, with the result that the railroads concerned would cause an exception to be issued which would be applicable only to those particular carriers in the affected area.

However, competition between rail and motor carriers is not the only cause for the "almost innumerable" exceptions. More rigid enforcement of the long-and-short-haul provisions of Section 4 of the

_____

[7] Docket No. 28310, "General Reply of Respondent Eastern and Southern Railroads to Protests and Requests for Suspension of Cancellations of Exceptions Ratings, Scheduled to become Effective May 30, 1952, or thereafter as Indicated," before the Interstate Commerce Commission, Washington (mimeo.), May 21, 1952, p. 5.

Interstate Commerce Act, the expansion of freight forwarder operations, decentralization of production by establishment of branch manufacturing units, and "simple rate-making inertia resisting the effort to bring special rates into line with a general classification, have all contributed to the great growth of classification exceptions." [8]

Widespread adoption of the exceptions began during the early 1930's, and greater utilization of the device followed a general rate increase in 1938. In 1945, the Interstate Commerce Commission showed that the railroads in Southern Territory alone had in effect some 3,500 exceptions ratings on exclusively less-than-carload traffic which were lower than the ratings on the same articles contained in the basic Classification. They had been adopted "ostensibly to meet motor competition," but the motor carriers retaliated by issuing comparable exceptions. "The same situation" existed in Western Territory and to a lesser extent in Official Territory.[9]

Since an exception is a departure from some provision contained in the basic Classification, the matters included in an exception take precedence over those covered by the Classification. There may be remote instances, however, where the class rate on some article, determined by application of an appropriate Class Tariff to the proper classification rating, may be found to be less than a rate resulting from an exception or less than a published commodity rate on the same article between two particular points. In other words, there could be two or more legally published rates resulting from the classification rating, an exception, and/or a commodity rate. Since a shipper is entitled to the lowest rate duly published in tariffs as prescribed by the Interstate Commerce Commission, he is protected by a rule comparable to the following which is included in a Commodity Rate Tariff of motor carriers: [10]

If the charges accruing under the class rates published in the following tariff, including supplements to or successive issues thereof, from and to the same points via the same routes are lower than the charges accruing under the commodity rates published in this tariff the lower charges resulting from such rates apply.

An exception may cover only one phase or part of the over-all requirements pertaining to one or more articles, which necessitates reference to the basic Classification for complete information. For

---

[8] Docket No. 28300, *op. cit.*, 262 I.C.C. 447 (476), 1945.
[9] Docket No. 28300, *op. cit.*, 281 I.C.C. 213 (283–284), 1951.
[10] *South Commodity Tariff*, Motor Freight Tariff No. 6–1, MF I.C.C. No. 416, Southern Motor Carriers Rate Conference, Atlanta, effective August 20, 1947, Item 1830, p. 71.

example, only the minimum volume weight may be reduced by an exception, which means the general description of the item, its packing requirements, its rating, applicable rules, etc., all remain the same as published in the Classification itself; hence, provisions of the Classification continue to be of vital importance to shippers and carriers, regardless of an exception. It should be mentioned in passing that, strictly speaking, a commodity rate is an exception to a Classification; but general use of the word "exception" restricts it to a Classification and excludes reference to commodity rates.

As has been explained, a tariff, containing the actual rates in terms of dollars and/or cents, is governed by the provisions of the Classification to which the tariff specifically refers. Likewise, an exceptions tariff is stated in the tariff of rates and the latter will show the extent to which the former applies. It should be understood, however, that exceptions apply only to the extent authorized in the rate tariffs, which means it is necessary, in order to insure accuracy in rate determination, to examine a rate tariff to ascertain the exceptions tariff by which it is governed. "All exceptions tariffs are alike with respect to the principles and conditions governing their application; but they are not necessarily uniform in their provisions, for each is established to meet what are, or what are thought to be, the individual requirements of different rate territories within a Classification territory." [11]

Exceptions are required to be published in accordance with the tariff publishing rules of the Interstate Commerce Commission, either by an individual carrier or by a publishing agent in behalf of a group of carriers affected by its provisions.[12] An exception tariff has a title page showing the respective identification numbers of the Interstate Commerce Commission and state commissions, name of the publishing agent, effective date, etc. It contains a Table of Contents, indices to rules and articles involved, and a list of participating carriers. However, an exceptions tariff need not be issued by the same publishing agent as the Classification to which it refers. Generally, an item in an exceptions tariff corresponds to the same item number in the basic Classification.

As was indicated earlier, an exception usually is for some particular geographical area included within a classification territory which is identified by a prefix symbol, thus: "SFA" means the exception is applicable throughout Southern Freight Association Territory; the

---

[11] Middle Atlantic States Motor Carrier Conference, Inc.: *Construction and Interpretation of Freight Tariffs*, Washington, 1944, p. 28.
[12] See, p. 306, below.

letter "A" indicates it is applicable only in the State of Alabama, "F" stands for Florida, and so on. Therefore, each exception is restricted to a particular area.

It should never be assumed that an exception rating is of secondary importance to the rating of the same article shown in the basic Classification. To the contrary, an exception completely cancels application of the Classification's rating in the area specified and for the carriers named in the exceptions tariff. When published, issued, and filed according to law, an exceptions tariff is just as legal, within the scope of its applicability, as the basic Classification itself. It may be said that an exception is particular whereas a Classification is general in its application, for the former covers only certain specified items in a restricted area while the latter includes all articles of commerce on a nation-wide basis. This distinction has been recognized by the Interstate Commerce Commission in the following language: [13]

We correct a misapprehension growing out of use of the term "exceptions" to the classification or classification ratings. The commodities so "excepted" are just as truly classified as the remaining articles which do take class ratings and to which class rates are applied. Setting apart the "excepted" commodities, and "excepting" them from the classification simply substitutes another classification rating for the general, normal rating. The new "exception" rating, by whatever term called, is a classification rating, and is subject to all requirements of the act. Whatever ratings are established, however they are called, must each be just and reasonable as compared with the ratings in effect on all other commodities, and must be free from unjust and undue prejudice to any other species of traffic whatever. . . .

An important feature is both the effective and expiration dates, because many exceptions are for a temporary period of time on an experimental basis. By the time the expiration date arrives, the experiment may have proved satisfactory to shippers and carriers alike, and its provisions will then appear in a supplement to the Classification or in a new issue of the Classification; or, the experiment may be continued for another stated period, in which event the original expiration date will be extended. However, when an expiration date is shown or is not extended, the exception ceases to be effective thereafter.

Exceptions Violate Uniformity. It was pointed out in the preceding section that exceptions are caused by unusual situations which result in departure from certain provisions of the published Classifications. The same is true of commodity rates. Over half-century

---

[13] Docket No. 28300, *op. cit.*, 281 I.C.C. 213 (287), 1951.

ago, the Interstate Commerce Commission stated: "A classification is a universal tariff from which the schedules of individual carriers should not depart, *except in cases demanded by special conditions. Commodity tariffs in restricted number may always remain a necessity.*" [14] There can be no absolute uniformity of classification ratings as long as exceptions and commodity rates remain in effect; and it would be the wildest stretch of one's imagination to anticipate their complete withdrawal in the near future, if ever.

The ideal of classification uniformity is a noble one; but its complete, nation-wide attainment is doubtful. The Commission's insistence that the carriers adopt uniform ratings is certain to simplify rate determination and eliminate former discriminatory conditions which existed among the classification territories. The fact that shortly prior to establishment of uniformity in 1952, only about 5 percent of railroad carload traffic moved on class rates based directly upon the then existing ratings of the "Consolidated" Classification, in contrast to about 10 percent on exceptions ratings and 85 percent on commodity rates, [15] should be ample proof that the pre-uniform system of classification had become outmoded and was in dire need of drastic and complete revision. For reasons which, by now, should be obvious, entire scrapping or "moth-balling" of classification would be a calamity of most serious consequences to the commerce of the nation. Yet, the prolific growth of exceptions and commodity rates prior to 1952, had caused to be sounded the death knell which reverberated in unmistakable tones across the United States. It may be said that classification ratings not only had a "one foot in the grave," but, in fact, 95 percent of the entire carcass had been buried! As these words are being written, resurrection and rehabilitation of classification to its proper fundamental place in ratemaking is in progress. There can be no doubt that, at least, partial uniformity will result in the long run in greater prosperity for the nation as a whole through the reduction of discriminatory situations which have developed through the years. For its continued insistence upon some semblance of uniformity since its creation in 1887, the Interstate Commerce Commission is to be commended. Uniformity will cause, and already it has caused, a substantial reduction in the number of exceptions and thereby it enables classification to perform its proper and more useful functions. However, for reasons which are presented below, the desirability of

---

[14] *Suspension of Western Classification No. 51*, 25 I.C.C. 442 (458), 1912. (Italics supplied.)

[15] Locklin, D. P.: *Economics of Transportation*, Fourth Edition, Irwin, Inc., Chicago, 1954, pp. 173–174.

complete uniformity is questioned, notwithstanding that the accomplishments towards interterritorial consistency are to be lauded. Possibly, it is unfortunate that the word "uniform" has been adopted because, technically, it is a misnomer and, therefore, it is misleading. Continuation of the words "Consolidated" and "National" to the respective Rail and Motor Classifications might have been a bit more realistic.

It is agreed that differences in local situations will have to be recognized, *not* by an abortion of classification ratings as heretofore, but wherever possible by appropriate changes in the freight rates themselves as they apply to the governing Classification. For example, where carrier operating costs are high in some sections of the country, it would appear reasonable that rates in that particular area be increased above what might be termed the "national average"; or, where there is a heavy and regular movement of a certain article between two points or in a localized area, a lower rate could be justified; or market competition could be met by appropriate readjustment in freight rates. Either of these situations, and possibly others, should be considered as an exceptional case to be determined upon its own merits. Neither, *per se,* should warrant disruption of the basic Classification; but, it would appear inevitable that, sooner or later, establishment of a specific commodity rate would be the most practical solution to either situation. AND a commodity rate can only mean something different from the class rate that is applicable to the rating contained in the published Classification! Immediately, the ideal of "uniformity" is destroyed.

It is recognized that the need, if there is a need, for uniformity of commodity rates is less realistic than the need for classification uniformity; but it must be understood that a commodity rate removes the article to which it is applied from the rating specified in the Classification and, therefore, a very real departure from the Classification is created. It is believed, however, that commodity rates should be restricted to very special situations where such departures from the Classification, after due and impartial investigation, are found to be justified. Wherever possible, the assignment of a commodity rate to a positive percentage of the Class 100 rate would create a direct relationship to the basic Classification and thereby eliminate many such rates which have no relationship whatsoever to the Classification.

Conditions pertaining to production, distribution, and the necessary transportation of commodities vary to a more or less extent in all parts of the country. To provide absolute, nation-wide uniform ratings on some specific commodity which is produced and shipped in great quantities in one small segment of the country would be utterly discriminatory, depending, of course, upon the uniform rating. For the vast majority of the country where irregular and small shipments of the particular article occur, a relatively high rating is justified. But for that small area where great volume of the article is produced and shipped, a high rating thereon, just for the sake of national uniformity, completely ignores the fundamental concepts of classification which were presented in Chapter 5. It ignores the existence of unused capacity of a carrier as well as the sound economic principle of "Decreasing Costs" which characterizes the transportation industry and whereby revenue derived from any source, provided it is something above out-of-pocket costs, contributes to the fixed costs of the individual carrier. From the standpoint of the public, it is contended that producers and shippers located in an area of specialization who produce great volumes of regular traffic for the carriers are entitled to a lower rating on their product than the occasional and irregular shipper of like articles. When the latter becomes competitive, or is able to demonstrate that he could be competitive with the former, then the very important factor of market competition should, and undoubtedly would, be influential with a classification committee in considering a readjustment of the rating of his commodity. The answer is either an exception or a commodity rate. It is doubtful that both exceptions and commodity rates ever will be withdrawn in their entirety, for to do so would be complete disregard of "what the traffic will bear" with the inevitable result of abandonment of production at some places, unemployment, reduction of national income, and substantial reduction in revenues to carriers which would be reflected in inferior service and higher over-all costs to industry and the consuming public in general.

Despite the efforts for complete uniformity, apparently the Interstate Commerce Commission recognizes that exceptions will continue to exist well into the future, although on a more restricted scale. Many years ago, the Commission commented that "although the carriers in the past may have been unwisely liberal in establishing exceptions . . . , such exceptions cannot now be arbitrarily eliminated without due regard for conditions existing in consequence of tariff making of this character." [16] Long before uniformity of classification became an issue, the Commission said: "As we have observed before, a classification should apply universally in

[16] Western Trunk Line Rules, 34 I.C.C. 554 (556), 1915.

the territory which it purports to cover, and exceptions should be made by individual carriers only for exceptional reasons." [17] Shortly thereafter it was held that, "an exception to the Classification ordinarily in its very nature presupposes the existence with respect to the commodity affected by it of special conditions." [18] In the two reports, particular attention is directed to the words, *"exceptional reasons"* and *"special* conditions."

More recently, the Commission said: "It is not intended that the foregoing findings with respect to uniformity shall prevent the making of exceptional classification ratings when required either by the provisions of the Interstate Commerce Act or for commercial or competitive reasons. . . ." [19] Again in 1951, "Throughout the proceeding it has been made as clear as we knew how to make it that exception rates are not within the scope of the issues in this proceeding." [20] However, the Commission admonished the carriers in the same report by saying: [21]

The same technique which they (the carriers) followed in making the exceptions . . . is available if they wish to restore the excepted commodities to the application of the present classification, or to subject them to the provisions of the new uniform classification . . . The carriers not only have a legal duty under the Act but an ethical duty as well to their customers to relieve this unnecessarily involved situation . . . That is the task of management . . . As a general proposition, we repeat what we said in numerous previous cases, as well as our earlier reports in this proceeding, that a classification must cover all commodities generally, and that while classification exceptions may be proper, when they become the rule, they should be stated in classifications. . . . While the course necessary to be followed to get rid of the exceptions may be time consuming and troublesome to the carriers, the trouble is of their own creating and maintenance.

When the Uniform Classification became effective May 30, 1952, exceptions on more than 3,500 commodities were canceled by the railroads. The greatest difficulty in compiling the new Classification was caused by exceptions, for it is reported that at least 90 percent of the research, testimony, and debate related thereto. In the words of R. E. Boyle, Jr.: [22] "We could have compiled a very acceptable Uniform Classification in six weeks had no thought been

---

[17] *Portland Chamber of Commerce v. Chicago, Milwaukee & St. Paul Railway Company,* 32 I.C.C. 188 (190).
[18] Lettuce from Texas Points, 36 I.C.C. 511 (513), 1915.
[19] Docket No. 28300, *op. cit.,* 262 I.C.C. 447 (511), 1945.
[20] Docket No. 28300, *op. cit.,* 281 I.C.C. 213 (285), 1951.
[21] *Ibid.,* pp. 286–287.
[22] See, p. 98, above.

given to exceptions ratings," [23] whereas more than six years were consumed in its preparation. Some 1,500 exceptions are still in effect on certain carload shipments, but it is anticipated many of them will be canceled in the future and the new uniform ratings applied to those commodities after further investigation.[24] Both the motor and rail carriers are studying the remaining exceptions to determine whether or not they should be incorporated into the Classification itself or canceled and the Classification rating applied to those articles which formerly were covered by exceptions. Perhaps it may be found advisable to publish exceptions to the new uniform Classifications. It must be remembered that since the existing rail and motor exceptions refer to the old Classifications, continued use of the pre-uniform publications is necessary.

It will be recalled from Chapter 6 that the predominating reason for opposition to establishment of the Uniform Classification was the manner in which uniform ratings would affect various forms of competition.[25] There has existed in the past and there exists today competition between similar and substitute articles, shippers, producers, markets, and among the carriers; but, it has been contended that "none of these forms of competition justifies diverse ratings in different territories." [26]

While, unquestionably, complete uniformity of ratings for *all* articles of commerce would reduce the existing complexity both of ratemaking by the carriers and of tariff interpretation, and the finding of an applicable rate, by shippers (and, it might be added, by many carrier employees), it is believed that ultimate attainment of *absolute* uniformity is a bit idealistic. Competition of commodities and of markets MUST be recognized as a most realistic and exceedingly potent factor in the determination of both ratings and rates, and competition will continue to be the primary cause of some kind of exception which will nullify true uniformity. Whether fortunately or unfortunately, an analysis of which is far beyond the scope of this presentation, it must be admitted that a Utopian state does not exist. It must further be recognized that the basic concepts of anti-trust legislation and of carrier regulation in the

---

[23] Boyle, R. E., Jr.: "What Do I.C.C. '28300 & 28310' Rate Changes Mean to Shippers and Carriers in the Southeast," as published in Proceedings: *The First Annual Southeastern Transportation Clinic*, Atlanta Division, University of Georgia, Atlanta, 1952, p. 14.

[24] *Ibid.*, p. 15.

[25] See, p. 96, above.

[26] Morton, Mignon: *The Complicated ABC's of Changes in Class Railroad Rates*, Industrial Research Series No. 10, University of Kansas Publications, University of Kansas, Lawrence, 1948, p. 84.

United States reflect the very fundamental and inherent quality of the American citizen to insist, through his public servants, upon the continuance of competitive influences in price determination for transportation services as well as for tangible goods. There is no true monopoly in transportation services in the United States. Although there may be only one railroad, one airline, or one certificated motor carrier serving numerous communities, the private airplane, the private automobile, the private truck, the private barge, all collectively and each individually, completely break down any semblance of monopoly. If a railroad or certificated motor carrier rate is too high for shippers, which means a rate that is higher than the value of the service to potential shippers of freight, frequently they will acquire and use their own vehicles, which is obvious to the most casual observer anywhere in the country. Adaptability of the privately-owned vehicle as a real competitor to certificated common carrier motor truck lines and railroad companies was recognized by the Interstate Commerce Commission when it reported to Congress in 1939: ". . . under modern conditions the shipper often has the opportunity to furnish transportation with his own private facilities. He can hardly be expected to pay rates which rise materially above the cost of such private transportation." [27] That statement was in 1939, before establishment of many enormous private fleets of motor trucks and, to a lesser degree in so far as numbers of transportation units are concerned but greater from the standpoint of tonnage capacity, inland waterway barges by producers for the purpose of distributing their products!

It was mentioned at the beginning of this section that both exceptions and commodity rates result in non-uniformity of classification ratings by some carrier(s) at some place(s) in the country. It is the firm belief of the writer that exceptions and/or commodity rates *always* will exist for practical considerations pertaining to individual situations caused primarily by the existence of some form of competition. For the carriers to entirely abolish them would be utter (and foolish) disregard of another most practical aspect of ratemaking, "a rate which the traffic will bear"; and to do so would be injurious to carriers and shippers alike in those particular geographical areas so affected. Physical and transportation characteristics which influence the determination of a rating have been presented. The fact must be recognized that peculiar traffic conditions concerning certain individual commodities exist in different

---

[27] *Fifty-Third Annual Report of the Interstate Commerce Commission*, Government Printing Office, Washington, 1939, p. 28.

parts of the country which prohibit, if the traffic is to move, literal compliance with a uniform classification. Notwithstanding that in the future, uniform ratings may be extended westward from the Continental Divide to the Pacific Ocean, the real necessity for certain exceptions and/or commodity rates in particular instances should be apparent, although the number of such necessary exceptional ratings or rates undoubtedly will and should be reduced. The achievement of absolute uniformity of classification ratings therefore is considered to be more idealistic than realistic, for as long as a single exception or commodity rate is effective in some area for some article, there can never be true uniformity; and such exceptional situations are bound to occur and to be continued into the future.

It is agreed, however, that competition between carriers and between different modes of transportation generally constitutes little justification for non-uniform ratings; but, doubtless, they too will be continued into the future as exceptional or unusual situations arise. Disruption of uniform ratings by a carrier for the *sole* purpose of meeting competition of another carrier, as rail versus motor, amounts to a form of rate cutting which, *per se*, was condemned many years ago as being repugnant to the public interest. Where carrier competition alone is the deciding factor, appropriate adjustment of the freight rates themselves in the area affected would be more feasible than disruption of classification uniformity.

Likewise, where one mode of transportation possesses an "inherent" advantage over another—as the water carrier for bulk shipments, the railroad for movement of heavy commodities and mass transportation, the motor carrier for its convenience and flexibility of operations—its favorable position to earn reasonable revenues should not be jeopardized by the greediness of another kind of carrier to participate in the movement of certain traffic for which it is not particularly adapted. To do so can only cause reduction of carrier income; and the resulting rate-cutting tends to disregard the mandate contained in that portion of the National Transportation Policy adopted by Congress in 1940, "to provide for fair and impartial regulation of all modes of transportation subject to the provisions of this Act, so administered as to recognize and preserve the inherent advantages of each." [28] However, where carriers of two competing modes of transportation have comparable characteristics for providing a particular service or for handling certain commodi-

---

[28] *The Interstate Commerce Act,* Revised to November 1, 1951, Government Printing Office, Washington, 1951, p. 1.

ties—as, in some areas, rail and motor in the movement of textiles, steel, canned goods, liquor, tobacco products, etc.—and, therefore, are truly competitive, some diversion from absolute uniformity is justified to meet the particular situation. In the interest of classification uniformity, wherever practical such conditions should be reflected in the freight rates themselves rather than by modifying the classification, which is the position taken by the Interstate Commerce Commission.[29]

Classification Changes. A carrier, shipper, traffic association, or any interested person who desires a change in or an addition to an existing published Classification has the legal right to request such a change. He submits his proposal or complaint in writing on a prescribed form to the appropriate classification committee which, as was stated earlier, may settle the matter informally by correspondence or conference; but, if of sufficient importance or on request of the applicant, the proceeding will be placed on a Docket for hearing.[30]

Although the actual ratings are determined by a committee representing the carriers, all users of carrier services may express their views individually or collectively concerning matters of interest to them, and, furthermore, they have the right to be heard. Any person may appear at a public hearing where he may present his views either in support of or in opposition to the proposal under consideration. A hearing is not restricted to the proponent of an item on the Docket nor to carrier representative; hence, hearings are *public* in every sense of the word, and ratings are not allocated in an arbitrary manner. The carriers are anxious to obtain the views of their customers; but, unfortunately, many shippers do not avail themselves of the opportunity and, after a rating is changed or a new rating established, frequently they bitterly complain about alleged discriminatory and arbitrary action of the carriers. Shipper organizations, such as, the National Industrial Traffic League, Southern Traffic League, chambers of commerce, etc., actively participate in these proceedings in the interests of their membership.

It is believed a classification committee never will intentionally set a high rating on a given commodity for the sole reason of anticipated high revenues. The committee realizes thoroughly that an unduly high rating will reduce the volume of traffic, divert the business to competing carriers or modes of transportation, encourage public consumption of competing or substitute commodities,

---

[29] Docket No. 28300, *op. cit.*, 262 I.C.C. 447, 1945.
[30] See, p. 172, above.

or influence the producer of the article to move his plant to another location, either of which will result in an ultimate reduction of revenue to the carrier. Since, as has been frequently emphasized, the transportation industry is characterized by the economic principle of decreasing costs, traffic volume is always a matter of profound significance. Therefore, a committee would display lack of wisdom to assign a rating so high as to drive away shipments of the article. Generally, ratings are designed so that the applicable freight rates will yield the carriers sufficient revenues as a whole to cover all costs and provide a fair return; and, at the same time, to be sufficiently low as to attract the movement of traffic without discrimination or prejudice to any commodity, place, or person.

The public hearings conducted by the committees permit representations to be made on both sides of a matter under consideration; and the impartial weighing of the facts so presented enables the committee to arrive at an equitable rating or decision, fair to carriers and shippers alike. A committee cannot be expected to be aware of all problems confronting each individual shipper in producing, manufacturing, and/or distributing his product in a competitive market; and it is incumbent upon the industrial traffic manager to make his peculiar problems known to the committee. Committees are in desperate need of full and complete information from shippers concerning the shipment of their goods in order that fair ratings may be established and inequitable situations may be corrected. Failure of industrial traffic managers to participate in these hearings, when their products or competing products are on a Docket, both defeats the purpose of an adequate procedure and inevitably results in an increase in over-all shipping costs. As Cushman states: [81]

. . . an acute shortcoming in the form of shipper and consignee delinquency in attending such meetings all but completely denies attainment of the desired objectives of classification docket procedure. The lethargic attitude on the part of the users of transportation has led to a condition of unilateral rather than co-operative classification determination, a circumstance that perhaps has resulted in a lack of proper protection of the interests of the shipper and consignee when classification ratings are determined, but nonetheless a circumstance for which the users of the transportation service are themselves principally at fault.

In the final analysis, it is only from testimony presented at these public hearings by both carriers and shippers, opponents and proponents, that a committee can render impartial opinions and rulings on classification matters.

[81] Cushman, F. M.: *Transportation for Management*, Prentice-Hall, New York, 1953, p. 221.

In proceedings involving the Rail Classification, hearings are conducted by a territorial committee which submits its recommendations to the Consolidated Classification Committee, and the latter takes action on matters included on the Docket. However, if the proposal is strictly a territorial matter, action of the territorial committee is final. The decision of the Consolidated Committee is submitted back to the territorial committee which then submits it to the member lines for approval or rejection. If approved, the Consolidated Committee is notified and the change appears in the published classification or supplement.[32]

Proposals involving the Motor Classification are submitted directly to the National Classification Board in a manner comparable to the railroad procedure. Dockets are issued and public hearings are conducted "at such places as the Board may deem proper and adequate." However, since there are no territorial committees in the motor freight industry, the proposals are handled exclusively by the one Board, and a majority vote of its membership governs the action taken. When a matter is approved, the Publishing Agent is so instructed and the change appears in a supplement or in a new issue of the Classification. If a proposal is rejected by the Board, the proponent thereof may appeal the Board's decision to the National Classification Committee. Also, if a minimum of fifteen carriers participating in the Motor Classification or eight members of the Committee object to the Board's findings, under prescribed conditions their written objections cause an automatic appeal to the National Committee. A majority of the Committee present at a meeting decides whether an appealed proposal is approved, rejected, or re-submitted to the Board.[33]

Action of either the rail or motor classification organizations may be taken before the Interstate Commerce Commission, and the Commission's decision may be appealed in the courts.

---

[32] See, p. 177, above.

[33] "Rules of Procedure for Changes in the National Motor Freight Classification," American Trucking Associations, Inc., Washington, Article IV.

Chapter 11

CLASSIFICATION RULES—
Part I

Just as commercial banks prescribe rules covering deposits, and various industries determine procedures to aid them in the conduct of their business, so have carriers formulated regulations to assist them in their dealings with their customers in the shipment of freight. These carrier regulations are the Classification Rules which, in general, constitute the "Bible" of proper shipping practices.

Since the early days of for-hire transportation, common carriers have established regulations specifying the conditions under which goods will be accepted for transport, certain obligations of shippers, and other matters pertaining to the shipment of property. For years, there was no standardization of the regulations among carriers; and, generally, the rules were designed for the protection of the carrier at the expense of the shipper. As the railroad industry developed in the United States, these regulations appeared in the railroads' published Classifications, and they became known as the Rules of Freight Classification.

With the advent of federal regulation of carriers, Congress directed removal of the unreasonably discriminatory aspects of the rules; but, for many years there was no uniformity in the rules which were published in the different Classifications. These differences caused considerable confusion to shippers of interterritorial traffic, and they were a source of frequent discriminations. In fact, the lack of uniformity of the rules was even a greater evil than the lack of uniformity of ratings.[1] Uniformity was achieved in 1919, with publication of the first Consolidated Classification.[2]

---

[1] Jones, Eliot: *Principles of Railway Transportation*, The Macmillan Company, New York, 1931, p. 146.
[2] See, p. 84, above.

Today, the Interstate Commerce Act requires common carriers subject to the Act to "establish, observe, and enforce just and reasonable" rules and practices, and it specifically states that any violation thereof is unlawful.[3] In addition, Part II of the Act, governing motor carriers, states, in part, that "it shall be the duty of every common carrier of property by motor vehicle" to comply with such regulations as they apply "to the manner and method of presenting, marking, packing, and delivering property for transportation."[4] Therefore, since 1887 for railroads, 1906 for pipe lines and the present Railway Express Agency, 1935 for motor carriers, 1940 for domestic water carriers, and 1942 for freight forwarders, the Interstate Commerce Act has required "just and reasonable" rules and practices of all common carriers engaged in interstate commerce which are subject to the Act. Air carriers are subjected to a comparable provision in the Civil Aeronautics Act of 1938.[5]

Purpose of Rules. Classification rules are the basic regulations governing the shipment of goods, and they contain a wealth of highly technical information. They cover practically every situation which may occur in the shipment of freight.[6] As Colton comments, literal observance constitutes "good shipping practices."[7]

Classification rules are the "legal code" of shipping regulations. They set forth the conditions under which carriers will provide the service of transportation, together with the rights and obligations of both shippers and carriers. They have been compiled by, and represent the result of many years of technical experience on the part of traffic and classification experts. They have been devised to assist carriers in the conduct of their business and to enumerate certain responsibilities of shippers. Therefore, the rules may be said to supplement the terms and conditions of the bill of lading contract, and define the relationship which exists between carrier and shipper.

The subject matter covered by each rule is shown in the "Index to Rules" which is listed in the Table of Contents of the published Classifications. For example: if a shipper desires to forward his freight C.O.D., he should refer to the Index of the Classification

---

[3] Interstate Commerce Act, Sec. 1 (6), Sec. 216 (b), Sec. 305 (a), Sec. 404 (a).

[4] *Ibid.*, Sec. 216 (b).

[5] Civil Aeronautics Act, Sec. 404 (a).

[6] Van Metre, T. W.: *Transportation in the United States,* The Foundation Press, Chicago, 1939, pp. 218–219.

[7] Colton, R. C.: *Practical Handbook of Industrial Traffic Management,* Funk & Wagnalls Company, New York, 1948, p. 42.

governing the carrier he proposes to use, where he will find reference both to the appropriate rule and the page on which the rule appears. The steps involved in securing the desired information are, as follows: upon consulting the Table of Contents in the front of *National Motor Freight Classification No. A-2,* effective July 7, 1954, he will observe the Index to Rules are on pages 154-A and 155-A; after turning the page 154-A, he will find the numerous subjects covered by the rules listed in alphabetical order, and that C.O.D. shipments are subject to rule No. 31 on pages 166-A and 167-A; finally, he will obtain complete information as to regulations and charges for such shipments upon reference to those pages. Exactly the same procedure applies to rail shipments subject to *Uniform Freight Classification No. 2,* effective December 10, 1953, in which the C.O.D. rule will be found on pages 158–159.

Since every freight tariff is governed by some particular Classification, the rules of the latter are of utmost importance in the application of a tariff. It has been pointed out earlier that classification is the foundation of ratemaking.[8] Carriers are bound to comply with the rules contained in the published Classification to which they subscribe and in which they participate. It should be understood that a carrier participating in a Classification may modify application of any rule either by means of an exception[9] or by appropriate statement in some particular tariff. It should be obvious, therefore, that a thorough understanding of the principles contained in the rules is an absolute necessity for effective traffic management, regardless of whether the individual is in the service of a carrier or in the service of an industrial traffic department. However, it is not to be presumed that the rules should be committed to memory; in fact, no attempt should be made to memorize them, because, like ratings and rates, rules are changed from time to time, and if one depends upon his or her memory it is highly probable that resulting costly errors will be inevitable. The important points are to possess a general knowledge of the *principles* of the rules themselves, to know that a rule exists covering some particular shipping situation, to know where and how to find that rule in the applicable published Classification, and to know how to interpret it. As Dean William J. Knorst, of the College of Advanced Traffic in Chicago, has stated, "it is not uncommon that more than one construction may be given to a particular rule," with the result that the "many controversies which have arisen from time to time" have

---

[8] See, p. 75, above.
[9] See, pp. 185–186, above.

had to be interpreted by the Interstate Commerce Commission and by the courts of the land. "Common sense, practical application, and custom have served with respect to others." [10]

Interpretation of some of the rules, admittedly, is made difficult by the complicated language adopted by the authors thereof. One is tempted to wonder, particularly the layman, if the complex and confusing manner in which some rules are presented is intentional so that the occasional shipper gives up and leaves interpretation to the whims of some carrier employee! [11] It is worthy of note that the new rail Classification consumes 40 pages of 11 by 7½ inches per sheet to portray its rules, much of which is in fine print and in closely arrayed lines.[12] In contrast, the motor Classification requires only 14 pages for presentation of its rules.[13] This difference in space requirements for presentation may be attributed to the wider variety of rail rules.

Another purpose of the rules is to endeavor to reduce loss and damage to shipments. It will be observed later in analyzing the rules that great detail is devoted to proper marking of packages, and to differentiation of various types of containers, such as bags, bales, barrels, baskets, boxes, buckets, bundles, carboys, cartons, coils, crates, drums, hampers, kits, pails, reels, rolls, etc. The prevention of loss or damage is a vital matter of common interest to both carrier and shipper.

It should not be assumed that the Classification rules are static. Instead, they reflect the dynamic nature of the transportation industry, although one author states: "carriers are adept in thinking up new conditions which should be attached to their business relations with their customers." [14] From time to time, a rule may be modified or eliminated, and new rules are created to conform with new ship-

---

[10] Knorst, W. J.: *Transportation and Traffic Management*, Fourth Edition, College of Advanced Traffic, Chicago, 1952, Vol. 1, p. 123.

[11] An excellent appraisal of the complexity of the rail Classification has been made by Professor Thurman W. Van Metre, of Columbia University, as follows: "When one reads the present (rail) classification rules, one is inclined to believe that classification authorities, like lawyers and landlords, think that the more words employed in framing a document the more impressive and 'legal' the document becomes, and one is inclined to wish that the language of many of the rules could be overhauled in the interest of simplicity and clarity. As a matter of fact, rules have at times been published in such involved and muddy language that it has been impossible for all interested parties to agree upon their precise meaning." Van Metre, T. W.: *Industrial Traffic Management*, McGraw-Hill Book Company, New York, 1953, p. 65.

[12] *Uniform Freight Classification No. 2*, Consolidated Classification Committee, Chicago, effective December 10, 1953, pp. 124–163.

[13] *National Motor Freight Classification No. A-2*, American Trucking Associations, Inc., Washington, effective July 7, 1954, pp. 156-A–169-A.

[14] Van Metre, *Industrial Traffic Management, op. cit.*, p. 64.

ping practices and to meet changing transportation conditions. Any rule that is changed, deleted, or added during the period between publication of successive issues of a Classification is shown in a Supplement to the Classification [15] pending publication of a new Classification.

Extent of Rules. The current rail *Consolidated Freight Classification No. 20,* effective October 15, 1951, contains rules numbered 1 to 52; but since there is none numbered 23, 37, 44, or 51, the total is 48 rules. *Uniform Freight Classification No. 2,* effective December 10, 1953, has rules numbered 1 to 53, with none numbered 26, 33, 37, 51, leaving a total of 49.

For motor carriers, *National Motor Freight Classification No. 13,* effective July 7, 1955, contains rules consecutively numbered 1 to 34, except there is no No. 12; but there are also rules numbered 5½, 12½, and 14½, making a total of 36. There are 37 rules similarly numbered, including No. 12, in the uniform *National Motor Freight Classification No. A-2,* effective July 7, 1954. There are 29 consecutively numbered rules in the New England *Coordinated Motor Freight Classification No. 7,* effective January 8, 1954.

Motor & Rail Rules. With some exceptions, which will be described later, the rules of the major motor and rail Classifications are similar in scope. The differences are caused by the physical characteristics peculiar to the two modes of transportation. Correlation of the respective rules by subject matter is presented in the following table.

CLASSIFICATION RULES

Rule Numbers

Subject of Rule	National Motor Freight Classification Rule No.	New England Coord. Motor Freight Classification Rule No.	Uniform Rail Classification Rule No.
Bill of Lading...............	1	2, 26, 27, 28	1
Description of Articles.........	2	6	2
Property of Extraordinary Value.	3	16	3
Damage by Freight...........	4	15	4
General Packing Requirements...	5	4	5, 40, 41
Containers for Explosives.......	5½	4	40
Marking......................	6	5	6
Information on Bill of Lading....	7	3	7
Advancing of Charges..........	8	14	8
Guarantee of Charges..........	9	13	9

[15] See, p. 181, above.

CLASSIFICATION RULES

	Rule Numbers		
Subject of Rule	National Motor Freight Classification Rule No.	New England Coord. Motor Freight Classification Rule No.	Uniform Rail Classification Rule No.
Charges on Gross Weight.......	10	7	11
Mixed Shipments..............	11	8, 9	10, 12
Minimum Charges.............	12	29	13
Minimum Weights.............	12½	—	12
Definition of Shipments.........	13	1	14, 15, 16
Rule of Analogy..............	14	23	17
Iron, Steel, Rubber, Plastics, Metals......................	14½	1	25, 28
Combination Articles..........	15	11	18
Complete Articles.............	16	12	20
Knocked Down Articles.........	17	1	19
Nested Articles................	18	1	21
Wooden Articles...............	19	—	22
Glass & Earthenware Containers.	20	4	5
Heavy or Bulky Articles........	21	—	27
Dunnage......................	22	18	30
Capacity & Type of Vehicles....	23	17	31
Disposition of Fractions.........	24	24	36
Special & Terminal Charges.....	25	—	—
Commodity Rates..............	26	19	38
Explosives & Dangerous Articles.	27	—	39
Advertising Matter.............	28	10	45
Reshipping Documents.........	29	21	42
Articles of Large Dimensions....	30	—	29
C.O.D. Regulations............	31	20	47
Bags for Reconditioning Shipments......................	32	—	50
Test Shipments................	33	—	49
Minimum Weights.............	34	8	34
Freight in Bunkers of Refrigerator Cars............	—	—	23
Freight in Excess of Full Carload.	—	—	24
Ice for Refrigeration...........	—	—	32
Tank Car Freight..............	—	—	35
Attendants with Shipments......	—	—	43
Method of Canceling Items.....	—	—	44
Definitions....................	—	—	46
Reference to Contents..........	—	25	48
Weights on Liquefied Petroleum Gas......................	—	—	52
Weights on Butadiene..........	—	—	53
Density on "Compressed" Ratings.....................	—	22	—
Claims.......................	—	30	—

INDEX TO RULES

Rule No.	Motor (page)	Rail (page)	New England (page)	Rule No.	Motor (page)	Rail (page)	New England (page)
1	8	8	41, 48, 50, 52	25	60	48	76
2	8	8	8	26	53	—	8
3	11	11	12	27	29	23	8
4	22	22	16, 19, 21-A, 22	28	55	48	8
5	16	16, 21-A	19	29	14	29	39
5½	19	—	—	30	29	25	78
6	19	19	8	31	60	27	END
7	12	12	32	32	21-A	71	
8	57	57	34	33	21-A	—	
9	31	31	34	34	62	62	
10	32	34	55	35	END	71	
11	34	32	48	36		60	
12	39	34	49	38		53	
12½	40	—	—	39		29	
13	41	39	31	40		16, 19	
14	47	41	57	41		16	
14½	48	—	—	42		14	
15	48	41	22	43		74-A	
16	49	41	11	44		75	
17	50	47	27	45		55	
18	52	48	25	46		76	
19	53	50	53	47		60	
20	21-A	49	60	48		76	
21	23	52	14	49		21-A	
22	25	53	77	50		21-A	
23	27	29	29, 47	52		76	
24	60	29	29, 60	53		77	

Analysis of Rules. A better understanding and appreciation of the rules will be obtained by explaining them according to subject matter, rather than presenting them in the heterogeneous manner in which they appear in numerical order in the published Classifications. Furthermore, a glance at the above table reveals that the different Classifications do not present comparable rules in the same sequence and that there is no standardization in numbering. Major Charles C. Glasgow, Jr., and Professor Gilbert L. Gifford have grouped the rules according to subject matter into five categories, as outlined below.[16]

1. Billing Rules including
   Motor Rules 1, 2, 3, 7, 29.
   Rail Rules 1, 2, 3, 7, 42.

---

[16] Glasgow, C. C., Jr., and Gifford, G. L.: *An Analysis of Motor Carrier Tariffs,* Revised Edition, The University of Tennessee, Knoxville, 1952, p. 22.

2. Packing & Marking Regulations, including
    Motor Rules 5, 5½, 6, 20, 32, 33
    Rail Rules 5, 6, 40, 49, 50
3. Loading & Unloading Regulations, including
    Motor Rules 4, 21, 22, 23, 27, 30
    Rail Rules 4, 23, 24, 27, 29, 30, 31, 39
4. Rating of Goods, including
    Motor Rules 9, 10, 11, 12, 12½, 13, 14, 14½, 15, 16, 17, 18, 19,
        26, 28
    Rail Rules 9, 10, 11, 12, 13, 14, 15, 16, 17, 18, 19, 20, 21, 22, 25,
        28, 38, 45
5. Special Rules, including
    Motor Rules 8, 24, 25, 31, 34
    Rail Rules 8, 32, 34, 35, 36, 43, 44, 46, 47, 48, 52, 53

For convenience and simplicity in referring to rules by number, the letter "R" preceding a number will indicate the number of a rule in the rail *Uniform Freight Classification,* "M" will refer to the *National Motor Freight Classification,* and "NE" will represent the New England motor carriers' *Coordinated Motor Freight Classification,* thus: "M-2" will mean rule No. 2 in the Motor Classification. Since the complete rules are published in the respective Classifications, only appropriate excerpts will appear herein. Unless otherwise indicated, all quotations in the following explanations are taken directly from the rules themselves. For the sake of brevity, shipments moving on less-than-truckload, less-than-carload, or any quantity ratings will be referred to herein as "small" shipments; truckload and carload, as "volume" shipments.

When applying a rule in actual practice, the reader is cautioned to refer directly to the rule itself in the appropriate Classification.

BILLING RULES

Use of the Uniform Bill of Lading (M-1, R-1, NE-2-26-27-28). The provisions of this rule have been presented earlier in the discussion of bills of lading; but, for review at this time, the reader should refer to pages 30–31, above. In summary, use of the uniform bill of lading is required for all shipments by common carriers, unless the shipper elects to bind the carrier by the more inclusive liability requirements of the common law, in which event the shipper is required to pay ten percent above the applicable published tariff rate and so notify the initial carrier who must make appropriate endorsement on the face of the bill of lading as set forth in the rule. Shippers may print their own bills of lading, but the terms and conditions of the uniform bill of lading apply regardless of whether or not they are printed thereon. Marine insurance is not assumed by the carrier unless specifically stated in applicable tariffs, which means, in the absence of a tariff provision, shippers must make their own arrangements for insurance coverage of marine perils.

Descriptions on Bills of Lading and Inspection of Property (M-2, R-2, NE-6). There are two sections of this rule in the Rail and New England Classifications; three, in the Motor. Section 1 contains the requirement that descriptions of goods on the bill of lading must conform with those in the Ratings Section of the Classification.[17] "Including packing specifications where different rates are provided on the same article according to the manner in which it is prepared for shipment." Also, the bill of lading must show the "number of articles, packages or pieces."

Intentional misdescription of an article by a shipper in order to benefit from a lower rate is fraud, and, upon conviction, he is subject to a maximum fine of $5,000 or two years' imprisonment "in the penitentiary," or both; likewise, the same penalty is applicable to any carrier employee "who shall knowingly and willfully, directly or indirectly," connives to permit such fraud.[18] However, many honest errors occur in describing shipments; and, as indicated above, many articles carry different ratings according to the type of container or manner in which packed for shipment.

In order to be certain that the correct legal rate is assessed on a shipment, both the industrial traffic manager and the rate clerk of the carrier should be certain the shipment is described on the bill of lading in exactly the same technical language that is shown in the appropriate Classification. Otherwise, either the shipper exposes himself to an overcharge, or the carrier may not realize the full amount to which it is entitled for providing the service of transportation. Managements of carriers have no desire to overcharge their customers; but when a shipment is described in an inaccurate manner, they have no alternative other than to assess the rate applicable to the shipment as it is described on the bill of lading. Accurate description is strictly a shipper's responsibility! It should always be remembered that a carrier is required by law to collect the legal applicable charges, that the shipper (or owner of the goods) must pay those charges, that the rates published in tariffs are public information, and that ignorance of tariff and Classification provisions is no excuse for failure of the shipper to pay and the carrier to collect those charges.

A description, rating, or rate, when properly published in accord-

---

[17] See, p. 160, above.
[18] Interstate Commerce Act, Sections 10 (3), 222 (c), 421 (c).

ance with requirements of the Interstate Commerce Act, has the dignity of a statute; and no one has authority to deviate from either as long as it remains in effect. If there occurs an error in the description of an article in a duly published Classification, it is usually corrected through the Special Permission procedures of the Interstate Commerce Commission.

Section 1 of this rule is most important. In the rush and bustle of daily activities, both shipper and carrier employees may overlook it. It is quoted below:

To insure assessment of the correct freight charges and avoid infractions of Federal and State laws, shippers should acquaint themselves with the descriptions of articles in the tariffs under which they ship; and commodity descriptions in shipping orders and bills of lading should conform to those in the applicable tariff, including packing specifications where different rates are provided on the same article according to the manner in which it is prepared for shipment. Shipping orders and bills of lading must specify number of articles, packages or pieces.

Regardless of errors in describing a shipment on the bill of lading, it has long been well established that the nature of the article itself and the manner in which it is packed govern the application of freight charges. If, after acceptance of shipment by a carrier, an error in the description is discovered causing an overpayment of freight charges applicable to the correct description, the carrier is required to refund the difference to the party who paid the freight bill. Likewise, if the error resulted in payment of freight charges less than the amount provided in the applicable tariff, the owner of the shipment is required to reimburse the carrier for the amount of the undercharge. Some of the cases sustaining this requirement are listed in the footnote below.[19]

The carriers have organized autonomous bureaus on a regional basis which cooperate with shippers concerning correct descriptions and proper methods of packing. Representatives of the bureaus

---

[19] *Southern Pacific Terminal Company v. Interstate Commerce Commission,* 219, U. S. 498, 1911.
Ohio Railroad Commission v. Worthington, 225 U. S. 101, 1927.
Texas & New Orleans Railroad Company v. Sabine Tram Company, 227 U. S. 111, 1913.
Baer Brothers v. Denver & Rio Grande Railroad Company, 233 U. S. 479, 1914.
Railroad Commission of Louisiana v. Texas & Pacific Railway Company, 229 U. S. 336, 1913.
Illinois Central Railroad Company v. Louisana Railroad Commission, 236 U. S. 157, 1915.
Kanotex Refining Company v. Atchison, Topeka & Santa Fe Railway Company, 34 I.C.C. 271, 1915.
Rates on Railroad Fuel and Other Coal, 36 I.C.C. 1, 1915.

make spot inspections of shipments in the carriers' terminals or freight stations and when errors in descriptions, weights, or packaging are discovered, they are reported to the carrier's agent who should arrange for necessary correction of the bill of lading covering the particular shipment involved. Frequently, a representative of a bureau personally calls on shippers, particularly those who are habitual in making errors, explains the mistakes, and generally accomplishes good results for both shippers and carriers. Another reason for establishment of a bureau representing all carriers of the same mode of transportation in a given area is that its periodic inspections prevent any possible collusion between an individual carrier employee and a favored shipper. By permitting a shipper to misdescribe his freight in order to secure a rate which is lower than the lawful rate would be a simple means of rebating which, of course, is strictly forbidden by law. Sooner or later, an inspector of a bureau will discover and expose such discriminatory irregularities. The work of the bureaus is essentially constructive, definitely not subversive or punitive. In Southern Territory, the organization sponsored and financed by motor carriers is the Weighing & Research Branch of the Southern Motor Carriers Rate Conference; by railroads, the Southern Weighing & Inspection Bureau. Inquiries from shippers regarding their problems of preparing goods for shipment always are welcomed by these organizations, and their assistance in reducing shipping costs and in preventing damage to freight has been highly commendatory.

Correct description of a shipment on the bill of lading assures the shipper of the lowest lawful rate being applied to his shipment. There is only one correct description of an article for shipping purposes, and it is the one published in the appropriate Classification. The Motor Classification requires that the number of pieces comprising a shipment must be indicated on the bill of lading; but the Rail Classification prescribes that information only for less-than-carload shipments.

Section 2 of the rule gives the carrier the right to inspect the contents of any package when it is considered by the terminal manager or carrier's agent advisable to determine the actual character of a shipment in order to protect the carrier's interest from a revenue standpoint. If a shipment is found to be incorrectly described after such inspection, the rule is explicit in stating that "freight charges *MUST* be collected according to proper description." In effect, this provision supplements Section 7 of the terms and conditions of the bill of lading contract. Hence, if inspection reveals a shipment has been incorrectly described resulting in the rate applied to the shipment being different from that which should apply, the freight charges must be adjusted accordingly. If the corrected charges are less than those published in the applicable tariff, the difference between the erroneously stated rate and the legal rate must be paid by the shipper or consignee; but if the charges paid are greater than the legal rate, the shipper or consignee is entitled to an appropriate refund from the carrier.

Section 3 of the rule in the Motor Classification is comparable to a paragraph in Section 1 of the rule in the Rail and New England Classifications. It requires that the description of explosives and dangerous articles must conform to the descriptions contained in a special explosives tariff together with descriptions specified in the Classification or the tariff in which the applicable rate is published, when there is a difference in such descriptions.

Property of Extraordinary Value Not Accepted (M-3, R-3, NE-16). This is a simple rule by which carriers announce they will not accept for shipment such valuable articles as bank bills, coin or currency, deeds, drafts, notes, valuable papers, jewelry, postage stamps, revenue stamps, letters, precious metals, precious stones, etc. The rule is entirely proper, because the freight transportation service is not designed to handle articles of high value which require constant personal protection. The Railway Express Agency provides adequate facilities and, when necessary, guards to insure safe transportation of such shipments. Under conditions of a special contract, however, common carriers of general commodities may agree to transport such articles.[20]

Information to Be Shown on Bills of Lading & Shipping Orders, and the Handling of "Order" Bills of Lading (M-7, R-7, NE-3). The principles contained in this rule were presented in the discussion of bills of lading.[21] The rule provides that the bill of lading may contain only one consignor, one consignee, and one destination, and that the name of the county must be shown when there are two places of the same name in one state. It specifies the conditions under which an order bill of lading is issued, the requirement that the properly endorsed original copy thereof must be surrendered to the

---

[20] "It should be further understood that while a common carrier, as such, must transport all commodities for whomsoever may desire its service, the request for transportation must be reasonable. It is apparent that to request or demand a carrier to transport such articles is unreasonable, and, by proper tariff rule, the carrier may limit the service it holds itself out to perform subject, always, to review by the Commission and the bounds of reason." Knorst, *op. cit.*, Vol. 1, p. 129.

[21] See, pp. 40–47, above.

carrier prior to delivery of the freight, and the conditions under which delivery may be accomplished without surrender of the document. The rule in the Rail Classification also provides for conditions where freight may be delivered at some point other than the consignee's address; [22] and it is more detailed than the rule in the Motor Classification concerning delivery of shipments covered by either the straight or the order bill of lading.

This rule is an important safeguard to both the delivering carrier and the true owner of a shipment moving on an order bill of lading. As was pointed out earlier, if such a shipment is delivered without surrender to the carrier of the original copy of the order bill of lading, properly endorsed by the ultimate consignee, the carrier is liable for the invoice value of the goods. From the standpoint of risk in effecting delivery to the proper person, an "order notify" shipment is one of the most hazardous for a carrier to handle. This rule provides protection to the carrier.

If for any reason whatsoever the properly endorsed original order bill of lading cannot be surrendered, the terminal manager or carrier's agent at final destination of such a shipment, after he has satisfied himself that the person requesting delivery of the shipment is entitled to receive it, can do only one of three things specified in the rule, viz.:

(1) He can accept currency, a certified check, or a bank cashier's check in an amount equal to 125 percent of the invoice value of the shipment;

(2) He can accept a specific bond of indemnity with surety in an amount equal to twice the invoice value, subject to approval by the management of the carrier;

(3) He can accept a blanket bond of indemnity, when satisfactory to the carrier's management as to surety, amount, and form.

The local representative of a carrier has absolutely no authority to depart from the provisions of this rule. If he does, and delivery is made to an unauthorized person for which the carrier is found to be liable, in many instances regulations of the carrier hold the agent personally responsible for the full amount involved.[23]

---

[22] See, pp. 33–34, above.

[23] The writer recalls most vividly a sad personal experience at a time he was employed by a carrier when, after pleas of the consignee, he caused to be delivered an "order notify" shipment without surrender of the bill of lading on a Saturday afternoon. The following Monday happened to be a legal holiday when banks were closed, and the inconvenience resulting in the inevitable delay of waiting until Tuesday to effect delivery was appreciated. The consignee was a valued customer of the carrier who was known to be a "good fellow," and who promised faithfully to deliver the bill "First thing Tuesday morning after the bank opens." Instead, he went on an extended fishing trip!

Usually, the Treasurer of the carrier is the only person who is authorized by carrier management to advise a local terminal manager or agent that the bonds are acceptable, and without such approval there is nothing the local carrier representative can do but insist upon the cash deposit described in item (1), above. The cash deposit may be refunded only upon surrender of the endorsed bill of lading or, if the bill has been lost or destroyed, upon receipt of a specific bond of indemnity approved by the carrier's Treasurer, or other delegated officer. The bond remains in effect throughout the statute of limitations on claims, which is two years and one day. The reason for requiring more than 100 percent of the invoice value of the shipment is to provide ample protection for the carrier should a question arise at some future date concerning proper value of the goods.

Reshipping Documents, Instructions, Invoices, etc. (M-29, R-42, NE-21). Reshipping documents, invoices, assembly or operating instructions for the use and advice of the consignee when he receives the freight, and other relevant papers may accompany shipments without additional charge. Inclusion of such a rule might appear to be silly; but it serves a most useful purpose for certain situations.

This rule is particularly valuable to a carrier in the handling of consolidated shipments which break bulk at some intermediate point short of final destinations. Frequently, it is advantageous for a carrier to forward a solid trailerload or carload of small shipments from point X to point Y for ultimate delivery to other places in the general vicinity of Y. When the trailer or car is unloaded at Y, the necessary shipping documents are readily available to the carrier's agent handling the transfer.

The rule benefits a shipper by permitting invoices, assembly or operating instructions, and other papers of a similar nature to accompany the shipment. Such documents may be of vital importance for the operation or sale of the merchandise, and in recognition thereof the rule was established to permit the papers to travel with the article at the same rate. Without this rule, it would be necessary to assess applicable charges for the papers under another rule which is discussed later.[24] Hence, the shipper is protected, provided he is familiar with the rule and takes advantage thereof by appropriate notation on the bill of lading.

Of greater importance to the carrier in the long run, however, this rule can enable a carrier to help its customer, if ignorant of the existence of the rule, by applying the provisions of the rule and

---

[24] See, p. 241, below.

thereby creating a most pleasant customer relationship which should place the carrier in a more favorable competitive position to secure a preponderance of future shipments. Hence, this rule illustrates very vividly that a carrier employee is in an excellent position to establish unlimited good will for his company from a shipper who is confronted with conditions which the rule may alleviate. It should be remembered that the intangible value of good will is immeasurable, and that a large volume of traffic in forthcoming months and years produces greater total income.

From the industrial traffic manager's standpoint, this rule demonstrates the absolute importance of shippers being familiar with the principles contained in all rules in order to reduce actual shipping costs to a minimum.

Packing & Marking Regulations

General Packing Requirements (M-5, R-5-40-41, NE-4). This is a long, detailed rule pertaining to packing requirements. The Rail Classification utilizes 18 pages in setting forth its requirements in three rules. The primary purpose is to insure that goods are shipped in proper kinds of containers which will withstand the normal shocks inherent to the transportation service and thereby afford adequate protection to shipments while being transported from consignor to consignee. Goods arriving at destination in a damaged condition are an economic waste, costly both to carrier and owner of the freight and conducive to causing dissatisfied customers. This rule is designed to prevent injury to shipments caused by the use of flimsy containers or inadequate packing. Also, penalties are provided for failure to comply with these regulations.

The local pick-up driver, the receiving clerk, and other terminal employees who accept outbound shipments have a great responsibility. Of course, they obligate the carrier by signing the bill of lading and thereby make the carrier a party to the contract of carriage. Before signing that fundamental document, however, the employee should at least examine the freight and satisfy himself that it is in safe condition to be handled. It is unreasonable to expect every pick-up driver or terminal employee to be fully cognizant of all shipping rules; but it is the responsibility of the terminal manager or local agent to be certain that his employees who accept freight are familiar with the packing and marking requirements. Exactly the same is true for the industrial traffic manager as he should instruct his shipping personnel who prepare articles for shipment and deliver them to a carrier. Otherwise, claim payments by the carrier and additional costs to the shipper are inevitable. It is foolish, and definitely "poor business," for a shipper to spend sums of money for the production of an article and then have it damaged or destroyed because it was shipped in a poor container.

Many years ago, before the value of efficient industrial traffic management was recognized by the top-managements of both commercial establishments and carriers, proper packing of freight for domestic transportation was not considered to be of any great importance. Old boxes or crates which appeared sufficiently adequate to pass the superficial glances of the carrier's representative were used. As a result, goods were lost or pilfered from those old dilapidated containers, shipments were damaged because of insecure packing; and even the physical welfare of employees was endangered by projecting nails, splinters, and rough corners. Since those days, great progress has been made toward the goal of good packing by both carriers and shippers. In recent years, considerable time and study have been devoted to the improvement of containers by several organizations, such as, the Bureau of Standards, the United States Department of Commerce, the Forest Products Laboratory of the Department of Agriculture, the Association of American Railroads, and the American Trucking Associations, Inc. Yet, despite the many innovations in packaging procedures and the positive rules of the carriers, loss and damage to shipments continue to occur and the carriers pay millions of dollars each year in the settlement of claims. While a part of this appalling economic waste may be attributed to the shipper for inadequate packing or marking, it must be recognized that a considerable portion is caused by rough handling and carelessness on the part of carrier employees.

A summary of the provisions of the rule follows:

1. Descriptions of articles in the Ratings Section of the Classification show the acceptable forms by which goods should be shipped.

2. Containers must afford reasonable and proper protection to their contents.

3. There must be full compliance with any description which specifies a particular kind of container.

4. Unless there is a description containing provisions to the contrary, ratings for articles shipped "loose" or "in bulk" will also apply to the same articles shipped in packages.

5. All articles which may be damaged by ordinary handling must be prepared for shipment in a safe manner.

6. Except where caused by carrier's negligence, the carrier has

the right to recooper defective containers at shipper's expense. It is extremely rare that this provision of the rule is invoked; but whenever it is, the cost of recoopering would be added to the freight bill and the consignee would be expected to pay the amount involved. Of course, the consignee could claim reimbursement from the consignor, but that is a matter beyond the province of the carrier.

7. The carrier reserves the right to refuse to accept any article which is presented for shipment in a way that it cannot be transported in a reasonably safe and practicable manner. This paragraph is positive in stating the carrier *will refuse* to accept such shipments. Whether or not a carrier will refuse acceptance is a moot question, for many practical considerations necessarily are involved. For instance, it is difficult to imagine that a carrier arbitrarily would revert to the provisions of this paragraph where one of its large revenue-producing shippers is concerned, for the simple reason that the customer might divert his future traffic to a competitor. In such a case, it is probable the carrier would refer the matter to its regional inspection organization mentioned earlier,[25] and its representative would call on the shipper in an effort to straighten out the difficulty. Also, during the rush of business when outbound freight is being received at a terminal, it would be most impractical for the carrier's employees to examine in detail each individual container.

8. There are specific requirements for glassware, earthenware, or fragile articles shipped in fibreboard boxes. Specifications are laid down for construction of such boxes, and those that comply therewith must bear a certificate of the manufacturer showing his name and other prescribed information. Also, any fragile article must be adequately wrapped or otherwise protected within the container.

9. The carrier again reserves the right to refuse acceptance of shipments unless the containers are of sufficient strength to protect their contents from the ordinary hazards of the transportation service.

10. Articles which may liquefy or expand, such as molasses in hot weather, must be shipped in containers which will retain such liquefaction or expansion and which will prevent leakage therefrom.

11. In the absence of a packing requirement in the Classification, an article may be accepted at the carrier's option.

12. Where freight has been accepted by a carrier and later it is found to be in an unauthorized container, or not prepared for ship-

---

[25] See, pp. 211–212, above.

ment in accordance with the requirements of the Classification, the freight charges shall be increased by 20 percent for less-than-truckload and less-than-carload or 10 percent for truckload and carload shipments. When this section is invoked, the Motor Classification requires the carrier to report the facts to the National Classification Board. While this section may appear harsh or even a bit unreasonable to some shippers, penalties are required for the enforcement of any rule. The same is true in a court of law. It is probable that carriers would be happy never to have occasion to use this rule, but its existence is necessary to at least discourage the use of inadequate containers as well as to protect the carrier from its liability as an insurer of goods entrusted to its care. Definitely, it is not designed as a source of income for the carriers. The Rail Classification contains a much more elaborate system of penalties than does the Motor Classification.

There has been some litigation regarding this item which is found in Section 6 of the rule. Paragraph (a) thereof states in bold print that it applies *only* after freight has been accepted by a carrier and then found to be in an unauthorized container or form. Therefore, the purpose of this Section is "to provide a legal basis for determining charges on shipments inadvertently accepted, and does not in any sense negative the requirement that shipments in unauthorized packages should be rejected." [26] The Commission has sustained carriers for assessing the penalty charges when applicable. [27]

13. Articles shipped in authorized containers which are fastened to pallets or to skids for lift trucks take the same rating that applies to the article shipped in the container.

14. The many different types of acceptable containers are defined, and the specifications for their construction are established. Section 12, which is included in this item, deserves special consideration. The title of Section 12 is, "Definition of Term 'In Packages'"; but it does not define a "package"! It provides that where the term "in packages" appears in the Description of Articles section of the Classification, such articles will be accepted in any container, "other than trunks, or in any shipping form other than 'in bulk,' 'loose,' or 'on skids,' but including articles securely fastened on elevating truck platform, lift truck skids or pallets, providing such containers or form of shipment will render the transportation of the freight rea-

[26] Colquitt, *op. cit.*, p. 140.
[27] *Diamond T Motor Car Company v. Northwestern Transit, Inc.*, 49 M.C.C. 515, 1949; *Aetna Plywood & Veneer Company v. Indianapolis Forwarding Company*, 52 M.C.C. 591, 1951.

sonably safe and practicable." The following comment of Mr. Joseph C. Colquitt [28] is most enlightening on the subject:

In other words, this section of the rule is an affirmative rule stating that where freight is provided for "in packages" the ratings shown in connection therewith will apply on certain forms of freight. It is also a negative rule as it provides that such ratings will not apply on certain forms of freight. The Classification also provides for freight "in bundles." There is no rule, similar to Section 12, regarding bundles. It is doubtful that any rule could be phrased describing "packages" and "bundles" that should not be so technical as to fall of its own weight in that it would be open to so many interpretations that it would lead to more trouble than it would cure. Of course, there are dictionary definitions; but they are not always helpful in connection with a document like the Classification that is designed to meet commercial conditions rather than academic definitions and necessarily contains many terms well understood in transportation and commercial parlance. Common sense is the best guide.

The same situation exists with Section 9 concerning bales, bundles, coils, reels, or rolls.

Furthermore, the term "in bulk" is found frequently throughout the Classification, including the rules; but, again, there is no definition of it! The word "bulk" refers either to space occupied by an article or the nature (or form) of the article. Reference to "light and bulky articles" means they are of low density and occupy much space. A commodity "in bulk" means it can be poured or scooped. In the Classification, "in bulk" is used in contrast to shipping "in packages" or specified containers. Frequently, articles shipped "in bulk in barrels" are granted a lower rating than when shipped "in barrels" or "in boxes." The Interstate Commerce Commission has held that a higher rate on condensed milk when shipped "in bulk in barrels" than "in cans in boxes" was unreasonable.[29] Mr. Colquitt explains this apparently minor distinction, as follows: [30]

The reason for this is that generally the commodity shipped in bulk in barrels or some other bulk container represents what is termed a wholesale movement, such as goes to manufacturers or dealers who repack the goods for the retail or shelf trade, thus adding to the value as compared with the bulk package.

Continuing, Mr. Colquitt gives the carriers a most pointed warning: [31]

---

[28] See, p. 70, above, Colquitt, *op. cit.*
[29] *American Bakeries Company v. Norfolk & Western Railway Company,* 140 I.C.C. 69, 1928.
[30] Colquitt, *op. cit.,* p. 156.
[31] *Ibid.*

Some commodities should not be accepted in bulk, even in truckload shipments, because of their melting point. Such a commodity could leak from equipment or become solidified to the point where the carriers' equipment might be damaged in removing it. Again, some commodities are so foul in one respect or another that they could so contaminate carriers' equipment as to make it unusable for other commodities without unusual expense of cleaning it.

In conclusion, it should always be remembered that a shipper is entitled to a reasonable rate for the service of transportation, and that his demand for transportation cannot be denied him by a carrier simply because the carrier prefers a particular form in which the freight is to be shipped.[32] More detailed information pertaining to this important rule may be found by referring to the cases listed in the footnote below.[33]

Containers for Explosives (M-5½, R-40, NE-4). The motor rule requires that container specifications which are provided in a special explosives tariff must be observed for shipments of explosives

---

[32] *Auto Vehicle Company v. Chicago, Milwaukee & St. Paul Railway Company*, 21 I.C.C. 286 (288), 1911.

[33] Colquitt, *op. cit.*, p. 11. *Eastbound Perishables in Unauthorized Containers*, 225 I.C.C. 293, 1937.

Huston Peanut Company v. Southern Railway Company, 156 I.C.C. 307, 1929.

Huston Peanut Company v. Illinois Central Railroad Co., 173 I.C.C. 366, 1931.

O-So-Ezy Products Company v. Director General, 85 I.C.C. 187, 1923.

Western Classification Case, 25 I.C.C. 442, 1912.

Loose-Wiles Biscuit Company v. Eastern Steamship Lines, 174 I.C.C. 57, 1931.

Ratings on Fertilizer Compounds, 186 I.C.C. 391, 1932.

Indian Packing Corporation v. Director General, 64 I.C.C. 205, 1921.

Northwest Furniture Manufacturers Association, Inc., v. Atchison, Topeka & Santa Fe Railway Company, 277 I.C.C. 219, 1950.

Campbell Transportation Company Control, 250 I.C.C. 9, 1941.

Atwacoal Transport Company—Exemption Section 303 (e), 250 I.C.C. 33, 1941.

John L. Goss Corporation Contract Carrier Application, 250 I.C.C. 101, 1941.

Wholesale Fruit & Produce Company v. Atchison, Topeka & Santa Fe Railway Company, 14 I.C.C. 410, 1908.

Gottron Brothers v. Genesee & Wyoming Railroad Company, 28 I.C.C. 38, 1913.

Keystone Wood Company v. Pennsylvania Railroad Company, 37 I.C.C. 622, 1916.

Mulqueen Contract Carrier Application, 250 I.C.C. 436, 1942.

Swift & Company v. Baltimore & Ohio Railroad Company, 50 I.C.C. 103, 1918.

American Bakeries Company v. Norfolk & Western Railway Company, 140 I.C.C. 69, 1928.

Auto Vehicle Company v. Chicago, Milwaukee & St. Paul Railway Company, 21 I.C.C. 286, 1911.

Planters Compress Company v. Cleveland, Cincinnati, Chicago & St. Louis Railway Company, 11 I.C.C. 382, 1905.

Ratings on Paint or Varnish Spraying Booths, 63 I.C.C. 282, 1921.

or other dangerous articles. The rail rule, in Section 4 of Rule 40, states that containers for explosives are prescribed by the Interstate Commerce Commission, and refers the reader to Rule 39 which will be discussed later.[34]

Marking or Tagging Shipments (M-6, R-6, NE-5). Motor carriers require that "each package or piece of each shipment must be plainly and durably marked, stencilled or tagged" by the shipper, showing the names and addresses of consignor and consignee, respectively. An exception to this general rule provides that "a shipment, received complete at one time for transportation in one vehicle where the quantity of such shipment is sufficient to occupy the major capacity of such vehicle, need not be marked as to every piece in such shipment, if every piece is of easy identification as belonging to such shipment without the possibility of being confused with other freight." The rail rule contains a similar marking requirement for less-than-carload freight and for goods moving on "any quantity" ratings; but the railroads reserve the right to refuse acceptance of such shipments when not so marked. The rail rule also eliminates the necessity for marking a l.c.l. shipment weighing 6,000 pounds or more.

In order that carrier employees may be warned of the necessity for careful handling, containers of fragile articles must be marked, "FRAGILE—HANDLE WITH CARE, or with similar precautionary marks." The purpose of this requirement is obvious, for there is no way for carrier personnel to know that the contents of a container are breakable unless appropriate information is placed in a conspicuous manner on the outside of the package by the shipper. Another common warning is, "THIS SIDE UP." Without exception, carrier employees should always comply with these and other similar markings by handling the article more carefully than other pieces of freight and by stowing and bracing it inside the vehicle in a manner which will insure its safe arrival at destination under normal operating conditions. Failure to do so is an invitation for a claim against the carrier and possible loss of a valued customer. It is the direct responsibility of the carrier's warehouse foreman to instruct his employees on the proper handling of shipments marked in this manner, and continuous supervision is essential to prevent acts of carelessness. Fragile articles especially, that have proper markings on their containers, should receive the same treatment as though they were the personal property of the employee handling them. It is difficult to imagine, for example, that an individual would

---

[34] See, p. 235, below.

purchase an expensive television set for his home, and then nonchalantly throw it up-side-down into the trunk of his car! And his wife, who might be considered as the consignee in this illustration, conceivably could have some uncomplimentary remarks to make when he arrived at home!

A C.O.D. shipment or a shipment moving on an order bill of lading must be so marked, together with an identifying symbol which must also appear on the bill of lading.

If a shipment consigned to a foreign country is to be handled through a broker at the port of export, the broker's name and address must be shown on the packages. The rail rule requires that the marking include the name of the port.

Proper marking of freight is a direct responsibility of the shipper. It serves to expedite the handling of small shipments, and it is a protection to both shipper and carrier. As has been stated earlier, a common carrier is an insurer of goods and, therefore, the carrier is required to produce safe transportation service and effect delivery only to the party who is entitled to receive the goods. However, the common law and the bill of lading contract exempt the carrier from its liability when the reason for loss or damage to freight is caused by an act of the shipper. Since marking of packages is a responsibility of the shipper, his failure to do so relieves the carrier of its liability for consequent loss attributable directly to inadequate marking. The importance of proper marking cannot be overemphasized, and an efficient industrial traffic manager will never permit a small shipment to leave his place of business without complete marking. On the other hand, if a shipper can show that his shipment was properly marked at the time it was accepted by the carrier, and subsequently it is lost, misdelivered, or damaged, then the burden of proof is upon the carrier to establish its innocence, which is next to impossible to do.

An unmarked box arriving at a terminal with other miscellaneous freight immediately creates a serious problem for the warehouse foreman, or whoever is in charge of receiving freight. If he is unable to match the box with data contained on a waybill, he has two alternatives: (1) open the package in search of identifying information as to consignee and consignor and, if found, forward it to its proper destination or request disposition instructions from the consignor; (2) contact the originating terminal of the trailer or car in an effort to identify the package. If both fail, the carrier has a lost shipment on its hands, and sooner or later a claim will be filed by its owner. In the meantime, the consignee has not received his freight, the shipper may have to duplicate the order, and general dissatisfaction can be the only result.

The safe rule to follow is for the individual who is responsible for shipping goods of a firm to be certain the markings on his outgoing packages conform exactly with the information shown on the bill of lading, which either he has prepared himself or which has been prepared by some other person in his organization. Then, if he is satisfied as to proper packing, the freight is ready for delivery to a carrier. The pick-up driver or receiving clerk at the depot should check the markings on each package and the number against the information contained on the bill of lading; then, and only after all details are found to be correct, should he sign the bill of lading. Of course, this procedure is not necessary for volume shipments when loaded by the shipper.

Carriers' requirement that shipments be marked in a proper manner is not a new innovation. As early as 1836, a tariff required that iron bars must be "distinctly marked," together with such other articles as meat and sacked grain. "If such precautions were necessary under the leisurely practices of those days they are infinitely more necessary under the complications of freight transportation in the hustle and bustle of business today." [35]

Many years ago, the Commission ruled: [36]

. . . when a shipper prepares a bill of lading providing for the carriage of property to a particular destination and marks a different and erroneous address on the package, the carrier will not be held responsible for the freight charges incurred in transporting the property to the destination shown on the package, although the correct destination is shown on the bill of lading.

Earthenware Inner Containers (M-20, R-5, NE-4). The Motor Classification contains a separate rule authorizing that the ratings of articles shipped in glass inner containers will apply to the same articles packed in earthenware containers. The same provision is incorporated in Rule 5, Section 2 (b) of the Rail Classification.

Bags for Reconditioning Purposes (M-32, R-50). Empty bags, not exceeding 25 pounds in weight, may accompany a volume shipment when the bags may be needed for reconditioning of the shipment while in transit. For example, extra bags may be shipped with sacked grain or sugar to replace some of the original bags which may have become torn. This provision is comparable to the rule

---

[35] Colquitt, *op. cit.*, p. 174.
[36] *C. S. Brackett Company v. Great Northern Express Company*, 29 I.C.C. 667, 1914.

permitting certain papers to accompany a shipment without applying the rating of the primary shipment.

Test Shipments (M-33, R-49). This rule permits experimental use of new types of containers without penalty to the shipper for using unauthorized packages. The purpose is to determine the adaptability, adequacy, and general merits of a new kind of container.

The motor rule requires that, prior to shipment, a request for a permit to make a test shipment be addressed to the Chairman of the National Classification Board, with a complete description of the container. When practical, it is desirable to submit a sample container for examination. Only if the Board finds the container possesses sufficient merit will it issue the necessary permit; but such authorization does not require a carrier to accept the shipment. If it is accepted, however, the carrier is not liable for any loss or damage arising from inadequacy of the container. A copy of the permit, signed by the Chairman of the National Classification Board, must be furnished the carrier's agent at point of origin; and appropriate notation, as provided by the rule, must appear on the bill of lading and the freight bill. Upon arrival of the shipment at destination, the delivering carrier is required to notify both the Board and the originating carrier whether or not there was any loss or damage to the freight.

The rail rule contains similar provisions, except that application for a permit is sent to the chairman of the appropriate geographical classification committee, and it requires that each package be prominently marked, "TEST SHIPMENT."

Chapter 12

CLASSIFICATION RULES—
Part II

Loading & Unloading Regulations

Freight Liable to Damage Other Freight or Equipment (M-4, R-4, NE-15). A carrier is not obligated to accept freight which may cause damage to other shipments or to the carrier's equipment; otherwise, through no fault of its own, the carrier would be liable for damage to the other freight. However, such articles may be accepted "subject to delay for suitable equipment"; but if the required equipment is not obtainable, the shipment may be refused.

An article with an offensive odor, such as green hides, would be subject to this rule. When loaded in the same unit of equipment with other miscellaneous freight, the odor might be absorbed by another shipment causing the latter to be valueless, in which event the carrier would be liable for the damage. Likewise, the odor from a volume movement of some articles will remain inside the vehicle in which it was transported long after the shipment has been unloaded, resulting in the vehicle being unfit to handle many other articles until it has been deodorized. It should be understood that the cost of deodorizing is borne by the carrier and, further, the unit is not available to produce revenue for the carrier during the period it is being reconditioned for general service.

Many foodstuffs, such as candy and margarine, shipped in small quantities, when loaded in a contaminated trailer or box car become permeated with the offensive odor which makes them unfit for human consumption. The carrier pays the claim, and properly so. To illustrate: a motor carrier accepted and transported a volume shipment of chemicals possessing a most pungent odor. After delivery of the chemicals, a shipment consisting of a well known headache tablet was loaded into the same trailer. The odor of the chemicals remained in the vehicle and permeated the tablets, notwithstanding that the tablets were packed in proper containers as specified by the

Classification. Again, the carrier was faced with a legitimate claim for the value of the tablets. Another known case of a carrier's equipment being rendered unfit was a rail shipment of butter which was loaded into a refrigerator car soon after it had transported a load of sacked bermuda onions. In order to avoid possible damage or loss to shipments caused by offensive odors, some carriers handling regular movements of an article possessing a strong odor will assign separate equipment to that particular traffic, and on the back haul such equipment will be loaded with freight which cannot be damaged by the odor clinging to the inside of the transportation unit.

In addition to odors, certain articles may damage other freight or even the vehicle itself. Some powders or salt will stick to the floor and may cause the flooring to disintegrate. A metal shipment subsequently loaded on the floor of the same unit may become corroded, and the carrier will be required to pay for the loss.

Heavy or Bulky Articles, Loading or Unloading (M-21, R-27). This rule in both the Motor and Rail Classifications pertains to unloading and loading of freight, but under somewhat different circumstances; hence, they will be explained separately where the Classifications differ. Also, this rule is supplemented by another rule which will be discussed later.[1]

The rule in both Classifications requires that heavy or bulky small shipments shall be loaded by the shipper and unloaded by the consignee, when such shipments cannot be handled in a normal manner by carrier employees or at points where the carrier does not provide adequate facilities, such as a crane. The motor rule is more specific by stating the minimum weight, 500 pounds, and dimensions of a single container; but it provides that the motor carrier, when requested, will undertake to employ additional labor as may be necessary at a charge of $1.50 per hour, or fraction thereof, for each man furnished, exclusive of the truck driver.

The rail rule specifies that carload shipments shall be loaded and unloaded by the owner of the freight, which usually means the shipper loads and the consignee unloads. An exception is where a tariff provides loading or unloading will be performed by the carrier. The rail rule also requires observance of the carrier's regulations pertaining to safe loading. Usually, it is understood by all concerned that, as a general rule, carriers do not load or unload volume shipments, although in many instances motor carrier employees assist in loading and unloading them. It will be recalled that the difference between the rating and/or rate on volume and small ship-

---

[1] See, p. 235, below.

ments of the same commodity is influenced by the former involving less handling costs to the carrier than the latter, with the result that a volume shipment enjoys a rate per 100 pounds which is lower than that applied to a small shipment. Hence, it is the responsibility of the consignor and consignee, respectively, to furnish the necessary personnel, equipment, and facilities with which to load and unload truckload and carload shipments.

In contrast to volume freight, usually the carriers load and unload small shipments. On an inbound movement, the normal procedure is that the freight is unloaded from the over-the-road trailer or freight car at the carrier's terminal by carrier employees, and then delivered to the consignee by the carrier's local pick-up and delivery vehicle. An exception to the usual practice is provided by a section of this rule. An example would be a heavy piece of machinery weighing a ton or two, consigned to a place where the carrier does not provide a crane or other suitable facilities. Here, responsibility for unloading rests with the consignee. It would be unreasonable to expect the carrier to provide extra personnel and specialized facilities for only an occasional shipment of such a nature; but if there were a regular movement of the commodity, it is probable the carrier would install the necessary facilities at its terminal.

There is a group of motor common carriers, commonly known as "heavy haulers," which are engaged in the highly specialized movement of large or unwieldly articles, such as, heavy machinery, boilers, airplanes, prefabricated houses, bowling alley equipment, etc. The unusual size and weight of such shipments require the use of special vehicles, sometimes equipped with winches and other devices for loading and unloading. The service of transportation, of course, "necessarily includes loading and unloading" of the shipment.[2] Cranes or other mechanical devices used for loading and unloading articles of unusual size or weight are considered to be "special equipment."[3] Such loading devices normally are provided by the "heavy haulers" but not by carriers of general commodities, although there is "an overlapping of commodities which as a practical matter move in either or both types of service."[4] The term "special equipment" has been used in Certificates of Public Convenience and Necessity of "heavy haulers" to indicate the special type of

---

[2] *E. A. Gallagher Common Carrier Application*, 48 M.C.C. 413 (415), 1948.

[3] *Steel Transportation Company, Inc., Extension—Wisconsin*, 44 M.C.C. 835, 1945.

[4] *St. Johnsbury Trucking Company, Inc., Extention–Heavy Hauling*, 53 M.C.C. 277 (297), 1951.

service they perform and, at the same time, restricts the carrier from invading the field of another type of service, especially the general-commodity common carriers. In granting authority to a motor carrier of general commodities to engage in the heavy hauling business, the Interstate Commerce Commission stated: "The use of modern devices for the economical and expedient loading, unloading, and handling of freight should not be denied any class of carrier. The use of such equipment is not a true and practical test of the commodities which a general-commodity carrier may or may not transport." [5]

Illustrative of an article of unusual size, shape, and weight is airplane engines. A proceeding before the Commission involved an unsuccessful attempt of a group of motor carriers to increase the rating on internal combustion engines when released to values of over $1.00 per pound. The carriers showed that because of the unusual size and shape of the engines, there was considerable wasted space in transporting them, varying from 50 to 75 percent of vehicle capacity, resulting in less revenue than was derived from handling full truckloads of other commodities at comparable rates. On interline movements, special devices and the labor of several men were required to transfer the engines at interchange points, for the smallest engines weighed about 1,500 pounds; [6] but at origin and destination, the loading and unloading usually were performed by the consignor and consignee, respectively. [7]

In another case, the Commission commented: [8]

The hauling of extra large or very heavy articles poses a number of problems that must be overcome before the movement can begin. In those instances, where the shipment exceeds the maximum load limit permitted on the highways of the State or States involved special permission must be obtained therefrom. The same situation prevails in those instances where the size of the shipments exceed State limitations. In those instances, it is frequently necessary for the State authorities to specify the highways over which the movement may be performed. The problem of obtaining such permission rests with the carriers.

An interesting observation by the Commission concerning a rail case follows: [9]

---

[5] *Ibid.*, p. 298.
[6] This was before adoption of the present procedure of interchanging trailers among connecting motor carriers.
[7] *Released Ratings and Rates on Engines*, 47 I.C.C. 767 (773–774), 1948.
[8] Ex Parte No. MC-45, *Descriptions in Motor Carrier Certificates*, 61 M.C.C. 209 (249), 1952.
[9] *Peterson Construction Company v. Minneapolis, St. Paul & Sault Ste. Marie Railroad Company, et al.*, 160 I.C.C. 178 (179), 1929.

When bulky articles which require open cars for their transportation are shipped as less than carloads, carriers for obvious reasons seldom load smaller articles belonging to other shippers on the same car, even though they have the technical right to do so.

Dunnage or Temporary Blocking Racks, Standards, Supports, etc. (M-22, R-30, NE-18). This is commonly known as the "Dunnage Rule." Dunnage is defined by the rules as, "Any temporary blocking, flooring or lining, racks, standards, strips, stakes, or similar bracing or supports not constituting a part of the vehicle (or car) . . ." The Rail Classification adds, "The term 'dunnage' does not include excelsior, hay, sawdust, shavings, shredded paper, straw, packing cushions or pads or similar packing material." Dunnage is used to brace, block, protect, or otherwise make shipments secure so that they will not shift or fall while being transported by a carrier. The rule requires that dunnage must be furnished and installed by the shipper at his expense for volume shipments. The motor rule provides that the carrier will install whatever dunnage the shipper furnishes at the rate of $1.50 per hour per man. If the dunnage is provided by the motor carrier, there will be an additional charge in accordance with applicable tariffs.

The rail rule authorizes an allowance of actual weight of dunnage to a maximum of 500 pounds, *provided* the shipper specifies the actual weight thereof on the bill of lading. Therefore, if the required information appears on the bill of lading, up to 500 pounds of dunnage is handled free, and only the excess over 500 pounds, if any, is included in the total weight of the shipment for the application of freight charges. It should be remembered that complete information must be shown on the bill of lading by the shipper, otherwise no allowance will be granted by the carrier. As a practical matter, there is no way for the carrier to know the quantity of dunnage used in a carload shipment unless it is shown on the bill of lading because, usually, the shipment was loaded, braced, and the car, if a closed car, sealed by the shipper at his place of business. Should, however, application of the dunnage allowance cause the gross weight of the shipment to become less than the minimum carload weight as specified in the Ratings Section of the Classification, the carload rate based upon the established minimum weight would be charged.[10] The requirement that the weight of dunnage be shown on the bill of lading was upheld many years ago by the Interstate Commerce Commission in refusing to authorize a dunnage allow-

---

[10] Wilson, G. L.: *The Principles of Freight Traffic*, The Traffic World, Chicago (now, The Traffic Service Corporation, Washington), 1935, pp. 27-28.

ance to a consignee when the shipper had neglected to provide the information. The case involved shipment of a crane by rail, in which the Commission rules: "The consignee is not entitled to an allowance for dunnage, because the consignor failed to specify on the shipping order the weight of the material used, as required by the following rule in the governing Classification . . ." [11]

Rule No. 10 of the Motor Classification, which is discussed later, completely excludes the weight of dunnage in determining the gross weight of a shipment for the application of freight charges.[12]

The rail rule affords another excellent illustration of the importance of familiarity with all sections of the rules. To illustrate: assume a carload shipment weighs 40,000 pounds, including 700 pounds of dunnage. If the shipper shows on the bill of lading that there are 700 pounds of dunnage by actual weight, the freight rate will be assessed on the basis of 39,500 pounds of the article instead of the full 40,000 pounds, thus:

Weight of shipment......................	39,300 pounds
Weight of dunnage.......................	700 pounds
Gross weight........................	40,000 pounds
Allowance for dunnage..................	500 pounds
Net weight.........................	39,500 pounds

However, if the shipper were ignorant of the provision of this rule by reason of his failure to examine the Classification, or for any other reason, and the notation did not appear on the face of the bill of lading, he or the consignee would be required to pay for transporting the extra 500 pounds which otherwise would have been hauled without charge.

Another section of the rail rule prohibits an allowance for dunnage used in connection with bulk shipments in closed cars.

The Interstate Commerce Commission has upheld inclusion of the weight of dunnage with the weight of a shipment in the following forceful statement: [13]

There can be no doubt on this record that the primary and most important purpose of the dunnage used in varying forms by the shipping interests here represented is to make the load safe for transportation and to obviate injury to the goods, the prevention of damage to the carriers' equipment or property being a minor consideration. Under these circumstances and in view of the fact that the substitution of dunnage for

---

[11] *Joseph T. Ryerson & Sons, Inc., v. Chicago, Milwaukee & St. Paul Railway Company*, 157 I.C.C. 8, 1929.
[12] See, p. 239, below.
[13] *Dunnage Allowances*, 30 I.C.C. 538 (539), 1914.

the more expensive boxes and crates and other packing material . . .
is of advantage to the shipper . . . , we think it is not inconsistent that
the carriers should receive revenue for the total weight hauled.

**Acceptance Subject to Capacity & Appropriate Type of Vehicles
(M-23, NE-17); Freight Requiring Heat or Refrigeration (R-31).**
Section 1 of the motor rule reads, as follows: "The obligation to accept articles for shipment shall be subject to capacity and appropriate type of vehicles, and to requirements of ordinances or laws limit-
ing or regulating the transportation of the property or use of the
vehicles." A primary duty of a common carrier is to provide adequate and efficient service to the general public without unreasonable discrimination or undue preference. However, the general
obligation to serve the public, of necessity, is restricted to the capacity and availability of the required type of equipment. Likewise,
motor carriers are subject to the heterogeneous mass of state laws
and municipal ordinances as to weight, length, breadth, and height
of vehicles. Therefore, this section of the rule gives a motor carrier
the right to refuse acceptance of a shipment when the vehicle required for its safe transportation is not available and, if such equipment is available, when handling the shipment would involve violation of the law of some state or municipality through which the
shipment would pass between origin and destination.

The term "appropriate type of vehicle" warrants some consideration. In the discussion of motor Rule 21,[14] mention was made of
the specialized equipment used by the "heavy haulers." Those vehicles are illustrative of the above quoted term. Refrigerated equipment, automobile transporters' units, tank trucks, and household
goods vans are others and, with the exception of refrigerated units,
they are not used by common motor carriers of general commodities. In a case where a motor carrier of general commodities applied
for and was granted permission to operate refrigerated units, the
Commission said: [15]

In specifying the service to be rendered by applicant pursuant to the
certificate in question, we used the term "general commodities" to indicate
his general availability for the transportation of all types of freight, but
limited the term by excepting certain particular commodities, including
those requiring "special equipment," which such carriers of general commodities seldom hold themselves out to haul. In so defining the service to
be rendered, it was not our purpose to restrict the right of the carrier to

---

[14] See, p. 228, above.
[15] *Clarence Meddock Extension of Operations—Refrigerator Service,* 30
M.C.C. 301 (303–304), 1941.

add to his equipment or facilities . . . The limitation with respect to "special equipment" is the only one presenting any important difficulty in interpretation . . . we do not believe that it precludes a general-commodity carrier from rendering a more complete and adequate service to the public by providing equipment which serves to protect from deterioration commodities which are not otherwise within the terms of any of the exceptions and which he has from the outset transported. . . . The substitution of mechanical devices for ice in equipment possessed by applicant or the purchase of additional vehicles designed to provide temperature control does not, in our opinion, constitute the use of special equipment in the instant case. It is, therefore, a service which may properly be rendered by applicant under the terms of the certificate held by him, and the additional authority sought is unnecessary.

In an early case concerning use of refrigerated equipment by a carrier of general commodities, objection was made to authorizing the motor carrier the right to use special equipment, "particularly refrigerated equipment and tank trucks." Here, refrigerated units were held to be "special equipment," and its use was denied.[16]

A motor carrier of general commodities has been defined by the Commission as one which transports "commodities generally, except such commodities as require special equipment or service."[17] Motor carriers of general commodities have always considered "special equipment" as being synonymous with special types of vehicles. In contrast, such specialized carriers as the "heavy haulers" and household goods carriers interpret the term as being something in addition to the vehicle itself, such as, special devices and machinery used for loading and unloading shipments.[18] In the meantime, the Commission has not prescribed a precise definition of "special equipment."

It is, of course, the duty of a carrier, whether it be rail or motor, to furnish equipment that is suitable to transport the freight with which it is to be loaded. "Obviously this duty cannot be fulfilled by furnishing a car (or trailer) that leaks or one so full of projecting nails as to be unsuitable for the transportation of commodities properly packed . . . Cars (and trailers) should be physically fit for the transportation of the product with which they are to be loaded."[19]

---

[16] *United Trucking Service, Incorporated, Common Carrier Application,* 7 M.C.C. 98, 1938.
[17] Ex Parte No. MC-10, *Classification of Motor Carriers of Property,* 2 M.C.C. 703 (709), 1937.
[18] Ex Parte No. MC-45, *op. cit.,* pp. 268–269.
[19] *Southwestern Missouri Miller's Club v. St. Louis & San Francisco Railroad Company,* 26 I.C.C. 245, 1913; also, see *Balfour, Guthrie & Company v. Oregon-Washington Railroad & Navigation Company,* 21 I.C.C. 539, 1911.

It is incumbent upon motor carrier personnel who receive outbound freight to give close attention to any shipment requiring unusual equipment and especially to a shipment of great weight or excessive dimensions. Information, preferably in the form of a chart, should be available in every terminal showing the physical restrictions of all states in order that those data may be immediately accessible to employees. A shipment should be refused when its transport would cause violation of any state or local law, unless special arrangements can be made with the state or municipality for its movement. Once it is accepted, of course, the carrier is liable for its safe delivery to the consignee, and great costs to the carrier could result when the shipment does not conform to existing laws. To illustrate: assume a very heavy shipment was accepted by a carrier at Nashville, Tennessee, consigned to Indianapolis, Indiana, and that the carrier's Certificate of Public Convenience & Necessity granted it a direct route between the two points through the State of Kentucky.[20] So, if the shipment in question exceeded the Kentucky maximum weight restriction, the carrier would be forced to re-route the freight via a circuitous route, probably by using the services of another carrier, in order to avoid transporting it through Kentucky which, obviously, would result in great cost to the originating carrier; or else the carrier might violate the law by moving the load through Kentucky! It is most essential, therefore, that carrier employees have ready access to the legal restrictions of each state through which an unusually large or heavy shipment will move, and that those employees satisfy themselves that no law will be violated when they accept such a shipment.

Section 2 of the motor rule is somewhat similar to the entire rail rule. The motor rule states that motor carriers are not required to furnish refrigeration or heating service for the protection of shipments unless so provided in the carrier's tariffs. The rail rule contains similar provisions for small shipments; but, in addition, it stipulates that carload ratings do not include refrigeration expense and that the carrier is not obligated to provide heat except as stated in appropriate tariffs.

The motor rule contains a third section pertaining to volume shipments in tank trucks.

---

[20] For some reason, Kentucky highways must be softer than those of other states, because the gross weight of a motor vehicle, as authorized by that state's law, is considerably less than in Tennessee and Indiana. It is interesting to observe, however, that when the Louisville & Nashville Railroad virtually ceased operations because of a strike in 1955, weight restrictions on motor vehicles were raised during the period of emergency.

This rule is the basis for a carrier assessing extra charges for providing special services to protect perishable freight against cold or heat. Those special charges are published in separate tariffs and, ordinarily, are in addition to the regular freight rate. At the same time, the rule relieves the carrier of accepting perishable freight requiring refrigeration, heat, or ventilation when equipment affording that protection is not available, notwithstanding that the carrier may participate in a tariff in which such services are listed.[21]

Explosives & Dangerous Articles (M-27, R-39). This is a simple rule which provides that explosives and other dangerous articles will be transported only in accordance with named special tariffs covering such articles.

Articles, Irregular or of Large Dimensions (M-30); Shipments Requiring Two or More Open Cars, Long or Bulky Articles in or on One Car (R-29). Although the motor and rail rules are somewhat comparable, they will be treated separately.

The motor rule is short. "Unless provided in separate descriptions of articles," a shipment which is so large that it cannot be loaded into the end door of a conventional trailer without "removal of or substantial alterations in the body" thereof, shall be charged at actual weight subject to a minimum of 4,000 pounds at the first-class rate for the entire shipment. Such shipments are made subject to Rules 21 and 23, which have been described earlier; and the rule exempts flat bed or tarpaulin-covered equipments.

The rail rule consists of three sections. Section 1 sets forth the conditions under which charges are assessed on a carload shipment requiring two or more cars to handle it; and Section 2 specifies that a less-than-carload shipment necessitating more than one car will be handled on the basis of the Class 100 rate for each car with a minimum of 7,500 pounds. A shipment of long poles serves to illustrate each section. Section 3 contains various specifications of shipments.

The purpose of this rule is to provide reasonable revenue to the carriers for transporting articles of unusual size which cannot be handled in a normal manner in a single standardized piece of equipment. The Interstate Commerce Commission has held that ordinarily the rates on articles of unusual size "are usually somewhat higher than those on similar articles of normal dimensions."[22]

---

[21] Cushman, F. M.: *Transportation for Management*, Prentice-Hall, New York, 1953, p. 247.

[22] Ex Parte No. MC-23, *Midwestern Motor Carrier Rates*, 27 M.C.C. 297 (312), 1941.

Freight in Bunkers of Refrigerator Cars (R-23). This rule appears only in the Rail Classification. It prohibits freight being loaded in the bunkers of refrigerator cars.

Freight in Excess of Full Carload (R-24). This is an important rule for railroad shipments requiring more than one car, for it is the basis for freight charges on shipments in excess of a single car. It is not unusual for a single shipment to require more than one car and without this rule there would be a serious problem in determining how the excess freight should be billed. It is commonly known as the "Overflow" Rule, and it applies to carload freight only with a minimum of 30,000 pounds. There is no comparable rule in the Motor Classification.

It should be understood that the minimum weights assigned to articles in the Classification are determined by the volume of the particular article that can be loaded in or on a "standard" car; and it will be explained later in Rule 34 that provisions are made to take care of instances where cars larger than "standard" are required.[23] Rail Rule 24 applies when the volume of a single shipment necessitates the use of two or more cars to handle it, whereas Rule 34 applies to the size of a car ordered by a shipper. These two rules should not be confused because they cover entirely different situations.

Here, assume a shipment will consume the capacity of three cars plus an excess requiring only part of a fourth car. Clearly, the shipper should not be penalized by having to pay the higher less-than-carload rate on the excess that must move in the fourth car, because unquestionably he has a volume shipment considerably greater than the minimum weight prescribed in the Classification which entitles him to the carload rate on the entire shipment. After all, it is not the shipper's fault nor his responsibility if the carrier does not own or provide cars of sufficient capacity to accommodate his traffic without the necessity of loading a relatively small excess quantity into another car. In recognition of frequent situations of this nature, this rule has been adopted by the railroads; but still, the shipper is required to comply with certain regulations.

When a carload shipment physically cannot be loaded in or on a car, the rule requires that it be forwarded on one bill of lading as a single shipment[24] and each car, except the car carrying the excess, must be loaded to capacity as shown by the load limit weight sten-

---

[23] See, Rule 34, p. 277, below.
[24] For definition of "shipment," see Rail Rule 14, p. 254, below.

cilled on the sides of all freight cars. The freight rate is computed on the basis of the actual weight of the shipment. For the excess quantity of the shipment, over and above that which could be loaded in the other car or cars, the rule provides different regulations for open and closed cars, *viz.*: if a closed car is used, the carload rate applicable to the shipment applies, but subject to a minimum weight of 6,000 pounds of the excess loaded in the extra car; if an open car is used, the excess freight is subject to a minimum of 4,000 pounds and the Class 100 rate applies. The excess must be marked in the same manner as less-than-carload freight.[25] Although carriers give shippers the benefit of carload rates for overflow shipments, through carload service is not necessarily accorded the excess amount of freight for it may be handled as less-than-carload freight with frequent transfers between points of origin and destination. The excess may be handled through depots, and carriers participating in the movement have the right to load other shipments in the same car.

Section 5 of the rule further states:

This rule will not apply when specific items in this Classification provide otherwise; nor on bulk freight or live stock; nor on freight the character of any portion of which at time of transportation requires and is loaded in either heated, refrigerator, insulated, ventilator or tank cars, or cars specially prepared either by carrier or shipper; nor on freight the authorized minimum carload weight for which is less than 30,000 pounds, nor on freight the minimum carload weights for which are subject to Rule 34, nor on freight subject to Rule 29.

To illustrate the rule, assume there is a shipment of ordinary wrought iron conduit pipe weighing 60,000 pounds. According to the Classification, the article is assigned a carload rating of Class 35, minimum 40,000 pounds, and a less-than-carload rating of Class 50.[26] Also assume only the class rate applies, and the Class 100 rate is $1.00. If 45,000 pounds is the maximum that can be loaded in a box car, obviously the remaining 15,000 pounds will have to move in another car. The shipper loads 45,000 pounds in the first car and 15,-000 pounds in the second car. The rate for the entire shipment will be the carload rate of 35¢ per 100 pounds, or $210.00; *not* split as a part being a carload shipment and the other part as a less-than-carload shipment merely because the excess of 15,000 pounds was loaded in the second car, thus:

---

[25] See, Rule 6, p. 222, above.
[26] *Uniform Freight Classification No. 2, op. cit.,* Item 13365.

Correct Rate	Incorrect Rate
1st car, 45,000 lbs. @ 35¢..$157.50	1st car, 45,000 lbs. @ 35¢..$157.50
2nd car, 15,000 lbs. @ 35¢.. 52.50	2nd car, 15,000 lbs. @ 50¢.. 75.00
$210.00	$232.00

It should be remembered that all packages in the shipment, *including* the excess, are considered as one single shipment which must be covered by only one bill of lading. Section 4 stipulates that the carrier's "waybill for each car, whether for excess or full load, must give reference to waybill for each other car used in shipment."

RATING RULES

Prepayment or Guarantee of Charges (M-9, R-9, NE-13). There are two sections of this rule which read, as follows: (1) "All charges must be prepaid or guaranteed on any shipment which in the judgment of the carrier's agent at point of origin or diversion point would not, at forced sale, realize the total amount of charges due at destination"; (2) "Freight on which prepayment is required may, on approval of the originating carrier, be forwarded on the guarantee of shipper that all charges will be paid at destination, full explanation to be made on bill of lading."

Under the provisions of Section 2, the originating carrier which accepts an interline shipment on the basis of a guarantee of charges by the consignor is liable to the connecting carriers for their respective shares of the total applicable through rate. Should the shipper fail to make good his guarantee, the only alternative of the originating carrier is to bring suit against him in a court of competent jurisdiction.

This rule is directly related to the requirement of the Interstate Commerce Act that all legally applicable charges must be paid before a common carrier may "relinquish possession at destination of any freight transported by it." [27] The law permits certain exceptions, such as, where credit has been authorized to a shipper or consignee pursuant to rules of the Interstate Commerce Commission, freight moving on Government bills of lading, or traffic consigned to any political subdivision of government. Without this rule, a carrier might not be able to collect the charges due it from the consignee. It should be observed that responsibility for assessing charges on a prepaid or guaranteed basis rests with the originating carrier's terminal manager or agent.

Some articles which serve to illustrate this rule are porcelain signs,

---

[27] Interstate Commerce Act, Sections 3 (2), 223, 318, 414.

printed advertising matter, household goods when transported by a common carrier of general commodities, exclusive use of a motor vehicle, Christmas trees.

Charges on Gross Weights (M-10, R-11, NE-7). This rule is the authority of a carrier to determine freight charges on the basis of the gross weight of a shipment, *viz.:* "unless otherwise provided, charges shall be computed on gross weights"; but there are some exceptions. Gross weight includes the weight of the goods being shipped, the weight of the container, and the weight of material used for packing or otherwise protecting the goods.

The motor rule excludes the weight of temporary flooring, blocking, dunnage, etc., in determining the gross weight of a shipment. In effect, it supplements the "Dunnage Rule" which was described earlier, and therefore the motor rule is more liberal to the shipper than the rail rule in that the former excludes the entire weight of dunnage, whereas the latter grants an allowance of 500 pounds. Furthermore, there is no requirement in the motor rule, as there is in the rail rule, that the weight of dunnage must be shown on the bill of lading.[28]

In at least one instance, the Interstate Commerce Commission has handed down an opinion concerning dunnage used to protect shipment by motor carrier. The case involved a regular movement of steel containers, such as tubs, barrels, drums, and pails. The investigation brought out that the carrier's method of insulating and bracing these shipments had virtually eliminated scarring and other damage which the articles had sustained when being handled by other carriers, both motor and rail. The carrier herein involved requested authority to transport the dunnage and insulation materials, and since no charge had been assessed thereon, the carrier "evidently considers it a part of its equipment." The Commission held that, "whether dunnage in this instance be treated as carrier equipment or as part of the lading is immaterial, because it is incidental to the transportation of steel containers and no authority should be required for its transportation when so used. It cannot be regarded as a commodity separate and distinct from" the shipment itself.[29] Here, therefore, a highly specialized type of dunnage, designed and developed by the carrier to protect regular shipments of a particular commodity, and which presumably remained in the carrier's equipment assigned to the movement, was found to be a

---

[28] See, pp. 230–231, above.
[29] *Continental Transportation Company Extension of Operations,* 7 M.C.C. 248 (250–251), 1938.

part of such equipment, and could be transported free without its weight being included in the gross weight of the shipment for the purpose of assessing charges.

The rail rule grants use of estimated weights, when authorized, instead of actual gross weights. Estimated weights are prescribed for certain commodities shipped in specified standard containers as published in tariffs of the carriers. When so authorized by tariff, estimated weights supersede actual weights, and the necessity for weighing shipments of the particular commodity is eliminated; but the estimated weight must be published in a tariff before it may be used! The estimated weight, of course, is nearly equal to the actual weight of the commodity as possible; and, particularly on a carload shipment, the overages of some packages will tend to be offset by underweight of others, thereby balancing out all packages in the entire shipment. Hence, the estimated weight of an article, including its container, is the average weight per unit of all containers comprising the particular shipment. The Interstate Commerce Commission ruled over twenty years ago: "Use of estimated weights to facilitate and expedite movement of traffic or when use of actual weights is impracticable has long been approved. Estimated weights must approximate actual weights . . ." [30] Again in 1940, the Commission re-emphasized its former ruling by stating, "Estimated weights should reflect the averages of actual weights." [31] A considerable volume of fresh fruits and vegetables move on the basis of estimated weights, as, for example: on produce moving out of Florida, the estimated weight on celery has been established at 70 pounds per crate, tomatoes at 40 pounds per crate, oranges at 100 pounds per box. [32] Likewise, the estimated weight of a standard case containing 30 dozen eggs is 53 pounds, notwithstanding that the actual gross weight of a particular case of eggs may be more or less than 53 pounds. [33] Another example of estimated weights is petroleum products shipped in tank car lots where the weight per gallon is stated in the applicable tariff.

Another type of weight should be explained at this time. It is known as "Agreed Weight," which, as its name implies, is a formal agreement between shipper and carrier covering specified articles

[30] *Northwest Potato Exchange v. Great Northern Railway Company, et al.*, 172 I.C.C. 671 (672), 1931.
[31] *Estimated Weights on Citrus Fruits*, 237 I.C.C. 313 (316), 1940.
[32] *The Freight Traffic Red Book*, Traffic Publishing Company, New York, 1955 Edition, pp. 358–359.
[33] Knorst, W. J.: *Transportation and Traffic Management*, College of Advanced Traffic, Chicago, Vol. 1, Fourth Edition, 1952, p. 157.

shipped in certain kinds of containers. Unlike estimated weights, agreed weights are not published in tariffs. Under an agreed weight arrangement, carrier and shipper agree on what amounts to the average weight of a large number of identical packages containing a particular article, as certain kinds of canned goods. The gross weight of the shipment is determined by simply counting the number of containers and applying the agreed weight of each to the total number. The shipper is required to show on the face of the bill of lading that the shipment is covered by a weight agreement, together with the number assigned to the agreement. The originating terminal makes appropriate notation on the several copies of the waybill, usually by means of a rubber stamp, both to eliminate subsequent weighing and to enable the accounting office of the carrier to determine that proper weight has been applied to the shipment.

The rail rule further requires that the shipper must furnish at his expense any pallets or skids on which he may load his freight, and the extra weight thereof "will be charged for at rate applicable on the freight loaded thereon." The use of bracing and dunnage is made subject to the provisions of Rule No. 30, which was described earlier.[34]

Packages Containing Articles Classed or Rated Differently (M-11, R-12, NE-9). Where two or more differently rated articles are enclosed in the same package, the rating or rate applicable to the highest rated article will be assessed against the package. In other words, if two articles are packed in the same container, one of which carries a rating of Class 100 and the other Class 90, the rating of Class 100 will apply to the shipment. For the most part, the rail rule, consisting of seven sections, is similar to the motor rule. Its practicability has been upheld by the Interstate Commerce Commission in the following blunt statement: "For sound transportation reasons, the present rule . . . has proved satisfactory for many years." [35]

Mixed Volume Shipments (M-13, Sec 3 (b); R-10, NE-8). This is the important "mixed shipment" or "mixing" rule. Dean William J. Knorst, of the College of Advanced Traffic in Chicago, has made the significant comment that it "is one of the most important as well as one of the most misunderstood rules." [36] A mixed shipment consists of two or more articles for which the same or different ratings, rates, or volume minimum weights are provided when shipped to-

[34] See, pp. 230–231, above.
[35] *Mixed Freight in Packages*, 251 I.C.C. 461, 1942.
[36] Knorst, *op. cit.*, Vol. 1, p. 150.

gether as a single shipment. Hence, if the several articles were shipped independently of each other, they would constitute separate and distinct shipments, and the respective ratings, etc., would apply to each article. A mixed shipment, therefore, is the consolidation of any number of commodities into a single shipment. The motor rule states:

Unless otherwise provided, when a number of different articles, for which volume or truckload ratings or rates are provided when in straight volume or truckload shipments, are shipped . . . on one bill of lading as a mixed volume or a mixed truckload shipment, the entire shipment will be charged at the highest straight volume or truckload rate and subject to the highest straight volume or truckload minimum weight that would be applicable to any article in the shipment if that quantity of each article in the mixed shipment were tendered as a straight volume or straight truckload shipment; however, when the aggregate charge upon the entire shipment is less on basis of volume or truckload rate and volume of truckload minimum weight . . . for one or more of the articles and on the basis of less than truckload rate or rates on the actual or authorized estimated weight of the other article or articles, the shipment will be charged accordingly.

Section 4 of motor rule 13 provides:

Subject to the provisions of (the above quoted) Section 3 (b), when the aggregate charge upon the entire shipment is made lower by considering the articles as if they were divided into two or more separate shipments subject to other than LTL or AQ ratings, the shipment will be charged for accordingly.

Attention is called to the phrase, "or rates," in the above quotation. This means that application is not based exclusively on the Classification ratings, but it may also include published commodity rates or Classification exceptions. Should there be a commodity rate applicable to one of the articles which is higher than the rates on all the other articles involved, the higher commodity rate would apply to the entire mixed shipment.

An interesting case concerning rates applicable to mixed shipments was decided by the Interstate Commerce Commission in 1948, in which the intent of this rule was upheld. A motor common carrier, which the proceeding developed did not possess appropriate operating authority, transported dismantled dwelling houses from one federal housing project to another, a distance of 203 miles, requiring 1,300 truckload shipments of which 885 were mixed shipments. A tariff issued by the carrier provided that movement of the house sections from and to the specified points would be at the rate of $154 per house section on a truckload basis, and that a rate of $14.41 per ton would apply to component parts of the house sections, with a minimum of 10,000 pounds per load. All the shipments moved on the uniform bill of lading. The Commission held that since the carrier had no operating authority to perform the service, its rates were inapplicable, as well as being unreasonably high on the "component parts." However, it was found that the 885 mixed shipment loads included some 27 different articles, such as, flooring, doors, girders, nails, pipe, shingles; and the Commission prescribed a reasonable rate for those mixed shipments.[37]

Where the motor rule is applicable for assessing charges on mixed volume or truckload shipments, there are the following possible methods of determining the lowest charges: [38]

1. The shipment may be rated as one volume shipment and charges assessed at the highest straight volume rate or rating applicable to any article in the shipment.* The highest rate shall apply against the total actual weight of the shipment, but not less than the highest volume minimum weight provided for any rate or rating in the mixture.
2. The shipment may be rated as provided in No. 1, above, except where lower charges result by removing, for rating purposes only, one or more articles from the volume portion of the shipment, and rating such article or articles separately at the less-than-truckload rate or rating applicable to each such article, the shipment may be charged for accordingly.
3. The shipment may be rated as two or more volume shipments if lower charges result. When using this optional method, each such volume shipment must be rated separately as provided in No. 1, above. The total amount for the entire shipment shall be accumulated after each such volume shipment has been fully rated.
4. Charges may be assessed as provided in No. 3, above; and in connection with each such volume shipment, the less-than-truckload provisions of No. 2, above, may be invoked.

The lowest charge determined under any of the foregoing paragraphs is the applicable charge to assess on a given shipment. Less-than-truckload or "any quantity" rates or ratings may not be used in determining the charges for the volume rated portion of a ship-

---

[37] *Bush Construction Company, Inc., v. Arthur J. Platten, Doing Business as Trailer Transport Company*, 48 M.C.C. 155, 1948.

[38] Information furnished by C. J. Ackerman, Chief Rate Analyst, Southern Motor Carrier Rate Conference, Atlanta, September 9, 1955.

* A "straight rate or rating" is one that has application where the shipment consists of one commodity only. Where, in the rate or exceptions tariff, the wording "straight or mixed" is used in connection with the rate, rating, or description it may be considered as a straight rating for the purpose of applying the provisions of the rule or exceptions thereto.

ment under the above four methods, nor may the weight of any article which is rated l.t.l. or "AQ" in the shipment be used to make up the volume minimum weight.

Exceptions to the rule, which provide a more lenient basis of determining charges for mixed shipments, may be employed where the following conditions exist: [39]

1. All rate tariffs where applicable volume rates or ratings are found must provide the exceptions to provisions of the rule.
2. Carrier or carriers participating in the movement must also participate in the exceptions rule in each of the rate tariffs or governing publications where applicable rates are found.
3. Where the conditions stated in the two foregoing paragraphs do not exist, the tariff user may revert to the rule in determining charges on mixed shipments except where lower charges result from a specific mixture rate or rating, or where the shipment is charged for at less-than-truckload rates or ratings. A specific mixture rating is well illustrated by the Class 65 rating for "Mixed volume of bakers' peels; bung starters; butter ladles, molds or spades, chopping trays; . . ." [40]

Generally, lower charges result from the use of exceptions to the rule because of the provision that charges will be assessed for the actual weight of each article and at the straight volume rate attached to each article. The volume minimum weight will be the highest provided for any article in the mixed volume shipment, and any deficit in the minimum weight will be charged for at the highest volume rate or rating applicable to any article in the mixed volume shipment. Of course, where the total actual weight of a volume shipment is greater than the volume minimum weight, such actual weight must be used.

Rail rule No. 10 states that, except as elsewhere provided, if two or more articles carrying different ratings or rates constitute a carload shipment, the freight charges will be on the basis of the highest rating or rate, and the minimum weight for the entire shipment will be the highest provided for any article in the carload shipment. However, subject to the above conditions, "when the aggregate charge upon the entire shipment is made lower by considering the articles as if they were divided into two or more separate carloads, the shipment will be charged accordingly," provided the minimum weight of each separate shipment is no less than that applicable to a standard box car of 40 feet 7 inches in length. Two other sections contain further details which make alternative charges possible

---

[39] *Ibid.*
[40] *National Motor Freight Classification No. A-2, op. cit.,* Item 98380.

244

under specified circumstances. Professor G. Lloyd Wilson, of the University of Pennsylvania, has summarized five ways by which charges may be assessed under the rule whereby the shipper is entitled to the lowest basis of charges, as follows: [41]

1. The shipment may be considered as a single shipment and charged at the highest rate and highest carload minimum applicable to any article in the mixture.
2. The shipment may be rated as a number of less-than-carload shipments and the L.C.L. rate may be applied to each article.
3. The shipment may be divided into a number of carload shipments and the rates assessed on the basis of the rate applicable to the highest rated article and the highest carload minimum applicable to any article.
4. The shipment may be considered as one carload and several less-than-carload shipments and rated accordingly.
5. It may be rated as several carloads and several less-than-carload shipments.

The purpose of the "mixing" rule is to insure that carriers receive full revenues to which they are entitled for performing the service of transportation. As has been pointed out, under the law a common carrier is required to assess on an article the legal rate published in the applicable tariff. If, with a mixed shipment consisting of one article carrying a high rating and another article with a low rating and only the latter is shown on the bill of lading, the carrier may not receive the complete remuneration it should. Furthermore, the higher rated article may have involved an element of risk.

On the other hand, the "mixing" rule gives a positive advantage to the industrial traffic manager. Usually, utilization of the provisions of the rule involves shipment of two or more articles which individually would constitute a number of small shipments, but which collectively constitute a volume shipment by meeting the highest minimum truckload or carload weight applicable to either of the several articles on a volume basis. The small shipments would move at a higher rate per 100 pounds than the consolidated shipment on a volume basis, with consequent savings in total transportation costs. However, depending entirely upon the ratings or rates on the several small shipments involved, it might prove less expensive to ship one l.t.l. or l.c.l. and the others as a single volume shipment. To illustrate:

Assume a hardware store at point Y orders 30,000 pounds of wire rods, 5,000 pounds of certain aluminum articles, and 10,000 pounds of smoke house doors from a wholesaler at point X; that the

---

[41] Wilson, G. L.: *The Principles of Freight Traffic*, The Traffic World, Chicago (now, The Traffic Service Corporation, Washington), 1935, p. 29.

Class 100 freight rate from X to Y is $1.00; and that there are no exceptions ratings or commodity rates, necessitating that the traffic move on class rates. Upon reference to Uniform Freight Classification No. 2, effective December 10, 1953, the following will be found:

Wire rods, item 25670, l.c.l. rating 50, c.l. rating 35, minimum 40,000 pounds;
Aluminum, item 1540, l.c.l. rating 100, c.l. rating 77½, minimum 14,000 pounds;
The doors, item 7040, l.c.l. rating 85, c.l. rating 45, minimum 24,000 pounds.

If all three articles were shipped together as a mixed shipment, the rating on aluminum and the minimum weight on wire rods would govern; hence, the total freight charges would be computed on the basis of the total weight of 40,000 pounds multiplied by 77½ cents per 100 pounds, or $310. However, if the aluminum were shipped separately as an l.c.l. shipment and the other two articles consolidated into a single carload shipment, the total charges would be, as follows:

Aluminum, 5,000 pounds @ $1.00 per 100 pounds...$ 50
Rods, 30,000 pounds
Doors, 10,000 pounds
Total, 40,000 pounds @ 45¢ per 100 pounds........ 180
Total charges..........$230

Hence, by separating the aluminum from the rods and doors, it will be seen the shipper saves the difference between $310 and $230, or $80.

It cannot be said, however, that the "mixing" rule has been satisfactory as it applies to truckload and carload traffic. Today, there are many variations of the "mixing" principle which have been brought about by exceptions and by commodity tariffs.[42] For all practical purposes, carriers in the East and South have abandoned rail Rule 10 through the issuance of exceptions.[43]

Essentially to meet competition of motor carriers, the railroads have published exceptions to Rule 10 which provide more lenient treatment to mixed carload shipments. What is known as "modified" Rule 10 provides that, instead of making the rate on the highest rated article apply to the entire shipment as is stated in the regular

[42] Colquitt, *op. cit.*, p. 126.
[43] Van Metre, T. W.: *Industrial Traffic Management*, McGraw-Hill Book Company, New York, 1953, p. 74.

rule, the charges on a mixed carload shipment are determined by applying the straight carload class or commodity rate to each article individually. It further provides that the carload minimum weight shall be the highest applicable to any article in the mixed shipment, and that any deficiency in the weight will be assessed on the basis of the highest rating or rate applicable to any commodity included in the shipment. The advantage to a shipper of "modified" Rule 10 over the regular rule may be illustrated by using the same shipment to a hardware store described above. Application of the "modified" rule would enable the merchant to realize a further saving of $41.25 in his freight charges, as follows:

30,000 pounds of rods,	@ 35¢ per 100 pounds	$105.00
5,000 pounds of aluminum,	@ 77½¢ per 100 pounds	38.75
10,000 pounds of doors,	@ 45¢ per 100 pounds	45.00
	Total charges	$188.75

A further modification of the rule is found in "all-commodity" or "all-freight" rates which also have been adopted by railroads to meet motor carrier competition. These rates apply to mixed carloads of all commodities, except for a few restricted articles, the rate decreasing as the total weight increases, thus: 7¢ per 100 pounds between specified points for a minimum carload weight of 60,000 pounds, 8¢ for 50,000 pounds, 16¢ for 20,000 pounds.[44] Here, merely a flat rate is published for the entire mixture regardless of the articles being shipped, but depending upon the weight of the entire shipment. To illustrate:

Western Trunk Line and Southwestern Territories: [45]

Class 75—Minimum 12,000 pounds
Class 60—Minimum 25,000 pounds
Class 46—Minimum 30,000 pounds

From Chicago to Birmingham: [46]

$1.41—Minimum 12,000 pounds
$1.12—Minimum 25,000 pounds
86¢—Minimum 40,000 pounds

The Interstate Commerce Commission has held that, "The lawfulness of all-freight rates as such has been recognized and their place in railroad rate structures is well established." [47] Although

---

[44] *The Freight Traffic Red Book, op. cit.,* 1955, p. 36.
[45] *Ibid.,* pp. 112, 151.
[46] *Ibid.,* p. 71.
[47] *All-Freight to Pacific Coast,* 238 I.C.C. 327, 1940.

serving a useful purpose for the railroads, these all-commodity rates ignore the basic principles of freight classification. However, as the Commission has pointed out, a rate structure which was suitable twenty years or more ago need not necessarily be satisfactory to meet today's conditions.[48]

A third adaptation is known as "streamlined" Rule 10. It further liberalizes the "modified" version by permitting use of "all-freight" rates, which means either the straight carload rate or the "all-freight" rate is applicable to a mixed carload shipment. Generally, the "modified" rule is used in Western Classification Territory, and the "streamlined" rule in Official and Southern territories.[49] In effect, rail Rule 10 is commonly known as "modified" Rule 10, whereas the general exceptions are known as "streamlined" Rule 10.[50]

A more recent attempt to complete the destruction of Rule 10 was a rail proposal in 1954 which would allow the aggregate charges on mixed freight to be even lower than those resulting from application of an all-commodity rate to an entire carload shipment. The plan involved a combination of "modified" Rule 10 and all-commodity rates. The Commission ruled against it.[51]

A brief review of a few of the more important cases involving the "mixing" rule will be of interest. There have been instances where carriers and shippers have attempted to take advantage of the rule by applying the lower volume rates to a number of articles aggregating a volume shipment. In 1942, the Commission ruled against a motor common carrier which proposed to transport mixed truckload shipments of not more than five named articles at the truckload rate on each article. It was further proposed that the truckload rate on the *lowest* rated commodity in the mixture would apply to any deficit between actual weight of the mixed shipment and the required minimum weight. The Commission recognized that the rail rule required the carload rate be based upon the *highest* rated article in the mixed shipment. Here, the carrier had authority to transport freight in truckload quantities only, whereas the proposal would have resulted in its performing a less-than-truckload service. Said the Commission:[52]

---

[48] *I. & S. Docket No. 4315*, 232 I.C.C. 381, 1939.
[49] Taff, C. A.: *Traffic Management*, Irwin, Chicago, 1955, p. 160.
[50] Colquitt, *op. cit.*, p. 127.
[51] I.C.C. Docket No. 31006, *Eastern Central Motor Carriers Association v. Akron, Canton & Youngstown Railroad, et al.*, as reported in *Transport Topics, op. cit.*, Dec. 6, 1954, p. 18.
[52] *Rates and Rules—Barbour Transportation Company, Inc.*, 34 M.C.C. 87 (90), 1942.

The limitation upon the authority of the respondent herein precludes the aggregation by him of less-than-truckload shipments for one or more consignors. The proposed mixed-truckload rule would permit the aggregation of five less-than-truckload shipments, each destined to a different consignee. This exceeds the respondent's authority, and the proposed rule, therefore, would be unlawful.

Earlier, the Commission had issued an order in another case which would "preclude applicant from aggregating a number of smaller shipments from one or more consignors to make up the required minimum weight" of a truckload shipment.[53]

In a proceeding brought before the Commission shortly after enactment of the Motor Carrier Act of 1935, a motor carrier proposed a rate on tin plate which would be a part of mixed shipments of fiberboard boxes, can tappers, tin can covers, printing ink, rubber cement, stationery, and other items "used in connection with the manufacture and use of tin cans." In approving the proposal, the Commission said, "The grouping together of these particular commodities in mixed shipments does not appear to violate any provision of the Motor Carrier Act." [54]

A carrier proposed to establish commodity volume rates on articles rated first to fourth class, inclusive, and to establish the then existing class rates as commodity rates with a rule that "mixed shipments of two or more classes will be taken at rates applicable to each class on basis of the aggregate weight of the entire shipment." Said the Commission: [55]

It is well settled that the differences in the quantities transported as a single shipment may afford a fair and reasonable basis for differences in transportation rates. In rail transportation these differences are recognized as between carload and less-than-carload lots . . . Further, in rail transportation in connection with mixed carloads of allied, or commercially related, commodities generally transported for account of large shippers, the Commission has prescribed or approved the application of the respective carload rates to the actual weight of *each commodity* in the car.[56]

In suspending the proposal, the Commission, however, set up the following provisions for subsequent filing of a mixing rule: (1) the rates to apply only to small shipments rated first class or lower, (2)

[53] *Allen Conrad Bareford Contract Carrier Application,* 32 M.C.C. 611 (614), 1942.
[54] *Motor Express & Terminal Corporation Rates,* 14 M.C.C. 351 (354), 1939.
[55] *All Freight Between Portland, Oreg., and Seattle, Wash.,* 28 M.C.C. 55 (56–60), 1941.
[56] Italics supplied.

any deficiency in weight to be considered as fourth class, and (3) the proposed rates will not apply where specific commodity rates are applicable.[57] Only a few months prior to this decision, the Commission had rejected a somewhat similar proposal involving commodity rates, where the carriers felt that a shipper of mixed volume shipments under class rates was entitled to as much consideration as that usually accorded to shippers of single commodities under commodity volume rates.[58]

Again, the Commission approved a somewhat drastic exception to the mixing rule as stated in the Classification admittedly in order to meet competitive rail all-commodity rates. "So-called all-commodity freight rates have been approved in other proceedings, and where, as in the matter now before us, the rail carriers maintain such freight rates approved by the entire Commission, the motor carriers in fairness should be permitted to establish them on competitive traffic." [59]

In still another case, the Commission held: [60]

Mixing provisions generally stimulate volume movements, which are more profitable to the carriers than less-than-truckload shipments. The contention most vigorously advanced by the board (i.e., the National Classification Board), that one article could be included in an otherwise straight shipment of a higher-rated article for the purpose of defeating the higher rating on straight shipments, loses its force when consideration is given to the fact that any possible situation of this nature could as well or better be avoided by establishment of a reasonable limitation on the amount of the higher-rated articles which could be included in the mixed shipment.

A carrier is not permitted to establish rates on mixed truckloads when the carrier is not authorized to transport any of the articles included in the mixture.[61]

Admittedly, considerable emphasis has been devoted to this rule which, at least, should indicate its wide application, the many attempts to circumvent it, the numerous efforts to revise it, the uncertainty as to its interpretation, and the voluminous litigation it has caused. While it would be erroneous to imply that any one rule is more important than another, certainly it can be said that no other rule is of great practical significance than this "mixing" rule. For

[57] *Ibid.*, p. 60.
[58] *Mixed-Shipment Tonnage-Reduction Rule—Oregon*, 22 M.C.C. 533, 1940.
[59] Ex Parte No. MC-20, *Trunk Line Territory Motor Carrier Rates*, 29 M.C.C. 741 (743), 1941.
[60] *Classification, Boilers, Heaters, Tanks*, 49 M.C.C. 637 (648), 1949.
[61] *Minimum Rates and Charges—V. S. and V. R. Partridge*, 46 M.C.C. 245, 1946.

those who may wish to become better informed regarding the many aspects of freight mixtures, there is listed in the footnote below a number of railroad cases.[62]

In a recent case the Commission held, "There can be no doubt that a uniform mixing rule applicable throughout all, or practically all, of the country would be highly desirable"; but the carriers have not come up with, nor has the Commission prescribed, a practical rule which will meet the needs of the shipping public and, at the same time, be equitable to the carriers. In the words of the Commission, "Any attempt to re-establish (rail) Classification Rule 10 for general application would be impractical."[63]

---

[62] Colquitt, *op. cit.*, p. 131. *Investigation and Suspension Docket 76*, 25 I.C.C. 442, 1912.

In the Matter of Private Cars, 50 I.C.C. 652, 1918.

Consolidated Classification Case, 54 I.C.C. 1, 1919.

Rudy-Patrick Seed Company v. St. Louis–San Francisco Railway Company, 60 I.C.C. 411, 1920.

Classification of Paper Shopping Bags, 64 I.C.C. 423, 1921.

National Wholesale Grocers Association v. Director General, 69 I.C.C. 669, 1922.

Southern Class Rate Investigation, 100 I.C.C. 513, 1925.

Victor Manufacturing & Gasket Company v. Aberdeen & Rockfish Railroad Company, 147 I.C.C. 38, 1928.

McCormick Brothers Company v. Aroostook Valley Railway Company, 136 I.C.C. 79, 1927.

James Manufacturing Company v. Chicago & Northwestern Railway Company, 147 I.C.C. 271, 1928.

Welch Grape Juice Company v. Abilene & Southern Railway Company, 147 I.C.C. 361, 1928.

Nelson Manufacturing Company v. Missouri Pacific Railroad Company, 153 I.C.C. 272, 1929.

Armstrong Cork Company v. Pennsylvania Railroad Company, 153 I.C.C. 189, 1929.

Fisher Supply Company v. Alabama & Vicksburg Railway Company, 157 I.C.C. 711, 1929.

Merck & Company v. Baltimore & Ohio Railroad Company, 160 I.C.C. 639, 1929.

Bennett v. Michigan Central Railroad Company, 132 I.C.C. 400, 1927.

Cobb Company v. Missouri-Kansas-Texas Railroad Company, 163 I.C.C. 241, 1930.

Exceptions to Rule on Mixed Carloads, 163 I.C.C. 795, 1930.

Kohler v. Atchison, Topeka & Santa Fe Railway Company, 171 I.C.C. 241, 1930.

Crane Company v. Chicago & Alton Railroad Company, 171 I.C.C. 248, 1930.

Loose-Wiles Biscuit Company v. Atchison, Topeka & Santa Fe Railway Company, 177 I.C.C. 238, 1931.

Western Traffic Conference, Inc., v. Atchison, Topeka & Santa Fe Railway Company, 291 I.C.C. 427, 1954.

Mixed Freight in Packages, 251 I.C.C. 461, 1942.

[63] *Western Traffic Conference, Inc., v. Atchison, Topeka & Santa Fe Railway Company*, 291 I.C.C. 427, 1954.

Chapter 13

CLASSIFICATION RULES—
Part III

Minimum Charge (M-12, R-13, NE-29). The motor rule covers only small shipments moving strictly in intrastate commerce, and it emphasizes in bold print that it is "NOT APPLICABLE ON INTERSTATE COMMERCE." Minimum charges on interstate shipments are published in the motor carriers' tariffs.

Prior to cancellation of the minimum charge on interstate traffic, the Interstate Commerce Commission prescribed two bases of determination of the minimum charge for small shipments which are contained in the present rule on intrastate movements, viz.: (1) where the applicable class or commodity rate is Class 100 or lower, the charge will be for 100 pounds at the applicable rate; or (2) if the article is rated higher than Class 100, the charge will be for 100 pounds at the Class 100 rate.[1] A third provision of the rule refers to a mixed shipment, wherein if none of the articles is rated higher than Class 100, the charge will be for 100 pounds "at the class or commodity rate applicable to the article taking the highest rate"; but if rated higher than Class 100, the Class 100 rate will apply for 100 pounds. Hence, if a shipment weighs less than 100 pounds, it will be assessed a rate just as though its actual weight were 100 pounds; but if over 100 pounds, the actual weight will apply. The rule further specifies an absolute minimum charge of $1.25. There is no comparable absolute minimum, stated in terms of dollars and cents, for a volume shipment.

The New England rule refers only to mixed shipments, and it states that the "higher or highest minimum charge specified for any article in the shipment shall be the minimum charge applicable to the entire shipment."

The rail rule covers both small and large shipments, the former

---

[1] *Commodities from and to the Southwest,* 47 M.C.C. 155 (158), 1947.

being comparable to the provisions of the motor rule. The rail rule establishes an absolute minimum of $1.43 per less-than-carload shipment and, among other things, $28.60 per car for carload traffic, subject to increases authorized by the Interstate Commerce Commission in a proceeding known as "X-175." [2] Many articles moving in carload lots are excluded from the minimum charge provision of the rule by published Exceptions to the Classification, such as, brick, cement, coal, certain forest products, sand, gravel, stone, and others. The rail rule applies to both interstate and intrastate traffic.

The reason for establishing minimum charges is an attempt to cover actual carrier costs. Regardless of the size of a shipment, some costs remain the same, such as, for billing, receiving and delivery personnel, supervision, transportation, plus, of course, the constant costs or fixed costs common to the industry. It must be agreed that these minima are most nominal. When determining the applicable charges on a shipment, the regular or actual rate should be computed first, and then compared with the minimum prescribed in this rule. The actual charges will apply when higher than the minimum, but the minimum charge applies when it is higher than the regular charge.

Charges on Articles Subject to Individual Minimum Weights (M-12½). The motor rule is comparable to Sections 4, 5, and 7 of rail rule No. 12. In effect, it supplements the minimum charge rule, presented immediately above, by providing more detailed data concerning loose freight. It authorizes acceptance of packages or loose pieces of freight weighing less than the individual minimum weight thereof as specified in the Description of Articles section of the Classification. Concluding, Section 5 of the rule states: "The total charge for any shipment subject to the provisions of this rule shall not exceed by more than 50% the charges which would result from the use of the applicable rate or rating in connection with the actual weight on the entire shipment."

In 1938, the Interstate Commerce Commission instituted an investigation concerning the lawfulness of rates, rules, and practices of California carriers. Among other things, it was found that for a long period of time motor carriers had engaged in rate wars among themselves and with railroads, resulting "in unduly low and noncompensatory rates and charges, in an unstable rate structure, in unsound economic conditions in the transportation industry, and in unjust discrimination against various shippers and receivers of

---

[2] Ex Parte No. 175, *Increased Freight Rates and Charges, 1951,* 281 I.C.C. 557, 1952.

freight and their traffic." The California commission recommended a rule whereby minimum charges of carriers in the Los Angeles area would be based upon weight with the intent "to be competitive with parcel-post and express charges." Although the Interstate Commerce Commission recognized that the proposed minimum charge rule differed from requirements of the Classification rule, its adoption was ordered.[3] Furthermore, in prescribing just and reasonable minimum charges, the Commission took exception to the packaging provision of Rule No. 12½, to the general packing requirements of Rule No. 5, and to the "Mixed Shipment" rule.[4]

Definition of Shipment (M-13, R-14-15-16, NE-1). The motor rule defines a "shipment"; it describes the meaning of "truckload," "volume," "less-than-truckload," and "any quantity" ratings; it explains the manner in which rates are assessed against the ratings; and, as was presented earlier, a part of it relates to mixed shipments.[5] The three rail rules differentiate between carload and less-than-carload shipments, with provisions as to the charges applicable thereto.

The Interstate Commerce Commission has defined a shipment in the following language: [6]

A shipment is a quantity of freight received from one shipper at one time at one place consigned to one consignee at a single destination under one bill of lading. When the quantity of a shipment substantially fills the carrying capacity of a vehicle ordinarily used in intercity transportation it is generally considered a truckload, and when the quantity is substantially below the carrying capacity of a vehicle it is considered a less-than-truckload.

The above definition was handed down in a proceeding where a carrier possessing authority to transport general commodities in truckload quantities only had proposed to establish new rates on freight "aggregated" at Chicago for delivery to one or more of fifty destinations, but subject to a maximum of ten delivery points. The

---

[3] Ex Parte No. MC-24, *California Motor Carrier Rates,* 41 M.C.C. 19 (55–57), 1942.

[4] *Ibid.,* p. 69. Said the Commission: "For purpose of determining the minimum rates and charges prescribed herein, articles will not be subject to the packing requirements of the governing Classification or exception sheet but, except as otherwise provided herein, may be accepted in any containers or any shipping form, provided such containers or shipping form will render the transportation of the freight reasonably safe and practicable. If two or more ratings are provided in the governing Classification or exception sheet for an article, subject to different packing requirements, the lowest of such ratings shall be used."

[5] See, pp. 241–242, above.

[6] *Merchandise, Southwest Freight Lines, Inc.,* 51 M.C.C. 112 (115), 1949.

rates were designed to handle traffic from a large mail-order establishment to its retail stores and warehouses. They were to apply to shipments originating at one place in truckload lots with a minimum of 20,000 pounds, shipped from one consignor on one bill of lading to one consignee, but the consignee was located at any one of the fifty destinations. In declining the application, the Commission stated: [7]

Manifestly, 10 aggregated shipments from 1 consignor to the same consignee at 10 destinations would require approximately the same type of less-than-truckload service at 10 aggregated shipments from 1 consignor to different consignees at 10 destinations. . . . The provision for a 20,000 pound minimum and one consignee at more than one destination cannot tran(s)form a peddler service of multiple less-than-truckload shipments into a truckload service. On each of the separate shipments, less-than-truckload service would be performed. We conclude that respondent has no authority to perform that service.

In an earlier case the Commission commented as follows, regarding an attempt of a motor carrier to establish a minimum truckload weight of only 1,000 pounds: [8]

So far as pertinent, the defendants have authority to transport shipments in truckloads only, but, under the guise of designating less-than-truckload rates as truckload rates, they are attempting to obtain less-than-truckload shipments weighing not less than 1,000 pounds. . . . We find that the defendants' . . . rates, minimum 1,000 pounds, . . . apply to the transportation of less-than-truckload shipments; . . . and, accordingly, that such rates are unlawful.

Considerable emphasis was stressed by the Commission in the proper interpretation of a truckload (or carload) shipment when it ruled, as follows: [9]

There has been little, if any, consideration given to the proper construction of this ("truckloads") term. It clearly implies, however, the transportation by a carrier of a load of freight to the capacity of its vehicle, or the transportation of a load of freight at a minimum weight which removes the load from the category of less-than-truckload shipments. We do not believe that any question would arise as to the right of a carrier authorized to transport only "truckloads," to include in a load a mixture of several different articles of freight, provided the truckload moves from one consignor to one consignee. We doubt, however, that

---

[7] *Ibid.*, p. 116.

[8] *Intermountain-Coast Motor Freight Tariff Bureau v. George A. Sims and Milton K. Sims, Doing Business as Salt Lake Transfer Company*, 42 M.C.C. 589 (595), 1943.

[9] *Rates and Rules—Barbour Transportation Company, Inc.*, 34 M.C.C. 87 (90), 1942.

authority to transport "truckloads" may properly be construed as embracing the right to handle a load, mixed or straight, consigned to a number of different consignees. In that event, the consignor would be receiving less-than-truckload service in respect of each of the separate consignments.

The motor and rail rules distinguish between large and small shipments in accordance with the minimum weight provisions stated for each article in the Description of Articles section of the respective Classifications. It should always be remembered that the minimum truckload or carload weight stated in the applicable Classification is the lowest weight on which a truckload or carload rating or rate will apply. Likewise, a shipment loaded by a shipper and offered to a carrier as a volume shipment, but which does not weigh as much as the required minimum weight for a volume shipment of that particular commodity, will be charged on the basis of the applicable minimum weight. This is entirely proper because the excess space in the trailer or car cannot be utilized to transport other freight, for once the trailer or car is dispatched, the excess space from that individual movement is lost forever. Unused capacity of facilities is one of the most unfortunate characteristics of the transportation industry. A partially loaded unit of a carrier's equipment represents irretrievable loss because the unused space cannot be stored for future traffic.

An "Any Quantity" rating, commonly referred to as "AQ," applies to an article for which no minimum weight is provided in a Classification for a volume, truckload, or carload shipment. For that type of shipment, the freight rate is assessed on the basis of the actual weight of the shipment.

Both the motor and rail rules further provide that the charges on a small shipment shall not exceed in the aggregate those of a large shipment of the same commodity at the volume rate when the small shipments meet the minimum weight requirements for the same article. This is a most important provision because it permits the industrial traffic manager to determine his actual freight charges on either the higher basis of a small shipment or the lower basis of a large shipment, and whichever produces the lesser amount applies to the shipment. To illustrate, assuming the following conditions apply to an article being shipped from one city to another:

> Actual weight of shipment...........20,000 pounds
> Minimum volume weight............25,000 pounds
> Rate, for small shipment............60¢ per 100 pounds
> Rate, for large shipment.............40¢ per 100 pounds

If shipped as a small shipment, the charges would be on the basis of 60¢ for actual weight, or $120; as a large shipment, on the basis of 40¢ for the minimum weight of 25,000 pounds, or $100, producing an obvious saving of $20.

It is not unusual that a shipment of relatively small weight will move cheaper as a volume shipment than as a small shipment by paying the rate applicable to the minimum volume weight for the former, and this is especially true when the less-than-truckload or less-than-carload rating is over Class 100. Hence, it behooves the efficient industrial traffic manager always to figure the charges on shipments of this nature on both bases to determine which will produce the lower total charge. However, the shipper should keep in mind that he should show both weights on the bill of lading, thus:

Actual Weight, 20,000 pounds
as   (Truckload)
25,000 pounds   (Carload)—Minimum

A further incidental saving to the shipper by forwarding and billing the goods as a volume shipment is entire elimination of the expense, time, and trouble of marking each package which, it will be recalled, is required for small shipments.[10]

The provision of this rule again illustrates the utmost importance of familiarity with the general principles contained in the Classification rules. Without knowledge of the existence of this particular rule, it is conceivable the freight, in the above example, would have been forwarded as a small shipment. Of course, an alert billing clerk in the carrier's employ would have discovered the error and caused a refund of $20 to be made; and it is worthy of mention that such a refund would create inestimable goodwill for the carrier.

The last clause in the last sentence of Section 3 (a) of the motor rule is most significant, viz.: "When a Volume or Truckload rating is used, charges will be assessed at the volume or truckload minimum weight shown herein, *except that actual weight will apply when in excess of the volume or truckload minimum weight.*"[11] In contrast, a rule in the Rail Classification, No. 24,[12] provides that a shipment requiring more than one car, when the authorized minimum weight is 30,000 pounds or more, will be subject to a minimum of 6,000 pounds for the excess if loaded in a closed car, and 4,000

---

[10] See, Rule No. 6, p. 222, above.
[11] Italics supplied.
[12] See, p. 236, above.

pounds at the Class 100 rate if loaded in an open car. Since there is no minimum weight restriction on a truck shipment in excess of the physical capacity of the vehicle and no requirement of a Class 100 rate for open-top equipment, the motor rule is more liberal to shippers than the rail rule. Thus, if that portion of a volume shipment which could not be loaded within the physical capacity of the carrier's equipment weighed 2,000 pounds, by motor the excess weight would be charged at the straight truckload rate applicable to 2,000 pounds; but by rail, in the absence of published exceptions, the excess 2,000 pounds would be charged on the basis of 6,000 pounds.

Rail Rule No. 14, pertaining to carload freight, further states that carload ratings or rates will apply in accordance with applicable tariffs for shipments loaded or unloaded by the carrier, split deliveries, stopovers, and transit privileges.[13] This rule has been modified from time to time to meet changing conditions; hence, supplements and exceptions to the Classification should be consulted so that new provisions will not be overlooked.

Section 1 of rail Rule No. 15 adds to the general rule, that the charge on a less-than-carload shipment shall not exceed the carload rate, by stating: "The charge for a car fully loaded must not exceed the charge for the same lot of freight if taken as an LCL shipment." Continuing, the Section specifies the above provisions will not apply to small shipments where pick-up or delivery service has been performed, "except where otherwise provided in tariffs of individual carriers." This latter provision is mandatory and prohibits rescinding of pick-up or delivery service after it has been performed.[14]

Section 2 of the same rule provides that when it is discoverd at destination less-than-carload shipment qualifies as a carload shipment, the lower carload rate will apply, and Section 2 grants the carrier authority to assess a charge of 8 cents per 100 pounds for loading and a like amount for unloading the freight. One of the primary justifications for a lower rate on volume shipments than on small shipments is that the shipper loads and the receiver unloads the freight at their expense, and the carrier thereby is relieved of handling costs at both its origin and destination terminals, plus possible transfers at intermediate points. Rail Rule No. 27, which was

---

[13] Split deliveries, meaning delivery of the freight at destination to two or more persons, is an exception to the general rule that there be only one consignee.

[14] *American Sales Book Company, Incorporated, v. New York Central Railroad, et al.*, 263 I.C.C. 511 (513), 1945.

presented earlier,[15] requires that freight be loaded and unloaded by the shipper and receiver, respectively, in order for the carload rate to apply. Therefore, if a carload rate subsequently is applied to what was billed as a less-than-carload shipment, the railroad is entitled to the extra compensation for its costs and services incident to the physical handling of the goods which should have been billed as a carload shipment in the first place. The charge of 8 cents per 100 pounds is *not* a penalty assessment; rather, it is intended to cover actual costs incurred by the carrier. The motor rule contains no comparable provision.

Rail Rule No. 16 defines less-than-carload freight. Section 3 states: "Two or more single shipments shall not be combined and way-billed as one shipment, but must be carried as separate shipments and at not less than the established minimum charge for each shipment."

Classification By Analogy (M-14, R-17, NE-23). This is the famous Rule of Analogy. From time to time, it is inevitable that someone will wish to ship something which is not included in the Description of Articles section of a Classification. While the published Classifications list and provide ratings for all known articles of commerce, the ever-changing economy of the country results in new articles being produced and tendered to the carriers for shipment. This rule provides for such shipments by authorizing a means for rating unclassified commodities. Classification by analogy occurs when the rating of an existing article is applied to a new or unclassified article which possesses similar transportation characteristics of the existing article.

When an article which is not specifically described in a Classification is offered for shipment, the rating of the "most closely analogous" article in the judgment of the carrier will be applied to it. The resemblance of the classified article to the unclassified article must recognize such transportation similarities as, size, shape, weight, value, etc. This method of applying a rating is a temporary expedient in order to move the shipment promptly when tendered to a carrier, for it eliminates the delay of securing an official rating by means of the procedures of the appropriate classification committee or board.[16]

The motor rule requires that the "facts must be reported to the

[15] See, p. 227, above.

[16] The story is told of an Army officer who had to dispose of a large supply of gas mask bags. After diligent search through the Classification, they were shipped as haversacks subject to this rule, haversacks being the most closely analogous article to gas mask bags.

Chairman of the National Classification Board through the traffic officer of the carrier in order that the establishment of specific provisions may be considered." The rail rule provides that the facts shall be reported to the "proper officer of Freight Department" for the same purpose. This provision is necessary in order to establish a permanent rating for the article, if found justifiable by anticipated future shipments; and because local carrier employees are not expected to have the expert knowledge of classification matters as is possessed by members of the classification board and committees. Where a new or unclassified article is to be shipped, it should be referred to the proper classification body; but pending an official ruling, the freight is permitted to move under this rule.

Both the Motor and Rail Classifications state the rule will not apply to exceptions to the Classification nor to commodity rates; therefore, use of the rule is restricted to the Classification itself. This limitation was upheld by the Interstate Commerce Commission, as follows: ". . . the language of (rail) Rule 17 definitely restricts the application of its provisions to the *classification* of commodities. It can not be used to determine the application of commodity rates carried in commodity tariffs." [17]

Actual shipments of two articles serve to illustrate application of the rule. The first relates to terrazzo materials, which are marble chips used for flooring. The article does not appear in the Motor and Rail Classifications. Shipments are made under authority of this rule and the commodity is rated as crushed stone.[18] The second involved rail shipments of rocket propelling units. For a time this rule was applied and the commodity was rated as blank cannon cartridges.[19] Subsequently, a supplement to the then existing Classification established a new description to cover the article.[20] The latter case further illustrates constructive action by the classification committee to create a proper description for a new commodity and thereby eliminate the necessity for continued use of the rule.[21]

Iron vs. Steel, Rubber, Plastic, and Gauge of Metal (M-14½, R-25-28, NE-1). This rule merely explains use of the words contained in the subject, such as: "iron" and "steel" may be used inter-

---

[17] *Cullum & Boren Company, et al., v. Chicago, Burlington & Quincy Railroad, et al.*, 93 I.C.C. 354 (355), 1924.

[18] *National Motor Freight Classification No. A-2, op. cit.,* Item 47880; *Uniform Freight Classification No. 2, op. cit.,* Item 22070.

[19] *Uniform Freight Classification No. 2, op. cit.,* Item 1835.

[20] *Supplement 20 to Uniform Freight Classification No. 2,* Consolidated Classification Committee, Chicago, effective May 15, 1955, Item 1835-A.

[21] The author is indebted to Mr. Harry E. Dixon of Roanoke, Virginia, owner of a nation-wide traffic management service which bears his name and past president of Delta Nu Alpha Transportation Fraternity, for bringing this example to his attention.

changeably, "rubber" includes natural and various synthetic rubbers, etc.

Combination of Articles (M-15, R-18, NE-11). "When not specifically classified, articles which have been combined or attached to each other will be charged for at the rating for the highest classed article of the combination and on a shipment subject to volume or truckload (or carload) rating, the minimum weight will be the highest minimum weight provided for any article in the combination." Should the combined article be broken down into its different constituent parts and shipped accordingly, then the Mixed Shipment rule would apply.[22]

This rule is designed to take care of new products being placed on the market pending determination of a specific rating and, therefore, it may be considered as supplementing the Rule of Analogy.[23] If a shipper produces an article which, actually, is two separate articles combined into one, such as a combination radio and phonograph, and there is no provision in the Classification for the combination, then the freight rate would be assessed on the basis of the highest rating applicable to each of the component parts of the combination article. The Classifications contain descriptions for many combination articles; but when one which is not listed is offered for transportation, the rate will be determined in accordance with this rule. The first phrase of the rule, "when not specifically classified," is most significant, because it permits the rating on a combined article contained in the Classification to take precedence over the rule. Some examples are: "Mop wringers and wheeled tanks or trucks combined,"[24] "Chairs or stools and step ladders combined,"[25] "Air cleaners, coolers, dehumidifiers, heaters other than portable, humidifiers or washers combined with blowers or fans."[26]

Frequently, however, difficulties arise in the interpretation and actual application of the rule for many of today's modern devices. An article of dual design and function may be considered as one article just as well as another. Mr. Colquitt, in his book to which previous reference has been made, states:[27]

The rule involves the application of common sense. The general idea is that the combination rule applies only to articles which though physically combined retain their separate functions and identities. . . . Vari-

---

[22] See, pp. 241–251, above.
[23] See, p. 259, above.
[24] *National Motor Freight Classification No. A-2, op. cit.,* Item 92840.
[25] *Ibid.,* Item 43390.
[26] *Ibid.,* Item 58330.
[27] Colquitt, *op. cit.,* p. 188.

ous attempts have been made to apply the rule to *mixtures* of ingredients constituting a formula or solution, such as a mixture of chemical elements, or one or more ingredients which when mixed constitute a distinct commodity. Such was never the purpose of the rule. Application of it to a distinct commodity would amount to a perversion of the rule. Sometimes articles that are claimed to come under the rule really constitute two or more distinct and separate articles that in fact constitute mixed packages and that, therefore, are subject to the rule governing mixed packages.

A number of cases on the subject are shown in the footnote below.[28]

Parts or Pieces Constituting a Complete Article (M-16, R-20, NE-12). "Parts or pieces constituting a complete article, received on one bill of lading, will be charged for at the rating provided for the complete article." The rule appears simple and self-explanatory; yet, there has been considerable litigation concerning its interpretation.

Applicability of the rule is determined by two factors, namely: (1) the separate pieces actually comprise a complete article, and (2) all the pieces are shipped as one shipment covered by one bill of lading. The rule should not be interpreted so as to deny a shipper the right of dismantling an article and shipping its component parts as separate shipments on separate bills of lading if, by so doing, he is able to obtain lower total transportation charges.

There have been many cases before the Interstate Commerce Commission involving the rail rule in which the Commission has upheld its lawfulness.[29] One pertaining to the motor rule was de-

---

[28] Colquitt, *op. cit.*, p. 190. *Ford v. Michigan Central Railroad Company,* 19 I.C.C. 507, 1910.

American Flange & Manufacturing Company v. Atchison, Topeka & Santa Fe Railway Company, 178 I.C.C. 739, 1931.

Weaver Pants Corporation v. Alabama Great Southern Railway Company, 223 I.C.C. 566, 1937.

Oakland Truck Company v. Baltimore & Ohio Railroad Company, 270 I.C.C. 548, 1948.

National Radiator Company v. Pennsylvania Railroad Company, 256 I.C.C. 82, 1943.

Harrison Construction Company v. Cincinnati, New Orleans & Texas Pacific Railway Company, 266 I.C.C. 313, 1946.

Easy Washing Machine Corporation v. Red Star Express Lines of Auburn, Inc., 49 M.C.C. 259, 1949.

[29] Colquitt, *op. cit.*, pp. 192–196. *Western Classification Case,* 25 I.C.C. 442, 1912.

Ratings on Glove-Palm Reinforcements, 161 I.C.C. 696, 1930.

George E. Fern Company v. Cleveland, Cincinnati, Chicago & St. Louis Railway Company, 248 I.C.C. 679, 1942.

Classification Ratings on Airplane Seats, 266 I.C.C. 702, 1946.

Nutting Truck Company v. Chicago Great Western Railroad Company, 246 I.C.C. 479, 1941.

cided in 1943, which again illustrates how a shipper may reduce his freight charges by being familiar with the rules. A less-than-truck-load shipment on one bill of lading consisted of eight crates, including one crate of tools, and, except for the tools the articles were components of a neon electric sign. The carrier assessed charges on the basis of the rate applicable to neon signs, but later conceded there had been an overcharge on the tools and offered proper adjustment. The consignee (complainant) contended he was entitled to the lowest charges applicable to the constituent parts. Said the Commission in sustaining the carrier: [30]

The charges collected resulted from the application of rule 16, of the National Motor Freight Classification . . . The primary question is whether these various items constituted the parts and pieces of a complete article, i.e., a neon electric sign, as contemplated by rule 16. The bill of lading was not introduced in evidence, but the various components of the shipment are all listed on one paid freight bill. Defendant treated the shipment as a complete neon electric sign, and assessed the charges accordingly. At no stage of the proceeding has the complainant contended that the packages were forwarded on separate bills of lading . . . The conclusion is warranted that the various packages, except the tools, together constituted a complete article . . .
A shipper has the right to disassemble his product in any way which would make the shipment take a lower rate than if the article were in final form. The classification rule does not abridge that right, for it is inapplicable to shipments separately billed and shipped. However, if all, or substantially all, of the pieces constituting a complete article are offered as one shipment under one bill of lading, the freight charges should be calculated upon the rating for the complete article . . .
Complainant stresses the fact that the various items in the shipment were separately listed on the paid freight bill and apparently also listed separately on the bill of lading. This is not sufficient; they must also be separately shipped, and the separate shipments evidenced by separate bills of lading.

Dresser-Stacey Company v. Abilene & Southern Railway Company, 291 I.C.C. 677, 1954.
Algoma Plywood & Veneer Company v. Aberdeen & Rockfish Railroad Company, 274 I.C.C. 231, 1949.
Lakewood Engineering Company v. Director General, 57 I.C.C. 311, 1920.
Parkersburg Rig & Reel Company v. Baltimore & Ohio Railroad Company, 115 I.C.C. 539, 1926.
Memphis Freight Bureau v. Atchison, Topeka & Santa Fe Railway Company, 174 I.C.C. 171, 1931.
Diamond T Motor Company v. Michigan Central Railway Company, 200 I.C.C. 599, 1934.
Westinghouse Electric Supply Company v. Alton & Southern Railroad Company, 226 I.C.C. 367, 1938.
Associated Telegraph Company v. Chicago & North Western Railway Company, 251 I.C.C. 311, 1942.
[30] *Electrical Products Corporation v. Consolidated Copperstate Lines,* 42 M.C.C. 103 (104–106), 1943.

In the above case, if the consignor had shipped the component parts of the sign as separate shipments on separate bills of lading, the rate applicable to each individual article would have applied instead of the rate on neon signs. At the time of the occurrence, the less-than-truckload rating on neon signs was four times the first-class rate, which was considerably higher than that applicable to the component parts individually.

"Knocked Down" Articles (M-17, R-19, NE-1). A "knocked down" article is one which has been taken apart in order to reduce its original bulk and, by reason of reduction of its over-all measurements, it occupies less space than the entire assembled, or "set up" article in a carrier's equipment. Generally, the rating on a "knocked down" article is less than that on a "set up" article.

The rule is simple, for it states that ratings on "knocked down" articles will apply only when the article "is taken apart in such manner as to materially reduce space occupied." Mere separation of an article into parts without reducing its bulk does not entitle the shipment to a "knocked down" rating. The motor rule is more specific than the rail rule in that it requires for such a rating to apply, the normal cubage of the assembled article must be reduced by at least one-third. For example, suppose a kitchen cabinet is to be shipped. If the top is separated from the bottom without reducing its total cubic footage, it would not be entitled to a "knocked down" rating. In contrast, if a kitchen table were being shipped and its legs were removed and bundled together, obviously there would be considerable reduction in the space required to accommodate the "set up" table. The same principle applies to a conventional card table which, when its legs are folded, is easier to handle and occupies less space when stored in a closet.

The rule, therefore, encourages conservation of space. The quantity of freight that can be loaded into a trailer or car is restricted to the cubic capacity of the carrier's equipment. Carriers must protect themselves against shipments which are so light in proportion to space occupied that they fill the available space without producing adequate revenues. The expenses for pulling a light trailer or car are practically the same as for a heavy one, because, other than fuel consumption, the costs of equipment, terminal facilities, labor, etc., remain the same regardless of the kind of freight that is transported. Hence, other things being equal, an article of great bulk in relation to weight usually is assessed a higher rating or rate than an article of higher density.

Some articles are constructed so that they can be taken apart and thereby reduce their original bulk. Generally, both shipper and carrier benefit when such articles are "knocked down": the shipper, by lower freight charges; the carrier, either by requiring less equipment to move the shipment, or by being able to load other shipments in the same piece of equipment, or both. Another factor is that "knocked down" articles, when properly packed, are less susceptible to damage than when "set up."

The Classifications contain separate ratings for many articles which are capable of being shipped either "set up" or "knocked down," thus, for less-than-truckload shipments:

	Class	
Article	Set Up	Knocked Down
Corn Pickers..............	100	85 [31]
Cotton Pickers............	200	100 [32]
Children's Sand Boxes.....	100	85 [33]
Bee Hives................	150	55 [34]
Steel Telephone Booths....	100	70 [35]
Children's Tricycles........	200	100 [36]

A decision of the Commission in 1911, involving church altars, is of historical importance both because it defined a "knocked down" article and led to establishment of the present rule. The first rule was in the Rail Southern Classification in 1915.[37] Said the Commission: [38]

Complainant does not object to the rating of altars, set up, at double first class, but contends that altars, knocked down, ought not to be rated higher than first class. Some evidence was introduced to the effect that certain altars may be so packed when knocked down as to occupy but one-half the space required when they are set up . . . The term "knocked down" has a definite and well understood meaning in railroad terminology; it involves taking apart the article shipped in such manner as to reduce materially the space occupied. Merely separating the article into parts and crating them, without reducing the bulk, would not constitute knocking down in such a manner as to justify a reduction in the rate. . . . These wooden altars have been given the double first class rate because of the considerable space occupied by them in proportion to

[31] *National Motor Freight Classification No. A-2, op. cit.,* Item 1400.
[32] *Ibid.,* Item 1450.
[33] *Ibid.,* Item 5600.
[34] *Ibid.,* Item 9250.
[35] *Ibid.,* Item 12060.
[36] *Ibid.,* Item 92970.
[37] Colquitt, *op. cit.,* pp. 198–199.
[38] *Fond du Lac Church Furnishing Company v. Chicago, Milwaukee & St. Paul Railway Company,* 21 I.C.C. 481, 1911.

their weight. When that ratio is reduced there should be a corresponding reduction in rate.

An amusing proceeding, in which the Commission ruled against the shipper, was where a consignor demanded a "knocked down" rating on a row-boat because the seats and oar locks had been removed! [39]

"Nested" or "Nested Solid" Articles (M-18, R-21, NE-1). The purpose of this rule is the same as the previous "Knocked Down" rule: conservation of shipping space. Here, provisions are made for "nested" articles which are defined, as follows:

NESTED: Three or more different sizes of the article enclosed each smaller within the next larger, or three or more of the articles placed one within the other so that each upper article will not project above the next lower article more than one-third of its height.

NESTED SOLID: Three or more of the articles placed one within or upon the other so that the outer side surface of the one above will be in contact with the inner side surfaces of the one below and so that each upper article will not project above the next lower more than one-quarter inch.

It will be observed there must be at least three articles in order for the rule to be used. Tin lamp shades furnish an excellent illustration. Both the Motor and Rail Classifications carry three ratings, depending entirely upon how the shades are prepared for shipment, viz.: [40]

```
Not Nested.......Class 100
Nested...........Class 85
Nested Solid......Class 70 for motor, Class 77½ for rail
```

Section 2 specifies that the "nested" articles must be of the same name or made of the same material in order for the rule to apply. Again using lamp shades for illustrative purposes, if they were made of cloth, parchment, and tin, respectively, this rule would not apply.

A "nested" article should not be confused with an "interlaced" one. The latter is used where a commodity cannot actually be "nested," but which complies with the spirit of "nesting" by increasing its density and thereby occupying less space. Illustrative are chair frames: when "interlaced," both the Motor and Rail Classifications provide a volume rating of Class 45; but when "not inter-

---

[39] *Keller v. St. Louis Southwestern Railway Company*, 21 I.C.C. 488, 1911.
[40] *Ibid.*, Item 56110; *Uniform Freight Classification No. 2*, op. cit., Item 25830.

laced," the motor rating is Class 100 and the rail rating is Class 70.[41]

Usually, a "nested" article carries a lower rating than an "un-nested" article. As was the case in the "knocked down" rule,[42] the Classifications differentiate between the two in the following manner:

Article	Class Not Nested	Class Nested
Automobile Hoods.............	150	85 [43]
Wooden Barrels...............	200	100 [44]
Coal Delivery Chutes.........	100	70 [45]
Garden Heaters...............	100	85 [46]
Garbage Cans.................	200	100 [47]
Steel Pails..................	100	85 [48]

Wooden Articles "In the Rough," "In the White," or "Finished" (M-19, R-22). This rule distinguishes between different stages of manufacture of wooden articles, as follows:

(1) "In the Rough"—when only sawed, hewn, planed, or bent.
(2) "In the White"—when further manufactured than in No. 1, but contains not more than one coat of priming.
(3) "Finished" —after the stage of manufacture provided in No. 2.

The ratings on such articles increase as they reach the "finished" stage. The following less-than-truckload ratings on certain kinds of woodenware are illustrative: [49]

Finished.............................Class 70
In the White........................Class 60
In the Rough........................Class 50

It has long been established that usually the ratings on manufactured articles are higher than the ratings on the materials from which such articles are made,[50] although there are occasions where a user of a product will consider an article as being a raw material while another party considers the same product as being

---

[41] *National Motor Freight Classification No. A-2, op. cit.,* Item 44710; *Uniform Freight Classification No. 2, op. cit.,* Item 20555.
[42] See, p. 264, above.
[43] *National Motor Freight Classification No. A-2, op. cit.,* Item 6500.
[44] *Ibid.,* Item 8390.
[45] *Ibid.,* Item 25970.
[46] *Ibid.,* Item 36160.
[47] *Ibid.,* Item 85540.
[48] *Ibid.,* Item 85750.
[49] *Ibid.,* Item 98360.
[50] *Breading Compounds, Classification Ratings,* 51 M.C.C. 634 (636), 1950.

a manufactured article.[51] This general understanding is the basis for the three categories of wooden articles.

There can be a very fine distinction as to whether an article is "in the rough" or "finished"; and, commercially, the terms are not restricted to wooden articles. In a case involving steel castings, it was brought out that a carrier might consider the article as being "finished" instead of still "in the rough," notwithstanding that "as much as ¼ inch of the surface would have to be removed to finish the article for a specific use." [52] Again, where a shipper contended the lower rate on Plaster of Paris should apply to Dental Plaster, the Commission said: [53]

Dental Plaster is further processed than Plaster of Paris and is usually scented before it is ready for use by the dental profession and that, when so processed, it is of course sold in much smaller units and at a much higher price.

In still another case, the Commission stated: [54]

To admit correctness of complainant's position, that the addition of a comparatively small amount of foreign and much more valuable substance does not change the nature of a commodity, not only does violence to this principle but opens the way to countless claims that articles which have been subjected to further stages of manufacture nevertheless remain entitled to the rates applicable to the less-manufactured article.

There has been considerable litigation with rail carriers concerning interpretation of the Classification rule. Years ago, the Commission remarked, "Throughout the country the lack of uniformity in the relationship of rates on wood articles and lumber is marked." [55] A few other cases on the subject are listed in the footnote below.[56]

[51] *Chicago Rawhide Manufacturing Company v. Long Transportation Company*, 48 M.C.C. 646 (649), 1948.

[52] *Description of Castings and Forgings in Central Territory*, 51 M.C.C. 441 (443), 1950.

[53] *United States Gypsum Company v. Staten Island Rapid Transit Railway Company, et al.*, 151 I.C.C. 641, 1929.

[54] *Lockport Fittings Company, Inc., v. Akron, Canton & Youngstown Railroad Company, et al.*, 241 I.C.C. 653, 1940.

[55] *Eastern Wheel Manufacturers Association v. Albama & Vicksburg Railway Company*, 27 I.C.C. 370, 1913.

[56] *Anson, Gilkey & Hurd Company v. Southern Pacific Company*, 33 I.C.C. 332, 1915.

Yellow Pine Sash Door & Blind Manufacturers Association v. Southern Railway Company, 35 I.C.C. 150, 1915.

Rates on Lumber and Lumber Products, 52 I.C.C. 598, 1919.

Wichita Wholesale Furniture Company v. Atchison, Topeka & Santa Fe Railway Company, 51 I.C.C. 586, 1918.

National Broom Company v. Atchison, Topeka & Santa Fe Railway Company, 128 I.C.C. 98, 1927.

One interesting case pertains to motor carriers. The freight consisted of flat plywood faced with walnut or poplar, packed in crates, and cut to size according to the consignee's specifications. The plywood was used in the manufacture of tables, desks, and other pieces of furniture. The shipments were described on bills of lading as "Built-up Wood n.o.i.b.n.," whereas the carrier contended the proper description should have been "Furniture Parts, n.o.i.," and alleged a total undercharge of over $25,000. The Commission, in ruling in favor of the shipper, found the lower rate applicable to wooden furniture stock "in the white" was proper, because: "The pieces shipped had ceased to be built-up wood or plywood and the issue presented is whether they had become furniture stock or furniture parts. We are of the opinion they constitute the former. Although the pieces were intended for use as furniture parts, their actual character while in transit, and not their intended use, is controlling as to the proper description to be accorded them." [57]

Application of Rates, Ratings, and Exceptions, Volume or Truckload Minimum Weights (M-26, R-38, NE-19). Although the intent is the same, the motor and rail rules read differently. With only two exceptions, a published commodity rate supersedes a class rate. One exception is when a commodity tariff specifically authorizes alternative use of both the applicable class and commodity rates. Generally, this means that if the class rate, or a combination of class and commodity rates, should be lower than the commodity rate, the lower will apply. It should be remembered that class rates are in effect between practically all points, and that commodity rates are published to meet certain situations. A commodity rate may be either higher or lower than the class rate on the same article between the same points; but in most instances, the commodity rate is lower. If this were not the case, there would have been no need to disrupt the Classification rating by adoption of a commodity rate. In this respect, the Interstate Commerce Commission has said: [58]

Hudson Manufacturing Company v. Chicago, Milwaukee & St. Paul Railway Company, 146 I.C.C. 635, 1928.

Ames Shovel & Tool Company v. New York, New Haven & Hartford Railroad Company, 148 I.C.C. 487, 1928.

Ohio Wood Products Company v. Arcade & Attica Railroad Corporation, 167 I.C.C. 445, 1930.

United Lens Company, Inc., v. Pennsylvania Railroad Company, 256 I.C.C. 370, 1943.

Southwestern Rates, 173 I.C.C. 662, 1931.

Brown Shoe Company v. Southern Pacific Company, 159 I.C.C. 735, 1929.

[57] *William P. Huston, et al., v. Freight Ways, Inc., et al.*, 52 M.C.C. 263 (266), 1950.

[58] Ex Parte No. MC-21, *Central Territory Motor Carrier Rates*, 19 M.C.C. 545 (575), 1939.

In some cases, the commodity rates prescribed exceed the class rates. With respect to rail rates, we have held generally that a commodity rate higher than the class rate is unreasonable. We see no reason for the adoption of a different principle respecting motor carrier rates . . . A rule . . . permitting the alternative application of rates in two or more tariffs is objectionable as it would require shippers and others to search through several tariffs to determine the rate applicable on a shipment.

Furthermore, establishment of a commodity rate makes two rates available for use on the same article between the same points. Therefore, in most instances the commodity tariff will contain a provision authorizing application of the class rate if it is lower than the commodity rate. This rule was provided to resolve the question of which rate to apply when a commodity tariff contains no alternative use of a lower class rate; otherwise, in the absence of the alternative provision, the commodity rate would have to be used. The Interstate Commerce Commission has sustained superiority of a commodity rate over a class rate in the following language: "Publication of a commodity rate on an article, whether in specific or general terms, removes that article from application of class rates between the same points." [59]

The other exception to a commodity rate superseding a class rate is to the effect that rates on import, export, coastwise, or intercoastal traffic take precedence over "land" rates and, according to the Rail Classification, those rates "must be applied on such shipments to the exclusion of all other rates not so designated." Import and export traffic involve foreign trade and they are beyond the scope of this study. Coastwise traffic is that which moves by water carrier between United States ports located on the Atlantic Ocean, the Pacific Ocean, the Gulf of Mexico, or between Atlantic and Gulf ports. Intercoastal traffic is that which moves by water carrier between Atlantic or Gulf ports and Pacific ports.

The rail rule contains a third exception which does not appear in the motor rule, namely: the lowest rate, regardless of whether class or commodity, will apply on intrastate traffic in Illinois which is in accordance with the requirement of an Illinois statute. [60]

The motor rule further provides that an exceptions rating supersedes the particular provision of the Classification therein involved. Also, that establishment of a different quantity minimum weight re-

[59] *Sunbury Converting Works v. Central Railroad Company of New Jersey,* 167 I.C.C. 367 (368), 1930.
[60] Knorst, W. J.: *Transportation and Traffic Management,* Vol. 1, College of Advanced Traffic, Chicago, 1952, p. 193.

moves application of the minimum weight shown for the article in the motor classification. Eastern-Southern Class Tariff No. 504 of the Southern Motor Carriers Rate Conference, MF-I.C.C. No. 614, contains a rule numbered Item 10040 which carries a provision in connection with volume and truckload minimum weights, as follows: "Except as otherwise provided when on traffic moving on ratings published in the National Motor Freight Classification, the volume minimum weight will be that provided in the Classification, but not in excess of 22,000 pounds."

Advertising Matter or Premiums (M-28, R-45, NE-10). Advertising matter "(other than figures or images or electric signs)," store display racks or signs, and premiums may be shipped with the primary commodity to be advertised at the same rate or rating applicable to the main article.[61] Description and weight of the advertising matter, premiums, etc., must be shown on the bill of lading; and if such supplementary materials exceed ten percent of the weight of the entire shipment, the excess weight will be assessed at the rate applicable to such materials. The ten percent maximum weight for motor carriers was sustained in an early motor case by the Interstate Commerce Commission in 1939, "as is customarily done in rail tariffs."[62] A few restrictions pertaining to premiums are stated in the rule.

Upon reference to the rule, it will be observed there are different provisions for advertising materials when accompanying large and small shipments. When accompanying a large shipment (carload or truckload), the materials either may be included in the same package with the primary article, or they may be in separate packages; but for a small shipment (less-than-truckload or less-than-carload), they *must* be enclosed within the same container with the primary article. This requirement is entirely proper because of handling costs, it being kept in mind that the consignor loads and the consignee unloads volume shipments whereas small shipments must be handled a number of times by the carrier.

In effect, this rule is an exception to the Mixing Rule.[63] Under the Mixing Rule, advertising matter would be required to be recognized as a separate article in a mixed shipment, and the rate on the entire shipment would be assessed accordingly. However, this rule provides that if a lower charge results by application of either the

---

[61] The rail rule also excludes gift articles and stationery.
[62] *Food Products from Pittsburgh, Pa., to Trenton, N. J.,* 19 M.C.C. 463 (467), 1939.
[63] See, p. 241, above.

Mixing Rule or the Definition of Shipment rule,[64] those rules should be applied.

This rule, therefore, grants a distinct saving in shipping costs to many producers. Frequently, from a sales promotion standpoint, a manufacturer finds the availability of this rule highly desirable in his distributive process, for he is granted the privilege of including advertising matter in the same package with his merchandise without the trouble of additional packing and the extra costs inherent thereto. This rule permits successful operation of manufacturers' sales promotion programs, for application of the Mixing Rule might cause the shipping costs to be so prohibitive that a sales promotion program would be impractical. Carriers recognize that shippers are in business to sell their merchandise rather than to sell the advertising materials; and the higher the volume of sales, the greater will be the volume of traffic.

However, a for-hire carrier is not permitted to handle advertising materials free of charge. In a case where a motor carrier proposed to transport advertising matter without charge, the only limitation being that such matter not exceed the gross weight of the primary commodity by more than five percent, the Interstate Commerce Commission ruled: [65]

The transportation of advertising matter is a service of value to the shipper, for which the carrier should maintain a reasonable charge. Our order herein will require the cancellation of the proposed rule, without prejudice to the establishment of a rule permitting the transportation of advertising matter . . . at the rates applicable on the commodity advertised.

---

[64] See, p. 254, above.
[65] *Minimum Rates and Charges—V. S. and V. R. Partridge*, 46 M.C.C. 245 (249), 1946.

Chapter 14

CLASSIFICATION RULES—
Part IV

Charges Not Advanced, or Advancing Charges Not Permitted (M-8, R-8, NE-14). This is the shortest rule in the Classification. It states: "No charges of any description will be advanced to shippers, owners, consignees, their warehousemen or agents." The rail rule is preceded by the phrase, "Except as provided in tariffs."

There are two essential reasons for this rule. First, advancing of charges *could* be a form of rebating which is strictly forbidden by law. For example, a shipper might request the originating carrier to pay for drayage or packing costs, and add the amount to the sum to be collected from the consignee. Such drayage and packing costs could be utterly and intentionally exorbitant, and thereby used for rebating purposes.

Second, a carrier is not a collecting agency. Conceivably, a shipper might wish to be reimbursed by a carrier at time of shipment for expenses incurred by the shipper which have no relation to transportation, and expect the carrier to collect the amount advanced from consignee. The transaction might not have been approved by the consignee, or it might have been something in which the consignee had no interest or for which the consignee was in no way responsible. Should the consignee refuse to pay the amount involved, the carrier has no legal right on which to insist upon payment. A carrier very properly does not wish to obligate itself to collect funds which were expended for nontransportation purposes, unless, of course, so authorized by tariffs. A carrier may advance charges only to the extent provided by legally published tariffs.

In actual practice, however, the effectiveness of this rule has been reduced by the carriers themselves by publication of exceptions; but it should always be remembered that any sum which is advanced to anyone must be specifically authorized by a tariff. Some advances authorized by tariffs include customs and brokerage fees on import traffic which have accrued before the freight has been delivered to the carrier.[1] Also, tariffs authorize carriers to advance certain charges of freight forwarders. Sometimes where there is no joint rate for an interline shipment moving on a "freight charges collect" basis, one carrier may advance the charges of the preceding carrier, and the consignee is billed by the delivering carrier for the amounts advanced.[2]

It will be recalled the bill of lading contains a space designated, "Charges Advanced." Under conditions where an advance has been made, the amount must be shown in that space and collection is accomplished by the delivering carrier from the consignee.

A group of motor carriers endeavored to establish a rule which would authorize advancement of "accrued transportation and consolidating charges on shipments which are consolidated in transit." Such charges would be entered on the bill of lading as advances and collected from the consignee. The Interstate Commerce Commission rejected its adoption, saying: [3]

The rule was designed for the benefit of chain-store merchandising organizations which have established at certain points agencies for consolidating individual shipments to their various stores throughout the country into larger shipments in order to secure reduced freight charges . . . While the proposed rule is shown to have been designed for the benefit of the large merchandising chain stores, there is no provision in the rule which would debar its use by freight forwarders or by any other shippers having regular movements of shipments from a number of points of origin to a number of destinations which may conveniently be consolidated enroute. . . . In addition, the rule is negative in form and does not affirmatively provide for the advancement of these charges or, even by inference, provide for the collection and remittances of the charges after movement. It is therefore improperly designated as an exception to rule 8 of the Classification.

In an earlier proceeding, carriers had endeavored to establish an exception to the rule by providing for advancement of charges to a shipper when he guarantees the charges by endorsement on the bill of lading; but this proposal, too, was denied.[4] Later, however, the Commission ruled: [5]

---

[1] Taff, C. A.: *Traffic Management,* Irwin, Chicago, 1955, pp. 158–159.
[2] Van Metre, T. W.: *Industrial Traffic Management,* McGraw-Hill Book Company, New York, 1953, p. 71.
[3] Ex Parte No. MC-21, *Central Territory Motor Carrier Rates,* 29 M.C.C. 213 (214–216), 1941.
[4] Ex Parte No. MC-21, *op. cit.,* 19 M.C.C. 545 (576), 1939.
[5] *Freight Forwarding Investigation,* 256 I.C.C. 699 (701), 1944.

Enactment of Part IV of the Act has removed the grounds upon which the findings of unlawfulness in the prior reports were based, and they are modified so as to permit respondent rail and motor carriers to advance published charges of freight forwarders, prior to their collection from the consignee.

A recent rail shipment of fir doors from a point in the State of Washington to a destination in Virginia illustrates the principle of advanced charges.[6] Two advances were made by the carrier, one of $91.01 and the other of $13.80, totaling $105.81, which amount was added to the freight charges and collected from the consignee by the delivering carrier.

Dispositions of Fractions (M-24, R-36, NE-24). This rule provides a uniform means for disposing of fractions in determining rates, *viz.*: if the fraction is less than one-half of a cent, omit; if one-half of a cent or greater, increase the amount to the "next whole figure." This provision has been sustained by the Interstate Commerce Commission.[7] However, fractions must be used in computing a rate from an occasional tariff which is not subject to a Classification and which contains no comparable rule. As Dean Knorst has stated: [8]

The idea back of the rule is to dispense with fractions entirely in rate making. This saves the "splitting of hairs" in the computation of rates and reduces the likelihood of errors. It also permits the use of narrower columns when publishing tables of rates in freight tariffs. Consequently a greater number of columns may be shown on each page. This reduces the size of the tariff, saves thousands of dollars in printers' bills, and makes the computation of freight charges easier.

Demurrage, Storage, Terminal and Other Charges (M-25). The motor rule provides that the rates contained in tariffs governed by the Classification are subject to the rules and charges published by the carriers covering demurrage, storage, diversions, terminal, and other charges. There is no comparable rule in the Rail Classification; but tariffs are published by the railroads covering the several services mentioned in the motor rule.

C.O.D. (Collect on Delivery) Shipments (M-31, R-47, NE-20). A shipment moving on a c.o.d. basis should not be confused with one covered by an order bill of lading.[9] The amount of a c.o.d. shipment is collected from the consignee by the carrier at time of delivery of the freight, and after collection thereof the sum is remitted

---

[6] *Northern Pacific Railway, Elna, Washington, Waybill No. 840*, May 13, 1955.
[7] *Trunk Line Territory Motor Carrier Rates*, 24 M.C.C. 501 (625), 1940.
[8] Knorst, *op. cit.*, p. 192.
[9] See, pp. 40–47, above.

directly to the consignor, or other person designated by the consignor as payee; whereas, for freight shipped on an order bill of lading, the consignor receives the invoice value of his shipment at approximately the time it is shipped. The rule sets forth the regulations which apply to c.o.d. shipments, and every shipper should be familiar with them before offering such a shipment to a carrier. The rule also contains a schedule of charges for providing the service.

In 1949, the Interstate Commerce Commission handed down a decision resulting from a general investigation of c.o.d. practices of motor carriers in which "all common carriers of property subject to Part II of the (Interstate Commerce) Act were made respondents." The Commission found that the provisions of the motor rule had been modified by "numerous carriers" by means of exceptions; but the respondent carriers represented at the hearing agreed the regulations should be strengthened "because the record of the entire industry has been blackened by the actions of a small minority." The following is a summary of the regulations prescribed by the Commission: [10]

(1) Applicability. The regulations shall apply to all common carriers of property subject to Part II of the Act, "except such transportation which is auxiliary to or supplemental of transportation by railroad and performed on railroad bills of lading, and except such transportation which is performed for freight forwarders and on freight forwarder bills of lading."

(2) Tariff Requirements. Any carrier performing c.o.d. services must publish a tariff containing "the rates, charges and rules governing such service, which rules shall conform to these regulations."

(3) Remittance. Each c.o.d. collection must be remitted "directly to the consignor or other person designated by the consignor as payee promptly and within ten (10) days after delivery of the c.o.d. shipment to the consignee." If an interline movement is involved, the delivering carrier is required to notify the originating carrier when the remittance is made.

(4) Records. Delivering carriers must maintain a record of all c.o.d. shipments showing: "(a) number and date of freight bill; (b) name and address of shipper or other person designated as payee; (c) name and address of consignee; (d) date shipment delivered; (e) amount of c.o.d.; (f) date collected by delivering

---

[10] Ex Parte No. MC-42, *Handling of C.O.D. Shipments,* 51 M.C.C. 5 (8–24), 1949.

276

carrier; (g) date remitted to payee; and (h) check number or other identification of remittance to payee."

The above regulations of the Commission *and* the provisions of the Classification rule govern the handling of c.o.d. shipments.

Application of Minimum Weight Factors (M-34, R-34). This rule is commonly known as the "Graduated Minimum" rule. As has been frequently mentioned, a ton of light or low density freight occupies more space than a ton of heavy or high density freight. For example, 50,000 pounds of pig iron may be loaded in a conventional trailer or car, but it would be impossible to load 50,000 pounds of feathered pillows or dry cereals into the same equipment. While 50,000 pounds may be a reasonable minimum weight for a volume shipment of pig iron, the same minimum weight would be most unreasonable for the pillows or dry cereals. Therefore, in order to provide a fair basis of weight for light and bulky articles, a graduated scale of minimum weights dependent upon the size of a carrier's equipment has been established by this rule.

The motor specifications are determined by the cubic capacity of a vehicle; the rail, by length of a car. It should be understood the maximum weight a motor carrier may transport is governed by state laws; but that of a railroad is indicated by the "load limit" in pounds stencilled on each side of a freight car. This rule refers exclusively to truckload or carload shipments. Its primary purpose is to encourage the loading of equipment to capacity, for it pre-scribes greater minimum weights for certain articles when shipped in larger than smaller units of equipment. By its establishment, car-riers recognize the wide differences in the density of articles in relation to the costs of transporting them. Larger and a greater num-ber of trailers and cars are required to transport a given weight of light, bulky articles than heavy articles, and the carriers must with-stand greater costs for purchasing or constructing those larger and additional pieces of equipment.

This rule is of utmost importance in computing the correct rate on volume shipments or articles which are subject to the rule. Illustrative of its significance is that it governs the minimum weight of 1,371 articles in the Motor Classification [11] and 4,427 articles in the Rail Classification.[12] The motor and rail rules will be discussed separately, it being noted that both are numbered 34.

A part of the motor rule is reproduced on page 279 below. The

[11] *National Motor Freight Classification No. A-2, op. cit.,* pp. 2–273.
[12] *Uniform Freight Classification No. 2, op. cit.,* pp. 187–451.

rule establishes the minimum weight of a truckload of freight depending upon the size of the vehicle. The Interstate Commerce Commission has recognized that safety requirements and the varying state laws pertaining to gross weight and size place limitations upon the carrying capacities of motor carrier equipment.[13] Therefore, the cubic footage of trailers must be considered in applying reasonable ratings to certain articles, particularly bulky articles. The Commission has said: [14]

We believe it inescapable that, in the light of the limited capacities of motor carrier equipment, as compared with the capacities of railroad freight cars, density, which has always been regarded as an important factor in determining rail classification ratings, merits more consideration, in determining the reasonableness of motor classification ratings, than it has heretofore been accorded.

Upon reference to the reproduced rule on the next page, it will be observed that there are several columns. The first column calls for a "minimum weight factor." It is based essentially upon density of the article and the minimum weight assigned to the article by competitive modes of transportation, primarily the railroads. The density factor is represented by the number after the decimal point; the competitive minimum weight, by the figures before the decimal point. The maximum capacity of a vehicle in terms of cubic feet of available space is indicated by the density figure.[15] The minimum weight factor itself is found in the Description of Articles section of the Classification, and it is always preceded by the letter "w" enclosed within a circle. The latter reference is explained in the Explanation of Abbreviations section of the Classification.[16] To illustrate, the truckload minimum weight for Christmas tree ornaments is *not* shown in pounds, but by " Ⓦ 12.2." [17] Hence, 12.2 is the minimum weight factor for the article.

Again referring to the rule, there will be found six columns of figures designated as Tables A to F, inclusive. Those tables are based directly upon the capacity of trailers of different sizes, *viz.:*

Table A—2,000 cubic feet capacity
Table B—1,800 cubic feet capacity
Table C—1,600 cubic feet capacity
Table D—1,400 cubic feet capacity
Table E—1,200 cubic feet capacity
Table F—1,000 cubic feet capacity

---

[13] *Incandescent Electric Lamps or Bulbs,* 47 M.C.C. 601 (602), 1947.
[14] *Ibid.,* p. 603.
[15] Knorst, *op. cit.,* p. 186.
[16] See, *National Motor Freight Classification No. A-2, op. cit.,* p. 1.
[17] *Ibid.,* Item 81750.

RULE 34

APPLICATION OF MINIMUM WEIGHT FACTORS

Sec. 1. The minimum weight factors named in connection with the individual descriptions and ratings herein apply as set forth in tables shown in Section 3 of this rule.

Sec. 2. Carriers' tariffs must be consulted in order to determine the table designating the applicable truckload minimum weight. Where carriers' tariff does not make provisions for application of this rule, Table F, Section 3, will apply.

Sec. 3. Tables of Truckload Minimum Weights:

WHEN MIN. WT. FACTOR IS:	TRUCKLOAD MINIMUM WEIGHT, IN POUNDS, WILL BE:					
	TABLE A	TABLE B	TABLE C	TABLE D	TABLE E	TABLE F
10.0	10,000	8,000	7,000	6,000	5,000	4,000
10.1	10,000	9,000	8,000	7,000	6,000	5,000
10.2	10,000	10,000	8,800	7,700	6,600	5,600
10.3	10,000	10,000	10,000	8,700	7,500	6,000
10.4	10,000	10,000	10,000	10,000	8,600	7,100
10.5	10,000	10,000	10,000	10,000	10,000	8,300
10.6	10,000	10,000	10,000	10,000	10,000	10,000
12.1	12,000	10,800	9,600	8,400	7,200	6,000
12.2	12,000	12,000	10,700	9,300	8,000	6,700
12.3	12,000	12,000	12,000	10,500	9,000	7,500
12.4	12,000	12,000	12,000	12,000	10,300	8,600
12.5	12,000	12,000	12,000	12,000	12,000	10,000
12.6	12,000	12,000	12,000	12,000	12,000	12,000
14.1	14,000	12,600	11,200	9,800	8,400	7,000
14.2	14,000	14,000	12,400	10,900	9,300	7,800
14.3	14,000	14,000	14,000	12,300	10,500	8,700
14.4	14,000	14,000	14,000	14,000	12,000	10,000
14.5	14,000	14,000	14,000	14,000	14,000	11,700
14.6	14,000	14,000	14,000	14,000	14,000	14,000
15.1	15,000	13,500	12,000	10,500	9,000	7,500
15.2	15,000	15,000	13,300	11,700	10,000	8,300
15.3	15,000	15,000	15,000	13,100	11,200	9,400
15.4	15,000	15,000	15,000	15,000	12,900	10,700
15.5	15,000	15,000	15,000	15,000	15,000	12,500
15.6	15,000	15,000	15,000	15,000	15,000	15,000
16.1	16,000	14,400	12,800	11,200	9,600	8,000
16.2	16,000	16,000	14,200	12,400	10,600	8,900
16.3	16,000	16,000	16,000	14,000	12,000	10,000
16.4	16,000	16,000	16,000	16,000	13,700	11,400
16.5	16,000	16,000	16,000	16,000	16,000	13,300
16.6	16,000	16,000	16,000	16,000	16,000	16,000
18.1	18,000	16,200	14,400	12,600	10,800	9,000
18.2	18,000	18,000	16,000	14,000	12,000	10,000
18.3	18,000	18,000	18,000	15,700	13,500	11,200
18.4	18,000	18,000	18,000	18,000	15,400	12,900
18.5	18,000	18,000	18,000	18,000	18,000	15,000
18.6	18,000	18,000	18,000	18,000	18,000	18,000
20.1	20,000	18,000	16,000	14,000	12,000	10,000
20.2	20,000	20,000	17,800	15,600	13,300	11,100
20.3	20,000	20,000	20,000	17,500	15,000	12,500
20.4	20,000	20,000	20,000	20,000	17,100	14,300
20.5	20,000	20,000	20,000	20,000	20,000	16,700
20.6	20,000	20,000	20,000	20,000	20,000	20,000
21.1	21,000	18,900	16,800	14,700	12,600	10,500
21.2	21,000	21,000	18,700	16,300	14,000	11,700
21.3	21,000	21,000	21,000	18,400	15,700	13,100
21.4	21,000	21,000	21,000	21,000	18,000	15,000
21.5	21,000	21,000	21,000	21,000	21,000	17,500
21.6	21,000	21,000	21,000	21,000	21,000	21,000
22.1	22,000	19,800	17,600	15,400	13,200	11,000
22.2	22,000	22,000	19,600	17,100	14,700	12,200
22.3	22,000	22,000	22,000	19,200	16,500	13,700
22.4	22,000	22,000	22,000	22,000	18,900	15,700
22.5	22,000	22,000	22,000	22,000	22,000	18,300
22.6	22,000	22,000	22,000	22,000	22,000	22,000
24.1	24,000	21,600	19,200	16,800	14,400	12,000
24.2	24,000	24,000	21,300	18,700	16,000	13,300
24.3	24,000	24,000	24,000	21,000	18,000	15,000
24.4	24,000	24,000	24,000	24,000	20,600	17,100
24.5	24,000	24,000	24,000	24,000	24,000	20,000
24.6	24,000	24,000	24,000	24,000	24,000	24,000
26.1	26,000	23,400	20,800	18,200	15,600	13,000
26.2	26,000	26,000	23,100	20,200	17,300	14,400
26.3	26,000	26,000	26,000	22,700	19,500	16,200
26.4	26,000	26,000	26,000	26,000	22,300	18,600
26.5	26,000	26,000	26,000	26,000	26,000	21,700
26.6	26,000	26,000	26,000	26,000	26,000	26,000

168-A   See page 1 for explanation of abbreviations and various characters.

As is stated in Section 2 of the rule, the next step is to consult the applicable tariff in order to determine which table to use in establishing the truckload minimum weight of the shipment. For example, *Central-Southern Class Tariff No. 100* contains the provision in its Item No. 5 that the tariff is governed by the *National Motor*

Freight Classification and that, "Table D of Rule 34 of said Classification will be used in determining truckload minimum weights in connection with commodities provided with a 'minimum weight factor' in said Classification, except that such truckload minimum weights shall not exceed 22,000 lbs." [18] Thus, a movement of Christmas tree ornaments, mentioned above, would be subject to a truckload minimum weight of 9,300 pounds. In order for the rule to be used, the applicable tariff of rates should contain a provision somewhat similar to the one quoted above. However, in cases where a tariff does *not* provide for application of the rule, Section 2 of the rule specifies that the truckload minimum weights shown in Table F will apply.

In order to clarify any possible misunderstanding, the following points should be remembered: (1) every tariff must be governed by some Classification; (2) a tariff contains a reference to the Classification by which it is governed; (3) where a weight factor instead of an actual minimum weight in pounds is shown for an article in the Description of Articles section of a Classification, the applicable tariff governed by the Motor Classification is expected to contain a provision specifying which Table in Rule 34 will be used in determining the minimum truckload weight; and (4) Table F will apply when no Table or actual weight is specified in the tariff.

With the recent development of "high-cube" trailers of some 2,200 cubic feet capacity, it is probable an additional Table will be added to the rule. Obviously, increases in the cubic capacity of vehicles will have an effect on the scale of truckload minimum weights provided by this rule. As this volume goes to press, the National Classification Board is giving consideration to the matter. [19]

The rail rule consists of ten sections. Sections 1–4 relate to closed cars, Sections 5–8 to open cars, and Sections 9–10 to both closed and open cars. There are some differences in the provisions pertaining to closed and open cars which necessitate care in applying the appropriate Section.

Carload minimum weights of all articles are based upon the cubic capacity of a so-called "standard" car. A standard closed car is 40 feet 7 inches in length, with a maximum of 3925 cubic feet capacity. Since some standard closed cars are higher than others, the cubic capacity varies accordingly to a low of about 3000 cubic feet.

---

[18] Central & Southern Motor Freight Tariff Association, Inc., Agent, Louisville: Tariff No. 100, *Central-Southern Class Tariff*, effective November 18, 1952, p. 90.

[19] *Transport Topics,* March 7, 1955, p. 18.

The standard open car is 41 feet 6 inches in length. The same minimum weight applicable to a standard car applies to cars which are shorter in length. Generally, the rule applies to low-density articles which have been assigned a minimum carload weight of less than 30,000 pounds, and they are identified in the Description of Articles section of the Classification by the letter "R," thus: the minimum carload weight for Paper Advertising Matter is shown as, "24,-000R." [20] Articles which are not subject to the rule carry the minimum weight shown in the Classification regardless of the size of car.

When an article that is subject to the rule is loaded in or on a standard car, the minimum carload weight, as shown for the article in the Classification, applies. However, when such articles are loaded in or on cars that are larger than standard, the minimum weight of the shipment is graduated upward in accordance with scales provided in the rule for closed and open cars, respectively. The scales are reproduced on the next page. To illustrate with a closed car:

Assume there is a shipment of beer barrels weighing 22,000 pounds and that the Class 100 rate is $1.00 per 100 pounds. Upon reference to the Classification, it will be found that the carload rating on beer barrels is Class 35, and that the carload minimum weight is shown as 20,000R.[21] If a standard box car is ordered by the shipper and furnished by the carrier, the freight rate would be computed on the basis of actual weight, or 35¢ times 220, resulting in a charge of $77.00. However, if a larger car were ordered and furnished, say what is commonly known as a "50-foot" car, although it may be 50 feet 6 inches in length, then the freight rate would be computed in accordance with the scale, *viz.*: since the minimum weight stated in the Classification is 20,000 pounds, subject to Rule 34 by the identifying letter "R," and the shipment weighs 22,000 pounds, the rate would be based upon the column headed "20,000 lbs.," which specifies that for a 50-foot car the "charge shall not be less than" for 32,400 pounds. Therefore, the rate would be 35¢ times 324, or $113.40. Exactly the same principle is followed for application of the scale pertaining to open cars.

Immediately, two points should be obvious. First, the shipper should know without question the size of car which is necessary to accommodate his shipment if subject to the rule. If he is not certain and orders a car of excess capacity just to provide leeway for his inaccuracies in figuring, he is causing himself undue expense. The

[20] *Uniform Freight Classification No. 2, op. cit.*, Item 230.
[21] *Ibid.*, Item 3930.

second point is that he must refer to and be governed by the sliding scales for closed and open cars whenever the letter "R" is shown with the minimum carload weight of the article in the Classification, or when an exception or a tariff specifically refers to the rule.

It should be observed there are positive percentage relationships in the sliding scales. For closed cars, the minimum for cars roughly between 40 and 50 feet is 162 percent of the base weight of a standard car; and for cars over 50½ feet, 200 percent. For open cars, there is the following:

Cars 41 ft. 6 in. or less......................—100% of base weight
Cars over 41 ft. 6 in., and not over 42 ft. 6 in.—122% of base weight
Cars over 42 ft. 6 in., and not over 46 ft. 6 in.—142% of base weight
Cars over 46 ft. 6 in., and not over 50 ft. 6 in.—162% of base weight
Cars over 50 ft. 6 in., and not over 52 ft. 6 in.—172% of base weight
Cars over 52 ft. 6 in........................—200% of base weight

Length of Closed Car	When Minimum CL. Weight provided in Classification, exceptions thereto or applicable tariff for articles shipped is:						
	10,000 lbs. Charge not less than	11,000 lbs. Charge not less than	12,000 lbs. Charge not less than	13,000 lbs. Charge not less than	14,000 lbs. Charge not less than	15,000 lbs. Charge not less than	16,000 lbs. Charge not less than
	lbs.	lbs.	lbs.	lbs.	lbs.	lbs.	lbs.
Cars over 40 ft. 7 in. and not over 50 ft. 6 in. long...............	16,200	17,820	19,440	21,060	22,680	24,300	25,920
Cars over 50 ft. 6 in. in length.................................	20,000	22,000	24,000	26,000	28,000	30,000	32,000

Length of Closed Car	When Minimum CL Weight provided in Classification, exceptions thereto or applicable tariff for articles shipped is:							
	18,000 lbs. Charge not less than	20,000 lbs. Charge not less than	22,000 lbs. Charge not less than	24,000 lbs. Charge not less than	26,000 lbs. Charge not less than	30,000 lbs. Charge not less than	36,000 lbs. Charge not less than	40,000 lbs. Charge not less than
	lbs.	lbs.	lbs.	lbs.	lbs.	lbs.	lbs.	lbs.
Cars over 40 ft. 7 in. and not over 50 ft. 6 in. long.	29,160	32,400	35,640	38,880	42,120	45,360	48,600	58,320	64,800
Cars over 50 ft. 6 in. in length.................	36,000	40,000	44,000	48,000	52,000	56,000	60,000	72,000	80,000

Length of Open Car	When Minimum CL Weight provided in Classification, exceptions thereto or applicable tariff for articles shipped is:								
	18,000 lbs. Charge not less than	20,000 lbs. Charge not less than	22,000 lbs. Charge not less than	24,000 lbs. Charge not less than	26,000 lbs. Charge not less than	28,000 lbs. Charge not less than	30,000 lbs. Charge not less than	36,000 lbs. Charge not less than	40,000 lbs. Charge not less than
	lbs.	lbs.	lbs.	lbs.	lbs.	lbs.	lbs.	lbs.	lbs.
Over 41 ft. 6 in. and not over 42 ft. 6 in.........	21,960	24,400	26,840	29,280	31,720	34,160	36,600	43,920	48,800
Over 42 ft. 6 in. and not over 46 ft. 6 in.........	25,560	28,400	31,240	34,080	36,920	39,760	42,600	51,120	56,800
Over 46 ft. 6 in. and not over 50 ft. 6 in.........	29,160	32,400	35,640	38,880	42,120	45,360	48,600	58,320	64,800
Over 50 ft. 6 in. and not over 52 ft. 6 in.........	30,960	34,400	37,840	41,280	44,720	48,160	51,600	61,920	68,800
Over 52 ft. 6 inches in length.................	36,000	40,000	44,000	48,000	52,000	56,000	60,000	72,000	80,000

(b) Where CL minimum weight is not shown as a base weight in Section 8 (a) and the articles are subject to Rule 34, the minimum weight for cars exceeding 41 feet 6 inches in length will be as follows (see Note 3):

	Example using 44,000 lbs. as base weight
Cars over 41 ft. 6 in. and not over 42 ft. 6 in., 122% of base weight.....................	53,680
Cars over 42 ft. 6 in. and not over 46 ft. 6 in., 142% of base weight.....................	62,480
Cars over 46 ft. 6 in. and not over 50 ft. 6 in., 162% of base weight.....................	71,280
Cars over 50 ft. 6 in. and not over 52 ft. 6 in., 172% of base weight.....................	75,680
Cars over 52 ft. 6 inches in length, 200% of base weight.................................	88,000

When a shipper orders a standard car and the carrier, for its convenience or otherwise, furnishes a larger car, the minimum weight shall be on the basis of the size car ordered, "except that when loading capacity of car is used, minimum weight shall be that fixed for car furnished." In such cases, however, in order for the shipper to benefit by the lower charge applicable to the smaller car which he ordered, a notation must appear on the bill of lading as stated in Sections 2 and 6 of the rule.

Furthermore, when a shipper orders a car longer than a standard car and the carrier is unable to provide it, the carrier may furnish two smaller cars without penalty to the shipper, but one of the cars shall be charged on the basis of its minimum weight and the applicable carload rate shall be charged for the remainder of the shipment that is loaded in the other car; "but in no case shall total weight charged for the two cars be less than minimum weight fixed for car ordered." Again, a notation, as provided by the rule, must appear on the bill of lading. In contrast, if a larger than standard car is loaded with articles subject to Rule 34 without the shipper having placed an order for a car of any specified length, the "minimum weight shall be that fixed for car used."

The utmost importance of both shippers and appropriate carrier employees being familiar with this rule cannot be overemphasized. It is essential that a shipper of articles subject to Rule 34 determine the size of car required to accommodate his shipment *before* the equipment is ordered. Then he should specify the length of car desired when placing his car order with the carrier. If cars are furnished in variance with the car-order, the carrier's representative at point of origin should be certain that an appropriate notation appears on the bill of lading and the waybill. Omission thereof from those documents can result in controversies and overcharges. For example, if a car larger than the one ordered were furnished without proper notation on the bill, the agent at destination would assume the shipper had not ordered a car of specified length, and charges based on the minimum weight fixed for the car would be assessed against the consignee.

A final illustration should suffice. Assume there is a shipment of an article subject to Rule 34 weighing 26,000 pounds, the authorized minimum weight of the article is 24,000 pounds for a standard closed car, the applicable rate is 50¢ per 100 pounds, the shipper orders a 50-foot box car, and such a car is furnished by the carrier. According to the table in Section 3, where the minimum weight for a standard car is 24,000 pounds, the minimum weight for a 50-foot car is 38,800 pounds. Therefore, the shipment would be charged on the basis of 38,800 pounds, or $194.00; whereas, had a standard car been ordered, and capable of accommodating the load, the charge would have been on the basis of the actual weight of 26,000 pounds, or $130.00. Now, further assume a 50-foot car actually was necessary to handle the shipment, but the carrier, for its own convenience, provided two standard cars. If the shipper loaded 16,000 pounds in one car and 10,000 pounds in the other, the charges would be:

1st car—16,000 lbs. as 24,000 lbs. @ 50¢—$120.00
2nd car—10,000 lbs. @ 50¢............— 50.00
                                        $170.00

However, and this is extremely important, Section 2 provides that "in no case shall total weight charged for the two cars be *LESS* [22] than the minimum weight fixed for the car ordered." As shown above, the minimum for the 50-foot car that was ordered amounted to $194.00 and, therefore, the proper charge for the shipment moving in two cars would be $194.00 instead of $170.00.

Since the world contains persons of varying degrees of honesty, cases of fraudulent use of Rule 34 are a matter of official record. A few unscrupulous shippers have resorted to the subterfuge of inserting false notations on bills of lading to the effect that standard cars were ordered but longer cars were furnished for carrier's convenience; whereas, in fact, the carrier had provided large cars exactly in accordance with car orders. Also, a false notation would be inserted on a bill of lading that a long car had been ordered, but two standard cars were furnished when actually the shipper desired two standard cars. During one year, over forty indictments were returned against both railroads and shippers, all of whom entered pleas of guilty and fines aggregating over $150,000 were imposed and paid.[23]

In conclusion, it should be understood that whenever a Classification or a commodity tariff provides that the minimum weight of an article is subject to Rule 34, the rule *must* be applied. On the other hand, articles not subject to the rule may be loaded in carrier's equipment of any size that will contain the shipment without application of the graduated scale of minimum weights.

....

The remaining rules discussed in this chapter are applicable only to rail shipments, except the last two which apply to freight moving by New England motor carriers.

Ice or Preservative Used for Protection of Freight (R-32). Under the provisions of this rule, there is no charge for the transportation of ice, or other preservatives, in bunkers of cars when used for handling perishable commodities. In other words, the weight of ice in refrigerator cars is not included with the weight of the shipment, and the ice becomes the property of the carrier after the car is un-

---

[22] Italics supplied.
[23] *55th Annual Report of the Interstate Commerce Commission,* Government Printing Office, Washington, 1941, pp. 79–80.

loaded. However, if the consignee removes or otherwise uses the ice at destination, then charges will be assessed on the basis of the weight of the ice that is in the car bunkers on arrival at destination at the same rate as that applicable to contents of the car.

In contrast, no allowance is granted for the weight of ice, or other preservatives, when it is placed in the same container with the freight. Thus, the weight of ice placed in a crate of lettuce is included in the weight of the shipment, and freight charges are based on the combined total of the weights of the lettuce and the ice at time of loading.

Tank Car Freight (R-35). This is a long and complex rule pertaining to the matter covered by the subject. It should be studied in detail by a shipper who contemplates the shipment of liquids or gases in tank cars. Notwithstanding that there are many tank truck operations, there is no comparable rule in the Motor Classification. Many articles are shipped in tank equipment, such as, vegetable oils, vinegar, molasses, asphalt, acids, gases, chemicals, milk, gasoline. For those commodities, bulk shipments in the tank equipment are more practical than packaging in barrels, cans or other containers.

Although the Interstate Commerce Act requires all railroads subject to the Act to "furnish safe and adequate car service," [24] and "it shall be the duty of every common carrier subject to this part to provide and furnish transportation upon reasonable request therefor," [25] a railroad is *not* obligated to furnish tank cars, even though ratings and rates for tank car freight are provided in tariffs. The use of a tank car mainly is for the convenience of the shipping public. A carrier fulfills its obligation as a common carrier by providing equipment, such as a box car, which could transport liquid shipments in barrels or cans.

In 1916, the Supreme Court of the United States ruled that a carrier was not obligated by the Interstate Commerce Act to provide tank cars.[26] Therefore a shipper must provide or make his own arrangements to secure the tank cars he desires to transport his products. Railroads, generally, do not own tank cars for commercial purposes. Shippers who require the use of tank cars either own them themselves or secure them on a rental basis from private car companies which make a specialty of leasing railroad equipment to shippers.[27] When non-railroad owned tank cars are made available to

---

[24] Interstate Commerce Act, Section 1 (11).
[25] *Ibid.*, Section 1 (4).
[26] *United States v. Pennsylvania Railroad Company*, 242 U.S. 208, 1916.
[27] Companies owning their own tank cars, to mention a few, are Koppers Company, Allied Chemical & Dye Corporation, Armour & Company, Atlas

shippers, the carriers are required to compensate the owners for the use of such equipment. Remuneration is computed on mileage. These "mileage allowances," as they are called, are in no way associated with the freight rate. Mileage allowance is payment by a carrier for use of equipment, whereas a freight rate is payment to the carrier for transporting goods. The two should not be confused. Private car allowances are beyond the scope of this chapter and will not be discussed further.

A carrier is not required to clean the interior of a privately owned tank car furnished for loading. Whatever cleaning that may be necessary must be performed by and at the expense of the shipper.

Gallonage capacities of tank cars are shown in a separate tariff. Assume there is a volume shipment of crude oil by tank car. The estimated weight per gallon is 7.4 pounds. If the capacity of the car is 8,000 gallons and it is completely loaded, the rate will be based on 7.4 times 8,000, or 59,200 pounds.

In order to determine which liquids are authorized a carload rating for shipment by tank car, it is necessary first to consult the Classification. In all cases where the Classification provides a rating for an article to be moved by tank car, there is reference to rail Rule 35, which means the freight can move only in accordance with this rule. For example, the Classification contains a provision for Nitric Acid to move by tank car in carload quantities only, subject to Rule 35, at a carload rating of Class 35, 30,000 pounds minimum.[28] Likewise, the Motor Classification provides for volume shipments of the same commodity by tank truck subject to motor Rule 23,[29] and only when individual motor carriers' tariffs provide applicable weights, rules, and rates. In addition to the Classification, there are many specific commodity tariffs which contain ratings or rates for articles capable of being shipped in tank equipment.

Except where the Classification refers specifically to rail Rule 35, or where special tariffs specify minimum weights, minimum carload rates on tank shipments generally are based upon the full capacity of the tank, exclusive of the dome which projects above the tank proper. If the contents extend into the dome, the amount

---

Powder Company, The Dow Chemical Company, Jones & Laughlin Steel Corporation, the Army and the Navy, most of the large oil companies. Some leasing companies include General American Transportation Corporation, North American Car Corporation, Union Tank Car Company, Shippers' Car Line Corporation. See, *The Official Railway Equipment Register*, M. A. Zenobia, Agent, published quarterly by the Railway Equipment and Publication Company, New York.
[28] *Uniform Freight Classification No. 2, op. cit.*, Item 165.
[29] *National Motor Freight Classification No. A-2, op. cit.*, Item 350.

thereof is added to the weight of the contents of the "shell" of the tank; [30] and it is the responsibility of the shipper to so add the extra weight in computing total weight of the shipment. The capacity of tank cars, as reported in the *Railway Equipment Register* and other official publications, does not include freight that is handled in the domes. Likewise, the minimum carload weight of articles shipped by tank car includes only the "shell" gallonage capacity of the tank proper. In other words, rates on tank car freight are predicated on the condition that cars are loaded to capacity, exclusive of the dome.

Where there is no weight agreement or estimated weight arrangement in effect,[31] the shipper is required to certify the actual weight per gallon on the bill of lading, and the weight so certified will be used as the basis for determining the freight rate. Or when a car is loaded to full "shell" capacity, or to the weight carrying capacity of the car, the shipper may so endorse on the bill of lading and the car will be weighed on track scales.

Sometimes drainage difficulties prevent complete unloading of a car at destination. Under such circumstances, a three percent tolerance is allowed—that is, if the substance remaining in the car does not exceed three percent of the inbound weight, no charge will be assessed by the carrier for a subsequent movement of the car. However, if the residue is greater than three percent, and the car is shipped to any other point for reloading, cleaning, or repairing, "the weight thereof must be declared by the shipper or receiver and will be charged for" at the applicable rate. Should the weight be less than the carload minimum weight, as would probably be the case, the less-than-carload rate applies.

The rule contains other sections pertaining to weights per gallon, compartment tank cars, compressed gasses, preparation of cars for loading, and other highly technical matters pertaining to tank car freight. It should be mentioned in passing that some tank cars are constructed with two or more compartments, thereby making it possible to ship two or more different commodities in the same car, depending upon the number of compartments. When a compartment is shipped empty, the freight charges for it are computed on the basis of the highest carload rating or rate applicable to any other commodity being shipped in the same car with the highest minimum weight applicable to those articles.

Shipments moving in tank equipment require special considera-

---

[30] The "shell" is the inside lining of a tank which holds and comes in direct contact with the liquid that is loaded therein.
[31] See, pp. 239–240, above.

tions which are not necessary for other freight.[32] For example, all gases and some liquids are subject to expansion or contraction with changes in temperature. Obviously, sufficient space must be left in a tank car or truck at the time of loading to allow room for expansion. This excess space is commonly known as "outage." Also, many commodities shipped in tank cars are inflammable, corrosive, or poisonous. Such articles are subject to the strict regulations contained in a special tariff on explosives and dangerous articles.

Contracts with Men in Charge of Shipments Other Than Live Stock, Live Wild Animals or Ostriches (R-43). This rule contains the provisions of a contract which must be executed by persons accompanying a shipment on a freight train, exclusive of shipments of live animals.[33] The agreement releases the carrier from its liability as a common carrier in the event of injury to the individual. Illustrative is an attendant for shipments of bananas to control the interior temperature of cars.[34]

Rule 44. Rule No. 44 in the Uniform Classification is entirely different from Rule No. 44 in the Consolidated Classification. Since both Classifications are applicable under certain conditions, the two rules will be explained.

Uniform Classification: **Method of Cancelling Items.** This rule is merely an explanation of identifying new items in the Classification. It states: "As this Classification is supplemented, numbered items with letter suffixes cancel correspondingly numbered items in the original Classification or in a prior supplement. Letter suffixes will be used in alphabetical sequence starting with A." For example, an Item shown as 445-A cancels Item 445, and, in turn, Item 445-B cancels Item 445-A which might have appeared in a prior supplement.

Consolidated Classification: **Fourth Section Departures.** This rule refers to Section 4, commonly known as the "Long & Short Haul Clause," of the Interstate Commerce Act which reads, in part, as follows: [35]

It shall be unlawful for any common carrier subject to this part of part III to charge or receive any greater compensation in the aggregate for the transportation of passengers, or of like kind of property, for a shorter than for a longer distance over the same line or route in the same direction, the shorter being included within the longer distance . . .

[32] See, *Motor Carriers' Explosives and Dangerous Articles Tariff No. 8,* ATA Agent.

[33] A special contract is also required for attendants accompanying live stock shipments. See, p. 51, above.

[34] Singer, S. R.: *The Shipment of Bananas,* a Master's thesis, The University of Tennessee, Knoxville, 1955.

[35] Interstate Commerce Act, Section 4 (1).

At the beginning, the rule states in heavy print that, "changes which may be made in compliance with the requirements of this Rule will be published in the tariffs of carriers . . ." It provides that in the event any change in the Classification causes an unauthorized violation of Section 4 of the Act, such violation shall be corrected on one day's notice to the Interstate Commerce Commission, instead of the usual minimum of thirty days for a change; and that if an overcharge was paid by a consignor or consignee as a direct result of the error, prompt application will be submitted to the Commission for authority to refund the overcharge.[36] It is required by law that an interstate carrier secure an order from the Commission authorizing a refund.[37]

The rule contains some highly technical terms which have not been explained heretofore and which, therefore, will be ignored for the present.

There is no reason for this rule to be included in the new Uniform Classification because that Classification is applicable only for rates prescribed by the Commission in I.C.C. Docket 28300.[38] Those rates are protected by Fourth Section relief granted by the Commission in connection with the scale of rates prescribed therein.

Use of Words "and," "or," "Rate," "Rating," "Column," Parentheses and Indentations (R-46). This rule is self-explanatory, in that it explains the terms shown in the subject. Similar provisions are contained on page 1 of the Motor Classification under the heading of "Application of Classification Ratings."

Reference to Rules, Items, Notes, etc. (R-48), (NE-25). Both the rail and the New England Classifications contain the same rule, namely:

Reference herein (or in supplements hereto) to items, pages, rules, etc., in this publication, includes reference to successive issues of such items, pages, rules, etc.

Reference herein (or in supplements hereto) to other publications includes reference to supplements thereto or successive issues thereof.

A similar rule appears in most freight tariffs. Its purpose is to eliminate the necessity of repeating all reference items every time a tariff to which reference is made is re-issued. Hence, the references remain constant at all times.

Weights on Liquified Petroleum Gas (R-52). Rail Rules 52 and

---

[36] *Consolidated Freight Classification No. 20,* Consolidated Classification Committee, Chicago, effective October 15, 1951, p. 154.

[37] Interstate Commerce Act, Section 15 (7).

[38] See, pp. 86–101, above.

53 are new. Rule 52 provides the method of computing weights on liquified petroleum gas when shipped in tank cars and, therefore, it supplements the Tank Car Rule.[39]

This rule contains a table composed of two columns. Column 1 lists the specific gravity rating of the commodity at 60 degrees Fahrenheit. Column 2 is divided into two sub-columns, one applicable from April to October and the other from November to March, both inclusive. In each sub-column there are listed the weights per gallon for the specific gravity ratings shown in the adjoining Column 1. Shipments of the commodity are subject to a carload weight computed by multiplying the gallonage capacity of the tank car, including the dome, by the weight per gallon shown in Column 2 at the specific gravity shown in Column 1 existing at point of origin at the time of loading.

Weights on Butadiene (R-53). The principle of this rule is exactly the same as Rule 52, described above.

Definition of "Compressed" (NE-22). The Coordinated Motor Classification in New England contains special rule pertaining to "compressed" articles. It states that, "except as otherwise provided," whenever the term "compressed" is used in that Classification, it means the container and contents must have a corresponding density rating in accordance with a table included in the rule. If the density does not meet the specifications contained in the table, the article is considered as "not compressed" and the rating provided therefor will apply; otherwise, the "compressed" rating is applicable.[40] The purpose is to provide higher ratings for articles than are specified in the Description of Articles section when the density is not sufficient to meet those ratings. For example, ground Pimento in packages is assigned a Class 4 rating; likewise, a Class 4 rating is assigned to unground Pimento "in bales, compressed"; but a Class 3 rating is assigned to the article when shipped "in bags, bales, not compressed, barrels, boxes or pails." [41] As has been previously indicated, the New England Classification is based primarily upon a density factor, with other transportation characteristics tending to increase the rating. The rule was first published in its present form in the Classification No. 7 which became effective January 8, 1954.[42]

---

[39] See, Rail Rule 35, pp. 285–288, above.
[40] *Coordinated Motor Freight Classification No. 7,* The New England Motor Rate Bureau, Boston, effective January 8, 1954, p. 111.
[41] *Ibid.,* Item 32625.
[42] Information contained in letter from A. C. Gardner, Classification Section, New England Motor Rate Bureau, Inc., Boston, dated July 27, 1955.

Overcharge & Undercharge Claims on Intrastate Shipments (NE-30). This rule of the New England motor carriers specifies that overcharge and undercharge claims on intrastate shipments must be filed with the carrier within two years from the date of delivery or tender of delivery of the shipment involved.[43]

---

[43] *Coordinated Motor Freight Classification No. 7, op. cit.,* p. 112.

Chapter 15

RATES & TARIFFS

Earlier a tariff was compared to a price list.[1] That is exactly what it is: a price list of services which common carriers render to the public. However, a tariff may contain data other than prices. For example, the published Classifications are tariffs, yet there is no price stated therein. All those data, whether they be prices, regulations, or what not, when duly published in tariffs, as required by statute and prescribed by regulatory bodies, have the same force as law. They are binding both on carriers and the shipping public, and neither party may legally deviate from them. Many years ago, the Interstate Commerce Commission said: "No proposition respecting the requirements of this Act is more clearly and firmly settled than that rules duly established as therein required are absolutely binding upon carriers and shippers alike . . ."[2]

Likewise, a carrier may legally charge only the price contained in a tariff, and the user of the carrier's service is required to pay that price. Hence, there is no bargaining between the buyer (the public) and the seller (the carrier), the former attempting to drive down the price and the latter being equally determined to increase it. The prices are set well in advance, the contents of tariffs are considered to be public information, and, therefore, the user of any carrier's service is presumed to know the amount he will be required to pay. Many years ago the Commission commented on the matter, as follows:[3]

Regardless of the rate quoted or inserted in the bill of lading, the published rate must be paid by the shipper and actually collected by the

---

[1] See, p. 4, above.

[2] R. H. Coomes, et al., v. Chicago, Milwaukee & St. Paul Railway Company, et al., 13 I.C.C. 192 (193), 1908.

[3] A. J. Poor Grain Company v. Chicago, Burlington & Quincy Railway Company, et al., 12 I.C.C. 418 (422), 1907.

carrier. The failure on the part of the shipper to pay or the carrier to collect the full freight charges, based upon the lawfully published rate for the particular movement between two given points constitutes a breach of the law and will subject either one or the other, and sometimes both, to its penalties . . . When regularly published it (a rate) is no longer the rate imposed by the carrier, but the rate imposed by the law.

Frequent references have been made to tariffs in the preceding pages, and the term "applicable tariff" has been used with freedom. This chapter will endeavor to present a brief explanation of the relationship that exists between tariffs and rates. There is no doubt that freight tariffs are the most complex of all tariffs, and some are more complicated than others. "The layman, when first confronted with their seemingly baffling array, soon becomes hopelessly lost . . ." [4] Sometimes the framers of tariffs add to the confusion by including an array of references which, of course, must be consulted by the tariff reader to insure accuracy. Although it is recognized that some references can hardly be avoided, the necessity to check four or five in order to determine a single rate is not conducive to simplification.

Positive steps have been taken in recent years to simplify tariffs. In 1951, the Railroads' Tariff Research Group, consisting of three full-time members under the chairmanship of Charles S. Baxter, was established to investigate the complexity of tariffs. Its objectives are: (1) to achieve uniformity of tariff rules, (2) to make it easy to find the rules, and (3) to make rules understandable and easy to read.[5] The Group submits its recommendations to a 12-man administrative committee composed of carrier traffic experts and 11 representatives of the National Industrial Traffic League who represent the interests of the shipping public. Action of this joint committee is final and binding upon all tariff publishers! [6] Already, accomplishments of Mr. Baxter's group have been outstanding, and future progress towards tariff simplification seems assured. The following comment of Edward A. Starr, distinguished traffic consultant and Lecturer in Transportation at Texas Christian University, is significant: [7]

Although there are those, particularly among veteran tariff users who may have taken a somewhat cynical view of the possibilities of tariff simplification, without doubt there has been already considerable accomplishment along this line . . . Contrasted to the carrier-shipper

[4] Starr, E. A.: *The Tools of the Traffic Man*, Transportation Press, Dallas, 1953, p. 24.

[5] Morton, Newton, and Mossman, F. H.: *Industrial Traffic Management*, The Ronald Press Company, New York, 1954, pp. 36–37.

[6] Starr, *op. cit.*, pp. 224–227.

[7] *Ibid.*, pp. 16, 227.

turmoil (of former years) we now hear of the Joint Committee . . . where carrier and shipper meet to determine amicably just how to iron out existing tariff complexities. . . . We may improve the mechanical set-up of the tariff in our efforts toward its simplification, but as long as the tariff must be expressed in the printed word, and as long as words are written in by human beings, the business of rate-finding will never be a sinecure.

The Commission has adhered to the principle that if a tariff is so complex that its meaning is doubtful, "the construction will be applied that is most favorable to the shippers." [8] Efforts towards reduction of tariff complexity received a great boost with the publication of the rail and motor uniform Classifications, which have been said to constitute "the greatest step ever taken toward tariff simplification." [9]

Definitions. Since primary emphasis will be devoted to tariffs containing rates, a knowledge of the different kinds of rates is essential.

Rate. It will be recalled from Chapter 1 that a rate was defined as the price for shipping freight.[10] Freight rates are always stated in terms of dollars and/or cents, usually in cents per 100 pounds; but other bases may be used, such as, per ton of either 2,000 pounds or 2,240 pounds, per package, per stated truckload or carload, or other defined unit, except units of time. All rates generally fall within one of three categories, which have been explained earlier, namely: (1) carload, truckload or volume rates; (2) less-than-truckload or less-than-carload; and (3) any quantity.[11]

Class Rate. A rate applicable to the rating of an article provided in a published Classification. Class Tariffs contain class rates.

Commodity Rate. A rate applicable to a particular article or group of articles, between named points, which is specifically described in the tariff. Usually, but not always,[12] a commodity rate supersedes a class rate and it is lower than the class rate on the same article and between the same points of origin and destination via the same route. Commodity Tariffs contain commodity rates.

Column Rate. A form of commodity rate to which is assigned a fixed percentage of the Class 100 rate, instead of being published in terms of dollars and cents. Obviously, column rates are closely tied

---

[8] Knorst, W. J.: *Transportation and Traffic Management,* Vol. 3, 2nd Edition, College of Advanced Traffic, Chicago, 1950, p. 971.

[9] Interstate Commerce Commission, Docket No. 28310, "General Reply of Respondent Railroads to Protests and Requests for Suspension of Uniform Classification No. 1, or Parts Thereof," 1 Park Avenue, New York City, 1952, p. 3.

[10] See, p. 4, above.

[11] See, p. 5, above.

[12] See, p. 269, above.

to the class rate structure, but they differ from exceptions generally because they apply to named commodities.

Local Rate. A rate applicable between points located on the lines or routes of a single carrier, thus: Knoxville, Tennessee, to New York City via Mason & Dixon Lines, or San Francisco to Bombay via Trans World Airlines. Distance is of no significance; rather, the entire movement from origin to destination must be handled by only one carrier. Local Tariffs contain local rates.

Joint Rate. A rate applicable over the lines of two or more carriers which have been established by agreement between the carriers involved and so published in a tariff naming the carriers concerned, thus: Boston to Miami via, for example, Associated Transport to Atlanta, thence Central Truck Lines to Miami. Joint Tariffs contain joint rates. Usually, a joint rate is less than the sum of intermediate local rates.

Through Rate. A rate applicable from origin to destination. It may be a local rate, a joint rate, or a combination of any separately established rates, thus: a rate from Atlanta to Chicago may be considered as a through rate. If the freight it covers moves all the way by Huber & Huber Motor Express, it is a local rate as well as a through rate; but if the freight moves via Georgia Highway Express from Atlanta to Knoxville thence Silver Fleet Motor Express from Knoxville to Chicago, then the through rate is also a joint rate.

Combination Rate. A rate which is made by combining two or more published rates, thus: if there were no single rate published from Boston to Los Angeles, but there existed a class rate on the article being shipped from Boston to St. Louis and a commodity rate from St. Louis to Los Angeles, then the through rate from Boston to Los Angeles would be the sum of the Boston–St. Louis and St. Louis–Los Angeles rates, forming a combination rate. Hence, in the absence of a through rate from origin to destination, the lowest combination of separately established rates form the applicable combination rate which "is as binding, definite, and absolute as a joint rate." [13]

Released Rate. A rate on an article which varies directly with the value of the article as declared by the shipper, by which the carrier is relieved of its liability for full value of the freight.

Proportional Rate. A rate applicable only on specified traffic between two points destined beyond the point to which the rate applies, or originated beyond the point from which such rate applies,

[13] Shinn, G. L.: *Freight Rate Application,* Simmons-Boardman Publishing Corporation, New York, 1948, p. 28.

or which both originated beyond the point from which such rate applies and is destined beyond the point to which such rate applies. The application of a proportional rate must be specifically restricted by tariff publication. It can be used only as a part of a combination through rate, thus: a published rate on grain from Minneapolis to Cincinnati to apply only on shipments of grain destined to points beyond Cincinnati, such as Atlanta. This proportional rate from Minneapolis to Cincinnati is less than the "standard" Minneapolis-Cincinnati rate which applies on grain for use or consumption in Cincinnati. For years, rail rates on Florida citrus were proportionals from Jacksonville, Florida, to Richmond, Virginia, for destinations beyond, thus: on oranges, the proportional rate from Jacksonville to Richmond was 37½ cents per box when New York City was the ultimate destination, but only about 33½ cents when Buffalo was the destination.[14]

Only part of the route over which a shipment moves is covered by a proportional rate; and it can be used only in connection with another published rate or rates. Hence, a proportional rate may be considered as being a form of combination rate and, as its name implies, it is a portion or part of a through rate. Alone it means nothing, because it has to be associated with some other rate before it establishes a rate between any two points. The Commission has summarized a proportional rate as being either a local or joint rate dependent upon a previous transportation to the point from which the proportional rate applies, a subsequent transportation from the point to which the proportional rate applies, or both.[15] Proportional Tariffs contain proportional rates.

Export & Import Rates. These are rates especially established on export and import traffic which usually are lower than comparable domestic rates to and from ports.

Blanket Rate. A rate that is uniform over a large geographical area. All points included in the blanketed area take the same rate instead of a different rate being applied to each individual locality. A blanket rate is a form of commodity rate used particularly for long-haul traffic. Possibly the largest "blanket" in the country is the territory applied to rail commodity rates on wine from Fresno, California. When packed in glass, earthenware, or metal cans, boxed or in bulk in barrels, rates on wine are exactly the same from Fresno to all points east of Salt Lake City and the eastern border of Ari-

---

[14] Healy, K. T.: *The Economics of Transportation in America,* The Ronald Press Company, New York, 1940, pp. 248-249.
[15] *Swift & Company v. Alton Railroad Company, et al.,* 262 I.C.C. 783, 1945.

zona.[16] Admittedly, this is an extreme situation; but blanket rates are by no means uncommon, especially on transcontinental traffic. Possibly a more realistic illustration is that blanket rates apply to all points in Florida south of Jacksonville and Lake City on many articles originating in California and the Pacific Northwest. From a negative approach, years ago citrus fruit growers in Florida endeavored to have the entire producing area of the state blanketed so that the same rate would apply from practically all points south of Jacksonville, but the request was declined by the Commission.[17]

Group Rate. A rate that is uniform over a relatively small geographical area. A group rate follows the same principle as a blanket rate, only it covers much less territory. All points within an established group take the same rate. Size of a group is influenced by distance of the haul, type of traffic, and the area to be included. Group rates "are the predominant form of commodity rates."[18]

The reader should recall the prior discussion of the I.C.C. Docket 28300. One of the primary objectives of the Commission's investigation was to eliminate, or at least materially reduce, the many different kinds of commodity rates which have no direct relationship to distance. Within the last few years, many of those rates have disappeared or have been brought into direct relationship with class rates by being assigned a percentage of the Class 100 rate. The several variations of commodity rates, therefore, should tend to be reduced with the passing of time; but their entire elimination is questionable.

Arbitraries & Differentials. In general, carriers use the words "arbitrary" and "differential" interchangeably. Technically, however, they have different meanings which Dean Knorst has defined, as follows:[19]

An ARBITRARY is (1) a fixed amount which a transportation line agrees to accept in dividing joint rates, or (2) a fixed amount added to or deducted from a rate from (or to) one point to make a rate from (or to) another point.

A DIFFERENTIAL is the difference established between rates from related points of origin, or to related points of destination, or via different routes between the same points.

A DIFFERENTIAL RATE is a rate established via a route from one point to another by deducting a fixed amount from or adding a fixed

---

[16] Daggett, Stuart, & Carter, J. P.: *The Structure of Transcontinental Railroad Rates*, University of California Press, Berkeley, 1947, pp. 73–74.

[17] Bigham, T. C., and Roberts, M. J.: *Citrus Fruit Rates*, University of Florida Press, Gainesville, 1950, pp. 56–57.

[18] Landon, C. E.: *Transportation*, William Sloane Associates, Inc., New York, 1951, p. 321.

[19] Knorst, *op. cit.*, Vol. 3, p. 879.

amount to the rate via another (standard) route between the same points.

A DIFFERENTIAL ROUTE is the line or lines which maintain differential rates.

An example of an arbitrary may be found in northern New England where rail rates to and from points located north of an imaginary line extending roughly between Boston and Albany were determined by adding fixed amounts, based on mileage, to the "standard" rate.[20]

Sometimes a differential is a percentage of a rate, or it may be a fixed number of cents, which is deducted from another rate in order to determine the rate applicable for a point located in an area which has been granted the differential. Differential rates are commonly used by carriers whose routes are circuitous or so unfavorably located that they cannot compete with other carriers for traffic except by lower rates. It should be understood that an arbitrary or differential added to or deducted from a "standard" base rate is *not* a combination rate; [21] instead, either is a method of simply establishing a through rate.

Agency Tariff. A tariff issued by a publishing agent on behalf of any number of carriers.

Individual Tariff. A tariff issued by one carrier. However, it should not be interpreted that an individual tariff is restricted to the single carrier which issues it. Other carriers may participate in such a tariff under a concurrence to the carrier which issued it and, therefore, the tariff does not always necessarily apply only to one carrier. Of course, rates in an individual tariff may not duplicate or conflict with rates published in an agency tariff.

In general, the priority of rates on the same commodity between the same points is, as follows: (1) a commodity rate applies instead of a class rate; (2) a joint rate takes precedence over a combination rate; (3) a through local rate applies instead of a combination of local rates; (4) a proportional rate supersedes a local or prior joint rate in determining the applicable rate on through traffic; (5) an export or import rate applies to the exclusion of domestic rates in determining the rate on export or import traffic; [22] and (6) a class rate made by the use of an exception rating takes precedence over the class rate made by use of the Classification rating.

---

[20] *Eastern Class Rate Investigation*, 164 I.C.C. 314, 1930.
[21] *Wisconsin Lime & Cement Company v. Atchison, Topeka & Santa Fe Railway*, 148 I.C.C. 599 (601), 1928.
[22] Shinn, *op. cit.*, p. 13.

Finally, there are two other kinds of rates about which much has been written: "legal" and "lawful" rates. Although often used interchangeably, their meanings are not synonymous by any means. A legal rate is one which has been duly published in a tariff and filed with the Commission pursuant to provisions of the Interstate Commerce Act and rules of the Interstate Commerce Commission. A lawful rate is one which adheres to the reasonableness and non-discriminatory provisions of the Act. Hence a rate may be legal, but found to be unlawful by the Commission for being, for example, unreasonably discriminatory in violation of Sections 2 and 216 (d) of the Act. Conversely, a rate may be lawful, but it is not legal if it does not conform with Sections 6 and 217 concerning tariff requirements. A rate may be condemned by the Commission as being unlawful, and the Commission may prescribe a new lawful rate for application in the future; but such a rate does not become a legal rate until it is published in a tariff, the tariff filed with the Commission, and the tariff becomes effective.[23] The Commission has held that, "A rate published in a tariff on file with the Commission is a legal rate even though it contravenes an order of the Commission . . . or violates the Interstate Commerce Act."[24] Basically, the term "legal" refers to the form of the rate in a tariff, while "lawful" refers to the level of the rate.[25]

Tariff Regulation. There is stringent regulation by the federal government of tariffs used by common carriers engaged in interstate commerce. Those regulations pertaining to railroads, pipe lines, express lines, and sleeping car companies are found in Section 6 of the Interstate Commerce Act which, incidentally, has been amended no less than nine times. The regulations governing motor carriers are in Sections 217 and 218; water carriers, in Section 306; and freight forwarders, in Section 405. Somewhat comparable requirements for air carriers are in Section 403 of the Civil Aeronautics Act.

Railroads were the first common carriers to be regulated by the federal government. The original Interstate Commerce Act, then entitled "An Act to Regulate Commerce," was adopted by the Congress of the United States in 1887 essentially to curb discriminatory rate practices; and the same Act created the Interstate Commerce Commission. Prior to that time, there was no legal requirement that rates be published in tariffs; and even when they were, there was

---

[23] Tedrow, J. H.: *Regulation of Transportation,* 4th Edition, William C. Brown Company, Dubuque, 1951, pp. 144–145.
[24] *Chase v. Atlantic Coast Line Railroad Company,* 220 I.C.C. 400, 1937.
[25] Cushman, F. M.: *Manual of Transportation Law,* The Transportation Press, Dallas, 1951, pp. 176–177.

no legal means whereby the carriers could be forced to comply with the rates which were published. Motor carriers were brought under the jurisdiction of the Commission by the Motor Carrier Act of 1935, now Part II of the Interstate Commerce Act.[26] A summary of the provisions of the Act, pertaining particularly to motor carriers and railroads, is presented below.

1. Every common carrier subject to the Act is required to file with the Interstate Commerce Commission, to print, and to keep open to public inspection, "schedules (tariffs) showing all the rates, fares, and charges for transportation" and all other services, together with all rules and regulations in connection therewith.

2. The tariffs shall show the rates, fares, and charges of the carrier "for transportation between different points on its own route, and between points on its own route and points on the route of any other carrier . . . when a through route and joint rate have been established."

3. The rates, fares, and charges must be stated in terms of lawful United States currency.

4. The tariffs shall be "published, filed, and posted in such form and manner, and contain such information, as the Commission by regulations shall prescribe."

5. Authority is granted to the Commission to reject any tariff not complying with the Act and with the Commission's regulations, and "any tariff so rejected by the Commission shall be void and its use shall be unlawful."

6. Carriers are required to charge and collect the exact amount stated in a tariff which is in effect at the time of the transaction, which means there must be strict observance of the published rates.

7. Carriers are forbidden to refund in any manner any portion of the amount specified in an applicable tariff, nor may they extend "any privileges or facilities for transportation" to anyone except as specified in the tariffs.

8. No change may be made in a tariff on less than 30 days' notice to the Commission. However, the Commission is authorized, "at its discretion and for good cause," to permit a change to become effective in less than 30 days.

9. No common carrier subject to the Act is permitted to operate unless its tariffs are filed and published in accordance with the provisions of the Act and regulations prescribed by the Commission.

---

[26] For a comprehensive presentation of the development of carrier regulation in general, and rate and tariff regulation in particular, see, Johnson, E. R.: *Government Regulation of Transportation,* D. Appleton-Century Company, New York, 1938.

10. For failure to comply with these regulations, Paragraph 10 of Section 6 of the Act provides a penalty of $500 for each offense, and $25 "for each and every day of the continuance of such offense." For motor carriers the penalty, as stated in Section 222, is a fine of $100 for the first offense and a maximum of $500 for a subsequent offense.

11. Tariffs are required to be "plainly printed in large type, and copies for use of the public shall be kept posted in two public and conspicuous places in every depot, station, or office of such carrier where passengers or freight, respectively, are received for transportation, in such form that they shall be accessible to the public and can be conveniently inspected." The requirement for motor carriers differs somewhat from the above for railroads in that only one copy must be posted at stations maintained by motor carriers, and one complete copy maintained at each carrier's principal office.

12. "The names of the several carriers which are parties to any joint tariff shall be specified therein, and each of the parties thereto, other than the one filing the same, shall file with the Commission such evidence of concurrence therein or acceptance thereof as may be required or approved by the Commission."

13. "In time of war or threatened war . . . upon demand of the President of the United States . . . carriers shall adopt every means within their control to facilitate and expedite the military traffic."

Some misunderstanding may exist concerning the meaning of the words "file" and "post" as used herein. A tariff has been "filed" with the Interstate Commerce Commission, or any state regulatory body, when received by the Commission; and it serves formal notice that the carrier proposes to place the tariff into effect on a particular date shown on the face of the tariff. A tariff has been "posted" when it is made accessible to the public by a carrier at its general and local offices. When a tariff is "filed" in accordance with the law, its effectiveness is not voided if it has not been "posted." In other words, failure to "post" a tariff that has been duly "filed" does not void its application. The Supreme Court of the United States ruled about 50 years ago that "posting was of secondary importance." [27] However, the carrier is subject to fine for violation of the Act.

The interpretation described above is justified, for otherwise if "posting" were a prerequisite to a rate becoming effective, a disgruntled shipper or carrier employee could remove the "posted" tariff from the carrier's depot thereby causing the rate to no longer be in existence! "Posting" is nothing more than a means of letting the

[27] *Texas & Pacific Railway Company v. Cisco Oil Mill,* 204 U. S. 449, 1907.

public know about the establishment of rates, rules, etc. Long ago, the courts ruled that any rate which is published and filed in accordance with the Act is the lawful rate, regardless of whether or not it has been posted.[28] Therefore, publication and filing are the steps of primary consideration.

What a tariff actually states governs its application instead of what might have been intended. Once filed with the Commission, a tariff "must stand as it is written." [29] Many years ago, the Commission commented very forcefully on this matter, as follows: [30]

> The law compels carriers to publish and post their schedules of charges upon the theory that they will be informative. The shipper who consults them has a right to rely upon their obvious meaning. He cannot be charged with knowledge of the intention of the framers or the carriers canons of construction or of some other tariff not even referred to in the one carrying the rate. The public posting of tariffs will be largely useless if the carriers' interpretation is to be dependent upon tradition and the arbitrary practices of a general freight office. This Commission has long since repudiated the suggestion that railroad officials may be looked to as authority for the construction of their tariffs.

Later, in another case in point, the Commission said: [31]

> Defendants contend that the item covering mattresses was intended for new mattresses and does not, therefore, embrace old or new mattresses. That contention is unsound. Tariffs are construed according to their language and the intention of the framers is not controlling. The language used in that item neither restricts it to new mattresses nor excludes old mattresses therefrom.

By order of the Commission, a carrier is not required to post at each of its local stations, all tariffs containing all inbound and outbound rates applicable to the particular stations; instead, the requirement covers tariffs containing only all outbound rates, plus, of course, charges on all services applicable at the station.[32] The carrier's agent where tariffs are posted is required to show on the title page of each tariff the date on which it was received, and to maintain a record showing the date each tariff or supplement was received and posted. Continuing, the Commission has ordered: [33]

---

[28] *United States v. Miller*, 223 U. S. 599, 1912.

[29] Knorst, *op. cit.*, p. 975.

[30] *Newton Gum Company v. Chicago, Burlington & Quincy Railroad Company, et al.*, 16 I.C.C. 341 (346), 1909.

[31] *American Cotton Waste & Linter Exchange v. Baltimore & Ohio Railroad Company, et al.*, 169 I.C.C. 710 (712), 1930.

[32] "In the Matter of Modification of the Provisions of Section 6 of the Act with regard to Posting Freight or Passenger Tariffs at Stations," Interstate Commerce Commission, Washington, 1915.

[33] *Ibid.*

He (the agent) shall also be instructed and required to give any information contained in such schedules (tariffs), to lend assistance to seekers for information therefrom, and to accord inquirers opportunity to examine any of said schedules without requiring or requesting the inquirer to assign any reason for such desire and with all the promptness possible and consistent with proper performance of the other duties devolving upon him.

Compulsory publication of tariffs and compulsory compliance by carriers of their provisions are among the most important provisions of the Interstate Commerce Act. Unquestionably, this requirement enables shippers to determine exactly what their transportation costs will be, and permits them to enter into contracts without fear of a sudden rate increase wiping out their profits. At the same time, since tariffs are public information, one shipper can easily ascertain the shipping costs of his competitor. Before adoption of the Act, "the rates of railroads were often shrouded in fogs of uncertainty and mists of obscurity that only the favored could penetrate." [34]

Suspension of Tariffs. What is commonly known as the "suspension power" of the Commission is another important phase of regulation. The term means that the Commission may prohibit a tariff from going into effect on the date proposed. This power to suspend a proposed new rate or rule was first established by the Mann-Elkins Act of 1910. As the law stands today, whenever a carrier files a new rate or regulation, the Commission may postpone its becoming effective pending investigation of its lawfulness. The Commission may take this action either upon complaint of some interested party or on its own volition; but it must notify the carriers affected as to the reasons for the suspension. Then, the Commission must conduct a hearing regarding the lawfulness of the proposal, at which the burden of proof is upon the carrier to show that the proposed change is just and reasonable, after which the Commission will issue its order. The period of suspension may be no longer than seven months beyond the time the tariff was to have become effective. If the proceeding has not been concluded by the end of seven months, the proposal shall go into effect at that time in the manner originally desired by the carrier, unless the carrier voluntarily postpones the effective date to a date determined by the carrier.[35] However, for rail carrier only, Part I of the Act provides that if the proposal involves an increase in rates, the carrier(s) concerned may be required to keep a detailed record of amounts collected by reason of

---

[34] Wilson, G. L.: *Traffic Law and Procedure*, Vol. 2, The Traffic Service Corporation, Chicago, 1944, p. 155.

[35] Interstate Commerce Act, Sections 15 (7), 216 (g), 307 (g), 406 (e).

the increase, and from whom, because upon completion of the hearing the Commission may require appropriate refunds to persons who had paid the higher charges. Justification of this last provision is questionable because by the time a refund is made the earlier increase may have been passed along to the consumer through a higher price for the article, resulting in the refund amounting to nothing more than a windfall. Actually, this situation seldom occurs, because the carrier will agree to an extension of the suspension period rather than have the possibility of refunds hanging over them together with eliminating the additional expense of keeping such detailed records.[36]

Types of Tariffs. There are numerous kinds of tariffs which Professor Wilson, of the University of Pennsylvania, has classified into four groups, as follows: [37]

1. By publication source. (a) An individual tariff is published by a single carrier for local traffic moving over its lines, but other carriers may participate in it as was mentioned earlier. (b) A joint tariff shows joint rates, and usually it is published by an agent, or bureau, representing a group of carriers. (c) An agency tariff is published by an agent representing any number of carriers. (d) A joint agents' tariff is published jointly by agents representing carriers in two or more territories which quotes joint rates between the two territories.

2. According to information shown therein, such as, the published Classifications, exceptions to the Classifications, class rates, commodity rates, various directories, special services, explosives, and others.

3. According to size. Tariffs vary in size from a single page document to volumes of several hundred pages. There are three categories of size, *viz.*: (a) one-sheet, (b) pamphlet, and (c) book tariffs.

4. According to application of rates. This group includes local tariffs, and joint rate tariffs.

A recent publication of the Southern Motor Carriers Rate Conference classifies tariffs, as follows: [38]

1. Classification
2. Exception to Classification

---

[36] Bigham, T. C., and Roberts, M. J.: *Transportation,* McGraw-Hill Book Company, New York, 1952, p. 238.
[37] Wilson, G. L.: *The Principles of Freight Traffic,* The Traffic World, Chicago, 1935, pp. 44–47.
[38] *Form, Construction and General Application of the Tariffs of the Southern Motor Carriers Rate Conference,* Southern Motor Carriers Rate Conference, Atlanta, 1955, p. 7.

3. Class Rate Tariffs (For Classification Ratings)
4. Class Rate Tariffs (For Exception Ratings)
5. Class and Commodity Rate Tariffs
6. General Commodity Tariffs
7. Specific Commodity Tariffs
8. Commodity Column Tariffs
9. Grouping Tariffs
10. Routing Tariffs
11. Accessorial Charge or Allowance Tariffs
12. Scope of Operations Tariff
13. Participating Carrier Tariffs

Construction of Tariffs. The construction of tariffs involves a question of law. The distinguished Justice Brandeis, in delivering a majority opinion of the Supreme Court of the United States, said: [39]

When words of a written instrument are used in their ordinary meaning, their construction presents a question solely of law. But words are used sometimes in a peculiar meaning. Then extrinsic evidence may be necessary to determine the meaning of words appearing in the document. This is true where technical words or phrases not commonly understood are employed . . . where the document to be construed is a tariff of an interstate carrier, . . . the preliminary determination must be made by the Commission . . . For the effect to be given the tariff might depend, not upon construction of the language—a question of law—but upon whether or not a particular judge or jury had found, as a fact, that the words of the document were used in the peculiar sense attributed to them or that a particular usage existed.

The form in which tariffs are published is governed by detailed rules prescribed by the Interstate Commerce Commission. The form may be changed from time to time by the Commission as may be found expedient.[40] The regulations governing motor carriers are contained in a 111-page document usually referred to simply as "Tariff Circular No. 3," the complete title of which is shown in the footnote below.[41] Rules pertaining to railroads consume 134 pages in a publication commonly known as "Tariff Circular No. 20." [42] These rules are *most* meticulous. They prescribe, among other things, such items as the size (8 x 11 inches) of each page, the

[39] *Great Northern Railroad Company v. Merchants' Elevator Company*, 259 U. S. 285 (290), 1922.
[40] *Interstate Commerce Commission v. Cincinnati, New Orleans & Texas Pacific Railway Company*, 167 U. S. 479, 1897.
[41] Interstate Commerce Commission, Bureau of Motor Carriers: *Tariff Circular MF No. 3*, "REGULATIONS to Govern the Construction, Filing, and Posting of Common Carrier Freight Tariffs and Classification Publications," effective 1941, Government Printing Office, Washington, 1940.
[42] Interstate Commerce Commission: *Tariff Circular No. 20*, "RULES to Govern the Construction and Filing of Freight-Rate Publications Including Pipe-Line Schedules and Classifications," effective 1928, Government Printing Office, Washington, 1928.

quality of paper, size of type, width of margin, manner of presenting tables and columns of figures, symbols to be used to denote changes, and other details. Also, each tariff must be identified by an I.C.C. number "in not less that 12-point bold face type," and immediately thereunder the I.C.C. number of the tariff being cancelled. The new numbers run consecutively, and they indicate the number under which each tariff is filed with the Commission.[43] The numbers for motor carrier tariffs carry the prefix "MF," thus: "MF-I.C.C. No. 614" identifies the *Eastern-Southern Class Tariff* of the Southern Motor Carriers Rate Conference; whereas "I.C.C. No. 1300 identifies the *Class Rates Tariff* of the Southern Freight Tariff Bureau, a section of the Southern Freight Association, for railroads. In the same manner, tariffs on intrastate traffic are numbered for filing with state commissions. Carriers may adopt the I.C.C. numbers for their own purposes, or establish an entirely different series of numbers. Simply stated, there is complete uniformity in the form of all tariffs issued by and in behalf of carriers subject to the Interstate Commerce Act.

Publication of Tariffs. Although a carrier itself may publish, file, and post an individual tariff, the majority of tariffs are issued by agents acting for a group of carriers. However, there are instances where a state regulatory body has published tariffs, such as those of the Railroad Commission of Texas covering intrastate movements of household goods by motor carriers and petroleum in tank trucks.[44] In some cases, tariffs are published by national associations of carriers, examples of which are the explosives tariffs published by the American Trucking Associations, Inc., and the Association of American Railroads, respectively.

Agency tariffs greatly simplify the problem of making all rates, fares, charges, classifications, rules, regulations, etc., available to both shippers and carriers. There would be utter chaos if each carrier by each mode of transportation published only its own tariffs; and, without joint action, there could be no joint rates to facilitate the through movement of goods over the lines of more than one carrier. These tariff agents, or bureaus, function on a geographical basis. For example, the explosive tariffs mentioned in the preceding paragraph are nation-wide in scope. In the South, the Southern Motor Carriers Rate Conference, under the direction of W. M. Miller, Executive Vice President, and the Southern Freight Association,

---

[43] *Tariff Circular MF No. 3*, Rules 1 and 2 (b), pp. 4–5; *Tariff Circular No. 20*, pp. 2–3.

[44] Starr, *op. cit.*, p. 3.

headed by J. G. Kerr, Chairman, are the respective tariff publishing agencies of motor carriers and railroads. Regardless of who publishes a tariff, however, carriers are required to designate someone by name as agent for each tariff.

Before an agent or bureau may publish a tariff, it must have in its possession a power of attorney, in prescribed form, authorizing it to act in behalf of the carrier. A copy must be filed with the Interstate Commerce Commission and with the state commission of each state in which the carrier operates. Each form is identified by established letters, such as, "PX" for passenger traffic and "FX" for freight traffic by railroad; whereas the form for motor carriers is identified by the prefix letter "M," thus, "MFX." The symbol "FX1" indicates the power of attorney granted by a railroad in appointing a tariff publishing agent.[45] The symbol "FX1 No. 21" would mean the 21st consecutive power of attorney granted by the issuing carrier.

There are two forms of powers of attorney for motor carriers designated as "MFXA2" and "MFXA3." The first one is used when the agent appointed to issue and file tariffs in behalf of the carrier is an individual, such as an official of the carrier; the latter is used when the agent is a corporation. In addition to specifying by name the individual to whom power of attorney is granted, form MFXA2 names an alternate agent who is authorized to act in event of the death, disability, resignation, or other *permanent* absence of the principal agent.

In addition to the power of attorney, when a carrier wishes to concur in a tariff issued by another carrier, the first named carrier must file with the Commission, or appropriate state regulatory bodies as the case may be, another document known as a "concurrence." It shows the carrier desires to participate in the tariffs published by other carriers, and the carrier then becomes a party to the joint rates and other matters covered therein. The symbols designating concurrences applicable to motor carriers are "MFXC2" and "MFXC3." The former is specific and is used when giving concurrence "in a particular tariff that is issued and filed by another carrier"; and the latter is a general concurrence with a tariff when issued by another carrier or an agent, "naming rates from or to points on its lines or over its lines." [46]

A summary of the symbols applicable to railroads follows: [47]

---

[45] *Tariff Circular No. 20*, Rules 17–18, pp. 58–60.
[46] *Tariff Circular MF No. 3*, Rule 23, pp. 77–78.
[47] *Tariff Circular No. 20*, Rules 20–25, pp. 63–66.

FX1 is the power of attorney granted to appoint a tariff publishing agent, which was explained earlier.

FX2 is a form of concurrence used when concurring in specific tariffs issued by another carrier or agent for one carrier.

FX3 is a form of concurrence used when concurring in tariffs of other carriers, or their agent, publishing rates which apply to and via points on the concurring carrier's line, but not *from* points on its line.

FX4 is a form of concurrence which expands FX3 to include rates applicable to specifically described traffic from, at, to, or via its line.

FX5 is a form of concurrence which further expands FX3 to include rates to, via, and from points on its line.

FX6 is a form of concurrence used when two or more carriers appoint the same person as agent, in which the concurring carrier is an intermediate or destination line and not the originating carrier.

FX7 is a form of concurrence which is granted to an agent representing two or more carriers for tariffs publishing rates from, to, or via its lines.

FX8 is a form of concurrence which expands FX7 to include rates on specifically described traffic or between certain points or territories.

FX9 is a form of concurrence which grants concurrence in a tariff issued by an agent for two or more carriers.

Rule 26 (b) of the Tariff Circular further explains concurrences, as follows: [48]

Concurrence forms FX2 and FX9 concur in the entire publication named therein and may not be modified except as modified in rule 19 (which prescribes the different forms). Concurrence forms FX3 and FX6 confer authority to publish and file rates to, but not from, points on lines of concurring carrier and via its lines. Concurrence forms FX5 and FX7 confer authority to publish and file rates from and to points on lines of concurring carrier, and via its lines. Forms FX3, FX5, FX6, and FX7 are not to be modified. Forms FX4 and FX8 are provided for instances which the other forms do not exactly fit and shall be used only when none of the other forms provides for the exact authority it is desired to confer.

It is worthy of mention, however, when two or more carriers issue separate powers of attorney to an agent, the originals of which are filed with the Interstate Commerce Commission, it is not necessary for those carriers to file separate "formal" concurrences. Concurrences are rarely used in agency tariffs, because concurrences are

---

[48] *Ibid.*, p. 67.

primarily used to permit one carrier to participate in an individual tariff issued by another carrier.

Both powers of attorney and concurrences may be revoked by a carrier after 60 days' notice to the Commission, state regulatory bodies, and to the agent or carrier to whom either had been issued, on special "revocation notice" forms prescribed by the Commission.[49] The period of 60 days for revocations is necessary in order to enable the carrier(s) to have sufficient time to make the changes in compliance with the 30 days' notice requirement of the law.[50] After expiration of the 60 days, providing the revocation notices were submitted in the form prescribed by the Commission, the carrier cannot be held responsible to protect the prior rate or matter involved.

If a carrier is named as a party to a joint or agency tariff without its having submitted proper power of attorney or concurrences, the carrier is not bound by the provisions of such a tariff. Under such circumstances, the carrier should notify the issuing agent and the regulatory commissions concerned.[51]

In summary, a power of attorney authorizes the person or corporation to whom it is issued to publish tariffs in behalf of the carrier granting it. A concurrence is given by a carrier to another carrier to permit the rates published by such other carrier or by its agent to also apply jointly over the line giving the concurrence.

Tariff Supplements. As was the case with the published Classifications,[52] supplements to tariffs are issued from time to time to take care of changes that arise before an existing tariff is replaced with a new one. These changes may include anything, such as: cancellation of a previous item, a new adoption, or revision of some existing provision. Supplements portray the dynamic nature of the transportation industry, for frequent changes in rates, rules, etc., are essential in order for carriers to properly and efficiently serve the public under private ownership and operation. As Edward A. Starr has commented, "The supplement bears the same relation to the freight tariff that the pencil eraser does to the lead pencil." [53] There could be no more fitting an analogy.

The Commission has prescribed rules pertaining to supplements in the two Tariff Circulars previously mentioned. Generally, a supplement is constructed in the same manner as its basic tariff. Among

---

[49] Tariff Circular MF No. 3, Rules 22 (n), p. 76, and 23 (d), pp. 79–80; *Tariff Circular No. 20,* Rule 26 (c) and (e), pp. 67–68.
[50] See, p. 300, above.
[51] *Tariff Circular No. 20,* Rule 52, p. 78.
[52] See, p. 181, above.
[53] Starr, *op. cit.,* p. 129.

other things, the rules require that supplements be consecutively numbered with reference on the title page to the tariff involved, thus:

(for motor)	(for rail)
Supplement No. 1	Supplement No. 1
to	to
MF-I.C.C. No. 614	I.C.C. No. S-1011

Although supplements are numbered consecutively, each supplement carries the same I.C.C. number as the basic tariff.

A supplement must specify both the publications which it cancels and other supplements that continue in force. Cancellations must be specific! The contents of a supplement are required to be arranged in the same general manner and order as in the basic tariff, which are described later. A supplement of 5 pages or more must be properly indexed, and one of more than 23 pages must have a table of contents. The number of supplements which may be in effect at one time is, as follows: [54]

Pages in Tariff	Number of Supplements
4 or less	0
5 to 16	1
17 to 80	2
81 to 200	3
over 200	4

The Commission has modified the above rule by an order scheduled to expire July 1, 1957, as follows: [55]

Number of Pages in Tariff	Number of Supplements Permitted	Volume of Supplemental Matter Permitted
4 or less	None	None
5 and not more than 8	1	4 pages
9 and not more than 16	2	8 pages
17 and not more than 80	2 & 2 additional supplements of not to exceed 4 pages each.	50 per cent of pages in tariff.
81 and not more than 200	3 & 2 additional supplements of not to exceed 4 pages each	50 per cent of pages in tariff.
Over 200	4 & 2 additional supplements of not to exceed 4 pages each	50 per cent of pages in tariff.

---

[54] *Tariff Circular MF No. 3*, Rule 6 (d), p. 25; *Tariff Circular No. 20*, Rule 9 (e), pp. 26–27.
[55] *Form, Construction and General Application of the Tariffs of the Southern Motor Carriers Rate Conference*, Southern Motor Carriers Rate Conference, Atlanta, 1955, p. 6.

Some exceptions to the above rigid requirements are that limitation of the number of supplements does not apply when rates, classifications, rules, or regulations are to be covered, nor for cancellation of a tariff, discontinuance of a service, and others. Prior to adoption of these restrictions, it was not unusual for an "harassed traffic user" to be forced to examine as many as 100 supplements to a single tariff.[56] The exceptions, however, permit large numbers of supplements since the greatest number of changes involve the matters which are excepted. For instance, *Eastern-Southern Class Tariff*, MF-I.C.C. No. 614, became effective on April 15, 1953, and in slightly over two years Supplement No. 55 was issued on May 6, 1955, to become effective June 17, 1955. It should not be assumed, however, that a shipper or carrier employee would be required to examine all 55 supplements to be certain the correct rate has been determined, because, as of the time this volume goes to press, only four regular supplements are in effect.

The Tariff Circulars also restrict the size of supplements. Tariffs containing 5 to 12 pages may have not more than 4 pages of supplemental matter, and tariffs containing more than 12 pages may have supplemental matter "aggregating not more than 33⅓ percent of the number of pages in the tariff," except that the maximum figure may be exceeded in order for the total number of pages to be divisible by 4.[57] The Commission possessed authority to alter the above restrictions as conditions warrant. For example, the 33⅓ percent maximum figure was increased to 50 percent by a special order in 1950.

When a new tariff is issued, it will contain the data included in all supplements to the previous tariff which are still in effect and, of course, the former supplements are thereby cancelled.

Tariff Index. Unless one knows from experience which tariff to "pull" in order to "check" a rate, the Tariff Index is an invaluable aid in rate determination. It contains an authoritative list of tariffs used by common carriers, and its publication is required by the Commission. The Tariff Circulars prescribe that the Index be prepared in sections to show the following information: (1) I.C.C. or MF-I.C.C. number, (2) carrier's own number, (3) index number, (4) name of issuing carrier or agent, (5) issuing carrier or agent's number, (6) character of the tariff or description of the articles

---

[56] Starr, *op. cit.*, pp. 132–133.
[57] *Tariff Circular MF No. 3*, Rule 6 (d), p. 25; *Tariff Circular No. 20*, Rule 9 (e), p. 27.

upon which it applies, (7) where tariff applies from, and (8) where tariff applies to.[58]

There are innumerable tariffs in effect as of a particular time, and selection of the proper one to determine the correct rate on a shipment can involve complications. The task of finding a rate is made more difficult because the proper tariff is not necessarily the one which names a rate on the shipment; instead, the proper tariff is the one which shows the applicable *lowest* rate for the desired service. Use of a Tariff Index renders the task easier in locating the right tariff.

The First Section of a Tariff Index, as prescribed by the Commission, lists all tariffs to which the carrier is a party as the originating carrier, in the following order: (1) specific commodity tariffs, (2) general commodity tariffs, (3) class and commodity tariffs, (4) class tariffs, and (5) miscellaneous tariffs. The Second Section lists all tariffs to which the carrier is a party as the delivering carrier. The Third Section contains "a complete list of the numbers of effective tariffs of its own I.C.C. series arranged in numerical order." Carriers are required to revise the Index each month, either by re-issue or supplement, in order that information pertaining to changes may be kept current; and a new issue is prescribed annually.[59] Unlike other tariffs, a Tariff Index does not become effective at some future date after its issuance, for it merely contains a list of tariffs in effect at some particular time; therefore, no effective date appears on an Index.

Title Page of Tariffs. The Interstate Commerce Commission requires detailed information to be shown on the title page of all tariffs and supplements. Title page of the Eastern-Southern Class Tariff, referred to above, is reproduced on the next page. Provisions of the Tariff Circulars are summarized below: [60]

1. The title page or top cover of tariffs "shall consist of durable but flexible paper of sufficient weight and strength to withstand hard usage."

2. If the tariff contains less than 5 pages and for tariffs issued in loose-leaf form, the following must appear at the upper left-hand corner of the title page: "No supplement to this tariff will be issued except for the purpose of cancelling the tariff unless otherwise

[58] *Tariff Circular MF No. 3,* Rule 18 (a), p. 55; *Tariff Circular No. 20,* Rule 11, p. 47.
[59] *Tariff Circular MF No. 3,* Rule 18, pp. 55–56; *Tariff Circular No. 20* Rule 11, pp. 47–48.
[60] *Tariff Circular MF No. 3,* Rule 2, pp. 4–7; *Tariff Circular No. 20,* Rule 3, pp. 3–4.

SOUTHERN MOTOR CARRIERS RATE CONFERENCE, AGENT

FREIGHT TARIFF NO. 504
For cancellation, see Page 2A.

JOINT AND LOCAL CLASS RATES

FROM AND TO POINTS IN		TO AND FROM RATE BASIS POINTS IN	
ALABAMA ARKANSAS (Helena and West Helena only) FLORIDA GEORGIA KENTUCKY LOUISIANA (East of Mississippi River)	MISSISSIPPI NORTH CAROLINA OHIO SOUTH CAROLINA TENNESSEE VIRGINIA	CONNECTICUT DELAWARE DISTRICT OF COLUMBIA MAINE MARYLAND MASSACHUSETTS NEW HAMPSHIRE NEW JERSEY	NEW YORK OHIO (EASTERN) PENNSYLVANIA RHODE ISLAND VERMONT VIRGINIA WEST VIRGINIA
As shown in tariff and in SMCRC Tariff 500 (Southern Group Guide), MF-ICC 610.		and points taking same rates as provided in SMCRC Tariff 508 (Eastern Group Guide), MF-ICC 618 (MAC MF-ICC A-475).	

EASTERN - SOUTHERN CLASS TARIFF

For reference to governing classification and other governing publications, see Item 130, Page 4A, or as amended.

Rates, rules and regulations published in this tariff apply only on Interstate traffic.

Tariff circular departure authorized by I.C.C. permission No. M-82089.

ISSUED MARCH 1, 1953   **EFFECTIVE APRIL 15, 1953**

ISSUED BY

MIDDLE ATLANTIC CONFERENCE,
AGENT
R. R. RICE,
Chief of Tariff Bureau,
2111 E. STREET, N. W.,
WASHINGTON 7, D. C.

SOUTHERN MOTOR CARRIERS
RATE CONFERENCE, AGENT
EMORY C. MOSS,
Chief of Tariff Bureau,
873 SPRING ST., N. W.,
P. O. BOX 6265, STATION H,
ATLANTA, GA.

Communications regarding rates, ratings or other provisions published herein should be addressed to the traffic officials of the carriers parties to this tariff.

(4060)   58471—THE STEIN PRINTING CO., ATLANTA, GA.   (Printed in U.S.A.)

specifically authorized by the Commission." This provision does not appear in the motor rules.

3. The I.C.C. identification number appears in the upper right-hand corner. On the reproduced title page herein, it will be observed there are two I.C.C. numbers, which is caused by the two bureaus, shown at the bottom of the page, being joint parties to its issuance. It will also be noted that the reader is referred to page 2A

for cancellations, which deviation is authorized by the rule in both Circulars.

4. Name of the issuing carrier or agent appears in the upper center of the title page. In the illustration, it is the Southern Motor Carriers Rate Conference.

5. Below the name of the issuing party is the number of the tariff. Here, it is No. 504.

6. Next is a statement of the kind of tariff. If it is a tariff of rates, it must show the kind of rates contained in it.

7. A brief but reasonably complete statement of the geographical territory or points from and to which the tariff applies is required.

8. In the center of the page is the title of the tariff in heavy bold type.

9. Next is reference, by name and I.C.C. number, to the governing Classification and other publications. In the reproduced title page, reference is made to page 4A, where is found a list of 13 publications, including *National Motor Freight Classification No. A-1*. *Tariff Circular No. 20* reminds the reader that: "A tariff is not governed by a Classification . . . except when and to the extent stated on or in the tariff."

10. The date on which the tariff is issued is shown on the lower left-hand side, and the effective date on the lower right-hand side. The importance of these dates was presented in connection with the Classifications.[61] The Act authorizes the Commission to "reject and refuse" to accept for filing any tariff which does not "give lawful notice of its effective date"; and once rejected, the tariff is void and its use is unlawful.[62] The Commission has ruled that when a rejected tariff is returned to the carrier which issued it, the rates contained therein cannot be construed as having been in effect nor may they go into effect in the future.[63]

11. At the bottom of the title page, there must appear the name, title, and street address of the officer or agent issuing the tariff. The rule provides that the same information for a joint agent, if any, may be shown, as has been done in the reproduced illustration.

12. Finally, if the tariff is to expire on a certain date, expiration notice and date shall be shown, as follows: "Expires with (date), unless sooner canceled, changed, or extended."

---

[61] See, p. 156, above.

[62] Interstate Commerce Act, Sections 6 (9), 217 (a), 306 (b), 405 (b).

[63] *Kaseman v. Atchison, Topeka & Santa Fe Railway Company, et al.*, 102 I.C.C. 315, 1925.

Contents of Tariffs. Like other phases of a tariff, the Commission has prescribed the general topics a tariff shall contain and the manner in which the contents shall be presented. Familiarity with the arrangement of the contents of tariffs is desirable for effective use of the publications.

Requirements of the two Tariff Circulars are outlined below. Since, for the most part, the need and reasons for the several items were presented in the discussion of the published Classifications,[64] further analysis is not necessary here. The Circulars provide that tariffs shall contain the following information in the order shown: [65]

1. Table of contents, in alphabetical order.

2. Names of participating carriers, in alphabetical order, "together with the form and number of power of attorney or concurrence of each" carrier.

3. Where a tariff provides commodity rates, an alphabetical index of all articles for which commodity rates are named.

4. Alphabetical indexes of all points (stations) from and to which rates apply, respectively.

5. Explanation of symbols, reference marks, and abbreviations of technical terms. Uniform symbols prescribed by the Commission are, as follows:

    ↓ to denote reductions.
    ♦ to denote increases.
    ▲ to denote changes in wording which result in neither increases nor reductions in charges.
    ● to denote no change in rate. (See rule 2 (a).)
    ∗ to denote prepay stations or points.
    ✛ to denote intrastate application only.
    □ to denote reissued matter. (See rule 9 (d).)

It is of utmost importance that the above and other reference marks be observed. A reference may limit or restrict application of a rate which was to have been applied to a shipment, and failure to observe its provisions can easily result in unnecessary increased charges which could and should have been avoided.

6. Provision for referring to "any separately published classification, tariff of classification exceptions, tariff of rules, or similar publication affecting the provisions of the tariff." This is applicable only to motor carriers.

7. A list of exceptions to classification ratings or rules, if any, which apply to rates contained in a particular tariff.

---

[64] See, pp. 146–171, above.
[65] *Tariff Circular MF No. 3,* Rule 3, pp. 7–13; *Tariff Circular No. 20,* Rule 4, pp. 5–16.

8. "Such explanatory statements as may be necessary to remove all doubt as to the proper application of the rates and rules contained in the tariff."

9. Rules and regulations which govern the tariff. Each rule should be given a separate number and they may be designated as "items." When it is not practicable to include the rules in the rate tariff, they may be published in separate tariffs, "provided specific reference is made in the rate tariff to such separate publication."

10. A statement of rates applicable to the articles for which rates are named in the tariff.

11. Provision for grouping by states of points of origin and destination. This does not apply to motor carriers.

12. A statement of the routes over which the published rates apply.

Statement of Rates. The next topic to appear in a tariff is the statement of rates. The Tariff Circular pertaining to motor carriers contains a separate rule governing this subject, whereas the rail Circular covers the same matter in a separate paragraph in the "Contents of Tariffs" rule. Both Circulars are substantially the same. A summary of the provisions of the rule follows: [66]

1. Rates must be "clearly and explicitly" stated in terms of dollars and/or cents for a definite unit of measure, usually per 100 pounds, together with names of the places to and from which they apply, "all arranged in a simple and systematic manner. Complicated plans or ambiguous terms must not be used." In this connection, many years ago the Commission said: "It is the duty of railroad companies under the Act to Regulate Commerce, to print, publish and file tariffs showing rates which are so simplified that persons of ordinary comprehension can understand them." [67] More recently, the Commission has held, "The law not only requires that tariff provisions shall be reasonable, but also that they shall be plainly stated." [68] Because of the indefiniteness of expression in a tariff, the Commission ruled that, "The statement that a rate or charge shall not be less than a certain amount is in no sense a clear and definite statement of what the charge will be." [69]

---

[66] *Tariff Circular MF No. 3,* Rule 4, pp. 13–21; *Tariff Circular No. 20,* Rule 4 (i), pp. 9–12.

[67] *H. B. Pitts & Sons v. St. Louis & San Francisco Railroad Company and Texas & Pacific Railway Company,* 10 I.C.C. 684, 1905.

[68] *N. O. Nelson Manufacturing Company v. Missouri Pacific Railroad Company, et al.,* 153 I.C.C. 272 (275), 1929.

[69] *Mixed Car Dealers Association v. Delaware, Lackawanna & Western Railroad Company, et al.,* 33 I.C.C. 133 (144), 1915.

2. Under certain specified conditions, a tariff may contain through rates.

3. A tariff may provide rates to or from designated points by the addition or deduction of artibraries or differentials, but there must be a clear statement of the manner in which the arbitraries or differentials are applied.

4. When articles are subject to percentages of class rates, such rates must be shown in Class Rates Tariffs just as if those percentages were additional numbered classes.

5. Commodity Rates Tariffs must contain minimum weights on which volume or truckload, or carload commodity rates apply.

6. Grouping of articles under a generic head is permitted under certain conditions. Packing house products is an example.

7. A tariff naming rates on a single commodity, or group of related commodities, must contain all the commodity rates applicable to the same commodity.

8. "A general commodity tariff or a combined class and commodity tariff shall contain reference to any other tariffs published by the same carrier or agent in which rates on other commodities are published from any point of origin to any point of destination named therein over the same route."

9. Publication of conflicting or duplicating rates is prohibited. The remainder apply only to motor carriers.

10. "When commodity rates are established, the description of the commodity must be specific and the rates thereon may not be applied to analogous articles."

11. A tariff may contain different rates based on different minimum quantities, under certain conditions.

12. Commodity rates may be established on mixed shipments, and the tariff must show the truckload minimum weight.

13. Alternative application of class rates in one tariff with commodity rates in another tariff is permitted under prescribed conditions, but the practice "should be resorted to only where there is real necessity therefor."

14. A published local or joint through rate is the applicable rate, even if higher than the aggregate of intermediate rates. A comparable provision is found in Rule 55 of the rail Circular. Frequently, however, tariffs will contain a provision authorizing application of the aggregate of intermediate rates when lower than the published through rate. Both Tariff Circulars state: [70]

---

[70] *Tariff Circular MF No. 3*, Rule 4 (m), p. 21; *Tariff Circular No. 20*, Rule 27, p. 73.

Class rates should be provided between practically all points and there appears little occasion for the employment of intermediate-point rules in connection with class rates except for the purpose of establishing rates from and to new points.

15. Tariffs containing proportional rates must clearly show their application.

16. Paragraph (k) provides a rule for application of rates at points not named in tariffs.

Tariff Interpretation. There is no single formula for reading and interpreting freight tariffs. In addition to the tariffs of rates covering the line-haul of a shipment, it has been pointed out earlier [71] there are tariffs pertaining to various special and terminal charges, rules and regulations governing numerous services, and others. It is not the purpose here to attempt to establish a check-list or manner of procedure in reading a freight tariff; however, the following steps may give some idea of what is involved.

1. Determine the proper tariff to be used from the Tariff Index, and "pull" that particular tariff from the files.

2. Close scrutiny of the title page is of absolute importance, and it should be examined with great care for the following reasons: (a) To ascertain if it contains the proper type of rate applicable to the shipment and applicable to the territories or points from and to which the rate applies. (b) To determine whether or not it was filed with the Interstate Commerce Commission or state regulatory bodies. If the tariff contains an MF-ICC number for motor carriers, or an ICC number for railroads, the tariff user can be assured that the tariff was filed with the Commission and that it applies on interstate traffic. If it also contains a state commission number, it applies on intrastate traffic within the state or states so indicated. If the tariff contains both an MF-ICC or ICC number and a state commission number, the rates contained therein apply on both interstate and intrastate traffic within the state or states so indicated, unless it is otherwise restricted. (c) To identify the tariff by the number of the issuing agent or individual. (d) To determine the governing Classification and exceptions thereto, if any. (e) To determine the effective date of the tariff.

3. Determine from the appropriate Classification, the rating, minimum weight, packing specifications, etc.

4. Check all supplements of both the Classification and tariff to determine the effective supplements which contain changes in the original publications, and apply them as may be found necessary.

---

[71] See, p. 304, above.

The items or index numbers in the effective supplements should be examined because they take precedence over the corresponding items in earlier supplements or in the original publications.

5. Consult the Table of Contents of the tariff in order that the sections of the tariff, the rules and regulations governing the tariff, and other information, can be readily located.

6. Check the list of participating carriers to be certain that all carriers selected to handle the shipment, if the shipment is to move over the lines of more than one carrier, are included in the list. An additional safeguard is to ascertain that proper powers of attorney or concurrences have been filed with the Interstate Commerce Commission.

7. Special rules, regulations, and exceptions to the Classification, if any (published in the front of the tariff), should be examined and if any are found to apply to the shipment, compliance therewith is required.

8. Determine if the points of origin and destination are shown in the section on Rate Basis Numbers, or in an alphabetical list of stations if the tariff contains one; if either the points of origin or destination is not shown, then it is necessary to consult the appropriate Group Guide. If the tariff refers to other tariffs for origin or destination points, or lists of commodities, or other pertinent data, the tariffs referred to must be checked to determine whether or not those matters are covered.

9. Reference marks and symbols pertaining to points of origin and destination must be checked because one of them might completely change what, at first, was thought to be applicable.

10. Determine if commodity rates or exceptions to the Classification apply by referring to the appropriate commodity or exceptions tariff as listed in the Tariff Index. If it is determined that neither applies, then the shipment will move on a class rate as published in a class tariff. If the tariff that is selected contains a reference to some other tariff, the latter should be checked without fail.

11. Routing instructions should be checked to insure that the rate applies over the route selected.

12. If the shipment is not local to one carrier, the routing tariff to which the rate tariff is subject must be examined to be certain that the rate applies via the particular combination of carriers and the junctions through which it is proposed to route the freight.

13. Determine from the tariff whether or not the rates shown as local rates to and from the points named can be used as proportional rates or factors in combination with other rates.

14. If the tariff contains rules or charges for terminal and other special services, or if reference is made to another tariff in regard thereto, those provisions must be checked to determine if any apply to the shipment.

15. Sometimes a rate applies only in one direction. Especially is this true for specific commodity rates. Hence, particular attention should be given to the tariff to ascertain if the rate applies in the desired direction of the movement.

16. If a class rate is to be used, determine the rate basis number which is applicable from point of origin to destination from the Rate Bases section of the class tariff. It is recognized that a mere description of this process is inadequate; therefore, a page from the *Eastern-Southern Class Tariff*, to which earlier reference was made, is reproduced herein on page 321.

17. In the back of the class tariffs there is another section containing scales of rates based upon classes. The next step is to turn to this section, and the class rate is determined by applying the rate found therein to the rate basis number, which was ascertained as described in the preceding paragraph. Rate base numbers are listed in a column in numerical order. The rates, in cents per 100 pounds, are listed in several columns according to the class rating prescribed by the Classification.

18. If a commodity rate applies, the index of points of origin, if the commodity tariff contains one, should be consulted in order to locate the index numbers or item numbers in the tariff containing reference to the particular point from which rates are desired.

19. The index of points of destination should be consulted for the same reason in connection with the point to which rates are desired.

20. The alphabetical index of commodities should be examined to find the desired rate. If the article to be shipped is not found, the commodity tariff does not contain a rate on the particular commodity.

21. It should always be kept in mind that when interpreting a Classification or a freight tariff, the publication must be considered as a whole.[72]

The reader should examine with care the two reproduced pages of the Southern Motor Carriers Rate Conference's Eastern-Southern Class Tariff No. 504, MF-I.C.C. No. 614, on the two accompanying pages. Page 1 of the tariff is shown on page 321 of this volume, and page 297 of the tariff on page 322. Tariff page 1 is preceded by 29

[72] *Form, Construction and General Application of the Tariffs of the Southern Motor Carriers Rate Conference, op. cit.,* pp. 9–13.

RATE BASIS NUMBERS
(For application, see Items 100 and 110)
(Apply rates opposite corresponding rate basis numbers in Section 1)

BETWEEN / AND	Albany, N. Y.	Allenstown, N. H.	Allingdale, W. Va.	Altamont, Md.-Chaffee, W. Va.	Altoona, Pa.	Annapolis, Md.	Anaconia, Pa.	Arcade, N. Y.	Arlington, Vt.	Atlantic City, N. J.	Augusta, Me.	Avondale, Pa.	Baltimore, Md.	Bangor, Me.	Batavia, N. Y.
Abbeville............Ga.	1075	1237p	896	848	899	799	997	1101	1126	912	1331	821	763	1406	1103
Aberdeen............Miss.	1255	1417p	878	910	971	979	1073	1005	1300	1092	1511	1000	943	1586	1007
Aberdeen............N. C.	707	869p	581	501	552	431	631	744	758	544	963	452	395	1038	758
Ackerman............Miss.	1286	1448p	907	939	1000	1010	1102	1034	1329	1123	1542	1031	974	1617	1036
Ahoskie............N. C.	541	703p	601	423	479	322	522	635	592	378	797	289	286	872	649
Aiken.............S. C.	865	1027p	719	638	689	589	787	907	916	702	1121	610	553	1196	914
Akron.............Ala.	1202	1364p	836	897	977	926	1079	1011	1253	1039	1458	947	890	1533	1013
Alachua............Fla.	1152	1314p	1031	950	1001	876	1076	1182	1203	989	1408	897	840	1483	1203
Albany.............Ga.	1140	1302p	897	913	964	864	1062	1102	1191	977	1396	885	828	1471	1104
Albemarle..........N. C.	714	876p	568	487	538	438	636	752	765	551	970	459	402	1045	763
Alberta (S)..........Va.	539	701p	492	368	420	263	463	576	590	376	795	284	227	870	590
Alexander City......Ala.	1147	1309p	807	864	938	871	1036	983	1198	984	1403	892	835	1478	985
Aliceville...........Ala.	1227	1389p	861	924	1002	951	1104	1036	1278	1064	1483	972	915	1558	1038
Allendale..........S. C.	903	1065p	779	698	749	627	827	940	954	740	1159	648	591	1234	954
Alma...............Ga.	1062	1224p	923	860	911	786	986	1099	1113	899	1318	807	750	1393	1113
Almond.............N. C.	911	1073p	637	684	735	635	833	903	962	748	1167	656	599	1242	907
Altavista (S)........Va.	556	718p	410	329	380	280	478	593	607	393	812	301	244	887	605
Altha..............Fla.	1261	1423p	1023	1043	1094	985	1185	1203	1312	1098	1517	1006	949	1592	1205
Altoona............Ala.	1082	1244p	716	780	857	806	959	891	1133	919	1338	827	770	1413	893
Americus...........Ga.	1110	1272p	862	883	934	834	1032	1067	1161	947	1366	855	798	1441	1069
Amite..............La.	1484	1646p	1108	1140	1201	1208	1303	1235	1530	1321	1740	1229	1172	1815	1237
Amory ....Miss.	1244	1406p	865	897	958	968	1060	992	1287	1081	1500	989	932	1575	994
Anchor.............Ky.	897	1059p	461	524	631	621	736	668	948	734	1153	642	585	1228	670
Andalusia..........Ala.	1248	1410p	944	1007	1072	972	1170	1119	1299	1085	1504	993	936	1579	1121
Anderson..........S. C.	880	1032p	682	653	704	604	802	918	931	717	1136	625	568	1211	929
Andrews............N. C.	934	1096p	660	707	758	658	856	893	985	771	1190	687	622	1265	895
Andrews...........S. C.	812	974p	704	624	675	536	736	849	863	649	1068	558	500	1143	863
Anniston...........Ala.	1079	1241p	732	789	863	803	961	909	1130	916	1335	824	767	1410	911
Apalachicola........Fla.	1300	1462p	1077	1082	1133	1024	1224	1276	1351	1137	1556	1045	988	1631	1278
Appalachia..........Va.	798	960p	410	467	582	522	680	676	849	365	1054	543	486	1129	680
Arcadia............Fla.	1332	1494p	1211	1130	1181	1056	1256	1369	1383	1169	1588	1077	1020	1663	1383
Arlington...........Ga.	1176	1338p	920	949	1000	900	1098	1119	1227	1013	1432	921	864	1507	1121
Arlington..........Tenn.	1165	1363p	782	814	875	1040	977	909	1203	1153	1480	1061	1004	1555	910
Armona............Tenn.	883	1045p	536	593	667	607	765	750	934	720	1139	628	571	1214	752
Arthur.............N. C.	612f	774fp	605f	464f	516f	359f	559f	672f	663f	449f	868f	360f	323f	943f	686f
Asheboro...........N. C.	684	846p	538	457	508	408	606	722	735	521	940	429	372	1015	733
Asheville...........N. C.	832	994p	561	605	656	556	754	827	883	669	1088	577	520	1163	831
Ashford............N. C.	808	970p	539	575	626	532	724	705	859	645	1064	553	496	1139	809
Ashland City.......Tenn.	1020n	1218np	636n	668n	729n	836n	831n	763n	1058n	949n	1335n	857n	800n	1410n	763n
Athens.............Ga.	936	1098p	761	709	760	660	858	974	987	773	1192	681	624	1267	985
Athens............Tenn.	922	1084p	575	632	706	646	804	789	973	759	1178	667	610	1253	791
Atlanta............Ga.	997	1159p	715	770	821	721	919	920	1048	834	1253	742	685	1328	922
Atmore............Ala.	1302	1464p	977	1040	1118	1026	1220	1152	1353	1139	1558	1047	990	1633	1154
Augusta............Ga.	914	1026p	739	687	738	638	836	952	965	751	1170	659	602	1245	963
Avon Park..........Fla.	1306	1468p	1185	1104	1155	1030	1230	1346	1357	1143	1562	1051	994	1637	1357
Bainbridge.........Ga.	1197	1359p	958	980	1031	921	1121	1157	1248	1034	1453	942	885	1528	1159
Barber.............N. C.	704	866p	548	477	528	428	626	742	755	541	960	449	392	1035	753
Bardstown..........Ky.	854	1052p	480	502	563	743	665	597	892	678	1169	757	707	1244	599
Barnwell...........S. C.	888	1050p	763	682	733	612	812	925	939	725	1144	633	576	1219	939
Barrineau Park.....Fla.	1302	1464p	977	1040	1118	1026	1220	1152	1353	1139	1558	1047	990	1633	1154
Bartow.............Fla.	1286	1448p	1165	1084	1135	1010	1210	1323	1337	1123	1542	1031	974	1617	1337
Batesburg..........S. C.	871	1033p	733	652	703	595	795	908	922	708	1127	616	559	1202	922
Batesville.........Miss.	1236	1434p	865	897	958	1073	1053	979	1274	1186	1551	1094	1037	1626	981
Baton Rouge........La.	1537	1699p	1161	1193	1254	1261	1356	1285	1580	1374	1793	1282	1225	1868	1287
Baton Rouge (E)....La.	1537	1699p	1161	1193	1254	1261	1356	1285	1580	1374	1793	1282	1225	1868	1287
Baxley.............Ga.	1048	1210p	884	832	883	772	972	1085	1099	885	1304	793	736	1379	1089
Baxter.............Fla.	1107	1269p	986	905	956	831	1031	1144	1158	944	1363	852	795	1438	1158
Bayard.............Fla.	1113	1275p	992	911	962	837	1037	1150	1164	950	1369	859	801	1444	1164
Bayboro........... N. C.	658f	820fp	671f	513f	565f	408f	608f	721f	709f	495f	914f	406f	372f	989f	735f
Bayou La Batre.....Ala.	1372	1534p	1037	1100	1178	1096	1280	1212	1423	1210	1628	1117	1060	1703	1214
Beaumont ....Miss.	1372	1534p	1006	1069	1147	1096	1249	1181	1423	1209	1628	1117	1060	1703	1183

1

pages, numbered 2A–30A, of exceptions, rules, and other matters required to appear in a tariff. Tariff page 1 shows the rate base numbers assigned to the different places shown, starting with Albany, New York, across the top and Abbeville, Georgia, in the vertical column; and the rate base numbers terminate at page 294 with Youngwood, Pennsylvania, and Yukon, Florida, respectively.

SMCRC FREIGHT TARIFF NO. 504

SECTION 1 (For application, see Item 15000, Page 295).

CLASS RATES IN CENTS PER 100 POUNDS.

RATE BASES NUMBERS (Numbers inclusive)	CLASSES												
	100	92¼	85	77½	70	65	60	55	50	45	40	37½	35
926 to 950	335	310	285	260	235	218	201	184	168	151	134	134	134
951 to 975	340	315	289	264	238	221	204	187	170	153	136	136	136
976 to 1000	345	319	293	267	242	224	207	190	173	155	138	138	138
1001 to 1025	350	324	298	271	245	228	210	193	175	158	140	140	140
1026 to 1050	355	328	302	275	249	231	213	195	178	160	142	142	142
1051 to 1075	360	333	306	279	252	234	216	198	180	162	144	144	144
1076 to 1100	365	338	310	283	256	237	219	201	183	164	146	146	146
1101 to 1125	370	342	315	287	259	241	222	204	185	167	148	148	148
1126 to 1150	375	347	319	291	263	244	225	206	188	169	150	150	150
1151 to 1175	380	352	323	295	266	247	228	209	190	171	152	152	152
1176 to 1200	385	356	327	298	270	250	231	212	193	173	154	154	154
1201 to 1225	390	361	332	302	273	254	234	215	195	176	176	176	176
1226 to 1250	395	365	336	306	277	257	237	217	198	176	176	176	176
1251 to 1275	400	370	340	310	280	260	240	220	200	178	178	178	178
1276 to 1300	405	375	344	314	284	263	243	223	203	180	180	180	180
1301 to 1325	410	379	349	318	287	267	246	226	205	185	185	185	185
1326 to 1350	415	384	353	322	291	270	249	228	208	187	187	187	187
1351 to 1375	420	389	357	326	294	273	252	231	210	189	189	189	189
1376 to 1400	425	393	361	329	298	276	255	234	213	191	191	191	191
1401 to 1425	430	398	366	333	301	280	258	237	215	194	194	194	194
1426 to 1450	435	402	370	337	306	283	261	239	218	196	196	196	196
1451 to 1475	440	407	374	341	308	286	264	242	220	198	198	198	198
1476 to 1500	445	412	378	345	312	289	267	245	223	200	200	200	200
1501 to 1525	450	416	383	349	315	293	270	248	225	203	203	203	203
1526 to 1550	455	421	387	353	319	296	273	250	228	205	205	205	205
1551 to 1575	460	426	391	357	322	299	276	253	230	207	207	207	207
1576 to 1600	465	430	395	360	326	302	279	256	233	209	209	209	209
1601 to 1625	470	435	400	364	329	306	282	259	235	212	212	212	212
1626 to 1650	475	439	404	368	333	309	285	261	238	214	214	214	214
1651 to 1675	480	444	408	372	336	312	288	264	240	216	216	216	216
1676 to 1700	485	449	412	376	340	315	291	267	243	218	218	218	218
1701 to 1725	490	453	417	380	343	319	294	270	245	221	221	221	221
1726 to 1750	495	458	421	384	347	322	297	272	248	223	223	223	223
1751 to 1775	500	463	425	388	350	325	300	275	250	225	225	225	225
1776 to 1800	505	467	429	391	354	328	303	278	253	227	227	227	227
1801 to 1825	510	472	434	395	357	332	306	281	255	230	230	230	230
1826 to 1850	515	476	438	399	361	335	309	283	258	232	232	232	232
1851 to 1875	520	481	442	403	364	338	312	286	260	234	234	234	234
1876 to 1900	525	486	446	407	368	341	315	289	263	236	236	236	236
1901 to 1925	530	490	451	411	371	345	318	292	265	239	239	239	239
1926 to 1950	535	495	455	415	375	348	321	294	268	241	241	241	241
1951 to 1975	540	500	459	419	378	351	324	297	270	243	243	243	243
1976 to 2000	545	504	463	422	382	354	327	300	273	245	245	245	245
2001 to 2025	550	509	468	426	385	358	330	303	275	248	248	248	248
2026 to 2050	555	513	472	430	389	361	333	305	278	250	250	250	250
2051 to 2075	560	518	476	434	392	364	336	308	280	252	252	252	252
2076 to 2100	565	523	480	438	396	367	339	311	283	254	254	254	254
2101 to 2125	570	527	485	442	399	371	342	314	285	257	257	257	257
2126 to 2150	575	532	489	446	403	374	345	316	288	259	259	259	259
2151 to 2175	580	537	493	450	406	377	348	319	290	261	261	261	261
2176 to 2200	585	541	497	453	410	380	351	322	293	263	263	263	263
781a to 800a	307	284	261	238	215	200	184	169	154	138	123	122	122
801a to 825a	312	289	265	242	218	203	187	172	156	140	125	124	124
826a to 850a	317	293	269	246	222	206	190	174	159	143	127	126	126
851a to 875a	322	298	274	250	225	209	193	177	161	145	129	128	128
876a to 900a	327	302	278	253	229	213	196	180	164	147	131	130	130
901a to 925a	332	307	282	257	232	216	199	183	166	149	133	132	132
926a to 950a	337	312	286	261	236	219	202	185	169	152	135	134	134
951a to 975a	342	316	291	265	239	222	205	188	171	154	137	136	136
976a to 1000a	347	321	295	269	243	226	208	191	174	156	139	138	138

297

Tariff page 297 contains rates according to classes in cents per 100 pounds applicable to the rate basis numbers listed in the preceding section. The rate basis numbers are listed in the column on the left of the page, and the classification ratings head the other columns across the page. Upon reference to the tariff itself it will be found the part containing the rates is divided into three sections. Section 1 contains rates based on Class 100 and lower. Section 2 lists rates based on classes higher than Class 100. Section 3, prior to its recent cancellation, shows the application of minimum rate provisions.

Now, using the same article as in the Classification illustration [73] suppose there is a shipment of steel corset stays packed in boxes, by motor carrier from Baltimore to Atlanta. The Classification reveals the article has a less-than-truckload rating of Class 85, and a truckload rating of Class 55 with a minimum weight of 30,000 pounds.[74] The rate base number for rates between Baltimore and Atlanta is shown on tariff page 1 to be 685. Upon reference to tariff page 296 it will be found that the Class 85 rate is 238¢ ($2.38) per 100 pounds, and the Class 55 rate is 154¢ ($1.54) per 100 pounds. Any increases or decreases in rates which have occurred since the basic tariff became effective in 1953 would have to be applied in accordance with effective supplements. It so happened that a supplement in 1955 increased the above rate from $2.38 to $2.74 for less-than-truckload shipments, and from $1.54 to $1.77 for truckload traffic.[75] Although the "A-2" Classification was not effective at the time the tariff became effective, the ratings in the "A-1" Classification were the same as those of the "A-2." Item 8060 of the tariff states, in part, that "where reference is made in this tariff to another tariff, such reference will also embrace supplements to or successive issues of such other tariff, unless otherwise specifically indicated." In the event the shipment had been consigned to some small town which is not listed in the tariff, reference would have to be made to the *Southern Group Guide* which is authorized by Item 130 (c) on page 4A of the tariff.

Exactly the same principle is followed to ascertain the rate of a shipment moving by rail. After it has been determined that only a class rate applies to the article, then the Class Tariff is used. Suppose the corset stays are to be shipped from Atlanta to Paducah. The Rail Classification shows the article is rated exactly the same as in the Motor Classification, Class 85 for less-than-carload and Class 55 for carload with a minimum weight of 30,000 pounds.[76] The rate base from Atlanta to Paducah is found to be 434, and the rates are $1.84 per 100 pounds for Class 85 and $1.19 for Class 55.[77]

---

[73] See, p. 166, above.

[74] *National Motor Freight Classification No. A-2*, effective July 7, 1954, Item 87930.

[75] Supplement No. 50 to Freight Tariff No. 504, *Eastern-Southern Class Tariff*, MF-I.C.C. No. 614, effective March 23, 1955.

[76] *Uniform Freight Classification No. 2*, effective December 10, 1953, Item 41295.

[77] Southern Freight Tariff Bureau, Freight Tariff No. S-1011, I.C.C. No. 1300, *Class Rates* Tariff, effective January 1, 1953, C. A. Spaninger, Agent, Atlanta, Georgia.

In order to ascertain if a commodity rate is authorized, the first step is to look for a description of the article in the Index of Commodities of the appropriate tariff. However, an alternative is to check the Index of Origins and the Index of Destinations in the front of the tariff containing commodity rates on the article in question. If both origin and destination points are found and if the commodity is described in the tariff, it is probable that a commodity rate is published on the article between the points concerned. The same item number will appear in connection with the commodity, the origin, and the destination. Upon turning to the rates section of the tariff where item numbers are listed in numerical order, it will be found that the article is again described, and points of origin and destination are indicated. The applicable rate is shown following this index number.

Rate Quotations. From time to time, shippers call on carriers for rate information. The shipper may not have an adequate tariff file of his own, or he may be doubtful of a rate he has found, or he may be either too lazy to look up the rate or utterly ignorant of rates and tariffs. There are occasions when a rate man in industry will wish to check his findings of a complicated situation with the opinion of a carrier's rate expert. Regardless of the causes, carriers' freight traffic departments, local traffic representatives, and local terminals or agencies receive many requests from shippers for rate information. Although the information may be furnished in writing over the signature of the highest traffic officer of the carrier, rates so quoted are *not* binding upon the carrier. Furthermore, carriers are required to furnish rate quotations upon request within a reasonable time.[78] This requirement is not new, for shippers had suffered losses from erroneous rate quotations furnished by carriers by having to pay the published rate instead of the lower rate which had been quoted. In recognition of this situation Congress included in the Mann-Elkins Act of 1910, a provision, which was later repealed, that upon written request a carrier must quote in writing the rate applicable to a proposed shipment; and if any loss were sustained by the shipper attributable to the misquoted rate, the carrier would be subject to penalty.[79]

At first glance, one might think the carrier should be held responsible for its mistake in furnishing an incorrect rate, particularly

---

[78] Wilson, G. L.: *Industrial Traffic Management,* The Traffic Service Corporation, Washington, 1949, pp. 101–102.
[79] Sharfman, I. L.: *The Interstate Commerce Commission,* Part I, The Commonwealth Fund, New York, 1931, p. 53.

when a prospective shipper makes a contract based upon the freight charges furnished by the carrier. To illustrate: assume a manufacturer in Chicago desires to furnish his product for use on a large construction job in Boston, in competition with producers located elsewhere. He requests and receives a rate quotation on his goods from the carrier, and on the basis thereof he submits a bid on the Boston job which will net him a reasonable profit. It develops that he is the low bidder and he is awarded the contract. Subsequently, it is found that the rates quoted him by the carrier were erroneous in that they were considerably lower than the actual rate. Here, the Chicago manufacturer has entered into a contract to furnish his product in Boston at a price which was directly influenced by the cost of transporting his commodity from Chicago to Boston; the freight rate quoted him by a representative of the carrier was in good faith, but an honest error occurred and compliance with the terms of the Boston contract results in considerable monetary loss to the Chicago producer. Can he sue the carrier or otherwise be reimbursed for his loss which is directly attributable to misinformation furnished by the carrier? The answer is, No!

As Professor Bryan has said, "the shipper has no vested rights in the (rate) quotation, as such, that will give him an action for damages against the carrier in event of loss as a result of such quotation." [80] Hence, misquotation by a carrier does not excuse the shipper from paying any sum other than the lawful applicable rate, and both shipper and carrier are expected to have complete knowledge of the applicable rate.[81] The Interstate Commerce Commission has said there can be only one applicable rate on an article at the same time, over the same route, and between the same points on the same traffic.[82]

It is well established that the only legal rate applicable to a particular shipment is the rate published in a duly issued tariff effective at the time; and any other rate that may be quoted by a carrier is illegal. Therefore, a rate quoted to a shipper cannot be considered as a price offer, or a bid, for providing transportation service.[83] As was stated earlier, since tariffs contain information which is available to the public, it is presumed the shipper will have examined the

---

[80] Bryan, L. A.: *Industrial Traffic Management*, A. W. Shaw Company, Chicago, 1929, p. 138; also, Bryan, L. A.: *Traffic Management in Industry*, The Dryden Press, New York, 1953, p. 173.
[81] Shinn, *op. cit.*, p. 2.
[82] *United States Industrial Alcohol Company v. Director General*, 68 I.C.C. 389, 1922.
[83] Bryan, L. A.: *Traffic Management in Industry, op. cit.*, p. 173.

proper tariff in order to have determined the applicable rate. Ignorance of the provisions of a tariff is no excuse, and the law expects the shipper to be just as familiar with those provisions as the carrier.

Another justification for not making a rate quotation binding is it could be used as an excellent subterfuge for rebating. If permitted, a carrier might intentionally quote a rate to a favored customer that is lower than the standard rate contained in the applicable tariff, and then at a later date claim the lower rate was quoted in error. In the meantime, the favored shipper would have had his goods transported at a rate less than that which his competitors had paid. Such instances of undue preference, and unreasonable and unjust discrimination are strictly prohibited by the Interstate Commerce Act, and heavy penalties may be inflicted on both carrier and shipper if found guilty of intentional violation of the Act. The Supreme Court of the United States has ruled on the matter of misquoting rates in the following forceful language: [84]

> Under the Interstate Commerce Act, the rate of the carrier, duly filed, is the only lawful charge. Deviation from it is not permitted under any pretext. Shippers and travelers are charged with notice of it and they, as well as the carrier, must abide by it, unless it is found by the Commission to be unreasonable. Ignorance or misquotation of rates is not an excuse for paying or charging more or less than the rate filed.

Previously, the high court had ruled that an error in quoting a rate by a carrier's agent did not alter the rate published in a tariff.[85]

Conclusion. The Interstate Commerce Act prohibits any interstate common carrier subject to the Act from engaging in the service of transportation without first having published and filed its rates and other charges in accordance with provisions of the Act and regulations of the Interstate Commerce Commission.[86] Therefore, if the Commission does not approve the tariff of a carrier, the carrier can be kept out of business. Stated differently, the legal publication, filing, and posting of tariffs are prerequisites to operation by a carrier, for a carrier has no legal rates or charges until they are duly published and filed.[87] Not only are interstate carriers prohibited from transporting property and passengers unless their rates and

---

[84] *Louisville & Nashville Railroad Company v. Maxwell*, 237 U. S. 94, 1915.
[85] *Illinois Central Railroad Company v. Henderson Elevator Company*, 226 U. S. 441, 1913.
[86] Interstate Commerce Act, Sections 6 (7), 217 (d), 306 (d), 405 (e).
[87] See, pp. 300–302, above.

fares have been duly published and filed,[88] but also willful failure to publish and file rates is unlawful.[89]

Frequently, there may be two legally published rates on the same commodity; but under those circumstances, provision is usually made for the lower rate to apply. In this connection, the Commission has said: "Generally speaking, where a tariff contains conflicting rates established on the same date, the lower of the rates so published is the legal rate." [90] Glenn L. Shinn, Attorney-Examiner of the Interstate Commerce Commission, has consolidated the following rules from decisions of the Commission and the courts in regard to the meaning of ambiguous language used in tariffs.[91]

Rule A. When two constructions of a tariff are possible, one of which would result in violation of law and the other would not, preference will be given to the interpretation which complies with the law.[92]

Rule B. All pertinent provisions of a tariff must be considered together, and the resulting reasonable construction is controlling.[93]

Rule C. An entire tariff must be visualized, with due emphasis being placed on every word, clause, and sentence.[94]

Rule D. The intention of the framers of a tariff, when reasonably determined, should be considered when ascertaining the meaning of a tariff.[95]

Rule E. Tariffs must be considered as a whole.[96]

Rule F. The title page should indicate the intent of the tariff's application.[97]

Rule G. Tariff terms must be read in the sense generally understood and accepted commercially.[98]

---

[88] *Southern Railway Company v. Reid*, 222 U. S. 424, 1912.

[89] *The Car Peddling Case*, 45 I.C.C. 494, 1917.

[90] *Abendroth Brothers v. Boston & Albany Railroad Company, et al.*, 161 I.C.C. 730 (732), 1930.

[91] Shinn, *op. cit.*, pp. 114–116.

[92] *Peter Fox Sons Company v. Cleveland, Cincinnati, Chicago & St. Louis Railway Company*, 201 I.C.C. 498, 1934.

[93] *Bacon Brothers v. Indiana Harbor Belt Railroad Company*, 139 I.C.C. 53, 1928.

[94] *Swift & Company v. Akron, Canton & Youngstown Railway Company*, 220 I.C.C. 778, 1937.

[95] *Forbes & Sons Piano Company v. Alabama Great Southern Railway Company, et al.*, 118 I.C.C. 185, 1926.

[96] *Kansas Flour Mill Corporation v. Abilene & Southern Railway Company*, 195 I.C.C. 277, 1933.

[97] *General Mills v. Chicago, Rock Island & Pacific Railway Company*, 185 I.C.C. 789, 1932.

[98] *Hill Motor Company v. Michigan Central Railroad Company, et al.*, 197 I.C.C. 259, 1933.

Rule H. A strained or unnatural tariff construction cannot be permitted by either carrier or shipper for its own purposes.[99]

Rule I. An ambiguous tariff is to be considered in the shipper's favor.[100]

Rule J. Tariffs must be construed strictly, but when reasonable doubt exists regarding the meaning of a provision, its construction shall be resolved in favor of the shipper.[101]

. . . .

---

[99] *Kroehler Manufacturing Company, et al., v. Baltimore & Ohio Railroad Company, et al.,* 200 I.C.C. 763, 1934.

[100] *McClamrock Company, et al., v. Atlantic & Yadkin Railway Company, et al.,* 195 I.C.C. 238, 1933.

[101] *Mississippi Farm Bureau Cotton Association v. Illinois Central Railroad Company,* 139 I.C.C. 344, 1928.

INDEX

A

Act to Regulate Commerce of 1887, 81, 146, 203, 299
Actual value ratings, 164
Advertising matter or premiums, 271
Agency tariff (*See* Tariffs)
Agreed weight, 240
Airbills, 27, 49, 61
Air classification, 107, 117–118
Air express receipt, 61
Air service uniform express receipt, 61
All-commodity rates, 247–248
Alldredge, J. Haden, 92, 137
Ambiguous tariffs, construction, 328
American Trucking Associations, Inc., 37, 103, 142, 178, 180, 217, 306
Any quantity (*See* Definitions)
Arbitraries (rate), 317
Arrival notice, 8, 63–64
Association of American Railroads, 37, 306

B

Bartel, W. P., 96
Baxter, Charles S., 293
Bigham & Roberts, 124, 138
Billing of shipments, 30, 161
Bill of lading (B/L)
  acceptance by shipper, 11
  airbill, 27, 61
  alternative form, 28
  background of, 21
  basis for claims, 18
  bill of lading liability, 31
  carrier practices, 28
  common law liability, 31
  contract of transportation, 11
  contract terms and conditions, 38
  copies, 36
  definition, 4
  description of shipment, 19, 210–211, 213
  development of uniformity, 23
  disclosure of information, 29

Bill of Lading (*continued*)
  exceptions, 22–23
  freight charges, 19
  full form, 27
  functions, 10–21
  government bill of lading, 49, 59, 60
  identification of consignee, 20
  information, non-disclosure, 29
  interline shipments, 12–13
  Interstate Commerce Commission requirements, 24, 26, 27, 30
  issuance, 37
  joint rate, 12
  joint routes, 12
  legal effect, 8, 12
  liability, 31
  nature, 7–8, 10
  necessity for signature, 12
  negotiability, 18, 44, 48
  non-bill of lading liability, 31
  non-disclosure of information, 29
  non-recourse clause, 12, 35
  notification instructions, 21
  on board bill, 53
  order bills of lading, 13, 17, 18, 40–48, 223
  preparation, 31–37
  protection of reduced rates, 31
  receipt for goods, 10–11
  route and routing, 20
  rules, 30, 208–216
  shipping document, 8
  short form, 27
  significance, 8
  special instructions, 20–21
  standard bill of lading, 24
  straight bill of lading, 13, 18, 39–40
  technical classification language, 35
  terms and conditions, 38, 49
  through export bill of lading, 49, 57–59
  title to goods, 13
  uniform bill of lading, 26–28, 40–48
  unit bill of lading, 37, 39

329

Bill of Lading (*continued*)
water carrier exceptions, 26
(*See also* Bill of Lading History,
Bills of Lading Act, Classifica-
tion Rules, Shipping Docu-
ments)
Bill of lading history
Admiralty Courts, 21
Alaska Steamship Company case, 25
Carmack Amendment, 24, 25
Cummins Amendments, 25
Customs of the Sea, 21
development of uniformity, 23–26,
27
exceptions, 22–23, 26
Law Merchant, 21
original function, 22
Ship's Book, 21–22
Bills of Lading Act, 19, 20, 25, 38–39,
46
Board of Investigation and Research,
87, 91
Brussels Rules, 52
Bugan, Thomas G., 13
Bureaus, 306, 307

C

California Commission, 254
Car ferry services (railroads), 56
Carload rates, 294
Carload shipments, 34, 118
Carmack Amendment (*See* Bill of
Lading History)
Carriage of Goods by Sea Act of
1936, 52
Civil Aeronautics Act of 1938, 203,
299
Civil Aeronautics Board
bill of lading requirements, 30
classification, authority, 107
uniform bill of lading, authority, 27
Claims
bill of lading as basis, 18
definition, 5
overcharge and undercharge-intra-
state, 291
Classes of the classifications, 72
Classification
billing of shipments, 7, 161
definition, 4, 69, 70, 73, 192
exceptions, 72
grouping of commodities, 74, 121
misdescription, 161
motor carrier's use, 75
nature, 69, 73–74, 120
necessity, 75

Classification (*continued*)
procedure for changes, 199–201
purpose, 70
railroads, 75
relation to rates and tariffs, 115,
118, 143–146, 155, 204, 269
simplification of tariffs, 76, 294
territories, classification, 83–84
uniformity, advantages, 100, 294
(*See also* Classification History,
Classification Ratings, Exceptions, Motor Freight Classification)
Classification application, 160, 163,
190, 204, 259, 320
Classification by analogy, 259–260
Classification committees
Committee on Uniform Classification, 89
Consolidated Freight Committee,
174, 201
National Classification Board, 178,
179, 201, 219, 260
National Classification Committee,
201
National Traffic Committee, 178
Railroad Committees, 201–202
Southern Classification Committee,
97, 176–178
Classification exceptions
adoption, 189
affects, 186
contents, 190
definition, 189
effective date, 191
expiration date, 191
legality, 191
publication, 190
reasons for, 186, 188
Classification factors
commercial factors listed, 126
competition, 126–128, 196
cost as classification factor, 132
express classification, 143
history, 122–123
Interstate Commerce Commission,
74, 121–122, 201
judgment factors, 131
New England classification, 132–
143
physical factors
other physical factors listed, 126
value of the service, 123, 139
value of the shipment, 124–126,
133
transportation factors

Combination rates, 115, 298
Commercial usage of terms, 327
Committee on uniform classification, 89
Commodity rates, 197, 269–270, 294, 299, 317, 320
Competition, 53, 103, 125–128, 139, 186–189, 194–197
Comptroller General of the United States, 59
Concurrences (tariff), 307–309
Conn, Donald D., 1
Consolidated freight classification, 84–85, 90, 94, 99, 100, 108, 149, 165–168, 192, 202, 288
Costs of carrier operation, 119, 136–139, 140–143
Court jurisdiction (classification), 201
Credit, extension of, 64, 238
Cullum Committee report, 87
Cummins Amendments (*See* Bill of Lading History)
Cushman, Frank M., 122, 134, 200
Customs of the Sea (*See* Bill of Lading History)

D

Definitions
    any quantity, 5, 120, 165, 256
    arbitraries, 297
    bill of lading, 4
    blanket rate, 296
    carrier, 4
    charge, 4
    c.i.f., 58
    claim, 5
    class, 70
    classification, 4, 69
    classification ratings, 121
    class rate, 294
    column rate, 294
    combination rate, 295
    commodity rate, 294
    compressed, 290
    concurrent (tariff), 307
    consignee, 5, 14
    consignor, 5, 14
    demurrage, 63
    differential, 297
    differential rate, 297
    differential route, 298
    export traffic, 3, 296
    fare, 4
    f.o.b. destination, 17
    f.o.b. point of origin, 15
    f.o.b. point of origin, c.o.d., 16

Definitions (*continued*)
    f.o.b. point of origin, freight charges to be deducted by consignee, 16
    foreign commerce, 5
    group rate, 297
    in bulk, 220
    in packages, 219
    interline traffic, 5
    interstate commerce, 5
    intrastate commerce, 5
    joint rates, 12, 295
    K.D., 159, 264–266
    less-than-truckload, 5
    local rates, 295
    NOIBN, NOI, 160
    order bill of lading, 13
    perishable traffic, 2, 3
    proportional rate, 295–296
    rate, 4, 70, 71, 94, 118, 294
    released rate, 295
    route, 4
    set up, 159
    shipment, 4, 254–259
    straight bill of lading, 13
    tariff, 4, 76, 292
    through rate, 295
    traffic, 2, 3
    transportation, 3
    truckload, 5, 112, 119–120, 255
    volume, 164
    waybill, 9
Delivery receipt, 8, 66–68
Demurrage, 63
Density, 128, 133
Description of shipment, 19, 35, 159
Differentials, 297, 317
Domestic services, bill of lading, 53
Dunnage, 239–240

E

Estimated weights, 240
Exceptions
    application principles, 190, 191
    competition, 186–189, 194, 196
    costs of operation, 194
    effect, 189
    example, 187
    general, 72, 100, 125, 185–199, 204, 269, 315
    history, 189, 196
    inherent advantages, transportation, 198
    nature, 185–186, 195
    reason for, 186, 198–199
    regulation by I.C.C., 190

Interstate Commerce Commission
(*continued*)
on costs, 136–139
order bills of lading (domestic),
44–45
packaging decisions, 219–220
parts or pieces constituting a
complete article, 262–263
posting of tariffs, 302–303
powers of attorney (tariffs),
307–309
publication of tariffs, 303, 326–
327
rate regulation, 299
rate schedules, 316
rough vs. finished articles, 268
shipment defined, 254–255
Southern Governors case, 235
ICC 253, 92
suspension of tariffs, 303–304
tank car equipment, 285
tariff application, 292
tariff circulars, 147, 185, 305–
306, 308–312, 315–318
tariff regulations, 300–303
through export bills of lading, 56
uniform classification, 86–88, 90,
192, 199
uniform live stock contract, 50
Issuance of bills of lading, 37

J

Joint rates, 12, 295

K

Knorst, William J., 12, 204, 241, 275,
297

L

Lawful rate, 299, 326
Legal and lawful rate, 299, 326
Light and bulky traffic, 102, 129, 227,
278
Locklin, D. P., 137
Long and bulky articles, 235
Loss and damage to shipments, 205

M

Mann-Elkins Act of 1910, 24, 81, 303,
324
Manufacturer's description as identi-
fication of shipments, 161–163
Market competition, 195, 196
McDonald, Walter G., 100
Miller, John M., 14, 34, 67
Minimum charge rules, 252–253

Minimum weights, 148, 164, 253–
254, 269, 277–284
Misdescription of shipments, 36, 161
(*See also* Truckload, Volume Shipments)
Misquotation of rates, 324–326
Mixed volume shipments, 241–251
Money classification of Railway Express Agency, 117
Motor Carrier Act of 1935, 101, 146,
203, 249, 300
Motor carrier statistics, 2, 140–142
Motor carriers, use of classification, 75
Motor freight classification
density of freight, 102
history, 101–105
New England classification, 71,
102, 105, 116, 132–141, 154,
181, 186, 206–208, 252, 290,
291
railroad competition as factor, 103
routing, 20
sample pages, 114, 151–152, 183
truckload ratings, 112
uniform classification ratings, 104,
113
(*See also* Classification, Classification Form and Contents, Classification Ratings, Interstate
Commerce Commission, Na-
tional Motor Freight Classification)

N

National Association of Railroad
Commissioners, 89
National Classification Board, 178,
201, 219, 225, 260
National Industrial Traffic League,
37, 199, 293
National motor freight classification,
5, 10, 19, 27, 30, 39, 46, 55, 86,
103–104, 112, 113, 114, 129,
143, 146, 151–152, 158, 168,
183, 204, 206–208, 244, 261,
267, 277–279, 323
National motor freight traffic agree-
ment, 178
National Traffic Committee, 178–179
National Transportation Policy, 198
Nested or nested solid articles, 266
New England classification, 71, 102,
105, 116, 132–141, 154, 181,
186, 206–208, 252, 290, 291
Non-recourse clause, 12, 35
Notification instructions, 21

Volume shipments, 118, 119, 164, 227–228, 241, 257, 277, 280, 286
Volume of movement as factor, 136
Volume ratings, 5, 120

W

Water carriers
  domestic, 203
  legislation, 53–54

Water carriers (*continued*)
  liability for loss and damage exceptions, 55
  uniform bill of lading, use, 55
Waybill, 9, 37
Western Classification Committee (*See* Classification Committees)
What the traffic will bear (*See* Classification Factors)
Wilson, G. Lloyd, 32, 65, 245, 304